MANHATTAN DATING GAME

An Unofficial and Unauthorised
Guide to Every Episode of
Sex and the City

Also by Jim Smith

(with Mark Clapham)

SOUL SEARCHING: The Unofficial Guide to the Life
and Trials of Ally McBeal

MANHATTAN DATING GAME

An Unofficial and Unauthorised Guide to Every Episode of *Sex and the City*

Jim Smith

This updated edition first published in 2004 by
Virgin Books Ltd
Thames Wharf Studios
Rainville Road
London
W6 9HA

First published by Virgin Books Ltd in 2002

A catalogue record for this book is available from the British
Library.

ISBN 0 7535 0925 3

Typeset by TW Typesetting, Plymouth, Devon
Printed and bound in Great Britain by
Clays Ltd, St Ives PLC

For Louisa
who shouldn't have had to ask

Contents

Acknowledgements

This book, like all 'solo projects', is actually the work of many hands; from those who look after me at Virgin Books to those in my social circle who've had to put up with not one, but two, periods of out-and-out *Sex and the City* fixation from yours truly. I am especially indebted to all those *Sex and the City* fans who've watched, discussed and debated this series with me over the last couple of years, providing alternative points of view and squaring the circle that is a guy's view on this girliest of television shows.

Kirstie Addis, my editor (without whom), Sarah Archibald, Jahanara Begum, Lizzie Bennett, Katie Bramall, Joanne Brooks (who invited me to write this book way back when), Kate Chilton, Mark Clapham, Laura Cook, Lucy Cohen, Melanie Davies, Jane Dunton, Becky Howard, Davinder Jalaf, Becki Kneale, Stephen Lavington, Sarah McAllister, David McCambridge (US research hero), James Clive Matthews, Steven Moffat, Dr Henry Potts, Kathryn Pozzi, Eddie Robson, Dr Catherine Spooner, Matt Symonds, Maria Wasilewski, Harris Watson and Mark Wyman.

Introduction

Hello, and welcome to the revised, updated and all-encompassing book about the TV series that was based on the book. When *Sex and the City* began on US Television in 1998 it was difficult to know what to make of it. Stylistically somewhere between the traditions of sitcom and drama, and based upon a best-selling novel, it featured recognisable movie talent in its lead roles and was hyped by the media in both the US and UK as being 'racy' to the point of being almost pornographic.

Even the most enthusiastic fans of Candace Bushnell's book and columns must have tuned in with little idea of what they were actually going to get. As star Sarah Jessica Parker told the London *Evening Standard* in February 2001, 'I have to admit, I was slightly nervous before the show started. I didn't know if people would find it saucy and smart or if they'd say, "Well, this is just completely inappropriate. Who are these dirty, awful people who pollute our airwaves?" '

This level of hype surrounding the series' 'house style' and the suggestion that it would both remain true to the book and deal frankly and directly with the subject matter demanded by its concept and title was only possible because *Sex and the City* was produced by and for HBO.

HBO is an acronym for 'Home Box Office'. It's a cable channel which was launched on 8 November 1972. It initially specialised in showing Hollywood movies uncut and uninterrupted by commercials (a luxury then unknown on US television) but the station swiftly moved into original programming. After a few false starts (its first own-generated production was a Polka Dance Festival) HBO soon carved itself a niche as a place where quality TV Movies could be made and shown away from the strictures and conservatism of Network TV (which the creator of *Sex and the City*, Darren Star, has been known to compare unfavourably with censorship in Soviet bloc countries during the Cold War).

The reasoning behind HBO's liberal attitude to censorship appeared to be simple. HBO was showing Hollywood product uncut anyway, product that often dealt in extremes of sex or violence, of language or theme that would have been unacceptable on one of the traditional 'Big' networks. There seemed to be no sensible reason to censor HBO's own-generated programming, to bring it into line with network norms, when it inevitably would have to run alongside NC-17 or R rated movies a lot of the time anyway.

From 'Movie of the Week' it was a short step to serial television, and thence to *Sex and the City*, one of a tiny number of US TV shows to use the word 'fuck' (and surely the only one to use it in an episode title) and the first to enrage opinion by using the dreaded 'cunt' (and that five times in one sentence in one particular episode).

HBO promised to give *Sex and the City* the freedom to explore its subject matter with honesty, wit and depth and, from the perspective of the observer at least, they didn't renege on that through 6 seasons and 94 episodes. The first results of that freedom, which a startled audience observed on 6 June 1998, was something really quite unlike anything else ever to air on US TV.

Detractors can claim that *Sex and the City* was lucky. That it gained press exposure by being shown during the 'off season' of June to October (when the main networks are generally running repeats) and that it trades on its reputation for sex to garner audience interest. That it's shallow, unfunny and cynical, and even that the series' premise is insulting to women (who in reality make up the bulk of its audience) or that merely having the word 'sex' in the title of a TV show is in bad taste. Judging by the nature of such criticisms, it's perhaps likely their perpetrators never actually watched one of the most consistently clever TV series of the last decade.

So, *that* was the show, and *this* is the guide, an *aide-mémoire* and critical journey through six seasons of

often superb television. The format of the book goes
something like this:

We (that is, you and I – we're in this together) go through
every episode, in order, noting the best and worst moments
in the lives of Carrie and her friends. How they deal with the
men they encounter and how they fare in their professional
lives. How they cope, day to day, with life in the buzzing,
humming, dirty, big, beautiful conurbation that is New York
City, both before and after the events of 11 September 2001.

Each episode of every series is divided into categories,
which allow us to break down each thirty-minute instalment into a few pages of witty, pithy, informative chunks.
Or at least, that's the general idea. The section for each
episode looks something like this.

Title

1st US Transmission Date
Writer
Director

Guest Cast: In the interests of accuracy I'll point out that
these listings aren't always exactly the same as those
accredited on screen, or necessarily in the order in which
they appear in the credits. I tend to group recurring
characters (e.g. Stanford) at the beginning of the cast list.
Sometimes cast members are uncredited, so I've added
them. Equally there are occasions where a character's first
name only is used on the cast list, but the episode itself tells
us their surname. In these cases extra information gleaned
from the episode has been added to the cast lists.

Carrie:

Samantha:

Charlotte:

Miranda:
One category for each of our heroines, charting what
happens to them in the episode, and what those events mean
to them.

Girl Talk: What the girls say about the guys when they're not there.

Guy Talk: And vice versa.

Men: Guys, short-term partners, long-term friends (such as Stanford or Skipper), particularly annoying people in Starbucks. This is a multi-purpose category for all the male characters.

Hey, Big Guy: Carrie's principal beau, Mr Big.

The City: Just before the series started, HBO's own publicity quoted Sarah Jessica Parker as saying, 'It's really a show about New York. New York is as important a character in the show as anybody.' With this in mind, this category will cover the geography of the town, where people go, and what it's like when they get there. As the series is largely shot on location, I'll also use it to point out interesting things about New York that are relevant to the episode under discussion.

Wine and Dine: Restaurants and bars, largely real ones, are a mainstay of this series. This category is to cover what goes on in them, and occasionally what I think of them.

Fetishes: We get a lot of them in this show, somewhat inevitably. They'll be recorded here. All in good taste, of course.

Fashion Victims: The clothes. The look of this show is so very important that it's worth referencing designer labels when they do turn up, as well as noting mentions, both sneering and complimentary, of the world of high fashion. I mean, let's face it, how is a discussion of Carrie Bradshaw going to be worthwhile if it doesn't mention her shoes?

Also Starring: A category for guest stars of note, be it *Buffy the Vampire Slayer* herself, Sarah Michelle Gellar's turn, or the appearance of an actor you don't quite recognise from another US TV show, this category is there to tell you who they are and where you've seen them before. Sometimes I'll go out on a limb and tell you what I think of their performance.

Kisses: This category is not to keep a tally of who's kissed whom, when and why, but to point out particularly significant bits of lip-play. As Miranda tells Carrie, (in **48**, 'Cock a Doodle Do!') 'Don't let him kiss you. That seems to be where you get into trouble.'

Other Categories: Will include **Trivia** (all the loose strands that won't fit into a category of their own), **Out and About** (when our heroines visit somewhere interesting) and **Fit to Print** (bits of Carrie's column we are privy to).

And So . . .: My final opinion on the episode: in these, I'll subjectively sum up its (relative) merits.

With me so far? Good. We've an appointment in New York in a couple of pages' time, but first let's find out a bit about our cast.

Principal Cast

Sarah Jessica Parker (Carrie) was born in Nelsonville, Ohio, on 25 March 1965, one of her mother's eight children. As a child she started acquiring bit-parts in theatre and TV after camera crews came to Ohio looking for kids to audition. 'I quickly discovered I enjoyed pretending to be someone else,' the actress told the London *Evening Standard* in February 2001. At the age of eight she was the *Little Match Girl* on TV, and by thirteen she was playing the title role in *Annie* on Broadway. The versatile actress's theatre work includes being directed by Harold Pinter in *The Innocents*; dancing in *Les Sylphides* and singing in several operas, such as *Pagliacci*. She is married to actor Matthew Broderick (for many to be forever associated with cult classic *Ferris Bueller's Day Off* (John Hughes, 1985) in which he played the eponymous hero). Long-time friends from the New York City theatre scene before becoming a couple, they starred together in the 1995 Broadway revival of *How to Succeed in Business Without Really Trying*. They have one child, son James.

Parker has appeared in more than two dozen movies, including memorable turns in *Ed Wood* (Tim Burton, 1994), *Hocus Pocus* (Kenny Ortega, 1993), *Mars Attacks!* (Tim Burton, 1996), *LA Story* with Steve Martin (Mick Jackson, 1991), *State and Main* (David Mamet, 2001), the shamefully underrated *Dudley Do-Right* (Hugh Wilson, 1999) with Brendan Fraser and the splitting-up comedy *Life Without Dick* (Bix Skahill, 2001). Series creator Darren Star feels that a big part of the series success is down to the appeal of SJP (as she is often referred to by her many fans) as Carrie and has been quoted as saying that the way the actress plays the character ensures that 'you love her, no matter what she does'.

Kim Cattrall (Samantha) was born in Liverpool, England, on 21 August 1956, and emigrated to Canada with her parents three months later. Trained at the London Academy of Musical and Dramatic Art, she has had a bewilderingly inconsistent film and television career. Guest spots in 70s TV staples such as *Charlie's Angels*, *The Incredible Hulk*, *Columbo*, *Quincy* and *Starsky and Hutch* led to the role of the sexually voracious gym teacher in 'sex comedy' *Porky's* (Bob Clark, 1981), but her subsequent career has sadly seen her appear in little that stretches her as an actress. The original *Police Academy* (Hugh Wilson, 1984) and bizarre reincarnation-themed romantic comedy *Mannequin* (Michael Gottlieb, 1987) are, amazingly, two of the less inconsequential movies in which she's appeared. Genuine career highlights include the Oliver Stone-produced television mini-series *Wild Palms* (1993) alongside James Belushi and Angie Dickinson; a memorable turn as a villainous Vulcan in *Star Trek VI: The Undiscovered Country* (Nicholas Meyer, 1991) and the very typical John Carpenter movie *Big Trouble in Little China* (1986). One of her movies is the astonishingly entitled *Live Nude Girls!* (Julianna Lavin, 1995) in which she appeared with former *Angel* and *Roseanne* star, the late Glenn Quinn. This is, despite the title, a talk-heavy, character-led comedy drama and not actually pornography.

*   *   *

Kristin Davis (Charlotte) was born on 24 February 1965 in Boulder, Colorado, and, before appearing in *Sex and the City*, was best known for her role as the scheming Brooke Armstrong in Aaron Spelling and Darren Star's *Melrose Place*. Her extensive CV of TV guest roles reads like a list of the very best that 90s television had to offer. 'Guest star' parts include *ER* ('The Luck of the Draw' shown 1 December 1994), *Friends* ('The One With Ross's Library Book', 16 November 2000) and *The Larry Sanders Show* ('The Breakdown: Part 2', 2 June 1993). She also made two appearances in the magnificent *Seinfeld*, playing Jenna, a one-time girlfriend of both Jerry Seinfeld and his loathed arch-rival Kenny Bania. ('The Pot Hole', 20 February 1997 and 'The Butter Shave', 25 September 1997). Her TV movie work includes *Alien Nation: Body & Soul* (Kenneth Johnson, 1995) and *Take Me Home: The John Denver Story* (Jerry London, 2000) in which she played Denver's wife, Annie, about whom he wrote his most famous song.

Native New Yorker Cynthia Nixon (Miranda) was born on 9 April 1966, making her the youngest of the four stars. Theatrical film roles include parts in the wonderful *Addams Family Values* (Barry Sonnenfeld, 1993), and the Oscar-winning *Amadeus* (Milos Forman, 1984). She also appeared in Steve Martin's ill-advised remake of Neil Simon's *The Out-of-Towners* (Sam Weissman, 1999) and popular indie hit *Igby Goes Down* (Burr Steers, 2002). TV movie work includes *Papa's Angels* (Dwight H Little, 2000) with Scott Bakula. An experienced theatrical actress, she has appeared in no less than seven Broadway productions, including *The Philadelphia Story*, for which she won a Theater World award.

Creator

Series creator Darren Star is one of American television's most respected 'showrunners'. (An industry and *Variety* term to describe a writer/producer credited as 'Executive

Producer' who acts as the absolute authority for, and often creator of, many TV shows throughout their career. Other examples would include *Buffy*'s Joss Whedon, *ER* and *The West Wing*'s John Wells or *The X-Files*' Chris Carter.) Star's early screenwriting credits include the film *Doin' Time on Planet Earth* (Charles Matthau, 1988) and the pilot for *Bill and Ted's Excellent Adventures*, an attempt to create a TV series spin-off from the 1989 Stephen Herek movie which ran for only seven more episodes. Television series that Star has contributed to as a writer, director and producer (or executive producer) include *Beverly Hills 90210* (which he created and worked on from 1990–95, though it ran for five more years) and *Melrose Place* (1992–95, a collaboration with legendary producer Aaron Spelling who had also replaced him on *90210*). Since creating, and while working on, *Sex and the City*, Star also created the short-lived *The $treet* (2000) about investment bankers, and the hit *Miss Match* (2003–) which successfully relaunched Alicia Silverstone as a TV star, albeit one who frequently has her small-screen vehicle stolen from under her nose by Charisma Carpenter.

List of Episodes

Season Three (June–October 2000)

31	4 Jun 00	Where There's Smoke . . .
32	11 Jun 00	Politically Erect
33	18 Jun 00	Attack of the 5'10" Woman
34	25 Jun 00	Boy, Girl, Boy, Girl . . .
35	9 Jul 00	No Ifs, Ands or Butts
36	16 Jul 00	Are We Sluts?
37	23 Jul 00	Drama Queens
38	30 Jul 00	The Big Time
39	6 Aug 00	Easy Come, Easy Go
40	13 Aug 00	All or Nothing
41	20 Aug 00	Running with Scissors
42	27 Aug 00	Don't Ask, Don't Tell
43	10 Sep 00	Escape From New York
44	17 Sep 00	Sex and Another City
45	24 Sep 00	Hot Child in the City
46	1 Oct 00	Frenemies
47	8 Oct 00	What Goes Around Comes Around
48	15 Oct 00	Cock a Doodle Do!

Season Four (June–August 2001/January–February 2002)

49	3 Jun 01	The Agony and the 'Ex'-tasy
50	3 Jun 01	The Real Me
51	10 Jun 01	Defining Moments
52	17 Jun 01	What's Sex Got To Do With It?
53	24 Jun 01	Ghost Town
54	1 Jul 01	Baby, Talk Is Cheap
55	8 Jul 01	Time and Punishment
56	15 Jul 01	My Motherboard, My Self
57	22 Jul 01	Sex and the Country
58	29 Jul 01	The Belles of the Balls
59	5 Aug 01	Coulda, Woulda, Shoulda
60	12 Aug 01	Just Say Yes
61	6 Jan 02	The Good Fight
62	13 Jan 02	All That Glitters . . .
63	20 Jan 02	Change of a Dress
64	27 Jan 02	Ring a Ding Ding
65	3 Feb 02	A 'Vogue' Idea
66	10 Feb 02	I Heart NY

Season Five (July–September 2002)

67	21 Jul 02	Anchors Away
68	28 Jul 02	Unoriginal Sin
69	4 Aug 02	Luck Be an Old Lady
70	11 Aug 02	Cover Girl
71	18 Aug 02	Plus One Is the Loneliest Number
72	25 Aug 02	Critical Condition
73	1 Sep 02	The Big Journey
74	8 Sep 02	I Love a Charade

Season Six (June–September 2003/January–February 2004)

75	22 Jun 03	To Market, to Market
76	29 Jun 03	Great Sexpectations
77	6 Jul 03	The Perfect Present
78	13 Jul 03	Pick-a-Little, Talk-a-Little
79	20 Jul 03	Lights, Camera, Relationship
80	27 Jul 03	Hop, Skip and a Week
81	3 Aug 03	The Post-it Always Sticks Twice
82	10 Aug 03	The Catch
83	17 Aug 03	A Woman's Right to Shoes
84	24 Aug 03	Boy, Interrupted
85	7 Sep 03	The Domino Effect
86	15 Sep 03	One
87	4 Jan 04	Let There Be Light
88	11 Jan 04	The Ick Factor
89	18 Jan 04	Catch-38
90	25 Jan 04	Out of the Frying Pan
91	1 Feb 04	The Cold War
92	8 Feb 04	Splat!
93	15 Feb 04	An American Girl in Paris (Part Une)
94	22 Feb 04	An American Girl in Paris (Part Deux)

Season One (1998)

Created by Darren Star
Based on the book by Candace Bushnell

Executive Producer: Darren Star
Executive Producer: Michael Patrick King
Co-Executive Producer: Barry Jossen
Producer: Judith Stevens
Co-Producer: Jane Raab
Co-Producer: Candace Bushnell (1)
Associate Producer: Mark McGann
Associate Producer: Amy B Harris

Regular Cast
Sarah Jessica Parker (Carrie Bradshaw) Kim Cattrall (Samantha Jones)
Kristin Davis (Charlotte York) Cynthia Nixon (Miranda Hobbes)

1
Sex and the City

6 June 1998

Written by Darren Star
Directed by Susan Seidelman

Guest Cast
Chris Noth (Mr Big) Willie Garson (Stanford Blatch)
Ben Weber (Skipper Johnston) Bruce McCarthy (Peter Mason)
Jeffrey Nordling (Capote Duncan) Bill Sage (Kurt Harrington)
Scott Bryce (Tim) Donna Hanover (Realtor) Sarah Wynter (Elizabeth)
Johnny Cienatiempo (Driver) Navia Nguyen (Tatiana)

Fit to Print: 'Once upon a time ...' Thirty-something journalist Carrie Bradshaw reads us a long section from one of her weekly *Sex and the City* columns, as printed in the *New York Star*. It's the story of an English journalist, Elizabeth, who came to New York and met a 42-year-old millionaire merchant banker named Tim. For weeks they snuggled, went to romantic restaurants and had amazing sex, and then one day they started looking at houses and he asked her to meet his parents. She was entranced – and after that day she never saw him again. Two weeks of waiting later she phoned him, and he told her he was snowed under at work and that he'd call her back. Carrie uses this story to illustrate the 'death of love in Manhattan'. One edition of her column is called 'Unmarried women, toxic bachelors'. She then takes us through some other events in her life, explaining that the stories in her column come to her from the best of sources: her friends.

Wine and Dine: 'Another thirty-something birthday with a group of unmarried female friends.' It's Miranda's birthday, and we see her and her three best friends Samantha, Charlotte and Carrie gathered together at a restaurant. The ensuing conversation highlights the differences between them clearly, and we're given a really good idea of who all the characters are and how they relate to each other.

Samantha: PR executive Samantha Jones is 'a New York inspiration' who regularly sleeps with 'good-looking guys in their twenties'. Carrie feels that Samantha has the kind of misplaced confidence that propels men like (multi-millionaire and self-funded Third Party Candidate, 1992 and 1996) Ross Perot to try to become president. In Carrie's opinion, Samantha has decided that all men are assholes, and everything in her life stems from this assumption. She's very cynical, but appears to enjoy the lack of inhibition that comes with that. She states, as point of fact, that she's as good-looking as any model and is unperturbed when her very direct advances are turned down by one of her targets. At dinner she tells her friends that they are alive in the first time in the history of Manhattan when women have had as much money and power as men, and the option of treating men as sex objects. She demands that her friends give up on love because 'the right guy is an illusion'; they should go out and have sex like men – 'without feeling'. She illustrates how liberating this can be by talking about a man she slept with, 'Drew', whom her friends immediately remember as 'Drew the sex god'. Sam says that after having sex with him her mood was essentially 'like, hey babe, gotta go, catch you later'. She then completely forgot about him. Charlotte thinks it's more likely that he simply didn't phone Sam, and says so.

Samantha talks about the infamous Linda Fiorentino movie *The Last Seduction* (John Dahl, 1994), a movie which Carrie claims Samantha is 'obsessed with', and which Charlotte claims to hate. It's worth a watch as an interesting insight into Samantha's character.

Miranda: Miranda tells a story about a friend of hers who enjoyed herself throughout her thirties, and just had fun. One day she woke up, she was 41 and there were no more dates. She had a total nervous breakdown and moved back to Wisconsin to live with her mother. This, she feels, is '. . . not a story that makes men feel bad'. Miranda seems sharp, clever and very, very funny. She's sceptical (and therefore prepared to be convinced) rather than cynical. At one point she angrily accuses Carrie's friend Skipper of saying that women fit into two categories, 'attractive' and 'interesting', and that no woman is both, when he clearly says no such thing. She also berates him for agreeing with her that everyone in the bar is painfully thin, arguing that he has effectively just called her fat. She is a corporate lawyer, and has lovely hair.

Charlotte: We are told that Charlotte is an art dealer, and is clearly the most naïve (or idealistic, depending on your point of view) of the four friends. She's visibly appalled when Samantha dismisses the very idea of romance out of hand. When Miranda tells her story about 'Jeremiah', a man who wanted to take her to dinner and read her his poetry, Charlotte is obviously quite attracted to the idea of dating a man like that. Her sweet, sensitive handling of her date with Capote Duncan doesn't deserve the appalling treatment that results from it. She claims that most men are threatened by successful women, and that the way to get one is by not talking too much and playing by *The Rules*, the 'dating guide book' for women; extremely conservative in nature, it has sold an enormous number of copies stateside.

Carrie: Last but not least our heroine, and our eyes on this world. Not as cynical as Samantha nor as naïve and romantic as Charlotte, she does feel that Samantha's professed attitude to life will vanish the moment she meets a man she can love. 'The right guy comes along . . . This whole thing? Out the window,' she says with a dismissive wave of her hand. After having been told by Samantha that women should go out and have sex like men (a proposal which, contrary to popular myths about the series, none of the other women explicitly sign up to), Carrie sees a man named Kurt Harrington in a bar. The dashing-looking Kurt is, Carrie claims, a mistake she made when she was 26. And 29. And 31. Her friend Stanford begs her not to go and talk to Kurt, as he couldn't bear to pick up the pieces for the fourth time. Stanford's hand-waving histrionics as he spies her talking to him are particularly amusing.

Carrie agrees to meet Kurt at his apartment as 3 p.m., where she lets him go down on her and then quickly leaves, 'feeling powerful, potent and incredibly alive'. This feeling is somewhat dented by how, when she next meets him, he seems delighted that she finally understands the kind of relationship he wants – all sex and no commitment. Carrie agrees to call him the next time she wants consequence-free sex, but is left wondering if all men actually want women to be 'promiscuous and emotionally detached' and what that says about them if this is true. She's also disturbed by the thought that even though she's trying to do what Samantha suggested, she doesn't feel any more in control. She carries a personal supply of ultra-textured Trojan condoms with a reservoir tip in her bag.

At the end of this episode she asks Big's chauffeur to drop her off at the junction of 72nd Street and Bank, which is presumably near her apartment (see **10**, 'The Baby Shower').

Men: 'Mr Big', who is apparently 'the next Donald Trump', except that he's younger and far more attractive. Sam tries it on with him but he's resolutely not interested, despite her very direct line of attack. Poor Sam is unaware that Carrie and Big have met before, briefly, when he helped her pick up the contents of her bag after another pedestrian knocked her over in the street. He clearly likes Carrie, and when he notices she's at Chaos, he waves at her. He gives her a lift home when she can't find a cab and is fairly gentlemanly about the whole thing. He smokes cigars and claims to have been smoking them since they 'were unfashionable'. The only brand he's interested in are Cohibas. According to executive producer/creator/this episode's writer Darren Star, Mr Big (whose full name we never discover, though we do learn his forename in **94**, 'An American Girl in Paris (Part Deux)', the show's last episode) is based on the publisher Ron Galotti, one-time boyfriend of *Sex and the City* book writer Candace Bushnell.

Skipper Johnston is an old, old friend of Carrie's and a self-professed 'nice guy'. Apparently too nice and unable to objectify women, it has been a whole year since he's had sex. He creates websites for a living, and is a born, and not at all closeted, romantic, who clearly finds all the cut and thrust of the dating game both painful and incomprehensible. He partially blames New York itself, saying that all love needs in order to conquer all is a bit of space: 'That's what's missing in Manhattan – the space for romance.' He asks Carrie to set him up with one of her friends, so she invites him to Chaos with the girls. He rather wittily describes the roomful of painfully thin women as a meeting of 'under-eaters anonymous'.

Stanford Blatch, another friend of Carrie's. He's the head of a talent agency that has only one client, Derek, an underwear model with his photograph on a billboard in Times Square. Stanford is very obviously gay, with great taste in shirts, and is emotionally very close to Carrie. He argues that the only place to find romance in New York is within the gay community. 'It's straight love that's become closeted,' he says, and then openly hits on the waiter.

Capote Duncan, a publishing executive who, according to Carrie, is one of New York's 'ungettable' bachelors. At one point he talks to camera, saying that he thinks women should forget about marriage and simply have a good time. He has a Ross Blechner painting which Charlotte wants to see, so she goes home with him. In her professional opinion, it could be sold for $100,000. After Charlotte decides to not sleep with him on their first date, he not only heads to a club because he feels he has to have sex that night but he tells her about it, and shares a cab with her because her apartment is quite near the club. He ends up going home with Samantha, who is happy about the fact that *post coitus* he doesn't want her to stay the night.

Kurt Harrington. In Stanford Blatch's opinion, 'the man is scum'.

Peter Mason, a thirty-something advertising exec, who believes in 'The Mid-Thirties Power Flip'. Essentially this means that until they reach their mid-thirties, women are in control of dating, they rarely have to do the chasing and have all the power. At about the age of 35, paranoia sets in about age, marriage, looks and children, and suddenly men are in control for the first time in their lives.

Fashion Victims: Skipper's hair, clothes and glasses are just awful. Carrie describes her kind of woman as being prepared to pay '$400 for a pair of Manolo Blahnik strappy sandals'. (Six years later it was $485, see **83**, 'A Woman's Right to Shoes'.) If any pair of sandals on earth is worth $400 then these are they. Charlotte's dress for her evening out with Capote Duncan is gorgeous.

Also Starring: Chris Noth who, as Mr Big, makes such a big impact on Carrie at the end of this episode, was born in Madison, Wisconsin, on 13 November 1954. He's best known to the TV-watching public as Detective Mike Logan in NBC's *Law & Order* from 1990 to 1995. Noth returned to the role in 1998 for *Exiled* (Jean de Segonzac, 1998), a *Law & Order* TV movie for which he also wrote the storyline. He has also played this character in an episode of *Homicide: Life on the Street* ('Law & Disorder', transmitted 24 February 1995). Other TV roles include a guest appearance in *Touched By an Angel* and three episodes of *Hill Street Blues* way back in 1986 ('Come & Get It', 'Slum Enchanted Evening' and 'Look Homeward, Ninja', shown 20 March to 3 April 1986). Noth's movies include the Tom Hanks hit *Cast Away* (Robert Zemeckis, 2001).

Born in New Jersey in 1964, the versatile Willie Garson (Stanford Blatch) has had an impressive career in film and television. Some of the many movies featuring Garson in supporting roles include *Being John Malkovich* (Spike Jonze, 1999), the sublime *Groundhog Day* (Harold Ramis, 1993), *Mars Attacks!* (Tim Burton, 1996) with Sarah Jessica Parker, *Things To Do in Denver When You're Dead* (Gary Fleder, 1995), and *There's Something About Mary* (Bobby Farrelly/Peter Farrelly, 1998). On TV he was Henry Coffield in *NYPD Blue* from 1996 to 1999, and has appeared as District Attorney Frank Shea in David E Kelley's *The Practice* on several occasions. He has also played Shea in Kelley's *other* Boston-based legal drama, *Ally McBeal* (in 'Compromising Positions', shown 15 September 1997). Confusingly he later appeared as another entirely separate character in *Ally McBeal* (Alan Farmer in 'These are the Days', shown 18 May 1998). Clearly one of those actors who appears to have been in *everything*, his notable guest-starring turns include appearances as an impressive comic turn in *Friends* (as Steve, in 'The One With the Girl Who Hits Joey', shown 18 February 1999), *The X-Files* (playing Henry Weems in 'The Goldberg Variation', shown 19 December 1999) and *Spin City* (Ned in 'Blind Faith', shown 15 November 2000), plus smaller roles in *Buffy the Vampire Slayer, Cheers, Family Ties, Melrose Place, Just Shoot Me, Star Trek: Voyager* and *Mad About You*. He has twice played supposed JFK assassin Lee Harvey Oswald, in *Ruby* (John Mackenzie, 1992) and in the *Quantum Leap* episode 'Lee Harvey Oswald' (shown 9 September 1992).

Ben Weber (Skipper Johnston), born 14 May 1972 in Washington, has a number of minor roles in successful movies to his credit, including parts in *Twister* (Jan de Bont, 1996) and *The Mirror Has Two Faces* (Barbra Streisand, 1996). Other notable TV guest roles include an appearance in *Law & Order* (playing Ethan Capp in the episode 'Sunday in the Park with Jorge', shown 24 January 2001).

The director of both this and many other episodes is Susan Seidelman, who is best known for directing *Desperately Seeking Susan* (1985), Madonna's first major movie role. Other films include *She-Devil* (1989) with Roseanne and Meryl Streep, and *Making Mr Right* (1987).

Out and About: A club called Chaos is situated near the junction of West Broadway and Broom, where the girls like to go on a Friday night. It's an intimate, sweaty place, and clearly quite expensive. It serves cocktails in abundance, and for some reason attracts a clientele of men in suits.

Trivia: Carrie refers to the movies *Breakfast at Tiffany's* (Blake Edwards, 1961) and *An Affair to Remember* (Leo Carey, 1957), and Edith Wharton's novel *The Age of Innocence* (1920). All, in their own ways, are influences on this series, and all are certainly worth your time.

In the series Carrie's columns are printed in the (fictional) *New York Star*. Candace Bushnell's original Sex and the City columns on which the book and the show are based were printed in the *New York Observer*.

Interviewed by HBO, series creator Darren Star claimed he was attracted to Candace Bushnell's novel because its thirty-something characters were 'looking at life with a slightly cynical point of view' and from it devised *Sex and the City* to be ' . . . a show that dealt in a really frank and funny manner with sex and relationships'. He later told *The Times*: 'Traditional sitcoms on television were, in a smirking kind of way, about sex. That's the subtext, but the jokes all come from euphemisms. I wanted to do a comedy about sex where you could say anything and go from there. And the hook was sex from a female point of view.'

It's interesting to note some of the changes made to Candace Bushnell's book in the process of adapting it into this episode's screenplay. Carrie meeting with Big at the party is, in the book, a simple case of her accosting him. On screen it's Samantha who directly attempts to seduce Big, while Carrie hangs shyly in the background. Also in the book Carrie goes home with Big straight away, whereas here she goes home alone, simply hoping that she'll re-encounter Big in the near future.

Kisses: Skipper, after having been pecked on the cheek and given the brush-off by Miranda (who thinks he's 'too nice'), pauses, turns around and then goes back to kiss her on the lips. Suddenly, she's kissing him back with equal fervour, proving, temporarily at least, that nice guys don't always finish last.

And So . . .: 'How the hell did we get into this mess?' Wow. By any normal standard this simply isn't television. Not just because of the enormous amounts of night and location filming and not just because Big says 'abso-fuckin'-lutely' before he drives away. The habit that several characters have of talking directly to camera, as if partici-pating in a documentary, is unusual for TV, but the way that Carrie looks at the camera and discusses *in the past tense* the events in which she is now participating is disconcerting and more like something out of French New Wave cinema than network television. It's also very careful to demonstrate different points of view, with the audience feeling they've glimpsed a bigger picture. This first episode is glossy and funny and you can practically *smell* New York City while watching it. Superb.

2
Models and Mortals

13 June 1998

Written by Darren Star
Directed by Alison Maclean

Guest Cast
Chris Noth (Mr Big) Willie Garson (Stanford Blatch)
Ben Weber (Skipper Johnston) Gabriel Macht (Barkley)
Josh Pais (Nick Waxler) Emily Cline (AshLeigh B)
Andre Boccaletti (Derek The Bone) Sandra Daley (Deanne)
Katie Finneran (Ellen) Andy Fowle (Dave) Michelle Griffin (Misha)
Amanda Harker (Marissa) Ryohei Hoshi (Korean Grocer)

Jo-Jo Loew (Cassie Fields) Montse Viader (Xandrella)
James Hyde (Brad Fox) Tully Jensen (Yvette)
David Andrew MacDonald (Greg)

Wine and Dine: Carrie and chums gather in her apartment
to eat Chinese food and discuss models and 'modelisers'.
Modelisers are, apparently, a breed of men set apart from
the pack. One step up from mere womanisers, they date
and/or have sex only with models. While Carrie wonders
what it is about models that makes normally rational people
crumble to dust, the girls discuss their attitudes to these two
hated subspecies of humankind. As Carrie says, 'There's
nothing like raising the subject of models among four single
women to spice up an otherwise dull Tuesday night.'

Miranda: 'The advantages given to models and to beautiful
women in general are so unfair it makes me wanna puke.'
She demands to know when all the men got together and
decided they were 'only going to get it up for giraffes with
big breasts'.

Carrie: Carrie claims that she came to terms with her looks
when she reached 30 and realised that she no longer had
the energy to be completely superficial.

Samantha: Samantha says that men have told her that she's
as beautiful as a model, but she has the added advantage
that she works for a living, so she is 'a model who took the
high road'. Later we learn that she never misses a major
fashion show in New York – which must keep her very busy.

Charlotte: Looking at pictures of supermodels makes
Charlotte want to give up, whereas Miranda wants to
forcefeed lard to the woman in question. This, Miranda
claims, is the very definition of the difference between the
two of them. Charlotte says she hates her thighs, leading
the others to chip in with their own pet hates about
themselves. Miranda hates her chin, Carrie loathes her
nose and Sam . . . Well, Sam loves the way she looks.

Men: Nick Waxler, a sports agent who has been a
modeliser for months, much to the chagrin of his friends;

they are sick of people who 'come to dinner, push their food around and pout'. He invites Miranda to a dinner party partially as an attempt to mollify his peer group; to provide them with a date of his who can 'carry on a decent conversation and eat without purging'. When Miranda finds out she is understandably less than impressed. 'What am I?' she demands. 'Your intellectual beard for the evening?' When pressed on the subject of being a modeliser, Waxler asks, 'Why fuck the girl in the skirt if you can fuck the girl in the advert for the skirt?' Charming.

Carrie meets Derek, Stanford's client and the object of his obsession, at a fashion show. He's rather sweet but clearly none too bright. He gets lonely in New York, and his ambitions stretch no further than going back to Iowa to have kids and become a local cop; far removed from Stanford's plans for him, both professional and personal. He's known as 'The Bone', apparently, and is no longer Stanford's only client (merely his 'most important one'), implying a small upturn in Mr Blatch's fortunes since the previous episode. Derek thinks most other models are stupid and isn't attracted to them. This leads Carrie to wonder if there is some kind of 'physics to models'. Does one model repel another, and are models therefore only attracted to 'normals'?

Hey, Big Guy: Carrie bumps into Big again at the fashion show. She describes him as a 'major tycoon, major dreamboat and majorly out of my league'. She asks him his opinion on her 'Modelisers' column, and makes a bit of a klutz of herself. Nevertheless he tracks her down to her favourite coffee shop in order to tell her that ultimately, when there are so many beautiful women in New York, after a while you just want to be with one who can make you laugh.

Skipper talks to Carrie about Miranda, and how she is 'so sexy', 'so smart', 'totally hot', and how she 'totally won't return my calls'. Later, in a 24-hour store beneath 14th St, he bumps into her. He confronts her about how she's been ignoring him, and she says he should date someone his own age. He points out that it isn't about age, and rather sweetly calls her 'luminous'. After a moment's hesitation, she takes him home with her. As Carrie points out, 'Miranda couldn't resist the vision of herself reflected in Skipper's slightly smudged lenses.'

Barkley, an artist Carrie knows who manages to carry on a fabulous SoHo lifestyle despite never having sold a single painting. He claims it's easier to get a model to have sex with you than it is a normal woman because 'that's what they do all the time'. They continually act 'like regular people do when they're on holiday'.

Fetishes: Barkley videos himself having sex with models, and then plays the results back on a huge bank of television screens which are grouped together and piled up on top of each other. It is, if you forgive the comparison, like something out of the Batcave. He namechecks some of the models he's slept with and taped – Vanessa, Tanya, Elena, Katrina. Carrie notes that he appears to have slept with half the perfume adverts in September's issue of *Vogue*. Samantha ends up having sex with him, and encourages him to tape them for his collection.

At his dinner party Nick initiates the classy parlour game of naming 'Old Actors Who You'd Have Liked To Fuck When They Were Young'. His choice is Veronica Lake, the year she made *Sullivan's Travels* (Preston Sturges, 1942). Nick's friend Dave opts for Sophia Loren, apparently because his dad had a big thing for her. Another party guest, Deanne, chooses Montgomery Clift, but is put off when it's pointed out he was gay. Other choices run from the predictable (Marilyn Monroe, 'before the Kennedys got to her') and the unusual (Bing Crosby). Miranda opts, with a grin, for 'Sean Connery, yesterday, today and tomorrow'.

Samantha uses the code question, 'Martini straight up, or with a twist?' in order to discover someone's sexuality.

Fashion Victims: Carrie's blue sweater when visiting Barkley is gorgeous, as is her square-topped little black dress. When Big introduces her to a model she suddenly feels inadequate, like she's 'wearing Patchouli in a room full of Chanel'.

The City: Carrie's favourite coffee shop is apparently on the corner of 73rd and Madison; near the Whitney Museum and her apartment. She implies her apartment is rent controlled (see **48**, 'Cock a Doodle Do!') and overlooking the park.

Trivia: In terms of Miranda and Skipper's relationship, it makes a lot more sense if this episode and the next one are transposed.

And So . . .: 'You were dating a modeliser and you didn't even know it?' Carrie deals with a complex although hardly pressing issue and comes out on top. This all works very well, but Charlotte hardly features at all, which is a shame. The episode's best moment comes when model AshLeigh B describes herself as 'very literary' because she can read a magazine from cover to cover (and sometimes she does, too). The moral of the story is that beauty is fleeting, but a rent-controlled apartment overlooking Central Park is for ever.

3
Bay of Married Pigs

21 June 1998

Written by Michael Patrick King
Directed by Nicole Holofcener

Guest Cast
Willie Garson (Stanford Blatch) Jennifer Guthrie (Patience)
Joanna P Adler (Syd) Remy Auberjonois (Waiter)
Kristen Behrendt (Rebecca) H Jon Benjamin (Jeff)
Karen Braga (Intellectual Woman)
John Connolly (David) Kerrianne Spellman Cort (Anne)
Andrew Fiscella (Working Class Guy)
David Forsyth (Senior Partner 'Chip') Karl Geary (Tommy)
Isabel Gillies (Elaine) Melora Griffis (Young 30s Woman)
David Healey (Peter) Lou Liberatore (Lou) Scott Rabinowitz (Sean)
Peter Reardon (Paul) Peter Rini (Joe) Stephanie Venditto (Lisa)

Carrie: 'One of the best things about living in a city like New York is leaving it.' Carrie goes to stay with married friends Patience and Peter. They are, in Carrie's eyes, the perfect couple. Fun, smart and looking like they've fallen out of a Jay Crew catalogue. In fact, if their house didn't overlook the beach, Carrie confidently predicts that she'd hate them. She has a very nice evening with the couple and wakes up feeling great. 'I couldn't wait,' she says, 'to go out and take in the spectacular view.' She gets rather more than she bargained for, when she emerges from the guest bedroom to find Peter standing in the hallway *sans* underwear. When Patience returns from her trip to buy fresh orange juice and muffins, Carrie tries to make light of it. 'I ran into Peter in the hallway without his underwear on. P.S. Congratulations.'

Wine and Dine: The girls meet in an Italian restaurant to discuss Carrie's recent experience. Samantha wonders if Peter merely wanted to 'show it off, like a monkey', then immediately starts hitting on the waiter. Carrie claims again that Peter is particularly well endowed, and this leads on to the topic of married men in general. Charlotte says that she would never sleep with a married man, and Samantha asks her how she knows she hasn't already. After all, wedding rings do come off.

Miranda: Miranda is obliged, as a company employee, to attend an annual softball game. What marks this occasion out as particularly irritating is that someone has fixed her up with someone called Syd, a blind date for the occasion. She's stunned when Syd turns out to be a woman; people in her office have assumed she's gay. 'When did being single translate into being gay?' she demands. However, the damage is done, and after playing rather well in the softball game, she and Syd are asked by the firm's senior partner, Charles (who asks her to call him Chip), to go to a 'couples only' dinner party with him, his wife and some friends. Unable to turn down this opportunity, Miranda says that 'they' will go.

Men: Sean, whom Carrie's friends David and Lisa 'surprise' fix her up with. His parents met at a 'fix-up'. Sean is the youngest of three brothers, has his own investment company and is about to move into a huge West Side apartment he's just purchased. Carrie dates him for a couple of weeks, slowly realising that he's 'the marrying guy, that elusive and rare Manhattan man whose sights were set on marriage'.

Stanford says that Carrie's wrong about her perceived 'cold war' between marrieds and singles; there's nothing cold about it. He tries to console her by telling her that it's not just in the straight arena that marriage is a big issue – every gay guy he knows is going to Hawaii, putting on a kaftan and pledging themselves for life. He now feels like an outcast among outcasts, and pines for the days when everyone was alone. While out walking through the Village with Stanford, Carrie bumps into an old friend, Joe, whom she hasn't seen since he was straight. He introduces her to his 'life partner' Lou (complete with wedding band) and asks her if she's willing to donate an egg so they can have a child. Carrie is amazed that she's been demoted so far that she's almost ceased to be a person and has become an opportunity instead.

Charlotte: Charlotte treats marriage like 'a sorority she was desperately hoping to pledge'. Once Carrie's persuaded Sean that she isn't right for him, she sets him up with Charlotte, who eventually breaks up with him because of his taste in crockery.

The City: Patience and Peter live in The Hamptons, the generic name for the affluent and expensive beach-fringed area at the top of Long Island, where Steven Spielberg, among others, has a house.

Fashion Victims: Carrie's blue striped top she wears to The Hamptons is great. Not sure about Samantha's blue party dress, but Charlotte's red velvet number is beautiful. Miranda's deliberately 'lesbian' clothes include a blue and white striped man's shirt and a red tie in which she actually looks rather fetching. At one point she wears a Harvard University sweat top, which when combined with the fact that she's a high-powered lawyer makes it likely she attended its famous law school (see **5**, 'The Power of Female Sex'). Carrie describes her relationship with Sean as being like a DKNY dress. 'You know it won't suit you but it's there so you try it on anyway.' Carrie also refers to Jay Crew, the mail-order catalogue for twenty- to thirty-something Americans. It sells practical and pseudo-practical casual wear for people who want to look like off-duty lumberjacks.

Out and About: Carrie takes Samantha and Charlotte to Sean's housewarming party on the West Side of the city. It's full of couples, Carrie describing it as 'Noah's Upper West Side Rent-Controlled Ark'.

Samantha: Sam gets amazingly drunk at Sean's party, sitting in the kitchen and downing tequila slammers. She announces that she has had sex with at least two of the 'happily married' men at the party and, for a change, seems to be something other than revelling in a fact like this. She's so drunk that Charlotte decides that she can't be trusted to get home alone, and makes her stay on the couch at her (fabulous) apartment block. Once Charlotte's asleep, a still-drunk Sam goes downstairs and seduces the young impressionable doorman by the subtle method of standing in front of him wearing only her underwear and demanding he come upstairs with her. It could be said that 'Bay of Married Pigs' is an unfortunate episode for Samantha, really. The initial attraction of the character as presented in **1**, 'Sex and the City', is her confidence and her no-holds-barred, no-string-attached enjoyment of her lifestyle. Yet here we see Samantha pathetically drunk and seemingly desperately unhappy with the way her life works. Later the episode goes out of its way to show that the doorman Tommy has been emotionally hurt by being used by Samantha so that she can feel better about herself. If the purpose of Samantha as a character is to validate her lifestyle choices as a healthy option, this is surely not the way to do it.

Kisses: While in the elevator at the end of their 'date', Miranda tentatively kisses Syd to see if it does anything for her. 'No, definitely straight,' she concludes.

Trivia: Movies on at the Greenwich Picture House include *Godzilla* (Roland Emmerich, 1998) and *City of Angels* (Brad Silberling, 1998).

The title is a pun on the abortive US military action in Cuba's Bay of Pigs in 1960. Planned by the outgoing Eisenhower/Nixon administration and followed through by the incoming Kennedy/Johnson one, it was a military and political disaster.

And So . . .: 'When someone gets married all bets are off.' Another episode, another issue; this is actually the funniest instalment yet, with loads of genuine 'laugh out loud' moments and even more excruciating ones. Stanford's single scene is amazing. Again the episode attempts a kind of 'moral equivalence', trying to look at the issue from every conceivable angle, and presenting both men and women with wildly differing views from others of their sex. There is, however, a somewhat unfortunate angle on Samantha (see **Samantha**). It's interesting that the people we've seen most hurt by rejection so far have been Tommy (the doorman) and Sean this week, and Skipper last week – all guys who don't behave in the way that Sam insists all men do and who then suffer for it being perceived that they should.

4
Valley of the Twenty-Something Guys

28 June 1998

Written by Michael Patrick King
Directed by Alison Maclean

Guest Cast
Chris Noth (Mr Big) Ben Weber (Skipper Johnston)
Daniel Gerroll (Mr Marvelous/Jack) Timothy Olyphant (Sam)

Kohl Sudduth (Jon) French Napier (Jock Guy)
Upendran Panicker (Cab Driver) Michael Parr (Groovy Guy)
Josh Stamberg (Brian) Robert Steinman (Salesperson)
Andre Vippolis (Underage Guy) James A Wolf Jr (Corporate Guy)

Hey, Big Guy: 'Once upon a time . . . a certain man and a slightly less certain woman kept bumping into one another . . . almost as if they were dating accidentally.' So Carrie and Mr Big decide to pick times to bump into each other on purpose. They agree to meet at the opening of what is guaranteed to be Manhattan's hottest restaurant, for which Samantha is handling the PR. He can only spare an hour, which, given that he spends half an hour outside queuing for entry and 20 minutes looking for her inside, means he only has enough time to tell her he's out of time before he leaves. They arrange to meet for dinner later, but this all goes wrong too (see **Men**).

Miranda: Apparently Miranda and Skipper aren't dating. 'It's a fuck thing,' she claims. She likes Martinis and hates rum, coke and rum and coke. She later claims that 'there are no available men in their thirties in New York. [Mayor Rudolph] Giuliani had them removed along with the homeless.'

Carrie: She sleeps in a black face mask, and smokes at least one Marlboro Light before getting out of bed in the morning. At one point she walks 48 blocks in $400 shoes because she left her cab fare behind.

Charlotte: Charlotte is dating a guy called Brian, who has all the things she desires in a man: looks, manners and money. He also wants to buy a painting from her gallery. 'Love and a commission,' Carrie observes. What else could Charlotte need?

Men: Jack (credited as 'Mr Marvelous') is a friend of Big's who is currently going through his second divorce: 'The bitch is getting everything the first bitch didn't.' He crashes Big and Carrie's dinner date because he phoned Big up crying and Big didn't have the heart to leave him alone. He's there less than five minutes before he starts hitting on random women. Carrie politely suggests that Jack and Big have a 'guys' night out' and that she and he get together some other time. She even leaves them enough money for a round of drinks on her.

'Jon', New York's hottest chef. He has no surname, but his blue crab strudel is so good he doesn't need one.

Sam, a friend of Jon's who takes a bit of a shine to Carrie. She goes shopping with him to the (seriously downmarket by her standards) Banana Republic to help him pick out a shirt. They briefly make out in the changing room, only to be interrupted by a sales assistant who reminds them, 'This isn't the Gap.' After her disastrous 'drink thing' with Big, Carrie catches up with Jon because she needs some fun and reassurance. She has a spectacular night of casual passion with him, but on waking up in his apartment realises what a cliché twenty-something guy he is: there's no paper in the bathroom, dirty laundry is scattered everywhere and cheap candles sit on every shelf. Initially confused that everything should seem so different in the morning, Carrie concludes that while the pace and excitement of dating a younger man has a short-term appeal, there's not really any substitute for emotional maturity. Sam's phone number (which he writes in bright blue biro on Carrie's arm) is 555-01981.

Carrie divides twenty-something guys into a number of categories: groovy guys, the corporate guys, the jock guys, the underage guys. She later adds an extra category: the really good kisser guys. We see a group of guys (including Skipper and everyone from the bar) playing basketball in what looks like the public ball court on West 14th St. Each of them tells the camera in turn what it is they like about older women.

- Jake Lewis (25), bass player and professional dog walker, finds older women '. . . grateful. Every bullshit nice thing you do is like throwing food to the starving.' Which is charming.
- Rick Stein (27), a stock analyst, claims that they all 'give great head' and know 'a lot about wine'.

- Tim Walker (24), a med student, claims they remind him of his mother.
- Fred King (17), still in high school, says somewhat abruptly, 'Two words: smart pussy,' and comes across as a dismal, faux-cynical jock who needs to do a lot of growing up.
- Skipper (27) strikes a reasonable note when he points out that 'they know who they are and what they want, and I like that'.

Samantha: Sam makes a point of snogging Jon in front of everyone just so they know that they're sleeping together. The next morning she phones Carrie to tell her, 'I am so fucked. Literally.' Eventually, she realises that if she always dates younger men, she will always be older, and gives up twenty-somethings on the spot.

Fetishes: Charlotte's perfect boyfriend tells her, 'We've been seeing each other for a couple of weeks, I really like you and tonight after dinner I want us to have anal sex.' Charlotte is appalled, and convenes an emergency meeting of her girlfriends to discuss what to do. Sam thinks she should do it because 'with the right guy and the right lubricant . . . it's fabulous', but Carrie and Miranda see that there are bigger issues at stake. Charlotte ultimately refuses. It isn't something she wants to do or feels comfortable being pressured into doing.

Fashion Victims: After yet another disappointment, Carrie shops for shoes, which she sees as swapping one vice for another.

Kisses: Carrie spends hours and hours 'just kissing' Jon's friend Sam. She ponders that she'd forgotten the sheer joy of just kissing.

Trivia: The opening narration invokes fairy tales, via *Star Wars* (George Lucas, 1977). Miranda is picked up by the girls' taxi on the corner of 62nd and Madison. The title suggests either *Beyond the Valley of the Dolls* (Russ Meyer, 1970) or its predecessor *Valley of the Dolls* (Mark Robson, 1967).

And So . . .: 'I would have been so cool if I hadn't looked back.' There are two standout sequences in this tale of thirty-something women in crisis: one is the discussion about anal sex in the back of a taxi ('Excuse me, you're driving!' barks Miranda when the cabman tries to listen in) and the other is the hilarious sequence of twenty-something Sam telling about his dream in which he had 'big aluminum hands. I could crush anything with these big aluminum hands'. Another feature of his dream was Carrie, represented as a 'unicorn woman with glass eyes', a phrase he then proceeds to sing. According to some women of my acquaintance this is actually the single funniest thing *ever*.

The Carrie/Big relationship really kicks into gear at last, and the final scene is charming and brilliant.

5
The Power of Female Sex

5 July 1998

Written by Darren Star & Jenji Kohan
Directed by Susan Seidelman

Guest Cast
Charles Keating (Neville Morgan)
Carole Raphaelle Davis (Amalita Amalfi) Ed Fry (Gilles)
Sean Arbuckle (Salesperson) Kennedy Brown (Waiter)
Jordi Caballero (Mario) Mimi Langeland (Hostess)
Phyllis Somerville (Gertrude)

Out and About: 'The most important woman in New York . . . the hostess at Balzac's, the only restaurant that matters.' Sam and Carrie try to get a table at Balzac's and are denied entry by the hostess. After waiting 45 minutes, and considering bribing her with between $20 and $50, they give up. Sam is enraged, saying that if the hostess were a man then she and Carrie would not only be eating by now, they'd be being sent free drinks by the bar. This leads Carrie to wonder about the validity of women using their sexuality to get ahead, and she arranges a poker night round at her place. The invited guests? Well, Miranda, Samantha and Charlotte. Who else?

Samantha: Apparently, sex is power and money is power, and the exchange of sex for money is therefore merely an exchange of power and a completely reasonable transaction to engage in. Samantha claims that it is a woman's right to use every means at her disposal to achieve power, including sleeping her way to the top if that's what it takes to get ahead. Charlotte is appalled, saying that this is exploitation. 'Of men,' qualifies Sam, 'which is perfectly legal.' Miranda angrily points out that Samantha is advocating a double standard: 'Women can use their sexuality to get ahead whenever possible but men should not be allowed to take advantage of it.' Miranda argues that Samantha's celebration of this double standard perpetuates divisions in, and problems with, society.

Samantha states that ten years ago she worked as a hostess in a restaurant, but that she used the power the position gave her 'in a beneficent fashion'.

Carrie: She has a theory that shopping is a way of unleashing the creative unconsciousness. This probably explains her credit card bills. While shopping for shoes in Dolce & Gabbana, Carrie bumps into Amalita Amalfi, a woman she's only met a few times but who claims to think of Carrie like 'a sister'. Amalita is an international jet-set kind of girl, a 'professional girlfriend'. Not actually an escort, just a woman with no job who lives entirely off whichever fabulously rich man she's dating at the time. She gets through two boyfriends in the course of this episode, and seems to have no problems getting a table at Balzac's on two separate occasions.

Men: Amalita is (initially) dating Carlo who owns a ranch in Argentina. He apparently has 'a tiny little penis, but he knows exactly how to use it' (see **12**, 'Oh Come All Ye Faithful'). He's bought Amalita a $12,000 diamond and gold bracelet from the amazingly exclusive store Van Cleef & Arpels.

Amalita introduces Carrie to Gilles, an architect from Paris. He's divorced and has a five-year-old daughter called Beatrice. On meeting him Carrie tells us, 'I suddenly remembered my terrible weakness for gorgeous French architects.' They spend a whole day together, one that she describes as 'like being in a Claude Lelouch film', one entitled *A Man and a Slightly Neurotic Woman*. She stays the night in his hotel room, and after he's left to get his early flight Carrie finds he's left her $1,000 in an envelope with a note saying 'Thanks for the beautiful day'. She worries that this was in some way planned by Amalita. Although she had no intention of taking money from Gilles when she went out with him, he has clearly (in some sense) just paid her for sex. 'I don't understand. What [is it] about me screams "Whore"?' she asks Samantha and Miranda. She knows that there's no way she can return the money, but when Amalita tries to hook her up with another man (Mario, who owns one of the palaces on the Grand Canal in Venice), she refuses.

The City: When she's with Carlo, Amalita Amalfi stays in the fabulous limestone Four Seasons hotel, which is 57 East 57th St. They're doubtlessly in one of the $1,000 a night suites.

Fetishes: Skipper is becoming obsessed, both personally and sexually, with Miranda. At one point he wonders aloud if you can become addicted to a person. He turns up early to collect her from the girls' poker night, and admits to Carrie that he doesn't like to wash after having sex with Miranda because he likes to smell of her for the rest of the day. On the up side, his sense of style is improving.

Charlotte: Legendary painter Neville Morgan is making his annual pilgrimage to Manhattan to check out what's new in the art world; he bumps into Charlotte in the street and fairly swiftly invites her to his ranch in Cincinnati to look at his most recent paintings. If they can reach an arrangement then it's possible he'll choose to exhibit through Charlotte's gallery, a major coup for her. Charlotte is worried that Morgan may attempt to make a move on her, or imply that he'll exhibit through her gallery only if she sleeps with him. Despite Samantha's urging that this is all fair game, Charlotte seems happier with Miranda's suggestion (see **Miranda**).

When she arrives at Morgan's ranch, Charlotte discovers that all of the old man's paintings are of one particular subject. 'Cunts,' rhapsodises Morgan. 'The source of all life and pleasure and beauty.' A slightly fazed Charlotte agrees. ('Charlotte,' comments Carrie afterwards, 'hated the C word'.)

Despite his crudity, Morgan actually behaves in a very gentlemanly and old-fashioned way towards Charlotte. He gets his doddering (and equally foul-mouthed) wife to bring her lemonade and cookies, and he clearly has no sexual interest in Charlotte at all.

He does however want to paint her . . . portrait.

Miranda: It's confirmed that Miranda studied law at Harvard. Which makes her very clever indeed. She tells Charlotte that if Neville Morgan suggests she should have sex with him in order to secure his work for her gallery she should instead call her so they can 'sue the hell out of him'.

Fashion Victims: Carrie's love of shoes. 'I have this little substance abuse problem,' she says. 'Expensive footwear.' It's clearly causing her problems, as when she tries to buy something in Dolce & Gabbana the credit card company authorise the store to cut the card up in front of her. She later says that 'dolce, dolce, dolce' is all the Italian she'll ever need to know. At one point Carrie finds herself in that common predicament: 'A closet full of clothes, nothing to wear.'

Trivia: This is, according to all authorities on the subject, the first time a US prime-time drama series uses the word 'cunt'.

And So . . .: 'Where's the line between professional girlfriend and just professional?' Visually dazzling, conceptually brilliant, thoughtful, truthful and really, really funny, this is the best episode of the first season. The point of the episode is that in the end a tiny act of simple kindness by Carrie (giving the hostess a tampon when she needs one) is worth more in the world than any cynical attempt to compete. The best favours are those done without obligation and the implication of reward. This could be seen as a deliberate validation of Miranda's attitudes over Samantha's, but the writers hold back from explicitly making that point. The inevitable ideological row between Samantha and Miranda that's been brewing since the series started actually breaks out as the girls play poker, and it looks for a moment as if it's going to turn quite nasty. It's also brilliant that Morgan turns out to be a sweet, genuine (if coarse) eccentric rather than a dirty old man.

6
Secret Sex

12 July 1998

Written by Darren Star
Directed by Michael Fields

Guest Cast
Chris Noth (Mr Big) Michael Port (Mike)
David Aaron Baker (Ted Baker) Heather Barclay (Libby Biyallick)
Philip Coccioletti (Mr Big's Friend) Glenn Fleschler (Schmuel)

Carrie: Carrie has had her picture taken as a promotional photo for her column. It is going to run on the side of a bus. 'I had misgivings, which were somewhat mollified when they told me I could keep the dress.'

Girl Talk: This dress, described by Charlotte as 'the naked dress', is the one Carrie decides to wear on her first proper date with Big. Samantha, Charlotte and Miranda gather to see Carrie off, and their meeting evolves into a discussion about 'sex on the first date'.
  Charlotte, as ever, is keen to stick to *The Rules*, pointing out that they make clear that if a woman is serious about a man she should keep him in a 'holding pattern' for at

least five dates. She explains that if a relationship starts with sex, it will never be about more than sex.

Samantha: 'The women who wrote that book wrote it because they couldn't get laid; so they constructed this whole bullshit theory to make women who can get laid feel bad.' She also argues that in any potentially long-term relationship it's important to establish if the sex is good right off the bat, before anyone's feelings get hurt.

Hey, Big Guy: Carrie gets into the cab with Mr Big. He calls her dress 'interesting' and then informs her that he's quite capable of restraining himself. She says that she is as well. And then they both totally fail to. After sex at Big's place, Carrie decides that if he never calls her again she will always think of him fondly . . . as an asshole. They then go for dinner at a Chinese restaurant, leading Carrie to worry that a) he's discovered her weaknesses for great sex and Chinese food and b) this is a diversionary tactic designed to stop her staying the night. Later, Big phones Carrie and tells her that he can't stop thinking about her ('I love trite,' she replies). He suggests they go for a 'proper' first date, a traditional American one: dinner and a movie.

Miranda: While kick boxing in the gym, Miranda accidentally belts someone round the head. That someone, Ted Baker, takes something of a shine to her, and they end up dating. He's 32, a sports medicine doctor, and has an apartment overlooking the National History Museum. He's had three previous serious relationships, none of which resulted in marriage.

Men: Mike Singer, the creative director of an ad agency and a man who has been a friend of Carrie's for ten years. She claims that they've never had sex because she wants to know him for another ten years. He's dating Libby Biyallik, whom he met over the cheese counter in a delicatessen while he was going through a bad break-up. He's hidden her from his friends because he doesn't think she's beautiful and he knows they have very little in common. He concedes that she's warm and unpretentious,

that she's one of the few women he's ever known that he
feels he can be himself with, and that they have the best sex
that he's ever had in his life, but he insists that she's not
right for him in a larger sense. Despite this he's been dating
her for three months and making sure she doesn't encounter any of his acquaintances. Does *anyone* think this is
reasonable behaviour on his part?

Fit to Print: Mike's activities lead Carrie to write a column
about 'Secret Sex'. Is it, she ponders, '. . . the purest form
of intimacy, since it exists . . . exempt from the judgement
of the world, or is it just another way in which we deny our
feelings and endlessly compartmentalise our lives?' She
begins to fear that she's simply Mr Big's secret sex girl, but
later concludes this is simply paranoia caused by Mike's
behaviour (but see **12**, 'Oh Come All Ye Faithful').

Fetishes: Looking through Ted's apartment, Miranda discovers a 'spanking video', a pornographic movie in which
most of the action consists of a man being spanked.
Initially appalled by this, she comes to the decision that she
may warm to the idea if he's worth the effort generally.
After a marvellous evening, she makes references to his
fetish and he panics. According to Carrie, he never spoke
to Miranda again, refused to take her calls and never
returned to the gym.

   Oh, Miranda in kick-boxing gear would clearly do it for
some people.

Wine and Dine: Big twice takes Carrie to Fung Wa's, which
he thinks does the best Chinese food in the whole of New
York City. It isn't a real restaurant.

Charlotte: Samantha tells Carrie that Charlotte had a
'secret sex' relationship with a rabbi. While this turns out
to be an exaggeration, it is true that she had an affair with
an orthodox Jewish painter whom she met by viewing his
paintings. She never introduced him to any of her friends
because their lifestyles were so incompatible. Carrie describes this as 'so forbidden, Daddy's little Episcopalian
princess in the arms of one of God's chosen people'.

Fashion Victims: At the launch of the bus with Carrie's picture on, the girls all wear silly pointy party hats.

Kisses: Carrie and Big failing to restrain themselves in the back of the limo. Wow.

And So . . .: 'Is this for real?' After last week this initially all seems a bit ordinary; Miranda's plotline is funny but clearly has nowhere to go and Samantha does nothing at all. However, the story of Charlotte and the rabbi is brilliant and Chris Noth gets his first real chance to shine as Mr Big, turning in a deadpan and charming performance. The big difference between Mike's 'secret sex' relationship with Libby and Charlotte's with Schmuel is that both Schmuel and Charlotte wanted the relationship kept secret, whereas Libby clearly doesn't like the situation with Mike, but can't change it except by dumping him (which ultimately she does). The final visual joke with Carrie's bus is brilliant, but you're going to have to watch the episode to find out what it is.

7
The Monogamists

19 July 1998

Written and Directed by Darren Star

Guest Cast
Chris Noth (Mr Big) Willie Garson (Stanford Blatch)
Ben Weber (Skipper Johnston) Caroline Aaron (Pamela Glock)
Jack Koenig (Michael Conway) Justin Theroux (Jared)
James McCaffrey (Max) Avalon (Julia) Todd Barry (Ordinary Guy)
Michael Dale (Rick Connelly)
Melissa Darling (Almost Together Woman)
Kate Jennings Grant (Allison Roth) Susan Malfitano (Ordinary Woman)
John Scurti (Chunky Gay Guy) Michael Spiller (Slick Guy)

Carrie: We are told that Manhattan Island is a cosy village of seven and a half million people who act as if they own the sidewalk, and also how somehow recently it has seemed as if there are only two people in the City: Carrie and Big.

Noting how quickly time spent with Big passes, Carrie wonders if Einstein's theories regarding relativity should be revised to take account of infatuation. She realises that she's 'become one of those women we hate' and that she's prioritising her new boyfriend over her longtime girl-friends, and has thus committed the cardinal sin of modern metropolitan life. She agrees to go to dinner with Sam, Miranda and Charlotte, an occasion she refers to as 'the tribunal'.

Wine and Dine: In the period since Carrie 'dropped off the map', Samantha has become obsessed with finding a new apartment, Miranda has presided over a terribly important merger of some kind or another and Charlotte has met a marvellous new man. Michael Conway is from a good New York family and obviously adores her, but there's a problem.

Fetishes: Charlotte can't and won't give Michael a blow job. 'She'll juggle, she'll spin plates, but she won't give head,' comments Carrie. Charlotte says that she has a very sensitive 'gag reflex' and subsequently can't bear to have a penis in her mouth. 'It makes me wanna puke,' she comments. She has frequently practised on bananas but it makes no difference in reality. Miranda says she likes oral sex, but won't swallow. Carrie points out that this is basically a lifestyle choice, and therefore clearly up to the individual, and Samantha counters that some guys don't give you the choice. 'It's not my favourite thing on the menu,' says Carrie, 'but I'll order it from time to time.' Sam claims to enjoy the sense of power it gives her. 'Maybe you're on your knees, but you've got them by the balls.'

Fit to Print: After dinner with the girls, Carrie bumps into Mr Big, who appears to be on a date with someone else. Initially shocked and appalled by this, Carrie then falls headlong into a crisis over monogamy. Is it a casualty of modern life, and is it too much for the citizens of Manhattan to expect it? How does Big really feel about her? Predictably it becomes the subject of her next column.

Guy Talk: 'Is it that men have an innate aversion to monogamy?' Asked in the street about the subject of monogamy, people come up with a wide variety of opinions. One guy claims that he believes in monogamy, but his definition includes sex with prostitutes. Another says that he and his partner have a kind of '90s monogamy' – they'll have sex with other people, but won't exchange bodily fluids or telephone numbers.

Girl Talk: Also asked in the street, a young woman responds that monogamy 'gives you a deep and profound connection to another human being, and you don't have to shave your legs as much'.

Samantha: Sam is apparently incapable of being monogamous with her real-estate dealers, as she's apartment hunting with several different agents while promising all of them that she'd never deal with anyone else. She flirts with her male broker and begins to have sex with him as they close the deal. This is completely in line with her comments in **5** 'The Power of Female Sex', and we can be sure that Miranda, at least, wouldn't approve.

Out and About: Big tries to make it up with Carrie, and takes her to a party at the house of his friends Max and Becky. Here she meets a woman who claims that Big still has her passport ('We travelled together,' he explains), and when Big introduces her to Max as 'someone special' he assumes she's 'Julia'. Put off and put out, Carrie leaves.

Men: Stanford claims that monogamy is on the way out. Again. It had a bit of a 90s renaissance but as the millennium approaches it's becoming unfashionable again. Carrie tells him he's a whore. 'I wish that were true,' he counters.

Stanford introduces Carrie to Jared, who is officially one of the 30 coolest people under 30 in NYC. He's written a novel called *Avenue B* and is taking the New York literary scene by storm. He has a terrible line in non-ironic slang ('ciao' and 'groovy') and great taste in shirts. He may be bisexual. He invites Carrie to a big party being held in his honour at the Luna Park Café, and promises to put her name on the door. After the incident with Big she decides to go, and then phones him to tell him that she's thinking of going home with Jared and that he can stop this by meeting her outside the club and talking with her about 'them'.

Miranda gets jealous when she sees Skipper out with another woman. Carrie points out that this is hardly fair, as it was she who dumped him. Skipper's new girlfriend Allison works in 'designer relations' at *Vogue* magazine, and is gorgeous.

Miranda: She calls Skipper's house while he's having sex with Allison, and asks him to go out with her some time. Skipper's resolve collapses and he tells Allison he's going back to Miranda. 'You're breaking up with me while you're still inside of me?' a justifiably astonished and appalled Allison bursts out.

After Skipper has gone to Miranda's place and they've had sex, he tells her about this. She tells him that he needn't have broken up with Allison as she'd assumed that 'we can see each other and still see other people, right?' Skipper tells her that he *can't*, such is his devotion to monogamy in general, and her in particular. The occasionally biting Johnston wit reappears as he calls her 'Miss Dial-A-Fuck' and then leaves.

Fashion Victims: There's a lot of tie-related stuff going on here, for some reason. Miranda's is ghastly but Big's is great. Stanford wears a pink tie and a red jumper that shouldn't be allowed in the same room together.

Trivia: According to executive producer/creator Darren Star, this episode was originally going to go rather further in pushing back the boundaries of sex on television. After Charlotte's departure from his apartment, Michael was to be seen being fellated by his dog, Buttercup. This was cut after HBO objected to the scene. According to Star, this was due to it being 'disturbingly realistic'. In June 2000 he told *The Times*, 'We shouldn't have cut it, but it was the first season and we'd gotten away with so much that I was like, "OK, whatever." ' He also admitted, 'I thought it was funny, y'know?'

And So . . .: 'Don't you wanna sit still with me?' A rollercoaster examination of Carrie's (ultimately justified) paranoia, paired with a quite disconcerting look at what some people consider to be 'monogamy'. It's hard to see how Charlotte's plotline isn't really just a re-run of **4**, 'Valley of the Twenty-Something Guys', and neither Miranda nor Skipper come out of their scenes with much credit at all. Her actions are motivated entirely by jealousy, whereas he's acting out of something quite close to unrequited love. This would possibly give him a slight edge if his actions resulting from it weren't so utterly appalling. His final scene with Miranda does seem to be there to knock a hole in the idea (advocated earlier in the episode by Carrie) that men have an innate aversion to monogamy. Big and Carrie's conversation in the car park of the Luna Park Café seems inconclusive but is intense and sweet, with both actors really giving it all they've got.

8
Three's a Crowd

26 July 1998

Written by Jenny Bicks
Directed by Nicole Holofcener

Guest Cast

Chris Noth (Mr Big) Gerry Bamman (Shrink) Noelle Beck (Barbara)
Joseph Murphy (Jack) Sherri Alexander (Peacock Woman)
Catherine Corpeny (Wife) Amy Delucia (Beautiful Woman)
Laura Ekstrand (Plain Woman) Lisa Emery (Ruth, Mid-Thirties Woman)
PJ Heslin (Husband) Toni James (Normal Woman)
Suzanne Smith (Long Island Woman) Matthew Sussman (Wall St Man)
Carmi Turchick (Scottie) Jonathan Walker (Ken)

Charlotte: 'Once upon a time, in a magical land called Manhattan, a young woman fell in love.' Charlotte is dating Jack, an architect and philanthropist, and the sex is amazing. One night he asks what her fantasies are.

Charlotte confesses that she's always wanted to have sex in her parents' bed, and Jack tells her that his ultimate fantasy is him, her and another woman in a threesome.

Girl Talk: Charlotte convenes a meeting of the usual suspects to discuss this. She tells them Jack wants to have a threesome. 'Of course he does, every guy does,' retorts Miranda, while Samantha points out that threesomes are 'the blow job of the 90s'. The blow job of the 80s was apparently anal sex. Miranda dismisses Jack's fantasy as 'a cheap ploy to watch you be a lesbian for a night', which based on what he himself says to Charlotte is actually a pretty accurate view.

Samantha admits that she's been involved in threesomes; Carrie hasn't, and Miranda says she may have done at college but she can't remember. All she knows is that one morning after getting very drunk she woke up wearing someone else's bra. Charlotte says that if she goes through with it, it would be easier on her if the third party were a friend, like Carrie. Carrie demurs and suggests the 'more experienced' Samantha. Miranda contrives to be offended that no one has suggested her. 'Everyone forget me!' she says. 'I'd do it with you guys. It's like picking teams for dodge ball all over again.'

Fit to Print: Carrie wonders if threesomes are the new sexual frontier, pondering that much of life is built on threes: fat, low fat, non-fat; first, business, economy; Moe, Larry and Curly (The Three Stooges). Carrie looks at the ads for threesomes in the paper: 'Wall St honcho seeks two horny gal pals for an East Hampton fuck fest ... No fatties please' and 'Me gorgeous with big boobs, you a couple with class .. I'm into museums, blow jobs, theatre and golden showers' are two of the funniest, but the most disturbing, is the '*X-Files* fanatic twosome' who 'seek Scully lookalike for abduction fantasy'. Scary.

Samantha: Sam's advice (if one is to take part in a threesome it should be as the 'guest star' so one doesn't have to deal with the relationship fall-out) is eminently, almost ruthlessly, practical. At the moment she's having regular sex with Ken, who's 37 and a wine importer. Ken is married to Ruth, who designs office furniture. Sam bumps into Ken and his wife in the street one day, and shortly afterwards he phones her to tell her that he's left his wife so that he and Sam can be together. Sam, of course, panics, refusing any such suggestion and pointing out that companionship was not what their relationship was about. She then fields a call from Ruth, who tells her that she's prepared to join Sam and Ken in a threesome if it will save her marriage. Sam panics some more.

Miranda: After the girls' discussion on threesomes, Miranda finds herself in a very vulnerable and paranoid place, emotionally speaking. Discussing her dreams with her therapist, she tells him of one where 'I'm in the sandbox with Charlotte, Sam and Carrie and they won't play with me'. Another finds her in a cab with the other three, and they won't let her sit in the back of the cab with them. Instead she has to ride up front with the cab driver instead. When her therapist insists on interpreting all this as Miranda being secretly attracted to her friends, it doesn't really help; worse, she finds that the more she analyses her dreams the more extreme her nightmares get. Eventually she answers an ad in a paper looking for a third party for a threesome; she meets the couple in a bar, and they seem very keen on her. Her ego boosted, Miranda makes her excuses and leaves. Clever.

Hey, Big Guy: Carrie discovers that Mr Big has an ex-wife called Barbara and that they once participated in a threesome. Unable to get this image out of her head, Carrie hunts her down and meets her. This is easier than it sounds because she works in publishing and Carrie pretends that she wants to pitch a book to her. On meeting her, Carrie is horrified that Barbara laughs at her jokes. 'Smart, beautiful and she got me. I have to kill her.' After a tense dinner where, as Big says, 'The food was terrible and we were talking to each other like strangers,' Carrie tells Big about her meeting with Barbara. What she's unaware of is that Big is still in regular contact with his ex-wife, and *she* has already told him.

Big tells Carrie that the reason he and Barbara had a threesome was because they were both looking for something or someone else. It was a symptom of the collapse of their relationship. We learn, somewhat worryingly, that Big cheated on his wife with her then best friend.

Trivia: The fact that Carrie is able to trace Big's ex-wife without his knowledge surely means that she knows his name even though we don't (see **94**, 'An American Girl in Paris (Part Deux)'. Charlotte's ambitions include owning her own gallery and having a cottage in Maine.

Out and About: The charity benefits that Jack and Charlotte attend include 'Circus for Cystic Fibrosis', 'A Night of a Thousand Tourettes' and (best of all) 'Hoe Down for Spina Bifida'.

Fetishes: Charlotte and Jack attend the 'Attention Deficit Disorder Masked Ball' where they jointly hit on women in order to try and get one into bed with them. 'It's amazing,' says Carrie, 'what some sequins on a stick can do to free up inhibitions.' Together Charlotte and Jack go upstairs and begin to make out in one of the bedrooms. A woman walks into the room behind them and asks if she can join in. Charlotte agrees, but the 'threesome' quickly degenerates into just the other woman and Jack having sex, and Charlotte walks away from it.

And So ...: 'Even if you're the only person in the bed, someone has always been there before you.' Greater than the sum of its parts, 'Three's a Crowd' often seems very contrived. The scene of Carrie pitching a book about a little girl who smokes magic cigarettes which take her to anywhere in the world is nowhere near as funny as it should be or as way out as it thinks it is. Also, are all of Charlotte's plotlines going to be about how she doesn't want to 'do' a particular sex act? Sam's sheer panic and Miranda's neuroses are very funny, completely in character and not overdone.

9
The Turtle and the Hare

2 August 1998

Written by Nicole Avril & Sue Kolinsky
Directed by Michael Fields

Guest Cast
Chris Noth (Mr Big) Willie Garson (Stanford Blatch)
Haviland Morris (Brooke) Tim Wheeler (Bernie Turtletaub 'The Turtle')
Sebastian Roche (Jerry) Merrill Holtzman (Personal Ad Guy)
Mimi Weddell (Stanford's Grandmother)

Out and About: It's said that in New York, 'a city of
perfect people', no one is 'more perfect than Brooke'. For
years, her every Saturday night was 'like senior prom' as
she dated a variety of guys in a variety of impressive
settings. Now she's getting married, to a guy she once
described to Carrie as 'more boring than exposed brick-
work'. The guest list at the wedding includes investment
bankers 'and the women who hate them' and ... Carrie,
Sam, Miranda and Charlotte, all of whom are placed on
the 'singles' table and none of whom are having a good
time. When talking to her after her vows, Carrie is
disturbed by Brooke's assertion that it is 'always better
to marry someone who loves you more than you love them'.

Carrie: Carrie and Big discuss Brooke's comment, and Big
admits to Carrie that the one thing marriage taught him is
that he should never again be married. Despite the fact
that she was not envisaging marrying him, this disturbs
Carrie, who wonders if (given that marriage is one of her
long-term goals) it's really a good idea for her to date a
man who will never get married. This, combined with
Brooke's comment, sends Carrie into a mini-crisis on the
subject of marriage. Inevitably a 'conference' of the four
friends is called, at which they discuss Carrie's dilemma
and its ramifications. Miranda thinks that marriage is
strictly for men who miss their mothers, while Charlotte is
convinced that any relationship has to be based on honesty

and communication if it has any chance of succeeding. In the episode's funniest line Samantha tells her, 'If you were twenty that would be adorable, but you're thirty-two now, so that's stupid.'

Miranda: It is Miranda's opinion that men will be obsolete within 50 years. Women already can't talk to them, don't need them to have children, and now don't even need them for sex. She tells her friends about The Rabbit, her new vibrator. She says she thinks she's in love. Carrie argues that she isn't going to replace a man with some battery-operated device, to which Miranda replies, 'You say that, but you haven't met The Rabbit.'

Charlotte: At the wedding Charlotte is desperately keen to catch the bridal bouquet. When out shopping with Miranda, Charlotte buys The Rabbit (only $92), partially because it's pink and partially because it has a cute face 'like Peter Rabbit'. After a few days Charlotte is spending more time alone in her apartment with The Rabbit than outside it with her friends. She even begins to miss appointments (and nearly a gallery opening in Chelsea). Eventually this begins to disturb even Miranda, and she and Carrie carry out the equivalent of a military strike on Charlotte's apartment, seizing the vibrator from her. They call this the 'Rabbit Intervention'. Miranda is appalled that Charlotte has hidden it inside a stuffed toy rabbit.

Men: Bernie Turtletaub, known as 'The Turtle', is famous in New York circles for two things – great investment advice and very bad breath. He has one chat-up line: 'Do you like this shirt? My ex-girlfriend picked it out for me.'

Stanford places a personal ad in a paper that describes him as an 'Ed Harris' type. He meets the only respondent, who then turns him down. 'Even guys like me don't want guys like me,' he complains, and says that he sometimes thinks of throwing the towel in, faking being straight and getting married. When Carrie queries this, he tells her that, as with the rest of his siblings and cousins, his grandmother will only release his share of their inheritance to him when he gets married. He suggests to Carrie that *they* marry. He'll get his money and she'll have a husband who shares all her passions, including men. They get as far as a meeting with Stanford's grandmother (who refers to him as 'My Stanny') but the old woman is clearly aware that Stanford is gay (although she'll never admit this to him). Her conversation with Carrie makes the younger woman realise that, yes, she does want to have children at some point. This is something of a surprise even to her, and rather puts a dampener on the idea of a lavender marriage between Stanford and herself.

Samantha: Sam has a date with Jerry whom she met at the wedding; they meet at the Luna Café (see **4**, 'Valley of the Twenty-Something Guys'). He's initially very charming and tells her that when he sees something that he wants he goes out and gets it. Sam is clearly impressed. When he fails to return from a trip to the restroom she eventually goes looking for him, only to discover him hitting on another woman. Visibly wounded by the casualness of this rejection, she goes to leave, only to be hollered at by The Turtle, who is sitting alone at a nearby table. After much persuading she joins him for dinner – and The Turtle explains his bad breath in terms of 'Chinese herbs' that he takes for longer life. Sam points out that although he may live longer, he'll need to as at the moment no one will go anywhere near him. After spending some time with The Turtle, Samantha decides she likes him, and begins to work on him, describing him to her friends as 'a cute little fixer-upper'. She gets him to buy Helmut Lang clothes and take regular facials at (exclusive beauty parlour) Bliss. Eventually she tires of his eccentricities and abandons him in a restaurant. After she leaves he immediately starts hitting on the first woman he sees.

Wine and Dine: The Turtle spends every meal attempting to identify the ingredients in his food and pondering on the source of the olive oil or the exact type of mushrooms used in the dish. No one on earth could blame Samantha for finding this extremely annoying.

Fashion Victims: At Brooke's wedding Carrie thinks that
she and her friends look like the witches of Eastwick,
referring to the Jack Nicholson horror/comedy (George
Miller, 1987). At one point Samantha refuses to sit down,
saying that her outfit (a little black dress) only works when
she's standing up. Stanford's grandmother wears a pink
twinset designed by Coco Chanel herself. She has dupli-
cates in a variety of colours including blue, black and
eggshell.

Trivia: Ed Harris is a balding, versatile actor who appeared
in, among other things, *Nixon* (Oliver Stone, 1995) and
Glengarry Glen Ross (James Foley, 1992).

And So . . .: 'Could I date a man who would never get
married?' This is the most traditionally 'sitcom' episode of
the first season. The diversion with Stanford's grandmother is brilliant; it's very funny, rather unexpected and
quite revealing in terms of Carrie's character. It's a
cunning reversal of expectations that Charlotte gets the
sexually loaded comic plotline and Samantha the slightly
fluffy relationship-based one, and this brings out aspects of
both their characters never really glimpsed before. The
problem between Big and Carrie that forms the core of the
episode is not so much dealt with as allowed to slip away,
to be dealt with in the fullness of time.

10
The Baby Shower

9 August 1998

Written by Terry Minsky
Directed by Susan Seidelman

Guest Cast
Dana Wheeler-Nicholson (Laney Berlin) Betsy Aidem (Susan)
Debbon Ayer (Mindy) Blair Hickey (Jonathan) Anne Lange (Gretchen)
Toby Poser (Mother) Lois Robbins (Brigid) Robin Ruzan (Roxanne)
Richard Toth (Fred) Welker White (Rebecca)

Fit to Print: 'Sometimes there is nothing harder in life than being happy for somebody else.' Carrie introduces us to Laney Berlin, a one-time New York City girl who ran with Carrie's crowd, and tells us how she changed her life completely. She married a Wall St investment banker and moved to Connecticut, whereas Carrie feels it would have been more in character for Laney to have sex with Sid Vicious and then move on to heroin. In swapping a lifestyle of bar chewing, bed hopping and taking her clothes off in public for suburban homemaking, Laney left her friends and her city behind. Once upon a time she was involved in A&R for a major record label, signing bands and sleeping with rock stars, and now, horror of horrors, she's having a baby.

(Outside) The City: Laney lives at 77 Hollyhock Lane in an affluent suburb. The tree-lined road distresses Carrie, who wonders how something involving so much nature could seem so unnatural. The suburban mothers the girls meet are wonderfully sinister – one tells Miranda with a kind of blank-eyed psychotic insistence that she tells her son he is 'a god' every single day. Another tries to paint herself as a rebel, telling how she'll climb into 'the kids' treehouse with [her] Walkman, light up a joint and listen to Peter Frampton'. We see that Laney has 'invisible electric fencing', some kind of alarm field that prevents her dog from leaving her grounds and sets off an alarm if unauthorised persons acquire access to her driveway.

Girl Talk: Samantha says that it's very sad that Laney needs to use a baby to validate herself, leaving Carrie to point out that it's obviously much better to use a cocktail and sex for this purpose like a normal person would. Miranda claims that if she sees another crepe-paper stork she's going to rip its little cardboard beak off.

Charlotte: Poor Charlotte is devastated when she hears that Laney may call her baby 'Shayla', a name that she invented for herself as a child. It's the name of the daughter she's always known she'll one day have. This shock causes her to open her 'dream box', a wooden chest containing photographs of ideal husbands, dream houses and gifts for her hypothetical baby, including a cushion with 'Shayla' embroidered on it.

Miranda: Miranda has a neat line in condemning thirty-something mothers. 'They think the same, dress the same, sacrifice themselves to the same cause. I've lost two sisters to The Motherhood,' she tells her friends. She argues that the witch in *Hansel and Gretel* is misunderstood, being simply a woman who takes just revenge on some children for spoiling her dream house. She gets the episode's best line, when she warns her friends that the mothers are a cult and that they'll try and convert them by forcing them to 'separate from the herd' and picking them off one by one.

Men: Ed, whom Samantha seduces so he'll do her tax returns for free.

    Jonathan, a 'trader' who meets Charlotte at a party; she uses an imagined version of him to 'mentally Scotch-tape her dream house back together'.

Fashion Victims: The flashback to the late 80s is amazing: Miranda's dreadful hair, Carrie's cowboy hat, Sam's entire outfit. Only Charlotte escapes with any dignity, chiefly by not being in the scene at all. We are told that Samantha has recently spent $395 on a pair of Gucci shoes, but sadly we don't get to see them.

Carrie: Carrie has a pregnancy scare when she realises her period is four days late. Wondering if she could cope with the responsibility and the changes in her life that would result from having a child, she does a huge amount of soul searching. 'What if I am?' she asks Miranda. 'If you am, you am,' her friend replies. Carrie feels she's unfit to be a parent, pointing out that as a child she taped her dog Pepper's jaw shut and shaved her Barbie's head because she was angry with her. At the very end of this episode there's a lovely scene as Carrie sits watching some children in a park, weighing up her possible future – although the wondering stops as, on her way home, she finally gets her period.

Trivia: Carrie's address (as printed on her baby shower invitation) is 245 East 73rd St, New York City. Recording artist Peter Frampton is mentioned.

Samantha: Carrie draws parallels between Samantha and the old Laney – 'both wild, both sexy, both incredibly insecure'. Samantha is the harshest on the new Laney and seems to regard her change in lifestyle as a personal betrayal. She's delighted by the idea that pregnant Laney will inevitably get very fat and takes a bottle of Scotch to the baby shower. Later she throws an I-don't-have-a-baby shower, at which she invites everyone to get drunk and celebrate his or her lack of offspring. Laney turns up at the party and makes a rather wretched fool of herself, getting very drunk and shouting, 'Who wants to see a pregnant woman's tits?' (No one does.) Sam watches approvingly, saying, 'This is, at once, so sad and the most fabulous validation I've ever gotten in my life.'

Also Starring: Dana Wheeler-Nicholson (Laney Berlin) is best known for playing the female lead in Chevy Chase's seminal *Fletch* (Michael Ritchie, 1985). Other film work of note includes playing Mattie Blaylock Earp (Wyatt's wife) in *Tombstone* (George P Cosmatos, 1993) with Kurt Russell, and playing half of *Nick and Jane* (Richard Mauro, 1997). TV work includes guest spots in *Seinfeld, Law & Order, NYPD Blue* and *The X-Files*. In 2001 she took the regular role of Ilene Pringle in popular US soap opera *All My Children*.

And So . . .: 'Oh, Toto, I don't think we're in Manhattan any more.' This episode takes a long hard look at the changes in lifestyle gone through by someone who was once, essentially, Samantha, and comes to the conclusion that she's made a mistake in becoming someone else. We're encouraged to feel sorry for Laney and her new life because it simply isn't right for her, but are also shown that her situation is Charlotte's ultimate ambition. Even Carrie may, in the right circumstances, want something similar. Dana Wheeler-Nicholson's performance is remarkably complex and assured given the small amount of time she's on screen. Carrie's final judgement on Laney is devastatingly effective: 'Despite her best efforts to be free, it seemed that Laney Berlin's invisible fencing stretched all the way to Manhattan.'

11
The Drought

16 August 1998

Written by Michael Green and Michael Patrick King
Directed by Matthew Harrison

Guest Cast
Chris Noth (Mr Big) Anthony DeSando (Siddhartha)
David Lee Russek (Kevin) Dann Fink (Man) Joe Gately (Wall St Guy)
Angela McNally (Early-Thirties Woman) Joe Mosso (Very Married Man)
Ellen Synn (Korean Woman) Ed Vassallo (Eddie)

Fit to Print: New York City is all about sex. It's the City That Never Sleeps because everybody is too busy trying to get laid. With 1.3 million single men sharing the city with 1.8 million single women, Carrie estimates that roughly 12 people in the whole of NYC think they are getting enough sex.

Guy Talk: We see some random people in the street discussing their sexual problems. One man says that he and his wife haven't had sex 'since the baby was born'. Unfortunately, 'the baby' is now of college age. Another guy claims that he has to masturbate 13 times every 24 hours just to get through the day. Most people have coffee breaks; he has 'jerk-off' breaks.

Carrie: Carrie has been seeing Mr Big for several weeks now. She likes the fact that they have become comfortable enough to sleep together instead of simply having sex. One morning, however, disaster strikes – she farts while they're in bed together. Big seems to find this very, very funny, but Carrie is horribly embarrassed. She rushes out of Big's place as fast as she can, and later claims that she hasn't got dressed that quickly since she was discovered in the boys' dorm during sophomore year. After briefly considering moving to another city where the shame of this awful event won't follow her, Carrie becomes increasingly fixated on what happened. One night Big is too tired for sex, and she interprets this as his being revolted by her since 'the incident'. She frets that she isn't perfect enough for this perfect man and his perfect life. 'I'm the girl who farts,' she tells Miranda. 'You're insane,' her friend replies. Carrie then redecorates her kitchen to take her mind off her problems, painting all her cabinets eggshell white. Eventually Big comes over, takes Carrie in his arms and assuages her worries about something he hasn't given a second thought to.

Samantha: When asked by Carrie for advice on how to deal with Big, Samantha argues that men quite simply aren't complicated and are more 'like plants' than anything else. They want women to be perfect and won't accept them if they aren't. This understandably doesn't really reassure Carrie at all. Samantha herself has a problem when she tries to seduce her yoga instructor, Siddhartha. He claims he's celibate. 'Why?' asks Sam. 'And again, why?' He has been celibate for three years, he explains, and practises tantric celibacy or 'Parmarchia', in which he never releases his sexual tension but allows it to flow around his body and renew him. Although initially sceptical, Sam is quite turned on by the idea of erotic readings and non-touching sessions with this guy, and so sits with him a few times. She quickly gets massively frustrated, horny and bored and eventually shags the first man out of her yoga class who'll say yes.

Miranda: She hasn't had sex for three months and one week. She claims that her first month of celibacy was 'interesting', the second 'numbing' and the third had her going out of her mind. She's resorted to renting lots of movies from Blockbuster Video, and is disturbed that she's built up enough loyalty points for the place to merit free bags of Gummi Bears. Movies she's rented include a five-hour documentary on the Nuremberg Trials of Nazi war criminals after World War II. She has an encounter with a workman who repeatedly shouts at her about how he has 'what you want', 'what you need'. She cracks, storming up to him and pointing out that what she needs is to get laid. Can he help? The workman points out that he's married and that he was joking, and Miranda storms off, having embarrassed the guy in front of all his buddies. When Miranda finds out about Samantha's tantric celibacy she's amazed, demanding to know why Sam is fasting when there are people out there starving.

Charlotte: Charlotte is dating a man who once dated Carrie. They haven't had sex yet, although they've become very close. Carrie finds this very confusing as she remembers him as being a sex maniac. Eventually the truth comes out when it is revealed that he is taking 'selective Seratonin re-uptake inhibiters' including Prozac. These drugs control his temper and mood swings but make it impossible for him to get an erection. After considering whether it's better to date a man who is kind and loving but who doesn't want sex, Charlotte gives up and leaves him. Carrie claims this is Charlotte discovering that she doesn't actually want something which she always thought she couldn't have.

Fashion Victims: While painting her kitchen Carrie wears a purple T-shirt emblazoned with the cover image from David Bowie's *Aladdin Sane* album.

And So . . .: 'I farted in front of my boyfriend.' Hmmm . . . There's occasionally some really funny 'laugh out loud' stuff in here, but it's a rather contrived and complacent episode that ultimately goes nowhere in terms of plot or characterisation. None of the individual plot strands have any real life, and Big seems bizarrely out of character a lot of the time (although the final scene with him and Carrie goes some way towards repairing the damage). 'The Drought' is the series' first real misfire, and not, frankly, one you'll want to re-watch very often.

12
Oh Come All Ye Faithful

23 August 1998

Written by Michael Patrick King
Directed by Matthew Harrison

Guest Cast
Chris Noth (Mr Big) Willie Garson (Stanford Blatch)
Ben Weber (Skipper Johnston) Jamie Goodwin (James)
John Benjamin Hickey (Thomas John Anderson)
Marian Seldes (Mrs Big) Duane Boutte (Allanne)
Marcia Jean Kurtz (Noanie) Novella Nelson (Mme Lordes)
Lazaro Perez (Interpreter) Christopher Wynkoop (Minister)

Samantha: One night in a jazz club, Samantha meets a handsome lawyer named James. They sit and listen to the music together, and after the club closes walk and talk for hours, and then Samantha does something that, according to Carrie, is extraordinary. She doesn't ask him to go back home with her. Over the next few weeks they date and talk, and Samantha is a changed woman. She claims she's in love and that James is the sort of man she could marry. She thanks Charlotte for talking 'all that bullshit', saying that some of it must have rubbed off on her. Carrie says that hearing Samantha say 'I'm in love' is an event as unfathomable as the parting of the Red Sea.

Charlotte: The possibility that Samantha might be in love, let alone the idea that she might get married before Charlotte does, sends the younger woman into a flat spin. She consults a number of highly regarded psychics, including Noanie Stine, who lives between Central Park West and Columbus and goes to the same kabbala class as Madonna, in order to discover when she'll get married. All agree that she never will. Ever. One even says that she is cursed, and then offers to remove the effects of the curse for $100. This is when Charlotte realises that the whole thing is just ridiculous and stops worrying.

Miranda: She's dating Thomas John Anderson, an up-and-coming New York playwright. Everything about him is perfect, except that immediately after sex he runs off and showers. And when Miranda says immediately she means *immediately*. Understandably she finds this rather disturbing and grows to resent it. Eventually she asks him what he's doing, and he tells her that while he was growing up, 'the nuns' told him sex was sinful, so he likes to take a shower straight afterwards to cleanse himself. Carrie later asks if this is a 'retro-baptism kind of thing', and Miranda admits that she has no idea. It disturbs her that she appears to be dating 'Catholic guy', the one religious person left in New York. It is suggested to Miranda that she shower with him, but she claims to be worried he'll pull out some garlic and a cross. Against this background, Anderson's frantic screams of 'Oh God!' every time we see them having sex become increasingly sinister, comical and disturbing.

Finally confronting Thomas, Miranda points out that his habit has some disturbing implications and that there's nothing sinful about sex. This sets off what can only be described as a 'Catholic guilt bomb' – Thomas rants about sex, sin, hell and repentance and then asks Miranda to leave. The guy has big issues, clearly. Carrie's narration mentions that this exact scene occurs in Anderson's later play, the wonderfully titled *Shower of Shame*.

Carrie: Miranda's religious concerns cause Carrie to spend one Sunday walking around Manhattan looking at churches. She's very surprised to see Mr Big coming out of Park Avenue Presbyterian, arm in arm with an old woman. He spots Carrie from the other side of the road and goes over to talk to her. She expresses her surprise that he's religious, saying that she thought he only believed in the Yankees. He tells her that he's an atheist but takes his mother to church every Sunday because she has no one else to go with. Carrie is initially impressed by this simple act of kindness, but it quickly sets off her paranoid streak. Worried because Big won't introduce her to his mother (and irritated that when she asks him outright to take her to church with them, he refuses, citing it as his and his mother's private time), she sneaks into the church one Sunday, hoping to get a better look at Mrs Big, and maybe force his hand when it comes to introducing them. He does, but tells his mother that Carrie is his 'friend'. After Mother has gone to talk to the pastor, Big tells Carrie that he doesn't want his mother to meet another girlfriend until he's 'sure', which upsets her as *she* is 'sure'.

Girl Talk: Everyone discusses their various religion-related traumas. Charlotte is impressed that Big attends Park Avenue Presbyterian as it's a 'very good' church. Carrie asks if there's a Zagat guide to churches, like the one for restaurants and hotels. This leads Miranda to speculate that some entries might read: 'Three stars, good bread, disappointing wine selection.'

Fashion Victims: As people pour out of the church, Carrie approvingly notes the labels responsible for their clothing – Valentino, Escada, Armani and Oscar de la Renta. When she and Miranda sneak a visit to Big's church, Carrie is wearing a shocking green and white striped summer dress with tiny white cotton gloves and a hat the size of a UFO. Special mention to Charlotte's wonderful square-topped deep maroon dress in her scene with Madonna's psychic.

Trivia: Carrie says that she was brought up in the 'Be nice to people and don't talk with your mouth full' church, indicating a distinctly secular upbringing.

Out and About: Stanford throws a huge party to celebrate the launch of a new fragrance, Fallen Angel, and to allow everyone to meet his new boyfriend, Allanne. He's very happy, telling Carrie, 'I've become one of those couples we hate and I'm loving it'. He describes the club they're in as 'like hell with a cover charge'.

Men: Miranda bumps into Skipper at Stanford's party; he tells her she looks wonderful, and she returns the compliment. It seems the intervening months have given her a new perspective on Skipper, or at least his shower-free attitude towards sex, and she asks him to go home with her and spend the night. 'The whole night?' he asks, and she nods. He tells her that he always knew they'd get back together, and that he lit a candle and prayed for it every day. She looks at him, justifiably appalled, and says, 'You're a freak'.

James, Samantha's dream guy, has a penis which is three inches when erect. Samantha is devastated, crying and wailing in the restrooms at a club. She loves 'a big dick', 'the feel of it . . . the look of it . . . *everything* about it'. She really likes James, maybe loves him, and she can almost certainly never be with him long term. When we last see her, she is having sex with James and looking utterly miserable. This whole plotline is quite funny but also strangely condemning. Samantha chucks out her world view and replaces it with Charlotte's at a few days' notice, much as Carrie predicted she would in **1**, 'Sex and the City'. She finds the right guy and gives up on everything that is proudly and uniquely 'her', then when she realises that he literally doesn't measure up, she's left deeply upset. It almost feels as if this is designed as her 'comeuppance': retribution meted out to her for her actions in the rest of the season. This is a shame, especially considering how non-judgemental the series usually is. One can't imagine fans of Samantha being all that impressed with this episode.

Hey, Big Guy: Big and Carrie plan to go to the Caribbean for a holiday – and he's paying. However, after their confrontation at the church, and Big's not being 'sure' about them, Carrie finds herself unable to go with him unless he says that he loves her, and admits that he feels she's 'the one'. Unable to bring himself to say any such thing, Big departs, leaving Carrie standing alone on the sidewalk. After he left she cried for a week, she tells us, but discovered that she still had faith in herself, and faith that she will one day meet someone who knows she's 'the one'.

And So . . .: 'Are relationships the religion of the nineties?' Clearly designed to function as both a series finale (should the show not have been renewed) and a springboard for a second season, this episode is often very funny indeed. However, Charlotte's little crisis is rather dull, especially when compared with, say, **10**, 'The Baby Shower'. Fortunately the Carrie/Big angst and some wonderful Miranda-based comedy (Cynthia Nixon is *exceptionally* brilliant in this episode) manage to pull the episode round. The final scene especially is rather wonderful.

Season Two (1999)

Created by Darren Star
Based on the book by Candace Bushnell

Executive Producer: Darren Star
Executive Producer: Michael Patrick King
Supervising Producer: Jenny Bicks
Supervising Producer: John Melfi
Co-Producer: Jane Raab
Co-Producer: Antonia Ellis
Associate Producer: Mark McGann
Associate Producer: Amy B Harris
Executive Consultant: Sarah Jessica Parker

Regular Cast
Sarah Jessica Parker (Carrie Bradshaw) Kim Cattrall (Samantha Jones)
Kristin Davis (Charlotte York) Cynthia Nixon (Miranda Hobbes)

13
Take Me Out to the Ball Game

6 June 1999

Written by Michael Patrick King
Directed by Allen Coulter

Guest Cast
Chris Noth (Mr Big) Rob Bogue (Paul Ericson)
Mark Devine ('New Yankee' Joe Stark) Jamie Goodwin (James)
Larry Doby Jr (Large Baseball Player) Marilyn Dobrin (Vendor Woman)
Maggie Kiley (Woman #1) Keira Naughton (Yuppie Woman)
Jason Testa (Pot Head Loser Guy)

Carrie: In somewhere like Manhattan, 'the chances of bumping into the one who broke your heart are incredibly high. The odds of bumping into him when you look like shit are even higher.' Carrie explains how, after a break-up, there are streets, locations and even times of day that seem off limits; as if New York is a battlefield loaded with emotional landmines, a place where you have to be careful where you tread for fear of being blown into tiny pieces.

Out and About: Miranda and Charlotte charge into Carrie's apartment and force her to go out with them. She agrees, as long they promise to take her somewhere where there's no chance of bumping into Big. Given this, Miranda's choice of destination, Yankee Stadium for a ball game, is somewhat odd. Big is a committed Yankees fan (as stated in **12**, 'Oh Come All Ye Faithful', and reiterated later in this episode). Carrie quite enjoys the game, but insists that it's being able to drink and smoke at 2 p.m. without fear of being judged that really appeals to her. Carrie uses her press pass to get them into the players' area, where she wants to get the match ball (which was foul hit into the stands near them) signed. Carrie persuades Joe Stark, one of the Yankees' new star pitchers, to go with her to the Dolce & Gabbana party.

Samantha: Samantha is still with James, he of the tiny penis and limited sexual repertoire. He's clearly besotted with her, calls her Princess and is seemingly quite fond of her friends. 'Me, James and his tiny penis, we're one big happy family', Sam says at one point. Carrie comments that Sam hasn't quite accepted James's shortcomings. Later Carrie stretches a baseball metaphor to breaking point, describing Samantha and James's relationship in terms of baseball coaching. 'Rather than quit mid-season, Samantha decided to attack the problem with the gusto of a seasoned coach training a rookie.' Like any good coach, she is giving him the benefit of her years of experience. James is not impressed when Samantha suggests that they use a vibrator as part of their lovemaking, but it is not made clear whether he agrees or not.

Girl Talk: Asked for their opinions on what to do during break-ups, a random sample of New York women have the following to say. One says it takes three months before you call or see him, because 'that's how long it takes to lose the weight you put on while breaking up.'

Another thinks you should 'Change your name, change your phone number, change your job. They're all bums.'

Guy Talk: When asked, the men come up with nothing better, one guy saying that you should under no circumstances cry, because you'll be known for ever as the 'guy who cried', while another is very forthright – 'Give her whatever she wants, but don't sign a mother-fucking thing.'

Men: Charlotte is dating Paul Ericson, a record-company executive who's obsessed with jazz music. He's handsome, rich, from a good New York family (very important to Charlotte, lest we forget), and nice. However, he has one flaw: he keeps cupping his crotch with his hands in public, which Charlotte finds acutely embarrassing. She buys him some support-base underwear (which she hopes will solve this problem), but he's freaked out that she's shopping for him and leaves her, fearing that she's on the verge of moving in with him. It's too fast, too much, too soon, as far as he's concerned.

Kisses: Carrie kisses Joe. 'Just four weeks out of my last relationship, I let the new Yankee get to first base.'

Wine and Dine: We see the girls at their Saturday morning ritual: eggs, coffee and discussion in a diner. Charlotte shows Carrie the day's paper which has, on page six, a photograph of her and Joe taken at the Dolce & Gabbana party the previous night. Carrie is described as a 'sex-pert'. 'A proud day for me,' Ms Bradshaw comments dryly. Sam says that Big will see the picture in the paper and die. Carrie says she doesn't want him to die, to which Sam replies, 'Cut the shit, it's me.'

Miranda is upset that the conversation inevitably comes back to Big over and over again. 'Why are we still talking about him? He hurt her; he's out of the picture. Let's talk about something else, OK?' Later she gets even more upset, demanding to know how four smart women can only talk about boyfriends. She calls it 'the seventh grade with bank accounts'.

Charlotte: Charlotte is a keen believer in the idea that it takes exactly half as long to get over someone as the time you were dating them. After Paul leaves her after exactly three weeks, she, true to form, recovers in exactly a week and a half. She tells Carrie that the only way to get over a relationship is to cry, feel bad, moan to your girlfriends and replay all the bad things about your ex in your head over and over again.

Miranda: Miranda is a committed Yankees supporter who often attends ball games, and she knows a great deal about the sport. She can rattle off statistics 'as well as any boy'. A few years ago, she dated a guy called Eric, who left her for another woman. She regarded him as the love of her life, and still finds it hard to talk about him. She sees him in the street at one point, and has to hide because she can't bear for him to see her.

Trivia: It has been four weeks since Carrie's break-up with Big. They dated for six months. Samantha has been with James for two months. None of these timings really coincide with what we're told in **12**, 'Oh Come All Ye Faithful'. Miranda calls Carrie 'Anne Frank', presumably because she's spending all her time locked in her home writing her diary. Tasteless.

Hey, Big Guy: Carrie and Big finally meet again for the first time since they split up. He's the model of reason and restraint, polite but not lingering. He shakes Joe's hand and tells him he's a big fan. After he leaves, Carrie gets very upset. It isn't that he's done anything; it's simply his presence. She tells Joe to leave her alone and goes and has coffee with Miranda. Miranda apologises for her earlier outburst and tells Carrie about her encounter with Eric. She says that Carrie is to take all the time she needs over this break-up, blaming her earlier insensitivity on having forgotten just how difficult it can be to get over someone. The episode ends with Carrie acknowledging that whenever you split up with someone, you'll never get through it without your friends.

And So . . .: 'What are the break-up rules?' Warmer and less distant than any episode in the first series, this is also staggeringly well shot, with Carrie's meeting with Big being a visual tour de force – the blurred photography and 'heartbeat' soundtrack giving an amazing representation of what Carrie is feeling. ('Never stop thinking about him, even for a moment, because that's the moment he'll appear.') Samantha is amazingly patient and loving with James because she really does like him but this continued rejection of her previously adhered-to lifestyle means Carrie was right about her all along – that she really was using cynicism to mask the fact that she'd never met 'the right guy' (see **1**, 'Sex and the City'). Charlotte's plotline again goes absolutely nowhere, but at least the discussion on jazz is funny. In total, this episode can be summed up by Yankee Joe's judgement on the Dolce & Gabbana party – 'kind of cool' and therefore implicitly nothing special.

14
The Awful Truth

13 June 1999

Written by Darren Star
Directed by Allen Coulter

Guest Cast
Chris Noth (Mr Big) Willie Garson (Stanford Blatch)
Daniel Gerroll (Mr Marvelous/Jack) Jamie Goodwin (James)
Molly Price (Susan Sharon) Robin Irwin (Woman #3)
Neal Jones (Richard) James Lee (Man) Neil Pepe (Aaron)
Amy Povich (Woman #1) Marilyn Sokol (Dr Velma Rubin)

Carrie: Carrie tells us abut Susan Sharon, an old friend of hers who is a rep for a cashmere clothing company. After a night out on the town, they go back to Susan's home so that she can give Carrie her birthday present, a $900 cashmere scarf. Carrie describes Susan Sharon's apartment as being so grown up that walking into it makes her feel as if she is 16 and visiting a friend's parents rather than a friend's home. What's more, she gets the feeling that these are the sort of parents who regard her as a bad influence

on their daughter. This feeling is only increased as Susan
Sharon's husband emerges form their bedroom and literally *screams* at them for making too much noise.
Appalled, Carrie goes to leave, but cannot resist calling
him 'Grumpy'. This unleashes another torrent of abuse.
'Taunting the psychotic spouse,' Carrie later comments,
'. . . was not a good idea.'

   Later, Susan Sharon apologises to Carrie by phone and
tells her that her husband is always like that. She asks her,
'What would you do if you were with a guy like that?
Would you leave?'

   Carrie's friends agree that Susan Sharon has placed her
in a no-win situation: if she leaves her husband she'll blame
Carrie, if she stays, she'll know that Carrie thinks she
should leave him. Any outcome from here on in is bad for
Carrie, basically.

Samantha: Sam is convinced that all relationships, especially her own, are based on a combination of lies and mutual
delusions. She still hasn't got round to telling James about
his problem. Carrie claims that 'Samantha dreaded the
shrink the way most people feared the dentist' – a bit rich
coming from Carrie, whose own attitude to psychiatry is
equally filled with fear (see **25**, 'Games People Play') – but
she agrees to visit noted couples' analyst Velma Rudin
(author, apparently, of the best-selling *In-to-Me-See*),
because James asks her to. All the way through the meeting
Samantha is desperate to tell James about his . . . shortcomings, but can't bring herself to hurt him. Eventually,
after much prodding, and claiming that she's not feeling
very sexual, she blurts out, 'Your dick is too small.'
Aghast, James replies angrily, 'Do you ever stop to think
that maybe your vagina is too big?' which is frankly
shocking, and very, very funny indeed. James storms out
and Sam apologises to Velma. 'What can I say? I need a
big dick,' she tells the shrink. The wizened old analyst
replies that she hears that.

Charlotte: 'Until she found the perfect man, Charlotte
would have the perfect dog.' Charlotte buys herself a small

dog, Henry, from whom she hopes she can get all the unconditional love she desperately craves. Initially, the plan seems to work – she can pet him, take him for walks and take him out with her friends, and whatever she says to him he just licks her face. Charlotte later finds that Henry is inconsistent, hopelessly stubborn and far too co-dependent, like a lot of the men she has dated. He also shits in her hallway and tears her bed to bits, something that, so far, no ex-boyfriends have been guilty of.

Fetishes: Miranda is dating 'Spring Roll Guy' (his real name is Richard), a man she met at the Vietnamese lunch truck outside her office building. She's embarrassed because he wants her to talk dirty to him during sex, something she's never really done before and is nervous about getting involved in. When her friends are amazed that someone as verbose as Miranda would have a problem with this, she points out that sex is the one time in her 'over-articulated and exceedingly verbal life where it is perfectly appropriate, if not preferable, to shut up'. After some encouragement, Miranda acquiesces to the idea of talking to Richard during sex. Everyone is very surprised that Charlotte uses the word 'cock' and seems generally very au fait with the whole concept of talking dirty.

Miranda begins to enjoy this new aspect of her love life, until one night after making love, Richard asks her to tell him what she knows he likes. She runs through a list of sex games she knows he enjoys and he gets increasingly turned on. Then she tells him that she's noticed that he likes it when she puts a finger up his ass. He freaks out, demanding to know what gave her that idea, shocked that she should even consider talking about it. Miranda is confused, as she knows from experience that this is something Richard *really* likes. Given that he loves dirty talk too, why is his reaction so bizarre and hostile?

Fit to Print: Recent developments with Miranda and Samantha and her own inability to confess to Big that she isn't over him lead Carrie to ponder in print, 'Are there still certain things, in a relationship, that one should never say?'

Girl Talk: A girl on the street tells us that her best friend just got engaged to a jerk. What is she supposed to say, 'Congratulations' or 'You're marrying an imbecile'?

Guy Talk: A fireman informs the audience that his wife has had two breast enlargements. In his opinion, they look great but feel like shit – he knows that he should keep that opinion to himself.

Miranda: Miranda discusses her little error in the arena of talking dirty with the other three. She can't understand why Spring Roll Guy is unable to accept what she said, especially as it's completely true. Why is he offended by the suggestion that he enjoys something when she knows, from personal experience, that he does? 'They enjoy it, they just don't want it brought to their attention,' counters Carrie. The obvious implication, never stated on screen, is that some men would regard an admission of enjoying such things as being close to an admission of closet homosexuality. It's therefore particularly wonderful and stereotype-assaulting to hear Stanford say, 'Speaking personally, I don't like anything up my ass.' The reaction in the room is spectacular laughter, leading him to follow his statement up with a grinning, 'I know this may come as a surprise.'

Hey, Big Guy: Big sends Carrie red roses for her birthday. They come with a card saying 'Best Wishes' and seem to be meant as a peace gesture rather than an incitement to renew the relationship. Charlotte interprets this as 'a grand gesture', an attempt at reconciliation. Miranda and Samantha, however, agree that this is actually a *selfish* act. Big is contriving to appear nice by doing something that is, on the surface, generous, but what he's actually trying to do is make Carrie think of him on her birthday. 'I don't want to play games,' wails a genuinely upset Carrie. She later phones Big to thank him for the flowers and, on impulse, invites him to her birthday dinner. He agrees and she instantly regrets it.

Wine and Dine: Carrie's birthday dinner, her 'Arabian Nights fantasy birthday' at Layla, a Moroccan restaurant, is attended by the usual four, plus Stanford, Susan Sharon and (eventually) Big and his arrogant friend Jack. Jack has just split up with another girlfriend, but this time it seems the bitch (as he terms her) didn't get any of his money, unlike the two ex-wives who defrauded him (see **4**, 'Valley of the Twenty-Something Guys'). As the night draws on, Carrie is forced to watch Big receive lap dances, with vodka as her only ally against the horror that is watching her day 'turning into *Midnight Express*' (Alan Parker, 1978). After being hit on by Jack, Susan Sharon decides her husband isn't so bad after all, and moves back in with him. She takes Charlotte's dog with her, and somehow shouting at the troublesome puppy brings the couple closer together.

And So . . .: 'In an intimate relationship you should be able to say anything.' This is fresh, sexy and very, very funny; almost certainly the series' best outright comedy episode to date. Everything works perfectly, with Carrie's angst over Big balancing out the sitcom of Charlotte, Miranda and Samantha's lives. The cast really push the material as far as they can go. The final scene with Big and Carrie alone in a New York street echoes the end of **1**, 'Sex and the City', and in a way brings the series full circle. Thanks to this, the heavy thematic links between what is happening in our heroines' lives seem particularly inspired this week. The point of the episode is that telling the truth is the best plan in almost any given situation, but aside from this basic nugget of wisdom there's an almost complete lack of anything resembling realism. Star's script treats its situations and characters as little more than cartoons. In fact, if he were treated with any seriousness at all, Susan Sharon's husband would be a rather disturbing figure. He's obviously a deeply unpleasant individual and a person whose actions would be, in reality, no laughing matter. However, the episode presents him as a ranting ogre, portrayed in an over-the-top manner and without a shred of realism, which rather takes the sting out of what could otherwise be seen as making light of a serious issue. It's only the episode's frantic nature that stops aspects of their relationship, and Susan's eventual return to him, from being a *completely* inappropriate subject matter for light entertainment. This is a wonderfully manic and very satisfying half-hour's television. Full marks.

15
The Freak Show

20 June 1999

Written by Jenny Bicks
Directed by Allen Coulter

Guest Cast

Ian Kahn (Ben) Marc Kurdisch (Harrison) Claudia Besso (Monica)
Jamie Denbo (Woman In Bathroom) Saidah Arrika Ekulona (Nurse)
Sam Freed (Doctor) James Joseph O'Neil (Date #2)
Thomas Pescod (Date #3) Charlie Schroeder (Mitchell Sailor)
Grant Varjas (Date #1/PJ) David Wike (Luke)

Fit to Print: 'Manhattan, for millions of our forefathers the gateway to hope, opportunity and happiness ... Today that hope is still alive: it's called the first date.' Carrie pens a column comparing immigrants of the nineteenth and early twentieth centuries with 90s women looking for a decent man. It's a long journey, with the final destination (marriage) rarely in sight, and only the occasional offer of a hot meal in transit to keep them going.

Samantha: According to Carrie, Sam doesn't believe in the first date but she does believe in sex after it. Having split up with James, she's back to her old self and making up for lost time. When we first encounter her, she's having dinner with Harrison, a litigator who takes steam baths with actor Ron Perlman, and owns an apartment on the 39th floor of the staggeringly exclusive Museum Tower. This is, Carrie feels, an 'excellent first-date pedigree'. After dinner he and Sam make out at his apartment. He thinks she should know that his speciality is sexual harassment.

'So's mine,' responds Sam lasciviously, and tells him she has a prior record of driving men crazy. Harrison claims not to be surprised. 'Most sexual harassment cases are brought by older women.'

Older women?

This gives Samantha a crisis. When she asks Carrie if she looks 40 Carrie knows enough to reply, 'You don't look a day over thirty-five.' Sam has been celebrating her 35th birthday for as long as Carrie can remember. Later Samantha meets an old friend in the street who has a secret behind her increasingly youthful appearance. She had the fat from her ass injected into her face, and the best thing about this technique is that you can eat what you want for a week before having the operation, as the more recent fat the surgeon has available to him to the better. An hour after this revelation Samantha is eating her first ever Big Mac and has made an appointment with the most expensive plastic surgeon on Upper Fifth. She later tells her friends where the excess fat from her rear has gone: 'It's sitting in a fat repository in Queens as we speak, and in three days it will be in my face and I will look fabulous.' Miranda wonders what happened to ageing gracefully. 'It got old,' replies Sam.

Sam is delighted with her new implants, and asks the surgeon what else he can do for her. This is because, according to Carrie, 'For Samantha, surgery was like being at [fashion store] Barney's. Once you were in the door, you might at well shop.' The surgeon uses a pen to draw various lines on Sam's naked body, indicating where and how she can have various procedures performed. After he leaves to discuss something with his secretary, she looks at her pen-marked, tattooed, scarred body in the mirror. According to Carrie, Samantha felt 'like she had walked into a fun house, only it wasn't particularly funny'.

Miranda: Miranda claims she doesn't date because all men are freaks. This is clearly a recent development. If a man is over 30 and single, there's something wrong with him, she claims. It's Darwinian – they're being weeded out from propagating the species. 'What about us?' demands Carrie, to which Miranda counters that they aren't being 'weeded out', they're just fussy.

Men: In contrast to Miranda, says Carrie, 'I wasn't ready to accept that all single men were freaks [so] I had actually agreed to go on my first blind date in two years.' In order to investigate Miranda's theory fully, Carrie goes on as many dates with as many people as possible. These are just some of them . . .

- Date #1: A successful independent movie producer, PJ, 'whose documentary on endangered seagulls has just aired to excellent reviews on CBS.' Carrie has dinner with this man, and makes the mistake of suggesting to him that she's interested in his work, but he tells her to be realistic – he's 'only doing this docu-bullshit to make a rep, y'know? I mean, ultimately I want to parley into the action – movie arena. I want to make money. I'm not afraid to say it! I love money! I would sell toilet bowls if it would make me a millionaire.' Carrie gently asks about the seagulls. 'Fuck the seagulls!' PJ replies. Carrie winces as hallucinatory fairground music fills her ears, and she imagines herself inviting punters to view the freak show that is masculinity. 'Step right up . . . the man with no soul!'
- Date #2: A guy with serious rage problems, who screams and yells at the people standing behind them in the queue for the movie theatre because they are standing too close to him, and we're talking the sort of anger fit that can lead to homicide. 'Stand far away from the man with two faces.'
- Date #3: Max, a broker, who made $2,000,000 last year. He and Carrie have 'a nice dinner in Little Italy', which is when she discovers he has 'a lending library in his pants'. Yes, this is a man of enormous wealth who, when in charity stores, steals used books for no reason. What a freak.

Later we see Miranda with a man who professes to hate the country. 'I haven't left Manhattan in ten years.'

Miranda, appalled, asks him if he's proud of that. He replies that everything he needs is available in Manhattan. 'Culture, food, the park, cabs at 3 a.m. Why leave?' Miranda suggests that by leaving he could experience the world outside Manhattan, but the guy shakes his head. 'There is no world outside Manhattan.' This man is 'Manhattan guy, a genetically mutant strain of single man'.

'Apparently,' Carrie reflects, 'the men in the dating world had devolved since the last time I visited. Miranda was right.' Later she ponders on the idea that maybe they should never have outlawed freak shows, because at least then the freaks were rounded up and kept in one place instead of roaming free.

Charlotte: Charlotte has met a guy called Mitchell Sailor. When Charlotte is very keen on someone, she uses their full name as it helps her to imagine her future monogrammed towels. Samantha has heard of Mitchell, who is known in New York dating folklore as 'Mr Pussy'. 'He loves going down on women', says Sam breathlessly. There are urban myths of women passing out due to the sheer force of an orgasm. Charlotte is determined to date him, and one night back at her apartment we see him indulging in his speciality. 'That night,' says Carrie, 'Charlotte came harder than she ever had before; that is until Tuesday, Thursday, Friday, Friday, Friday . . . That night Charlotte saw God seven times. For a lapsed Episcopalian, it was a Very Good Friday.' Carrie is unsure how this fits into her 'freak' theory, and acknowledges that if Mitch is a freak then Charlotte is clearly happy to run away and join the circus.

After a while Charlotte becomes convinced that she's in love with Mitchell, which Carrie refutes utterly, telling her that she's in the sex haze – the time in a relationship when 'the sex is really great [so] you start acting like a crazy person and you start thinking that the relationship is something that it isn't'. Charlotte realises that this is true, and tries unsuccessfully to change the nature of her relationship with Mitchell, suggesting that they have conversations or maybe go to see a play.

Fetishes: Samantha returns from 'freshening up' to see Harrison chained up and wearing leather inside a cupboard she later describes as 'a cedar-lined den of iniquity'. She quickly leaves, and later speculates that for all she knows he is still trapped in there.

Carrie: One day, while sitting in one of New York's squares, Carrie strikes up a conversation with a man called Ben. He thinks women are all freaks, and tells her about a woman he dated who slept with her shoes on, 'That's why I don't date any more,' he says. 'Women are bizarre.' Carrie tells him that she once saw the world's fattest twins at a state fair, and they were both married to very skinny women. She seems to find it offensive that they could find love and she can't. 'Maybe it was an optical illusion,' Ben offers by way of explanation. As they are both no longer dating, they decide to see each other for a 'non-date', and so, 'There in the middle of Manhattan, two complete strangers gave out their unlisted phone numbers.' Carrie discovers that Ben is the editor of a hip political magazine, and that he has the ability to make her laugh. As he walks her home one night it's pointed out that he can't kiss her as this is a 'non-date'. So they decide on a 'non-kiss', and Carrie comments, 'There was nothing non about it.'

After several non-dates, Carrie and Ben are sitting in his apartment, drawn together by their mutual distrust of 'freaks'. She jokingly demands to know what his freak power is, and he shows her a tattoo of Tweetie Pie (as in the Warner Bros cartoon characters Tweetie Pie and Sylvester) on his right shoulder. It's the result of a drunken bachelor party, and the tattoo has lasted longer than his friend's marriage. Carrie calls it adorable, and in return shows him the three stitches below her right knee she got as a result of an injury sustained in a grade-school fight. 'And then,' she tells us, 'the amazing tattooed man made love to me.'

One morning, weeks later, Ben leaves Carrie alone in his apartment as he has to go and play football with his friends. As soon as he is gone, Carrie ransacks the place as she tries to find something wrong with him. Eventually she finds a small, locked wooden box which she pronounces to be his 'secret box of freakdom, home of illicit photos, love letters, maybe an old marriage licence'. As she is struggling to open it, he returns unexpectedly and demands to know what she's done to his home. She can't explain it. 'I guess I was looking for something. Something freaky,' she stammers. He opens the box and shows her what it contains – his cub-scout badge collection, a normal relic of a normal childhood, kept for sentimental reasons. 'I was going to skip the game to be with you. I thought you were actually a normal one.' Appalled by her own actions, Carrie lets herself out of his apartment and out of his life.

That day Carrie came face to face with her freak. She realises that every single person in Manhattan, male or female, gets freaked out from time to time, but 'you have to figure, if the world's fattest twins can find love, there's hope for all of us. Somewhere out there is another little freak who'll love us, understand us and kiss our three heads and make it all better.'

Trivia: An instrumental version of 'The Look of Love', the ballad Burt Bacharach wrote for Dusty Springfield to sing, plays in Charlotte's apartment. When Samantha is at Harrison's place we hear the rather less distinguished 'I'm Too Sexy', as performed by British pop act Right Said Fred. We discover that Carrie and Miranda use the code-phrase 'I have to go and feed my cat' in order to back out of malfunctioning double dates.

And So . . .: 'Are all men freaks?' Or more appropriately, freak or clique? Carrie charges through a problem of the dating game in record time, and comes out with a renewed perspective. To some people, maybe all people, there are times when those who are not sufficiently 'like me' are judged as freaks, but there are also, unquestionably, some real freakazoids out there too. Carrie messes up with Ben because she can't trust her own judgement and comes to realise that, in her own way, she's a freak too. Jenny Bicks' script is rich in character and uses every second of its screen time well, while the use of obtrusive, slightly sinister fairground tunes as background music creates an occasionally disconcerting atmosphere. This is a bona-fide classic piece of television.

16
They Shoot Single People, Don't They?

27 June 1999

Written by Michael Patrick King
Directed by John David Coles

Guest Cast
Willie Garson (Stanford Blatch) Mark Feuerstein (Josh)
Tom Gilroy (Tom) Robert Montano (William)
Hope Adams (WASPy Woman) John Cleary (Deaf Man)
Teddy Coluca (Garbage Man) Bradley Cooper (Jake)
Adam Dannheiser (Editor) Camille Hickman (Woman)
Wendy Hoopes (Lennox) James Lascesne (Nevin) Ajay Mehta (Busboy)
Matthew Morrison (Young Busboy)
Lawrence Rosenberg (Downtown Guy) Seth Ullian (Cute Waiter)

Carrie: There are in life certain events that come along so rarely 'that when they do special attention must be paid'. These events apparently include Halley's Comet circling the earth, and Carrie, Miranda, Charlotte and Samantha all being single at the same time. They meet for drinks and toast 'to us without men'.

Carrie says that she can't stay late as the next morning she has an appointment to pose for photographs in *New York* magazine. The article is to be entitled 'Single & Fabulous' and will celebrate the lifestyles of thirty-something New York women who are single and happy to be so. Carrie is invited partially because she fits the bill and partially because Stanford's new boyfriend, Nevin, is the assistant photo editor of the magazine. Charlotte persuades her to stay for one more drink, and then 'one drink turned into many and before I knew it I was dragging my tired yet single and fabulous ass home at dawn'. Worn out,

Carrie decides that the way to avoid looking like she's been up all night is to stay up all morning. Inevitably she falls asleep, and is called by a concerned Stanford who tells her that she's 40 minutes late. 'I'm at the photo shoot and everyone is freaking out,' he complains. Carrie promises that she'll be with him in 20 minutes, and rushes out of the apartment in the clothes she partied and then slept in.

When she arrives, she apologises to Stanford and claims she couldn't get a cab. He looks her up and down and retorts, 'What did you do? Grab on to a bumper and get one to drag you here?' Stung by his sarcasm, she admits she was up all night. 'I need a coffee the size of my head.' She's then introduced to Nevin, who accuses her of being 'about a fucking month late'. Carrie looks to Stanford for support and he replies, 'Don't look at me, you're the one who's about a fucking month late.'

Fit to Print?: When the article and photographs are eventually printed, it has become 'Single & Fabulous?' rather than 'Single & Fabulous!' Explicitly critical of single women in their thirties and accompanied by a photograph of Carrie looking like a wreck, the article upsets the whole group, and while Miranda loudly protests, 'This piece of trash has nothing, I repeat, nothing, to do with us', Carrie can see that 'somehow the question mark has leapt off my cover and on to each one of them'.

Carrie's own column is about faking: faking friendships, faking relationships, faking orgasms. She ponders, 'Is being alone raising the bar on faking?'

Miranda: While power walking in the park with her friends (apparently being single frees up your time for such useful activities), Miranda runs into Josh, an ophthalmologist (eye doctor) whom she once briefly dated. He was nice but the sex wasn't good. She only slept with him twice, and she had to fake an orgasm both times. He reminds her that she's got his phone number, and she is sufficiently sick of being single to give him another try. She tries dating him again, but once more finds that he is completely unable to make her climax. After a few weeks of faking it, she tells him what's happening. Surprisingly he reacts rather well, asking her to teach him how to be a better lover, and apologising for his inadequacies.

Miranda discusses this with her friends; Samantha is quite sympathetic, pointing out that no one gives men an instruction manual for the female body, so how are they supposed to know what to do if you don't tell them? 'If I had a son,' she says, 'I'd teach him all about the vagina.' 'If you had a son,' Carrie responds, 'we'd call social services.'

Charlotte: When told about Josh and Miranda always having to fake orgasm with him, Charlotte is unimpressed. She claims that he's an ophthalmologist and therefore a prize catch, and shouldn't be dismissed on such trivial grounds. She says that orgasms are not the be all and end all of a relationship, and asks when an orgasm brings you a cup of coffee in the morning. Miranda points out that she'd 'take an orgasm over a cup of French drip Columbian any day'. 'You see,' jokes Carrie, 'for me it's a toss-up.'

Girl Talk: A woman talks about how her boyfriend preferred thin, blonde WASPy women, so she became one.

Guy Talk: A man describes his wife as an idiot; every day spent with her 'is like a trip to the idiot farm'. He later says that he doesn't want to tell her his real feelings. 'I'm pretty sure she'd leave me.'

Men: Tom is an out-of-work actor who lives in the same apartment block as Charlotte. She comes to rely on him because he can do all the household chores that she can't. Whenever she needs plugs rewiring or TVs tuning, Charlotte turns to him. Eventually she turns to him for something else too, but Carrie feels that Charlotte is faking a relationship, which is far more dishonest than faking an orgasm, and tells her so. Charlotte claims to really like Tom: 'He's strong and masculine and he can fix things around the house.' Eventually she realises that she can't carry on a relationship with him, and allows him to fly out of New York to pursue his acting dreams. They have a fake break-up, where they both say things the other already knows in a faintly cynical 'let's get it over with' way.

Samantha: Sam advises Charlotte: 'Slap on some armour and go through life like I do, enjoying men but not expecting them to fill you up. Except when . . .' Fortunately, everyone gets the picture so no further elaboration is required. Initially, Sam seems back to her old self post-James, rattling off wit and advice and determined to have a great time. She goes on a few dates with William, who is the owner of the exclusive New York salsa club responsible for Carrie being late for her photo shoot. One night Will is meant to meet her at her favourite romantic restaurant, but doesn't show up. After waiting for several hours, Samantha gets increasingly upset at her abandonment and eventually goes home alone. Carrie describes William as the worst kind of faker, 'one of those men who faked a future to get what they wanted in the present'.

Wine and Dine: Carrie sits on her own at an outside table in a restaurant, at one with being alone. The waiter asks her if she's waiting for someone, and she chirpily replies, 'No, it's just me.' She sits, 'no books, no man, no friends, no armour, no faking' and, happy being single, enjoys the solitude. This scene, although charming and subtle, doesn't really fit with the rest of the episode. (See **And So . . .**)

Trivia: One of the characters refers to WASPs, a common US acronym for White Anglo Saxon Protestant, perceived (arguably correctly) as the most privileged and numerous of the US's many ethnic and social groupings.

And So . . .: 'All these years lying to myself that I was happy being single.' A colossal thematic misfire, this is also the third episode written by Michael Patrick King in which Samantha is reduced to tears. Later episodes make it obvious that King's scripts don't mean to humiliate Sam (she seems, in fact, to be his favourite character) and that he principally sees her as a cartoon figure who can rebound from almost anything. There is an accidental thread of implicit disapproval at Sam's lifestyle running through this script. What's more, it isn't particularly inventive, being, in part, a rewrite of the concerns of **12**, 'Oh Come All Ye Faithful' and **14**, 'The Awful Truth'.

The title is taken from the movie *They Shoot Horses, Don't They?* (Sydney Pollack, 1969), which is about a Depression-era dance contest. The point of the movie is that people only engage in something as pointless as a dance contest because they are so desperately unhappy about their lives. Ultimately the contest is revealed as an exercise that nobody enjoys, a freak show that kills several of its participants. For contest read dating, for participants read Carrie, Samantha, Miranda and Charlotte? This may sound ridiculous, but consider the article in *New York* magazine that comments on how, for people like Carrie, though it was fun to be single at twenty, 'you want to ask these women, "How fun will nightclub hopping be at forty?" Filling their lives with an endless parade of decoys and distractions to avoid the fact that they're completely alone.' The strength of the four women's reactions to this piece would seem to indicate that they secretly 'know' it's the 'truth'. Which of course it isn't.

Thought-provoking for all the wrong reasons, 'They Shoot Single People, Don't They?' is downright unsettling; it seems to be trying to conclude that no matter how much it hurts, sometimes it's better to be alone than to fake it, but instead – perhaps accidentally – comes across as an outright condemnation of everything that our four hero-ines do. Is this a result of miscommunication between writer and director or does the script just need another draft?

17
Four Women and a Funeral

4 July 1999

Written by Jenny Bicks
Directed by Allen Coulter

Guest Cast
Chris Noth (Mr Big) Kurt Deutsch (Ned) Seth Barrish (Mortgage Guy)
Porter Beerman (Hostess) Lisa Butler (Maitre D')
Michael De Vries (Richard (Dick) Cranwell)
Felicity Lafortune (Sandy Cranwell) Jimmy Noonan (Bouncer)
Rhasaan Orange (Assistant) Barbara Spiegel (Realtor)
Ellen Tobie (Shippy Shipman) Shannon Williams (Josefine)
Susan Willis (Older Woman)

Fashion Victims: There are only two times at which it is
permissible to wear a little black dress in daylight. One
involves leaving a party very late, and the other involves
leaving the party very early, i.e. death. Carrie breaks her
little black dress out of storage to attend the funeral of
Javier, a Cuban designer who was the toast of New York,
and a very old friend of hers. She had, she informs us,
known him since he was 'Harvey'. Javier loved clothes, but
unfortunately he loved heroin more; a love that ultimately
killed him. Carrie, Charlotte and Samantha attend the
funeral.

Samantha: Dressed in a $2,000 suit designed by Javier on
the grounds that it would be rude not to wear something
designed by the dead man at his funeral, Sam notes that
the prices of Javier's lines have gone up 30 per cent since
the announcement of his death. (It is typical of New York,
claims Carrie, that someone is more popular when they're
not around.) Sam has to look fabulous at the funeral
because 'everybody will be there'. 'This is a funeral, not
Friday night at Bond Street!' splutters Carrie.

Javier's sister and heir, Josephine, announces the estab-
lishment of Javier House, a charity designed to help those
in the fashion industry affected by narcotics. Sam is
immediately enthused by the idea, hoping to grab a place
on the board. When Carrie describes this as uncharacteris-
tically nice of Samantha, Sam reminds her that the mailing
list for the organisation will be fabulously exclusive and
she'll have access to every unlisted (Manhattan area code)
212 phone number in the city.

However, it all quickly goes wrong for Ms Jones.
Attempting to get a donation from Richard Cranwell, she

allows herself to be seduced by him, and they are interrupted by his wife. In revenge, Mrs Cranwell engineers a 'social hit' on Samantha. In a matter of days, Sam goes from social A-list to social blacklist, her credit card is refused all across town, and she gets left off guest lists left, right and centre. According to Carrie, 'After a week of being a social pariah, Samantha realised [that] if she wanted her life back she'd have to beg for it.' She goes to Shippy Shipman, doyenne of the ladies-who-lunch and 'personally responsible for the death of at least seventy social lives'. Presumably her plan is to get Shipman to do to Cranwell what Cranwell has done to her, but the plan backfires spectacularly as Shipman remembers Samantha as having tried to seduce her husband at a charity benefit a few years before. Shipman refuses to help her, even after Samantha has humiliated herself by announcing, 'I'm a big whore. Now, will you help me?' Sam acknowledges that she is actually deader in this town than Javier and has no idea how to restore her once enviable status.

Charlotte: The hat that Charlotte borrows from Samantha for the funeral blows off her head and on to a woman's grave. Charlotte apologises to the sad-faced man standing there and asks, 'Your mother?' He shakes his head. 'My wife.' His name is Ned, he went to Princeton and Charlotte thinks he's very handsome. They go for drinks, and when he talks about his late wife, Ned cries. According to Carrie, Charlotte doesn't normally like seeing men cry, but it somehow makes Ned even more romantic. He apologises, and she tells him to take all the time he needs. It turns out that all the time he needs is around 45 minutes, as less than an hour later they're in bed together in a room dominated by photographs of his late wife. 'Under the watchful eyes of a dead woman,' Carrie's narration explains, 'Ned came back to life. Twice.'

Girl Talk: Miranda is unimpressed by Charlotte's widower, who has 'project written all over him'. Samantha invokes the 'dead wife factor': it doesn't matter what she was like in life, in death she'll be perfect. Charlotte counters that her hat blowing on to Liz's grave may have been a message from the dead woman, leading Miranda to comment that the message was probably, 'Don't fuck my husband, you hat-loving bitch.' Ned invites Charlotte to his wife's memorial service, and she agrees to attend. There she meets the three other women who are 'helping' Ned through his grief, and decides that this relationship is not for her. Or, more precisely, she slaps him with a huge bouquet of lilies and storms out. You go, girl!

Miranda: Miranda has bought her first apartment, a huge, amazingly expensive, positively palatial apartment in an exclusive block. That's the upside. The downside is that she's sick of being asked 'Just you?' at every turn. The estate agent, the mortgage broker, the neighbours – everybody is seemingly obsessed with and surprised by the fact that Miranda is single. When filling in her mortgage forms, Carrie comments that Miranda has 'checked more "Single Woman" boxes than her gynaecologist'.

On meeting her new neighbours, Miranda is told that the previous occupant of her apartment was a single woman, who never married, and who died in there. No one noticed that she'd died for a week, and when they found the body her cat had eaten half her face. Disturbed by this story, especially on top of all the 'Just you?' stuff, Miranda begins having panic attacks. Worse, she nearly chokes to death on some Chinese food. After this, just to be on the safe side, she goes to bed hungry and doesn't let the cat out of the kitchen for two days. 'I'm gonna die alone, Carrie!' Miranda wails. She points out that the first people on her list of people to call in case of emergency are her parents, which is pathetic, not just due to her age but also because she doesn't like them and they live in Pennsylvania. Her paranoia eventually recedes and, according to Carrie, 'She realised that she wouldn't die alone, but she kept overfeeding her cat just in case.'

Men: Leonardo DiCaprio. Yes, really ... OK, not really. But a young man appears in blazing sunlight, his face cast into silhouette as he arrives at the Javier House benefit. He shakes hands with Samantha, and Carrie informs us that this is indeed the star of *Titanic* (James Cameron, 1997). Sam and Leo become great friends, and in a matter of days he elevates her social status to previously unimagined levels.

Hey, Big Guy: 'In under thirty seconds we had resuscitated a relationship that took six months to die.' Troubled by thoughts of death, Carrie phones Big and asks him to dinner with her. They meet, eat and discuss death. Despite lots of flirting, Carrie tells Big she's not going to sleep with him. Nevertheless, she ends up in the doorway to his apartment, trying not to go in. Eventually she forces herself to leave, thinking, 'It felt great and weird and wrong. The first time I got involved with Big I got out just in time. Would I be so lucky the second?'

Kisses: After several days and a lot of call-screening, Big cracks and goes to Carrie's apartment. She opens the door, he looks at her and says, 'Good, you're alive,' and makes to leave. She grabs him by the arm, insists they go out, and drags him to a bowling alley because it's the least sexual place she can think of. They play one game, at which Big beats Carrie soundly, then he looks at her and says, 'You wanna play a second game?' 'Maybe,' she replies, and kisses him.

Trivia: The title is taken from *Four Weddings and a Funeral* (Mike Newell, 1994), the Hugh Grant comedy.

And So . . .: 'In a city that moves so fast they give you the Sunday paper on Saturday, how do any of us know how much time we have left?' A really rather clever rumination on different kinds of death (social death, actual death, the death of possibility) is held together by some very good jokes. The total abandonment of realism as Samantha meets Leonardo DiCaprio is wonderful; he appears, bathed in sunlight, to rescue her from social oblivion. Miranda's plotline allows us to both laugh at her and feel enormous sympathy for her without making her remotely pathetic, which is not an easy trick to pull off.

18
The Cheating Curve

11 July 1999

Written by Darren Star
Directed by John David Coles

Guest Cast
Chris Noth (Mr Big) Rob Campbell (Ethan Watson)
Mary McCann (Lydia) Tamara Tunie (Eileen)
Julianna Francis (Woman In Steam Room) Sean Haberle (Gareth Davis)
Chris John (Thor) Jodi Long (Patty Aston) Scott Lucy (Caterer)

Carrie: 'They say that most New Yorkers would attend the opening of an envelope as long as the champagne didn't run out.' Carrie says this is true, but Charlotte's gallery opening for a lesbian painter from Brooklyn Heights transcends such clichés. It does look like an impressive evening, one where 'lesbian chic meets art-world cool, a fabulous combustion that no one saw coming'. We are introduced to the Power Lesbians, New York's newest group with disposable income. They dominate the evening, with Carrie feeling that they're strong, sexy and know a) a lot about shoes and b) the secret of invisible make-up. Seeing that each of her friends is attached to an ostensibly suitable man, Carrie makes her excuses and sneaks off to see Mr Big.

Miranda: Miranda is dating a guy she met at a 'sparsely attended Harvard alumni mixer'. He has a passion for film, especially documentaries, and talks a lot of pseudo-intellectual guff about the nature of narrative film. She goes back to his place, where he insists on watching porn while they're having sex. For a while Miranda doesn't mind too much, but after several times she gets irritated. 'It's borderline humiliating,' she tells Carrie. 'You would think the real thing would be more entertaining than the tape.' Eventually deciding to confront him, she demands that it's her or the porn. He tells her that it isn't that easy, he's only known her for a few weeks, but his relationship with some of the porn models goes back years. Miranda stands up and walks out. 'I am *so* out of here.' Before the door closes he's gone back to his tapes.

Samantha: At the gallery opening, Samantha spots a man she knows – 'a trainer at my gym, and you should see his squat thrusts' – and rushes off to talk to him. Later, they have sex in a shower stall and he asks her if she's a dirty girl. 'I guess that depends on your definition of dirty,' she coolly replies. He then shaves her legs and trims her pubic hair into a lightning-flash shape, which Sam finds immensely sexy. Miranda says that men who prefer women to have no pubic hair are dubious: 'It's obvious they want a little girl.' Later, Samantha is in the steam room at the gym and spots another women with exactly the same shaved pattern. She instantly knows that he's cheating on her. 'Lightning does indeed strike twice.'

Fetishes: Samantha comments that straight guys often follow lesbians around 'to see what they're going to do'.

Girl Talk: 'Cheating' as a concept is discussed. Samantha claims that men cheat 'for the same reason dogs lick their balls: because they can. It's part of their biology.' This is, of course, exactly what you'd expect her to say. It's pointed out that women cheat too, and Charlotte claims this is different because women are not ruled by testosterone, and therefore don't go round throwing themselves at any man they are attracted to. 'Speak for yourself,' retorts Sam. She demands of Charlotte what it is Charlotte thinks does drive women. 'Emotions' is the reply. 'You mean hormones,' Sam corrects her.

Carrie argues that you can't define cheating in absolute terms: 'Someone's definition of what constitutes cheating is in direct proportion to how much they themselves want to cheat.' Miranda argues that this is moral relativism, and she's right. It may also be true.

Sam puts forward another theory, one that proposes that 'the act of cheating is defined by the act of getting caught – one doesn't exist without the other'. This is called 'quantum cheating' and is rather like the idea that any food secretly consumed while on a diet doesn't count towards calorie counting.

Charlotte: Charlotte is initially dating Gareth Davis, a toxic bachelor (see **1**, 'Sex and the City') and owner of a reasonably fashionable restaurant, the sort of place one finds second-tier models and the men who buy them salad. After she finds him kissing another woman in the storage room at her gallery, she dumps him. Later she is asked by Melissa, one of the group of Power Lesbians, if she would like to go for a drink with her and her friends. This leads on to an evening in G-Spot, the hottest new girl bar in town, followed by dinner at Luke's, 'a hot new French fusion restaurant with an even hotter Sapphic chef', followed by late-night dancing at Love Tunnel. Charlotte, Carrie says, finds 'something relaxing and liberating about travelling through an alternative universe with no thoughts of men'. She goes out with her lesbian friends three times in a week, and finds herself gently teased by her clique as a result. Miranda calls her a 'clit tease'.

Charlotte is introduced to Patty Aston, the queen bee of the Power Lesbians, who's on the board of 100 charities. She talks to Charlotte about her joining their group and going skiing with them. There's just one thing she needs to know first – is Charlotte gay? Charlotte admits that she isn't, but talks about the part of her that is linked, very powerfully, with a strong feminine identity. Patty looks at her a little contemptuously. 'Sweetheart, that's all very nice, but if you're not going to eat pussy you're not a dyke.'

Kisses: 'Maybe he doesn't consider kissing cheating,' says Sam when Charlotte tells them all about Gareth's betrayal. Miranda says that she was 'a major lesbian in fourth grade'. She knew a girl called Wendy Curtzon. 'We kissed. It was great.' This doesn't really fit with what she says in **3**, 'Bay of Married Pigs', but is very funny anyway.

Hey, Big Guy: Carrie is keeping her renewed relationship with Big a secret. She's seeing him a lot, but no one else has been informed. She finds the secrecy an aphrodisiac – it makes her feel sexier and more alive than she's ever felt. She decides that she wants to make Big a meal: 'That night in Mr Big's kitchen, I performed an unnatural act of my own. I cooked.'

After a while, Carrie realises that she can't keep this secret from her friends any longer. Not telling the truth is fine, but when she is forced to actually lie to Miranda (apparently for the first time in their long friendship), she doesn't like it at all. While walking through the street with her friends, she finally cracks and tells them about her and Big. They complain, and she tells them that this time it feels OK. 'If it feels OK, why are you sneaking behind our backs?' demands Miranda.

A few days later Big and Carrie go dancing. This, she feels, is because he knows she needs to talk and is putting her in a situation where she'll least likely be able to have a serious discussion with him. She asks him if they are back together 'officially', and he replies, 'I don't know what "officially" means.' They discuss their break-up, but she can't bring herself to tell him that the reason she didn't go away with him was because she was afraid that he could never love her in the way that she wants to be loved. Instead she tells him it was because she was afraid. She asks him if he cried after they broke up. After a pause, he answers, 'No, but I did listen to a *hell* of a lot of Sinatra.' They dance and kiss. Carrie tells us, 'There it was, I guess we were back together. Officially. Whatever that means.'

And So . . .: 'In a gravity-free world of "anything goes", what constitutes cheating?' Darren Star once again demonstrates that no one has a firmer grasp of this series and its characters than he does. The Carrie/Big scenes are wonderfully complex and romantic, Miranda's 'relationship' is utterly bizarre and very funny, Sam's plotline is a riot and Charlotte's involvement with the clique of Power Lesbians is handled with a deft, self-mocking awareness that carries you along with it. The discussion about cheating is a perfect example of how this series works when it's at its best.

19
The Chicken Dance

18 July 1999

Written by Cindy Chupack
Directed by Victoria Hochberg

Guest Cast
Chris Noth (Mr Big) Carrie Preston (Madeline Dunn)
Stephen Barker Turner (Jeremy Fields) David Beach (Bandleader)
Buzz Bovshow (Man) Mike Dooly (Martin Healy)
Paul Haber (Cute Investment Banker) Kevin Hagan (Mr Healy)
David McCann (Doorman) John Mese (Dave)
Grace Naughton (Busy Female Executive) Mary Jane Wells (Mrs Healy)

Miranda: 'There are seven million people in New York, not counting house guests.' Carrie explains how most single people in New York don't get round to buying furniture or hanging pictures until prompted to do so by the arrival of a house guest. Miranda is no exception; the imminent arrival of her old friend Jeremy has induced a controlled shopping frenzy. Now Miranda's new apartment is full of objects hand picked and arranged by a friend of Charlotte's, an up-and-coming interior designer named Madeline Dunn.

Men: Jeremy Fields, a college friend of Miranda's. He's been in London working on *The Economist*, and is now returning to New York. Miranda has offered him the new sofabed in her new apartment because his e-mails, which have always been friendly, have begun to take a distinctly flirtatious tone. When he arrives he is 'even more adorable than Miranda remembered', especially when he announces, 'I'm tired of dating. I'm ready to get married.'

Just as Jeremy and Miranda are getting ready to go for dinner, Madeline arrives with Miranda's last item of furniture; the much-awaited 'end table'. Jeremy invites Madeline to come to dinner with them and, to Miranda's mounting horror, they discover that they have a great deal in common. Later that night, Miranda discovers, in Carrie's words, that 'she was on a truly great first date – unfortunately it was somebody else's'.

Two weeks later, Jeremy no longer needs to stay with Miranda, so she throws him a going-away party on his last night, and in the middle of all the festivities Jeremy and Madeline unexpectedly announce their engagement.

Hey, Big Guy: In stark contrast, Carrie has once again become a regular house guest at Big's. One night she forgets her toothbrush, and he gives her the spare head for his electric one. Carrie is quietly delighted, as allowing her to keep a toothbrush at his apartment is the closest Big has come to admitting to any kind of substance in their relationship. She calls it 'the single most encouraging thing so far'.

Girl Talk: Sitting on the steps during the engagement party, Carrie, Samantha, Miranda and Charlotte discuss recent events. Samantha can't understand why women are so obsessed with getting married. 'Married people just want to be single again.' When you are single, 'The world is your smorgasbord,' she says. Miranda now believes that her apartment is going to be lucky for everyone except her, a sense of paranoia that only increases after Samantha meets a handsome man who takes an interest in her. 'Why not me? What am I doing wrong?' Miranda demands. The killer blow is when the doorman at her own building fails to recognise her. 'I live here!' she barks at him.

Guy Talk: Big is told about Jeremy and Madeline's speedy marriage and is somewhat philosophical about it, saying nothing is shocking in New York: 'We've embraced public urination.' Carrie tells him that Madeline and Jeremy believe themselves to be soul mates. 'Did they actually use the term "soul mates"?' Big asks, incredulous. When Carrie confirms this he smiles and says, 'Then I give them three months.'

Samantha: Having hooked up with a handsome man at the engagement party, Samantha finds herself experiencing a 'déjà fuck'. She suddenly realises that she's had sex with this man before, and completely forgotten about it. 'How could you forget a guy you had sex with?' Charlotte demands to know. 'I don't think we're in single figures any more,' explains Carrie gently. Samantha is irritated she is 'officially out of men to fuck' and considers her options to be either marriage or moving to another city.

Fit to Print: 'In a city as cynical as New York, is it possible to believe in love at first sight?' We hear a few different viewpoints from this week's interviewees. Madeline tells us that she now knows that people who don't believe in love at first sight have never experienced it. A corporate-looking guy claims that the whole concept is 'too flaky' for New York – it is, after all, a city where 'women want to see a blood test and an ATM receipt before they give up their number'. Another woman demands to know how you can believe in love at first sight in a city where people jerk off on you in the subway.

Carrie: Madeline asks Carrie to write a poem about her and Jeremy, and to read it at the reception. Seemingly both flattered and flabbergasted, Carrie agrees, but she later tells Miranda that although she was flattered to be asked, she doesn't consider herself a poet. The only reason she acquiesced was because she didn't know how to say no to such a request. How do you turn down someone who asks for help with their wedding? 'If I could answer that I wouldn't be in charge of the guest book,' Miranda replies. Carrie is worried about her task. 'I write about sex, not love,' she points out. 'What do I know?' She tries to compose the poem while in bed with Big, and his helpful suggestions include 'Love is like a dove, or a big fuzzy glove,' although he points out that she probably shouldn't use it as he is possibly plagiarising a greetings card. Big agrees to go to the wedding with Carrie, but seems unsure about whether to sign the card or not. Carrie tells him that it doesn't matter, even though she clearly wants him to, and so he doesn't. 'Two people were committing to a life together and I couldn't get a guy to be on a card with me.'

Out and About: All four of our heroines attend the wedding. 'The ceremony,' says Carrie, 'was short and sweet: like the engagement.' Miranda is amazed that it took Madeline six months to find her a table but only four weeks to plan a wedding at The Plaza. Carrie discovers to her horror that her poem is in the programme, sandwiched between the vows and the fish course.

Eventually she gets up to read it to the assembled crowd:

His hello was the end of her endings,
Her laugh their first step down the aisle,
His hand would be hers to hold forever,
His forever was as simple as her smile,
He said she was what was missing,
She said instantly, she knew,
She was a question to be answered,
And his answer was 'I do'.

During her reading, Big takes a call on his mobile phone and exits the hall, which causes Carrie to burst into tears. She passes them off as tears of joy for the happy couple but is deeply hurt by his thoughtlessness.

When Big returns, he asks if he missed anything, and Carrie points out that he missed her poem and almost all of the reception. She tells him there's nothing like a slow dance to make you forgive and forget, but he declines saying he doesn't like to dance while people are eating. She goes to the bar and drinks heavily, and although she and Big go home together she's now more uncertain about what he wants than ever before. 'I'm afraid we don't want the same things. I want someone who's going to be with me until the end . . . of a wedding,' she tells him.

Charlotte: Charlotte is going to be one of Madeline's bridesmaids; she gets an expensive black satin dress in which she looks fabulous, and what's more she gets to be walked up the aisle by best man Martin Healy. Charlotte and Martin really hit it off; with good family and great prospects he's exactly the sort of guy Charlotte has always looked for. They spend most of the wedding together and eventually end up having sex in the bridal suite. Carrie observes that although technically it wasn't the third date, they had 'already had dinner *and* been dancing', which is roughly in line with Charlotte's beloved *Rules*. Later Charlotte dances with Martin's father, and he feels her up as they dance. When Charlotte tells Martin this, Martin is furious. With her. He points out that his parents have been married for fifty years. 'My dad would not cop a feel because some girl is wearing a slutty dress.' He storms off. 'Did the last four and a half hours mean nothing to you?' she wails as he departs. This is the shortest, silliest relationship that any of the four characters have had yet.

And So . . .: 'Nothing is important to him.' The whirlwind romance of Madeline and Jeremy suddenly brings what's lacking in Carrie and Big's relationship into sharp relief. Something that starts off as a cunning comedy of manners, with Miranda dispensing wit from the sidelines, changes into a complex look at people's differing expectations. Carrie describes the hour she spends with Madeline helping to plan the wedding as 'a mind-boggling hour in the presence of absolute certainty', and it's clear that it's that *certainty* she craves above all else. A certainty that would steady her self-confessed 'slightly neurotic' nature and add balance to her life. Can Big provide this? The answer is looking more likely to be 'no' all the time. Chris Noth struggles manfully with the script, trying to make Big charming and likeable, but his emotional distance and insensitivity push him away from the viewer for exactly the same reasons they are pushing him away from Carrie. Or they do in this episode, anyway, his characterisation in next week's instalment being handled rather differently.

20
The Man, the Myth, the Viagra

25 July 1999

Written by Michael Patrick King
Directed by Victoria Hochberg

Guest Cast
Chris Noth (Mr Big) David Eigenberg (Steve Brady)
Bruce MacVittie (Allan Miller) Spiro Malas (Carlo) Bill McHugh (Ed)
Dina Paisner (Housekeeper) Sean Runnette (Comic)

Carrie: 'Once upon a second time around in a mythical land between Carmine and Mulberry Streets, two mere mortals were having a wonderful time.' Big takes Carrie to a family-run Italian restaurant where he is a regular. He introduces her to the patron as his girlfriend. She's surprised and delighted because he's never called her his girlfriend before. 'Sure I have, just not to your face.' She smiles.

The owner of the restaurant gets up and sings a song, and then pressurises Big into doing the same. He dedicates the song to Carrie, who is surprised that he can sing rather well. Carrie describes this evening as perfect. 'I felt like I was in heaven.'

Miranda: Meanwhile, across town, Miranda is in hell in a comedy club with an acerbic, unfunny stand-up comedian telling bad jokes. 'When does the comedy start?' Miranda asks her date, Alan, a divorced architect whom she met in aisle three at the food emporium. They'd immediately bonded over a mutual hatred of designer croutons. Alan and Miranda decide to leave. As he goes off to pick up the bill, she tells him, 'If you ditch me in this place I will hunt you down and kill you.' While he's gone, his phone, which he has left on the table, starts ringing. The stand-up comedian provokes Miranda into answering it, and she's appalled to discover it's Alan's wife. He admits that he and his wife are not divorced they're simply separated. 'No,' she says, '*we* are separated. See, this is me, separating,' and walks away.

Girl Talk: Everyone meets to discuss Miranda's trauma. Miranda says men are 'shit', and are all married, gay or burned by divorce. She points out that Alan told her what she needed to know, and she believed him. 'Am I that needy?' she asks. Charlotte tries to console her by talking about a friend of a friend who met a wonderful man, found out he was married, wanted to leave him, and then he divorced his wife for her and is now a magnificent husband and father. Samantha points out that these stories are modern-day urban dating myths 'concocted by women to make their love lives seem less hopeless'. Examples of these myths include 1) The one-night stand that became a relationship, 2) The married man who left his wife, and 3) The couple who get back together, and she discovered that he really had changed. Prompted by this, and with some needling from Charlotte, Carrie tells everyone how much she's enjoying her renewed relationship with Big. 'Something shifted,' she says. 'If we are together again it really must be for a reason.'

Samantha: Sam meets a 72-year-old man whom she spies in a bar – she's having her regular post-office cocktail, he's having a drinks meeting with Donald Trump. He asks if he can buy her a drink; she says that she already has one. 'Can I buy you an island?' he responds. 'I don't know, can you?' an intrigued Samantha replies. As Carrie later tells us, 'A bottle of their best champagne later and Samantha had learned that Ed was single, available and a millionaire many, many times over.' She goes for dinner at his house, where he gives her expensive jewellery and tells her that he knows that he only has 'a dozen' good years of life left to him. He's looking to have a little fun, and he hopes Samantha is someone he can have fun with. He has, he claims, 'a big old pocketful of Viagra'. Samantha squeezes his groin and notes, approvingly, 'That's not Viagra.' Reasoning that 'all cats look the same in the dark', Samantha decides that Ed may be the man for her. In bed, she discovers that his lips are not noticeably those of a 72-year-old man and his touch is not noticeably that of a 72-year-old man. Unfortunately for her, his butt is very much that of a 72-year-old man and this freaks her out so much she runs away.

Hey, Big Guy: Carrie asks Big if he'll get to know her friends better and become integrated into her life. He agrees and suggests they all go for dinner together at the fashionable Denial on Saturday. Delighted, Carrie tells her friends about this auspicious event, and uses it as an example of how Big is changing.

On Saturday she arrives at his apartment, only to discover him still slouching around in casuals. He claims he's been out all day and is tired, and devastates her by asking, 'Do you mind if I don't go?' Distraught, she leaves to meet up with her friends, unsure of what she'll tell them.

Men: Drinking alone in a bar, Miranda meets Steve Brady, a warmly sarcastic bartender, who asks her to say 'please' at the end of her requests for wine and begs her to stay and talk to him so he won't have to listen to the NYU students talking about (then fashionable singer/songwriter) Fiona Apple and smoking cheap cigarettes. Eventually they wind up doing more than talking; they go back to Miranda's apartment for sex and, in Carrie's words, 'Steve the bartender gave her two orgasms, straight up.'

As he's leaving, Steve asks Miranda if he can have her phone number. When she asks why, he replies, 'To call you up and ask you for a date.' Miranda refuses, telling him that he doesn't have to bullshit her, and that they should call this what it is – a one-night stand. She packs him off with the words, 'Sure. OK. Whatever. Thanks. Bye. Great sex.'

A couple of days later, Steve rings Miranda's doorbell and asks to speak to her. She demands to know why he is there. 'I didn't have your number and I wanted to tell you something,' he says. 'I like you,' and then tells her again that he does really like her, and that he'd like to see her. Miranda tells him that he's simply saying, 'I think you're an easy lay and I'd like to have sex again.' He wants to have dinner with her. Can he? Please? Again she asks him why they should go out and eat. 'Because we're hungry?' he offers. Beaten down by his earnest pestering, Miranda invites him to her dinner with Big and the girls at Denial.

Wine and Dine: Denial, the thematically monikered fashionable eatery where Carrie hopes Big will get to know her friends better. Also, the insanely exclusive Jean Georges, where Ed can get a table without booking.

Out and About: At the club, Carrie struggles with how to explain to her friends that Big, her 'fallen hero', isn't coming. 'How could I imagine that things would be different the second time around?' she berates herself. Meanwhile, Steve struggles with Miranda's relentless cynicism, and after she's spent a while verbally abusing him, he takes her to one side. 'Can you imagine for one second that you might be able to believe that I'm not a full-of-shit guy? That maybe I do like you? That maybe the other night was special?' he asks. She says that she can't and, frustrated and hurt, he leaves.

Then Big appears, dressed to the nines. Carrie is delighted, but it's the effect on Miranda that's extraordinary. As Carrie puts it, 'Seeing Big show up for me like that shook Miranda's lack-of-belief system to the core.' Realising that everything that Steve said may have been true, realising that she may have thrown away something beautiful and grand for the sake of being right, realising that she still has a chance to put this right, she dashes out of the club and into the rainy Manhattan street shouting his name, creating her own urban myth in the process – as she and Steve become 'the one-night stand that turned into a relationship'.

Kisses: Miranda and Steve, a jaw-droppingly perfect romantic moment as they embrace in the rain. Glorious.

Also Starring: David Eigenberg – so brilliant as Steve Brady – has played district attorney Harvey Welk in David E Kelley's legal drama *The Practice* on numerous occasions; in fact, his initial appearance was in the very first episode. He's also featured in two episodes of *Homicide: Life on the Street* (in 'Sniper: Part 2' shown 12 January 1996 and 'Prison Riot' shown 18 October 1996), both times as the same character, Alex Robey. Other guest appearances include *Cosby* (the US version of the UK's *One Foot in the Grave* with Bill Cosby), and two appearances in *Ed* (playing Jeff in 'Loyalties' and 'Live Deliberately' shown on 20 February and 28 February 2001). He remains with the show on and off, until the very end and is a *de facto* principal character for much of the series.

And So . . . : 'People *do* live happily ever after.' Things which are great about this episode: Big walking down the stairs towards Carrie; Steve Brady; Samantha's reaction to Ed's generosity; Bill McHugh's giggling, lecherous, somehow dignified performance; the amazing 'kissing in the rain' ending; Steve again; Big cooking for Carrie; Miranda's joke about 'politically incorrect meat'; the relentless visual flair; the discussion of urban myths; Carrie's dress. This is *perfect*. Romantic, funny, exciting, tense, pacey; it'll have you punching the air in delight and laughing out loud. This is one of the show's very best episodes *ever*.

21
Old Dogs, New Dicks

1 August 1999

Written by Jenny Bicks
Directed by Alan Taylor

Guest Cast
Chris Noth (Mr Big) David Eigenberg (Steve Brady)
Jackie Beat (Drag Caller) Alex Draper (Mike) Lorraine Farris (Waitress)
Lisa Gorlitsky (Brooklyn Woman) Amy B Harris (Bingo Woman)
Doan Mackenzie (Drag Queen #2) Hedda Lettuce (Drag Queen #1)
Chris McGinn (Testimonial)

Fit to Print: 'They say that the women in New York are the most beautiful women in the world, which explains why men in New York spend all their time looking at them.' Carrie is growing increasingly irritated with the way that Big looks at other women as they pass. Samantha tells her bluntly that if that is the biggest problem she's having with Big, she's *lucky*. 'You can't change that about a man . . . It's part of their genetic code.' She claims that you simply can't change a man. Ever. Alterations to their hair and clothing are a vague possibility, but even that is a 'constant struggle'. (She seems to, at least partially, be talking about Bernie (see **9**, 'The Turtle and the Hare').) When Carrie says she's going to try to change Big, Sam warns her to be careful with alterations – 'if you pull the wrong thread it can all fall apart'.

Charlotte: She is dating Mike, a 'cute but feared restaurant critic', famous for his 'five whisk' rating system. Charlotte is about to have sex with him when she discovers that his penis is uncircumcised. According to Carrie, 'The only uncut version of anything Charlotte had ever seen was the original *Gone with the Wind*' (Victor Fleming, 1939). She gets some sympathy from Miranda, who admits that she too has never had sex with an uncircumcised man and that it would freak her out, but she tells Charlotte she's overreacting. 'You're dating the guy, not the penis.' Carrie points out that 85 per cent of men aren't circumcised, and therefore Charlotte's reaction is not only disproportionate, but her never-having-seen-an-uncut-one is actually statistically massively unlikely. Samantha's response is simple – 'uncut men are the best'.

Talking to Mike later, Charlotte discovers that he has decided to get circumcised as he's had this reaction from several women. 'Apparently some men could budge an inch,' says Carrie, 'although in Mike's case it may have been more like an inch and a half . . .'

Charlotte takes Mike for a post-operative Scotch, where he tells her that on a scale of one to five his pain level is 72. A few weeks later Charlotte gets the chance to inspect what she calls the new merchandise. After they have sex, she asks him what he wants to do at the weekend, and he tells her that he doesn't think they should be exclusive. 'I just feel like I can't be tied down right now,' he says. 'There's a whole new me happening and I want to go out and share it.' Charlotte never sees Mike again.

Girl Talk: A woman tells us that her boyfriend was obsessed with watching sports 24/7. To change him she 'fooled around with his best friend'. Now, apparently, he's obsessed with watching her.

Guy Talk: A guy tells us that every girlfriend he ever had wanted him to change something – sometimes his job, sometimes his attitude, sometimes something else – but the only thing he ever changes is girlfriends.

Wine and Dine: Carrie and Big go out 'to celebrate absolutely nothing'. Halfway through the meal Big is asked by a waitress to stop smoking a huge cigar. He says that he's sure that their table is in the smoking area of the restaurant, and she replies that it's not her but other customers who are bothered. To prove his point, Big wanders round the restaurant, asking every other patron if they mind if he smokes his cigar. No one seems to mind, especially after he buys the entire room a round of drinks. He sits down in front of Carrie, convinced he's done good. Carrie grimaces – she minds that he's smoking but can't bring herself to say so. She tells him that he's very arrogant and he replies, 'I thought that was what you liked about me.' She tells us that she has reached that point in a relationship 'when all the little things you love about a person become huge liabilities'.

Fashion Victims: Big has an amazing black trench coat. Carrie wears a cute red skinny shirt with the Cookie Monster from *Sesame Street* on it.

Out and About: The girls go to Drag Queen Bingo, which is exactly what it sounds like. Charlotte complains that she never wins, while Samantha takes it all too seriously and is seemingly of the opinion that the house is deliberately cheating her.

Hey, Big Guy: Carrie and Big are supposed to meet at his place, but he's half an hour late. When he eventually arrives, Carrie is furious, telling him that the doorman thought she was a hooker. 'Did you make any money?' he deadpans. Carrie later tells us, 'That night something else changed. Neither of us wanted to make love. If this was all I was ever going to get out of Big . . . was it enough for me?'

Later that night as they sleep, Big rolls over and knocks Carrie out of bed. She shouts at him and then punches him in the face. He gets up and goes to sleep on the sofa.

A few hours later, she wakes him up and apologises for hitting him. She tells him that she hates that he looks at other women, hates that he's never stayed the night at hers, hates that he can't even make space for her in his bed, and she knows it's not his fault because she never says anything about it. 'I feel like I'm back in your life and nothing has really changed,' she says. 'I know you can't change a man and you definitely can't change a man like you, but I still want something to change a little bit. For me.' She then leaves. After several days Big still hasn't called her, leading Carrie to speculate that you *can* change a man – you can 'change him into not calling you'. Then Big turns up at her apartment out of the blue, and Carrie sees the extent of the bruising on his face. He tells her he understands that she needs him to give her a key to his place so that she'll know he's crazy about her, but explains that he's given out the key to his apartment five times in his life and never got them back. Carrie seems to understand that he's using the apartment key as a metaphor for a larger commitment to someone. He then tells her what it is he doesn't like about her. 'I hate that you eat oranges in my bed. They're sticky, and they make my sheets sticky.' She jokes that maybe they should discuss this, and that it might take a while . . . Big suggests that if that's the case, then maybe he should spend the night at her place.

Samantha: Sam doesn't get a lot to do this week, but she does get an amazing scene where she meets Brad, a semi-professional hockey player she once dated. In the intervening years he's become a drag queen. She demands to know when he made this lifestyle choice. 'Right after you,' he informs her. She then discovers that he calls himself 'Samantha'. 'Imitation is the sincerest form of flattery,' he tells her. This leads Samantha to realise that she has changed a man . . . into a woman. 'I am so much prettier than him,' the real Sam insists.

Miranda: Dating Steve means keeping to a schedule that is killing Miranda. 'Everything was great about Steve except for one thing. They had completely opposite schedules.'

She works during the day; he works at night. He has free time in the morning; she has to be in court. She wants to make love in the evening; he wants to make love in the morning. This, for Miranda, is unthinkable, according to Carrie: 'The only thing Miranda liked inside her in the morning was a cup of take-out coffee she drank on the way to the subway.'

One night Steve comes round after work, waking Miranda up in the process. 'How was your night?' he asks. 'I don't know, I was asleep,' is all she can say. He tells her that he's late because, although he intended to close the bar at 2 a.m., a large number of Japanese bankers turned up and ordered 'big flaming drinks', forcing him to keep the bar open. Later one of them was sick. This, it seems, is a typical day.

After a few days of this, and bolstered by coffee, Miranda decides to perform a 2 a.m. seduction of Steve, with candles and elaborate nightwear. Steve arrives and is impressed. Who wouldn't be? He then falls asleep before she's even touched him. She wakes him up and they have a row about their competing schedules. He walks out, telling her to let go, and to call him when she has a window in her schedule.

The next night Steve calls her from the bar and asks her to walk to her window. He wants to show her something – a blue moon hanging in the sky. He tells her how rare they are and she asks him to come by after work. They make love that night and again in the morning. 'Miranda was an hour late for work and didn't even notice, so maybe you can't change a man, but once in a blue moon you can change a woman.'

And So . . .: 'It wasn't just about the cigar . . . It never is.' This is messy. The Carrie and Big stuff is great, Samantha's comic subplot is totally bizarre and utterly inspired and Steve and Miranda continue to develop into a fascinating couple – but Charlotte's fear and disgust of uncircumcised men borders on incomprehensible. As Carrie points out, it's statistically massively unlikely that Charlotte should never have had sex with an uncircumcised man. Which begs the question, why write a plotline about it? And if you're going to, why debunk it *during* the episode by pointing out how implausible it is? Funny or not, it just makes Charlotte come across as a bit strange (although admittedly Mike comes across as a good deal stranger). Perhaps it's fortunate that she ends up married to a man of Jewish faith (see **92**, 'Splat!' et al). The central 'dilemma' (whether you can change a man) is also inconsistently handled. Carrie concludes that women can change but men can't, despite the fact that during the course of the episode Big, Steve and Mike (and, in a sense, Brad) all adapt because of the demands of a relationship. The real question appears to be, then, just what is this episode trying to say?

22
The Caste System

8 August 1999

Written by Darren Star
Directed by Allison Anders

Guest Cast
Chris Noth (Mr Big) David Eigenberg (Steve Brady)
Samuel Ball (Jeremiah) Brian Van Holt (Wylie Ford)
Harvey Bouvy (Cocktail Waiter) Pamela J Gray (Serena)
Philip Karner (Salesman) James McCauley (Harvey Terkell)
Jina Oh (Sum)

Carrie: It's spring in Manhattan, and Carrie tells us some of the things she loves about New York: 'that week in spring when it's warm but not hot . . . men in suits, three papers and twelve gossip columns. It's easy for me to say, "I love you, New York" but it's not so easy for me to say, "I love you, Mr Big".'

Carrie tells us that the first time she wanted to tell Big she loved him was when he took her to the ballet, because she knows just how much he hates ballet. She tries to say it but ends up with, 'I love . . . your hair like that.'

Then one day Big buys a gift for her – a thoroughly tacky spangly purse in the shape of a duck. Speechless, all

Carrie can think of to say is, 'I love you.' And Big ignores her.

Girl Talk: A crisis meeting is convened to discuss this accidental development. Carrie's friends suggest that maybe Big is ignoring her comment because he didn't clearly hear it. Maybe he thinks she said she loved the purse. 'I did not say I loved the purse,' maintains Carrie. Saying 'I love you' is, she claims, a 'laying down of the gauntlet', even when not intended as one. A silence, a non-reciprocation, has the 'shelf life of a dairy product', in that it will 'last about a week'.

Miranda: Miranda seems remarkably unconcerned about Carrie's dilemma, asking the others, 'Did you ever think that at this very moment the man might be trying to find his own way to tell Carrie he loves her?' Carrie explains that since going out with Steve, Miranda has had a 'romantic epiphany', changing from 'love's greatest sceptic' into something else entirely.

We are later told that in order to protect his masculine pride, Miranda has been letting Steve pay for their dates, 'but only at places she knew he could afford'. We see Miranda and Steve sitting outside a cheap pizza parlour, clearly having a wonderful time. Miranda asks Steve to go to a huge company function with her but tells him that it will be very boring. He rather sweetly responds that it's 'not going to be boring if I'm there with you'. Samantha thinks it's wonderful that Miranda is dating a bartender, especially one with whom the sex is fantastic. He can 'make you come and then he can make you a Cosmopolitan'.

Charlotte: Our Charlotte thinks it 'normal for the man to have more money' in a relationship, and is generally disapproving of Miranda's affair with a man with no prospects. Later, we see her swoon over actor Wylie Ford as he visits her gallery. Taken with him, not least because he calls her 'adorable', Charlotte starts hanging out with Ford and his cronies and groupies, drinking heavily and smoking dope (this is arguably an insanely sanitised view of a movie star's lifestyle). He calls her Charlene because he prefers the name. After Ford makes a request that Charlotte cannot acquiesce to (that she go to the bathroom, insert her fingers inside herself and then come back to the bar so he can sniff them in public), she walks out on him.

Samantha: Samantha is dating, in her own words, 'a guy with an actual servant'. His name is Harvey and he's 'a real-estate agent who's changed Chelsea sweatshops into trendy co-ops for the painfully trendy'. His servant is an exceptionally servile oriental woman called Sum, but the first night Samantha stays over at Harvey's she gets an unpleasant surprise. Once he's left for work Sum turns nasty, demanding she get out of bed so she can wash the sheets. She also refuses to cook breakfast for Samantha despite Harvey's insistence that she must.

On another occasion when Samantha stays over, Sum puts into action her masterplan to get Samantha out of her master's life. She starts screaming at Samantha, throwing condom wrappers at her and shouting, 'Dirty cock-sucking whore!' When Harvey comes into the room Sum starts crying, and tells him that Samantha hit her. Samantha tries to explain but Harvey won't have any of it. Samantha quickly leaves, realising that a) there is only room for one woman in Harvey's house and b) this is one master/servant relationship where the actual dynamic is really rather different from what you'd think.

Wine and Dine: Big takes Carrie out for a romantic dinner. She's convinced that this will be when he returns her affections. 'There's something I've been meaning to tell you ever since the night I came to you with the purse ...' Carrie waits, baited breath, for what Big is about to say. He loves her, surely? 'You can take it back if you don't like it,' he finishes. Sheesh!

Fashion Victims: Steve claims to have one suit, in 'gold corduroy'. Seeing Miranda's (justly) appalled face, he deadpans, 'What's wrong with corduroy?' 'I don't have enough time to tell you what's wrong with corduroy,' she replies.

Later Miranda takes Steve shopping and gets him to try on an Armani suit. 'I think it's kind of frightening how good I look,' he says, looking at himself in the mirror. Knowing that he can't afford the clothes she's got him to try on, Miranda tries to buy Steve the suit, but he won't let her, insisting that he pay the $18,000 tab himself. Embarrassingly his credit card is rejected, and he pays with a combination of cards, cheques and cash.

Out and About: Big takes Carrie to a fabulous society party thrown by Serena Bush, a woman apparently famous for her husband's money and close friendships with media royalty. Carrie points out that she knew her when she was 'famous for her father's money and a close personal friendship with her drug dealer'. After a few minutes in this God-awful environment, Carrie is desperate to escape. She is later astonished that Serena has a 'no brown food' policy in her house. This is clearly a new 'mutant strain of Upper East Side anal' that Carrie was unaware of.

Men: One of the waiters at the party is Jeremiah, an old friend of Carrie's who is a famous downtown performance artist, often known uptown as 'Hey, kid, another Scotch and soda' due to his habit of moonlighting as a waiter. Forbidden by Serena Bush from smoking in her home, Carrie goes on to the balcony in order to indulge her Marlboro habit. Here Jeremiah offers to show her his new tattoo, stretching from his waist and then . . . downward. Another guest sees Carrie inspecting Jeremiah's new piece of body art, and through a contrived set of circumstances belives that she is in fact giving him a blow job. The news spreads around the party, and Carrie is eventually asked by Big if this is really the case. Insulted that he even asked her, she leaves the party in the company of the recently sacked Jeremiah. They head downtown where they each consume a 'couple of pitchers of margaritas'. Walking back to Carrie's apartment together, both hugely drunk, they kiss. 'That was the last thing I could remember that night . . .' Carrie later tells us. She and Jeremiah both wake up in her bed and although they tell each other that they've obviously not had sex, neither seem very sure. Then the phone rings. It's Big saying he knows what it is she's pissed off about, but that 'it's something I have to do in my own time . . . I fucking love you, you know I do . . . It's just something I have difficulty saying because it always gets me in trouble . . .' Carrie listens to this while sitting in bed with Jeremiah and feels like the worst person in the whole world.

Steve takes Miranda back to his apartment for the first time in their relationship. It's a dump, and he jokes that he 'modelled it after De Niro's place in *Taxi Driver*' (Martin Scorsese, 1976). He excuses the place on the quite reasonable grounds that 'it's cheap, and near the bar, and you never have to come here again'. Carrie later tells us that 'that evening Miranda experienced her first pangs of yuppie guilt', fearing for the future of their relationship because she is so much more financially secure than Steve is. This, on top of their incompatible schedules, may cause them severe problems. Ultimately the decision is taken out of Miranda's hands. Steve arrives at her apartment one night and he tells her that she's 'going places' and that she deserves somebody who'll go places with her. He apologises, and then walks calmly out of her life.

And So . . .: 'We don't say things like working class any more.' BANG!! This is quick-fire, surefooted and *nasty*. It's a really great episode for Miranda (in character terms, at least), and you're either shouting at the TV or trying not to cry when Steve breaks up with her because *he* thinks that he's not good enough for her. Charlotte doesn't come across at all well, as we see that the flipside of her romantic idealism is a money-centric angle on dating. She's looking for love and love means husband and father, and husband and father means *provider*. Her brief fling with the world of celebrity groupies is very funny, though. In many ways the episode is a series of attacks on snobbery, both traditional and inverted, that really takes no prisoners in its depiction of just how destructive such things can be. One of Star's finest scripts for the series, this pulls out surprise after surprise and carries enormous emotional impact. Brilliant.

23
Evolution

15 August 1999

Written by Cindy Chupack
Directed by Pam Thomas

Guest Cast
Chris Noth (Mr Big) Willie Garson (Stanford Blatch)
John Shea (Dominic Del Monico) Dan Futterman (Stefan Bodeme)
Phillippe Brenninkmeyer (Bartender) Elaine Bromka (Dr Finch)
Harry O'Reilly (Joseph Adler)

Kisses: We see Charlotte, who has apparently tired of the Neanderthals she dates, spending her Saturday night with a gay friend who caters for parties at her gallery, dessert chef Stefan Bodeme. As Charlotte gets into her cab, Stefan turns and kisses her full on the lips.

Wine and Dine: Charlotte is confused about whether he is gay or straight. 'It's not that simple any more,' Carrie points out. 'The real question is, is he a straight/gay man or a gay/straight man?' She then goes on to define the difference. Gay/straight is a heterosexual 'spawned in Manhattan as the result of overexposure to fashion, exotic cuisine, musical theatre and antique furniture.' It's someone who is basically straight but who has gay qualities, Samantha continues, whereas a straight/gay guy is 'just a gay guy who plays sports and won't fuck you'. It's pointed out that Stefan must be gay/straight because he asked Charlotte out for a second date, but paranoia leads Charlotte to speculate that he could be a straight/gay man in denial. Despite a couple more dates and some serious kissing action, Charlotte is still worried, so she convenes 'a panel of experts', consisting of Carrie and Stanford, to meet him at his place of work. Stanford paraphrases *The Wizard of Oz* (Victor Fleming, 1939) in an obvious attempt to catch him out, but it doesn't work. Carrie is worried that Stefan not only reads her column but also notices that she has changed her hair since the photograph she uses in the paper was taken. This, she thinks, is not a good sign. However, Stanford is adamant that Stefan is straight. He says that he fancies him, and he usually only fancies straight men, and then points out that Stefan is quite obviously crazy about Charlotte. But what, wonders Charlotte, if he's gay but just doesn't know it yet? Stanford shakes his head, 'Honey . . . When I was a boy my father gave me a book about the female body to teach me about sex. I took one look at it and said, "No!"' He later comments, 'It's so not fair. All the good ones are straight, even the gay ones!'

Miranda: There is nothing more humiliating for a woman than a visit to the gynaecologist, except, as Miranda discovers, 'telling your gynaecologist you don't need the pill any more.' Steve leaving has hit Miranda quite hard; she describes him as the first real relationship she's had in years, and she admits to missing him. Her gynaecologist then drops a bombshell: Miranda has a 'lazy ovary'. The right one no longer produces eggs, meaning that she only produces an egg on alternate months. 'Is it possible that it's just on strike?' she asks. She later describes the situation to Carrie as her right ovary having given up hope that she's ever going to get married and have children. Yes, Carrie points out, but 'at least the left one still believes'.

Worried, Miranda agrees to go on a date with a guy from work whom she's turned down twice before. He's quite dull and has hair plug-ins. He rhapsodises endlessly about the benefits of his follicle surgery, so Miranda tells him about her ovary problem and how she's now taking hormones to try and rectify this. She confides that she's considering having some of her eggs frozen. He's massively unimpressed, even when she points out that this 'removes the whole biological clock issue'.

He has a social Darwinistic, vaguely eugenicist attitude to what he calls an 'abuse of science', arguing that maybe some people aren't supposed to reproduce and this is nature's way of weeding out the weak. Miranda is, quite rightly, unimpressed by this attitude, particularly coming from someone who appears to be performing 'crop rotation on his head!'

Heading home she concludes that 'maybe someday there would be eggs in her freezer, but not yet', and digs a bottle of vodka out of it instead.

Charlotte: As they are about to make love, Charlotte feels moved to ask Stefan whether he's gay. He shakes his head. 'Charlotte, I'm a thirty-five-year-old pastry chef who lives in Chelsea. If I were gay, I . . . would be gay.' It's pretty hard to argue with his logic here. After a fantastic night of sex, Charlotte wakes up to find Stefan cooking. She tells him that if she dates him she's going to put on ten pounds. He points out that she'll still be gorgeous. Just then there's a noise, a painful squeaking, and they both look down and see a mouse trapped in a mousetrap. They both panic, neither of them able to do anything about the injured rodent. Stefan jumps on a chair shrieking, and Charlotte concludes that the mouse-killing side of her personality isn't highly developed enough to date a man whose feminine side is as developed as Stefan's is.

Carrie: Carrie is tired of having to carry around all the stuff she needs to wake up and make up every night she stays at Big's. Samantha is amazed that, after all this time, she doesn't have so much as a drawer there. Carrie claims that 'Big is weird about stuff', and that her motto is 'walk softly and carry a big purse'. Deciding to confront this issue by stealth, Carrie hides a variety of items belonging to her in Big's apartment.

Samantha: While having cocktails in a bar, Samantha spots Dominic Del Monico, a publishing magnate and the only man she has ever really loved. He wined and dined her, set the bar for what she considered to be hot sex, and ultimately dumped her for an Icelandic supermodel named Anka. When told this story Charlotte is perplexed, as 'imagining Samantha with a broken heart was almost more confusing to Charlotte than a French kiss from a gay man'. Sam plans to date Dominic once, then refuse to have sex with him, putting him through a little of what he put her through. 'I'm the one with the power now. I've evolved past him,' she tells Carrie. Unfortunately not everything goes to plan and she discovers that her 'desire for revenge was not as strong as her desire for Dominic'. They sleep together, and she revises her plan. Now she's going to have sex with him a few times to remind him what he's missing and THEN crush him. But after another night of passion, Dominic informs Samantha that he is returning to Anka, mostly for financial reasons. She is once again devastated by his departure, and realises that she lacks his killer instinct and emotional detachment. 'She hadn't evolved past having feelings,' says Carrie, 'which in a way was nice to know . . .'

Fit to Print: Carrie's column ponders the problems of *fin de siècle* New York – a city in which gay men are 'so out, they're in,' and women are so single their ovaries 'become vestigial organs, we can have anything delivered at any hour, we can have our dogs walked, our clothes cleaned, our food cooked. Who needs a husband when you can have a doorman? Are New Yorkers evolving out of relationships?'

Fashion Victims: While cooking with Stefan, Charlotte wears a beautiful yet impractical Cynthia Ralle sheer silver dress.

Trivia: The 26th US President and native New Yorker Theodore Roosevelt (President 1901–1909), was often quoted as saying, 'Speak softly and carry a big stick . . .' It's this somewhat cryptic comment that Carrie paraphrases when talking about Big. Interesting fact: Roosevelt was so wedded to New York that he established a 'Summer White House' in The Hamptons during his Presidency, and is buried within the city.

Also Starring: John Shea, playing Dominic, is best known for playing Superman's nemesis Lex Luthor in the popular early 90s TV show *Lois & Clark* alongside Dean Cain and latter-day Bond girl Teri Hatcher.

Hey, Big Guy: 'Hey, beautiful.' 'Hi, handsome.' Big pops round to Carrie's place unexpectedly, a bag from (department store) Barney's in his hand. 'Just a few things you left at my place,' he says, handing it over. It contains all the objects Carrie stashed at his apartment. She speculates that Big's place is like 'Teflon for women', nothing sticks, and notes that she feels like she's been 'kicked out of the relationship fast lane'.

This provokes a discussion about Carrie's need to leave things at Big's apartment, and she tells him that he can leave stuff at her place if he likes. He points out that he doesn't want to. She asks him what the ideal domestic situation for two lovers is, and he tells her that it's exactly what they have. 'I have my place, you have yours, we're together when we want to be and apart when we want to be.' A sort of 'separate/togetherness'.

Later Carrie finds a photograph of her and Big that he's put in a drawer at his apartment and she realises that she doesn't need to leave objects behind because she's already made her mark.

And So . . . : 'Home is where my hairdryer is.' Unfocused, and with Charlotte centre-stage, 'Evolution' is a strange beast. Big's emotional inaccessibility and bizarre problems with intimacy are becoming more and more tiresome for both Carrie and the audience, while Samantha's collapsed revenge fantasy is very funny indeed. Stefan is wonderful, though, and it's both peculiar and rather a shame that Charlotte can't see a future with him. The episode's best line belongs to Samantha who, on seeing Miranda guzzling her hormone pills, asks, 'Are those recreational? Because this drink isn't doing it for me.' He he he.

24
La Douleur Exquise!

22 August 1999

Written by Ollie Levy & Michael Patrick King
Directed by Allison Anders

Guest Cast
Chris Noth (Mr Big) Willie Garson (Stanford Blatch) Will Arnett (Jack)
James Urbaniak (Buster) Matthew Beisner (Sexy Waiter)
Matt Conley (Older Man) Faith Geer (Elderly Woman)
Chris Payne Gilbert (Gorgeous Young Hunk)
Anthony J Ribustello (Large Imposing Man)

Out and About: New York city restaurants are always looking for that new angle with which to trap the jaded Manhattan patron. In 1998 it was Fusion Cajun, recently it was Mussels from Brussels, and tonight it's S&M. Samantha's PR firm does the opening for an S&M theme restaurant in Manhattan, La Douleur Exquise! Of course, Carrie et al are invited, and seem a bit freaked out by the place, but Samantha revels in it. She tells her friends not to be so judgmental. 'This is just a sexual expression; all these people have jobs and pay their bills, they're just having fun with fetishes ... I think it's healthy and fabulous.' She then teases Charlotte with a riding crop and says 'I wonder what your fetish is?' Charlotte replies by claiming not to have any fetishes, which is a bit odd given the events of **8**, 'Three's a Crowd'.

Hey, Big Guy: Carrie has to leave dinner early in order to see Big. He's heading for Paris the next day on business and she wants to say goodbye. As she watches him pack, he casually mentions to her that he 'may have to move to Paris for work, just for a while'. When pressed about how long a while is, he says, 'Seven months, maybe a year.' Carrie is furious, demanding to know when he was going to tell her this. He points out that he just has. She then asks how long he's known that this is a possibility. 'It's been in the works for a while' is all he can say.

Girl Talk: Carrie tells her friends how angry she is at Big, particularly as it is quite clear that she is not 'even a factor in his decision-making process'.

Charlotte: When a woman with a shoe fetish meets a shoe salesman with a foot fetish, expect *results*. According to Carrie, Charlotte, just 'like every other normal woman in Manhattan, has a thing for shoes'. She is size seven, and can spot shoes she wants to buy from the other side of the road. Tempted into a shop by the sight of something in the window, she tries on several pairs that she can't afford, especially as she's trying to start saving for a summer share in The Hamptons. After trying on a particularly beautiful pair, she asks the attendant (who introduces himself as 'Buster'), to 'please take it off before I start to cry'. He tells her that 'shoes are meant to be loved' and that it is she who should love them.

She later returns to the store to try something else on, and is amazed when Buster *gives* her a pair of shoes because he knows she can't afford them. After talking to Carrie about this, she realises that she has to return the $500 sandals, but when she tries to take them back Buster refuses to have them on the grounds that they've already been worn and are now in an unsellable condition. She asks him if there's anything she can do to repay him for the shoes – he tells her that she can model some new styles for him. Surrounded by 'exquisite shoes' and finding 'the smell of leather intoxicating', Charlotte agrees. As Buster puts more and more pairs of shoes on Charlotte's feet, and he becomes more and more excited by this, Carrie tells us that Charlotte 'felt like Cinderella – Cinderella in a dirty, kinky, freaked out, storybook parallel universe'. Yuck!

Men: Stanford claims that 'some fetishes can only flourish behind closed doors in the very late-night hours on a laptop'. At the S&M party, Stanford wants to know when wild sex came back in style; Carrie points out that this happened the weekend he spent at the Barney's sale. Later, Stanford tells Carrie that he has something to confess to her, and he asks her not to judge him . . . He's been having cyber-sex on the Internet, under the name Rick9plus. Carrie finds this hilariously funny, especially when he tells her that he's been chatting with a guy who styles himself Bigtool4U. Now, Bigtool4U wants to meet up, at an after-hours gay club in the meat-packing district (right by the Hudson River). He's unsure if he should go, as the real might not live up to the electronic. He eventually decides that he has to go, chiefly because, 'I haven't had good sex since before *Cats* was on Broadway.' He visits the club, only to find it has a mandatory 'underwear only' policy. If you're wearing clothes, you don't get in. Despite the fact that Stanford hasn't been seen in his underwear by a roomful of men since seventh-grade gym class, he agrees, and enters the club to look for Bigtool4U. He doesn't find him, but he does find a young man who appears to be very interested in both the design of his underwear and what it contains.

Samantha: Sam claims that women think in 'we', but that for a man, intrinsically selfish as they are, 'we' is him and his dick. This is slightly bizarre coming from a woman who has no interest in relationships and prefers men who are avoiding commitment.

Miranda: We discover that Miranda is obsessed with historical biographies. In fact, 'She spent all last weekend in bed with [King] Philip [II] of Spain.' While shopping at a second-hand book store for a copy of *Art & Scandal: The Life and Times of Isabella Stewart Gardner*, she bumps into a man called Jack, who shares her interest in the lives of the rich, famous and dead. They chat about *Crazy Horse and Custer: The Parallel Lives of Two American Warriors* by Stephen Ambrose, and his other book *Meriwether Lewis and Thomas Jefferson: Undaunted Courage*. And then, just after she picks up *Elizabeth I* by Jasper Riley, Miranda allows Jack to pick her up.

Miranda and Jack have what she believes will go down in history as the best first date of her life – they talk about books and ideas and he shows her the house that Mark

Twain lived in while resident in New York. It's while standing near this revered literary monument that Miranda discovers Jack's fetish – 'I like to have sex in places where I can get caught.'

Over a week or so of dating Jack, Miranda has sex in a public toilet, the back of a cab, Bond Street and God knows where else. This begins to unnerve her, so she tries to persuade him that they should go back to his apartment for more 'normal' sex. To her surprise Miranda has no difficulty getting Jack to go back to his apartment, but just as they are really going for it on the sofa, she hears a voice from another room . . . 'Son?' Jack's parents are visiting, and it seems that for him, the idea of being discovered having sex by them is the biggest turn-on of all.

Fashion Victims: Check out Miranda's orange dress. Orange dress, red hair, shouldn't work, should it? But it does. When with Buster the foot fetishist, Charlotte tries on a variety of (then very new and exclusive) shoes by Jimmy Choo and several pairs of Manolo Blahnik sandals. The pair he gives her (we never get that good a look at them) should cost $500 – they're white sandals, and almost certainly by Jimmy Choo.

Trivia: The French title means literally 'The Exquisite Pain!'

Fetishes: Oh, where to start! Samantha enjoys playing the mistress of pain, smacking both Charlotte and a waiter with her riding crop. Carrie takes a top hat and riding crop to Big's place, which certainly seems to do it for him. Then there's Jack's desire to be discovered, Buster's obsession with shoes, Stanford's flirtation with underwear clubs and cyber-sex . . .

Carrie: After Big comes back from Paris, Carrie goes over to his apartment to greet him, wearing a silly French hat and carrying a bag of McDonald's food. She tells him that they can work their relationship out, and that she is willing to go to Paris for a while if necessary and write 'le sex in le city'. Big tells her that if she moves to Paris it must be because she independently wants to, not because of him – he doesn't want her to uproot her life for him, and he warns her not to expect anything from him. Carrie is furious, and starts flinging takeaway food everywhere. 'You don't even care if I'm in your life!' she yells. He asks her to calm down, and she angrily tells him, 'I am so tired of calming down!' He tells her that Paris isn't about them, it's about work, and she retorts that her anger isn't about Paris, it's about them getting closer and him getting so freaked out about it that he feels the need to put an ocean between them. 'Why is it so hard for you to factor me into your life in any real way?' she asks, and Big looks shamefaced and says, 'I guess old habits die hard.' She says she can't do this any more, and goes to leave. 'You said you loved me,' she says, near to tears. Big replies that he does. 'Then why does it hurt so fucking much?' she asks.

Later Carrie wonders if she really loves Big, or if she is just addicted to the pain of wanting someone so exquisitely unobtainable. Big comes round in the middle of the night, and they make love without speaking, and then he leaves – walking out of her life again, for exactly the same reasons as before.

And So . . .: 'And just like that, I had untied myself from Mr Big.' A frantic mixture of pain and pleasure, this mixes some rich, delightfully off-the-wall comedy in with some of the most complex emotional material the series has ever dealt with. Here, Stanford is almost a fifth member of the normal group, with as much screen time devoted to him as the usual four – the scene where a handsome young man admires his underwear is brilliant and strangely sweet. Miranda and Charlotte's plotlines are skin-crawlingly funny, and Chris Noth and Sarah Jessica Parker have rarely been better than during their argument scene, or in its strangely tender immediate aftermath. The only flaw is that Samantha hardly features at all, and when she does she comes across as little better than a crude parody of her normal self. That aside, this is damn good stuff.

25
Games People Play

29 August 1999

Written by Jenny Bicks
Directed by Michael Spiller

Guest Cast

Willie Garson (Stanford Blatch) Jon Bon Jovi (Seth Robinson)
John Dossett (Don Siegler) Anne Lange (Dr Ellen Greenfield)
Steve Albert (Sports Announcer) Maureen Cassidy (Preppy Woman)
George Hahn (Great-Looking Guy) Steve Scionti (Wall Street Guy)
Jodi Stevens (Mid-20s Hot Girl) Oliver Vaquer (Waiter)

Girl Talk: 'In a town where everyone is dying to couple up,
sometimes there's nothing better than being out of a
relationship.' You have time to do your laundry, freedom
to play your favourite bad music, and best of all you have
time to talk to your friends. We see a montage of scenes of
Carrie obsessing about Big to her friends, mostly backed
with Gloria Gaynor's 'I Will Survive'. Eventually, while
sitting outside a cafe, the three bite the bullet. 'Honey,'
says Samantha as gently as possible, 'you're obsessed with
talking about Big and, frankly, we can't take it any more.'
They suggest that she gets a shrink, something that she's
loth to do as she doesn't buy 'the whole shrink thing'.
However, worried that she may have 'crossed a line from
pleasantly neurotic into annoying troubled', she agrees to
see a shrink recommended by Miranda's psychiatrist.

Carrie: Carrie meets with Dr Ellen Greenfield, who according to Stanford is also Gwyneth Paltrow's psychiatrist. Dr
G, as she likes to be termed, doesn't like the term 'normal',
and Carrie's belief that 'psychiatry is a self-indulgence'
seems to be borne out by the fact that the only thing that
Dr G is able to tell her is that she may be picking the
wrong men. Samantha points out that this is obvious, and
what's more, it's not as if any viewer of this series couldn't
have told you that months ago. Carrie worries about her
ability to attract and be attracted to the wrong men.
Miranda asks Carrie if she thinks that she is a fly strip for

the wrong guy, and Carrie responds that yes, she is, 'but a really pretty floral scented one'.

Hey, Big Guy: Carrie describes Big as 'smart, sexy, totally screwed up, playing all these games and I didn't know the rules'. This leads her to question whether you have to play games in order to make a relationship work. Is all this 'Don't call him until Thursday' and 'Don't be too keen' type stuff really necessary? Is it just an extension of the games played in childhood, but with higher stakes?

Charlotte: Charlotte claims she's a really good tennis player (see **48**, 'Cock a Doodle Do!'). Aside from this she hardly appears, although she is wearing the sandals given to her by Buster-the-shoe-fetishist in **24**, 'La Douleur Exquise!'

Miranda: One night Miranda finds herself being watched by her neighbour through a window. After a couple of nights of ignoring him, she begins a protracted game of 'Peek-a-Boo' with him. One night, he flashes his behind at her, and in response she flashes her left breast. Strangely turned on by this whole business, she later approaches her neighbour in a supermarket, reasoning the adult thing to do is to stop playing games and introduce herself. Her neighbour doesn't really know who she is, and it's only after she explains as best she can that he realises that she's the girl 'who lives above the guy I've been cruising'. Miranda is appalled, wondering if, like in childhood, she's just been playing with her imaginary friends because there's no one else around.

Men: In the waiting room for Dr G, Carrie encounters Seth Robinson, a photographer. After a couple of coy glances, they swap names and numbers. They have a great first date, followed by a couple of other really good dates, and then she invites him to hers and they play Twister and make love. Afterwards they discuss Dr G, and he tells her he's screwed up about women, because once he's slept with them he loses all interest. He then asks her what her problem is. 'I pick the wrong men,' she says sadly.

The ever-wonderful Stanford appears briefly, in order to give Carrie his opinion on whether or not she should get a psychiatrist: 'This is Manhattan!' he says, amazed. 'Even the shrinks have shrinks!' Carrie reluctantly concedes that 'in Manhattan a shrink was as ubiquitous as pirated cable'.

Fetishes: At the sports bar Samantha meets Don Siegler, an importer of Mexican handbags, who is fanatical about two things, 1) keeping the price of foreign labour down and 2) New York's premier basketball team, the Knicks. Samantha is initially quite interested in him and his basketball obsession, especially after she discovers that sex with him is amazing, but then a problem rears its ugly head. Or rather nothing rears its head. Don can only have sex when the Knicks win a game. Initially planning to ride this obsession out, Samantha leaves Don when she realises just how rarely the Knicks win a game.

Also Starring: Jon Bon Jovi was originally best known for having poodle-hair and being the lead singer with rock band Bon Jovi. In recent years he's turned his hand to acting, notably in historically inept World War II drama *U-571* (John Mostow, 2000), lame horror flick *John Carpenter's Vampires* (unsurprisingly, John Carpenter, 2000), and thesp-heavy sentimental tear-jerker *Pay it Forward* (Mimi Leder, 2000), with Kevin Spacey and Helen Hunt. None of these, of course, beat his uncredited, non-speaking role as a man who gets shot as he tries to escape prison in *Young Guns II: Blaze of Glory* (Geoff Murphy, 1990), for which he also wrote and performed some of the music.

Trivia: We hear the thumping 'Rock & Roll – Part One' by disgraced British Glam Rock artist Gary Glitter.

Out and About: Carrie leads her friends to sports night at the bar/diner where they often eat (to pick a random example, **13**, 'Take Me Out to the Ball Game'). When she's informed that on sports night ladies drink for free, Miranda is hugely impressed. 'Forget Disneyland, this is the happiest place on earth.'

And So ...: 'Maybe you're picking the wrong men.' Inconsequential, 'Games People Play' is a welcome dose of unadulterated sitcom after last week's traumas; Jon Bon Jovi is surprisingly good as Seth, but Miranda and Samantha's stories are disconcertingly brief and empty.

26
The Fuck Buddy

5 September 1999

Written by Merrill Markoe and Darren Star
Directed by Alan Taylor

Guest Cast
Ben Weber (Skipper Johnston) Dean Winters (John McFadden)
David Lansbury (Kevin) Louis Aguirre (George) Divina Cook (Marlene)
Abigail Lopez (Girlfriend #2) Kate Miller (Girlfriend #1)
Anne O'Sullivan (Mid-30s Woman) Victor Pagan (Jesus)
Lydia Radziul (WASPy Woman) Timmi Reifsnyder (13-Year-Old Boy)
Jon Patrick Walker (Eric)

Carrie: Miss Bradshaw has fallen into a rut since Big left, staying out until the early hours of the morning, sleeping until midday and eating a lot of Chinese takeaway food. This is the pattern into which she falls following every break-up, and a particular part of this pattern involves calling John McFadden, her 'fuck buddy', a guy with whom she can have consequence-free, high-quality sex for the cost of a phone call. Worried at the ease with which she slips into this pattern, Carrie discusses modes of behaviour with her friends ...

Charlotte: It is said that Charlotte's pattern is that she waits for a perfect guy to ask her on a perfect date, and then when this happens she projects a huge number of expectations on to him. These expectations inevitably blow up in her face. Struck by the truth of this observation, Charlotte decides to try and change her pattern. Emboldened by too many tantric headstands at her yoga class, Charlotte is moved to ask a man out for the first time in her life. She plans two dates in a single night, an early dinner with Bachelor #1, followed by late supper with Bachelor #2. This is daring, this is out of character, this is never going to work . . . Charlotte's first date overruns, so she has to rush to her second telling Bachelor #1 that she has a sore throat and has to go home. Later, she takes Bachelor #2 back to her place, but #1 emerges from her apartment block to find her kissing #2. Neither guy is particularly impressed, especially #1, who had called round with some chicken soup for Charlotte's throat. Dumped on the spot by both guys, Charlotte finds herself abandoned and alone while they share a cab back to the Upper East Side.

Miranda: Miranda dates yet another angry guy, who's sarcastic and obviously not as clever as he thinks he is. He bosses Miranda around terribly, which she hates except when they're having sex, when she absolutely loves it. For a while she excuses his appalling behaviour, wiping his beer glass for him so he doesn't berate the waitress for serving him spilt beer and generally clearing up after him. It is pointed out to her that her pattern is a tendency to date angry, unpleasant men and then complain about it. She realises this is true, and dumps him as he rants endlessly about how $100 champagne doesn't taste any different to the $30 stuff, and how Miranda doesn't appreciate how much pressure he is under.

Girl Talk: A woman is interviewed about her pattern and after some prodding admits to having dated several artists. All of them were narcissistic, and had both commitment issues *and* substance abuse problems, but she is convinced that the sculptors were very different to the painters. Another woman admits to a pattern of dating 'handsome, WASPy assholes who treat me like shit'.

Guy Talk: A 13-year-old boy informs us that he only dates girls who have Sony PlayStations or breasts. Or presumably both.

Men: John McFadden, the eponymous anti-hero. He's fun, comfortable and easy to be with, and from Carrie's point of view 'a real shot in the arm for my sexual self-esteem'. Tempted to try and make more of their relationship, Carrie invites John out to dinner, despite Samantha's loud protestations that she can't date her fuck buddy. After a dreadful dinner date and an even worse time at a movie, Carrie realises why John was simply 'Dial-a-Dick' all these years. He's boring. Appalled that someone so stimulating in bed could be so tedious in life she breaks up with him immediately, falling back into her pattern, only this time without her fuck buddy as a back-up.

A welcome return for Miranda's ex, Skipper Johnston, last seen in **12**, 'Oh Come All Ye Faithful', at the end of Season One. We actually get to see their break-up scene, which we didn't first time round. Carrie runs into Skipper on the street, bruised and frantic having just broken up with another girl, only a few months after being dumped by his previous girlfriend. He complains to Carrie that women 'wait for you to get relaxed and comfortable before they hit you in the face with an ice pick'. Carrie explains that he is a sweet guy who is perpetually attracted to women who are looking for jerks – this is his problem and his pattern. After dumping Kevin, Miranda runs into Skipper, who given his current mood, doesn't want anything to do with her. Having never seen him this angry Miranda is amazed at how much his ire attracts her to him. 'Have you been working out?' she bellows as he walks away from her down the street.

Samantha: Bored and alone, Samantha is disturbed by the noise of the people in the next apartment having very loud sex. Working on the philosophy of 'if you can't join them, beat it', Samantha starts masturbating to the sounds of her neighbours' lovemaking. After several nights of this game, she realises that they can hear her screams. Then one of them knocks on the wall in order to draw attention to the fact they can hear her. Tentatively, she knocks back. Desperate to find out more about the couple, especially after they leave her a note saying that they'd like to 'take down the wall' between them, she interrogates the cleaner.

He says that he is a musician, whereas she is a dancer. Thrilled with this information, Samantha goes next door, hoping to become the 'guest star' in a threesome. But when she meets the couple she discovers that they are quite old, and while the woman may have been a dancer, it was a long time ago and there's no sign of it on her body. Terrified, she politely asks them to keep the noise down and leaves.

Hey, Big Guy: It is now 'a few weeks' since Big left. Carrie says that he is 43 years old.

And So . . .: 'Were we all just dating the same person over and over again?' A cunning examination of 'patterns', explained here as bigger, more complex versions of people having a 'type'. There aren't many laughs, but those that there are (Samantha interrogating the cleaner, Charlotte's two dates leaving together to share a cab) are really effective.

27
Shortcomings

12 September 1999

Written by Terri Minsky
Directed by Dan Algrant

Guest Cast
Justin Theroux (Vaughn Weisel) David McCallum (Duncan Weisel)
Daniel McDonald (Roger Cobb) Valerie Harper (Wallis)
Leslie Beatty (Mother In Gym) Jake Burbage (Simon Cobb)
Mireille Enos (Jenna) Meg Gibson (Zooey Weisel)
Colleen Werthmann (Franny Weisel)

Carrie: Carrie is dating Vaughn Weisel, a Greenwich Village-based fiction writer whom she considers to be a suitable match for her. He's modelling clothes for *GQ* (men's lifestyle magazine) on the side, and has ambitions to win a Pulitzer Prize. He's written at least one volume of acclaimed short stories. One day Carrie is walking through the Village with him, and he tells her that he has to pop into his parents' house to deliver some books. Although she doesn't want to meet his parents yet, she reluctantly acquiesces.

Samantha: Carrie describes Samantha as the 'General Patton of sex' – she won't allow her troops to go into battle if they have no hope of winning, whereas Charlotte is less kind, saying that Sam has 'so many notches on her bedpost it's whittled down to a toothpick'. Charlotte has a reason for this, though: Samantha has had sex with Charlotte's married brother, Wesley, who has been in New York visiting her. This, however, is nowhere near as condemning as her enraged outburst: 'Is your vagina in the New York city guidebook? Because it should be – it's the hottest spot in town and it's always open!' OUCH.

Miranda: 'Everyone has a worst nightmare, for some it's bathing-suit season, for some it's that their birth certificate can never be destroyed, for Miranda it was family hour at her gym.' Yet, it's during family hour at the gym that Miranda meets a new man. Roger Cobb is in the middle of a divorce, and is in the gym with son Simon, whom he has a tendency to overindulge. Roger asks Miranda out on a date, and despite her distaste for kids in general, Miranda agrees. Samantha points out to her that all divorced men come with baggage, even if they don't come with kids, and suggests that society should round up all the divorced men and keep them in a pound. Here, single women could get a complete personal history of any man before they take a chance on him. Miranda dates Roger a couple of times, and is surprised to hear him describe himself as 'one of those weird male aberrations who like to be married' and that he likes routine. Miranda tells him he's 'the heterosexual Holy Grail' and even begins to get used to his son's tantrums and hysteria. One time after Simon hits her across her left temple with a branch, she deadpans, 'Fortunately I mostly use the right side of my brain.'

But when she's at Roger's house, Simon walks in on Miranda in the bathroom and she slams the door in his face, resulting in quite a large red weal on his forehead. Although Miranda is profusely apologetic, Roger asks her to leave. Miranda departs knowing that she can never date Roger with kids, and that Roger will never be without them.

Charlotte: After Samantha has sex with Wesley, Charlotte is furious; yet when she talks to her brother about this he explains that his marriage is on the rocks, his wife is frigid and they haven't had sex in two years. He needed Samantha that night – she was exactly the solution he required. (He's also her perfect man: good sex and an acrimony-free goodbye.) Charlotte apologises to Samantha for what she said to her, and gives her a huge basket of muffins. This, says Carrie, is Charlotte's way of saying, 'Thank you for fucking my brother.'

Wine and Dine: Meeting the Weisel family, Carrie discovers that they are this wonderful liberal ideal of a middle-class metropolitan American family. They have no hang-ups, tons of money, bags of ambition and they genuinely care for each other. Carrie enjoys their company so much that in a way Vaughn's family become more important to her relationship with Vaughn than Vaughn himself. Vaughn's father Duncan teaches at Columbia, and wants Carrie to speak at a seminar on the cultural zeitgeist. 'You are an icon!' he tells her. His mother is equally wonderful, at one point telling Carrie that when her daughter Franny 'told her she was a lesbian, she said, 'Fine, as long as you're not a Republican!'

Trivia: A rather literary episode, this; Roger suggests that 'Miranda' is the sort of name given to a princess. This is an oblique reference to the fact that the name Miranda originates in Shakespeare's play *The Tempest* (written c1609), where Miranda was the daughter of Prospero. As Prospero was an exiled Duke, Miranda *was* a princess, making Miranda exactly the sort of name a princess would have. Furthermore, Duncan Weisel's daughters Zooey and Franny are named after the title characters from J.D.

Salinger's lesser-known work *Franny and Zooey* (published in its complete form in 1961).

Also Starring: David McCallum (Duncan) has had one of the most successful and long-running careers in television history, playing leads in TV series produced on both sides of the Atlantic for over 30 years. For many he will forever be Illya Kuryakin, one of the heroes of *The Man From UNCLE.* For another generation he's the star of BBC1's grim POW drama *Colditz* in which he played Flight Lt Simon Carter, alongside Robert Wagner's tough Phil Carrington. Other roles include playing Diana Rigg's husband in the BAFTA-award-winning *Mother Love,* a grim tale of a mother's pathological obsession with her son. In the 70s he starred as supernatural investigator Steel in ITV's genuinely terrifying *Sapphire and Steel* alongside Joanna Lumley and was the eponymous lead of *The Invisible Man.* In the 90s he was a regular in both *Trainer* (for the BBC) and short-lived US sci-fi TV show *VR 5.* He's made guest appearances in everything from *The Twilight Zone* (the original 60s version) to *Babylon 5.* If you don't recognise him then you've probably never watched television. Ever.

The actor playing Charlotte's brother, Wesley York, is uncredited.

Men: Vaughn has a severe sexual problem, one alluded to in the title of this episode – premature ejaculation. This is something he's unable to talk to Carrie about, despite her extensive attempts to be patient and understanding with him. When he tries to start an argument with her while they are with his parents, she realises that she isn't going to be able to help him, and leaves. Before going, however, she promises to call his mother some-time.

And So . . .: 'I'll be scrutiny and you be ridicule.' This is a very funny and exceptionally well-played episode. The contrast between Miranda (who doesn't like her boy-friend's kid) and Carrie (who adores her boyfriend's parents) isn't overdone but it successfully gets across the point that while nothing is more important than family, it is up to the individual to decide what it is that constitutes 'family'. Charlotte's fury at Samantha is really, really funny, too.

28
Was It Good For You?

19 September 1999

Written by Michael Patrick King
Directed by Dan Algrant

Guest Cast
Richard Joseph Paul (Patrick Casey)
Elizbieta Czyzewska (Dr G Shapiro) Kevin Flynn (Bram Walker)
Sean Martin Hingston (David Shoffer) Brad Hurtado (David Tevis)
Bernard Wagner (Dr Ronny Shapiro)

Charlotte: Miss York is dating Bram Walker, a very hard-working orthopaedic surgeon who one night falls asleep while having sex with her. This understandably upsets Charlotte, who convinces herself that Bram's narcoleptic fit is her fault, rather than something to do with his being horribly overworked.

Samantha: Sam's reaction to Charlotte's problem is pretty straightforward. She thinks it's her fault. 'I can't say I'm surprised. Ever see her on a StairMaster? Nothing happening below the waist!' Carrie tries to argue with her, but Samantha is having none of it, explaining, in a condescending tone, 'No one ever took a nap while fucking me.' She goes on to illustrate her point with an example of her most recent validating experience. A gay couple she knows, David and David, have decided that they want to have sex with a woman. Neither has ever done it with a woman, 'and of all the beautiful women we know, you are probably the best in bed.' Samantha has agreed to a threesome, and despite herself, Carrie is shocked. 'For a sex columnist you have a very limited view of sexuality,' Sam reprimands her, and goes on to say that this new millennium won't be about sexual labels, it'll be about sexual expression.

As she prepares to have sex with David and David however, Samantha gets cold feet. She goes to talk to them about it but is so turned on by the sight of them in their identical jockey shorts that she decides to go ahead with it. Initially it all seems to be going well, with everyone enjoying themselves. Both Davids are impressed with the feel of Sam's breasts ('They're so soft!'), but when faced with the prospect of dealing with her vagina they both balk, and decide to go out for some food instead.

Out and About: Charlotte is trying to come to terms with the fact that she's a terrible lover. She claims she's mature enough to admit that she's good at some things, such as accessories, but bad at others, 'like fucking,' interrupts Samantha. 'I need help,' Charlotte claims, and she books herself a place on a tantric sex class entitled 'How To Please A Man'. She wants her friends to go with her. 'I could teach the damn class,' Sam objects, but she's eventually convinced to attend.

As the four sit together in an ageing woman's Manhattan apartment, being taught the secrets of tantric sex, Carrie and Miranda get repeated attacks of the giggles, while Samantha looks on unimpressed and Charlotte takes reams of notes. Carrie describes the experience as 'being unable to look away from a car crash'.

Dr G Shapiro talks them through her tantric masturbation of her husband Ronny, explaining about 'the root chakra' which is 'located between the anus and the genitals'. It's known medically as the perineum, which Miranda claims is Latin for 'not without an engagement ring'. Unfortunately for Miranda, as the aged Ronny Shapiro orgasms, she's looking right at him, and . . . well, as Carrie puts it, 'Just like that, Miranda got hit by old faithful.'

After trying the Shapiros' tricks on Bram, Charlotte declares the course to be the best 50 bucks she's ever spent; after having had Dr Shapiro's semen on her face, Miranda has to be talked down from the ledge . . .

Trivia: Samantha is compared to Jean Harlow in *Red Dust* (Victor Fleming, 1932), the famously raunchy movie in which Harlow made her name as a 'floozie' seduced by Clark Gable.

Fit to Print: Carrie's column is concerned with female sexual prowess. She wonders if we are secretly being graded. 'Is making love really nothing more than a pop quiz? How do we know if we're good in bed?'

Miranda: Miranda has spent a fortune on bed linen, the theory being that if she makes her bedroom somewhere that she wants to be, then other people will feel the same way. The problem is, she can't decide if she really loves or really hates the colour of her new sheets.

Men: Carrie meets Patrick Casey, a movie music composer, when he accidentally burns her with his cigarette. They go for coffee and she gives him her phone number. A few days later she's fretting because he hasn't called, when she bumps into him in Greenwich Village. He tells her that he's a recovering alcoholic. Carrie says that she doesn't mind him being an alcoholic. 'I love alcoholics,' she tactlessly jokes. 'I hope to be one some day . . .' He explains that he's been in 'the program' (presumably AA?) for eleven months. He's doing well, but his sponsor has advised him not to date anyone for at least a year. After some prodding by Carrie, he agrees to go on a date with her, but asks her to be patient with how compulsive he is. She tells him that this isn't a problem – she's compulsive about loads of things, such as Reese's Pieces and shoes. 'Aren't we all in recovery from something?' she says.

Kisses: Carrie tries several times to get Patrick to kiss her. While standing on her apartment steps after their first date, she tries her very best 'lean in and kiss me goodnight move' but it doesn't work. She tries again three or four times, and eventually he kisses her. They spend a night together and he admits to her that this is the first time he's ever had sex while sober. He decides it's amazing, and although Carrie is initially gratified by his fulsome praise ('You are the best!') and happy to spend every waking hour having sex with him, she soon realises that she is his latest compulsion, especially after he tells her that he loves her one and a half weeks into the relationship.

Carrie pushes Patrick away from her, telling him that they should spend a few days apart as he comes to terms with the fact that he doesn't love her – he loves him, not drinking, with her. The event pushes him off the wagon, and he ends the night naked and drunk, crying outside Carrie's apartment.

And So . . .: 'I did it, sex without beer!' Where to start? This has comic scenes depicting alcoholism, mocks Charlotte's (clearly very real) fears and portrays Carrie as selfish to the point of sociopathy. She pushes Patrick first into dating her against the advice of his doctor, and then into having sex with her when he feels he's not ready. She then proceeds to (a) be embarrassed for herself and (b) not care about the effects on him when he returns to drinking. (At the end she's unsure which is more important – if Patrick climbs back on the wagon or whether she's good in bed.) Oh, *and* the script humiliates Samantha in a horrible comedy fashion, although at least she's got another 66 episodes in which to re-assert her dignity. This is a horrid, awful episode. 'Was it good for you?' No, not good for me and not good *at all*.

29
Twenty-Something Girls vs. Thirty-Something Women

26 September 1999

Written and Directed by Darren Star

Guest Cast
Chris Noth (Mr Big) Bridget Moynahan (Natasha)
Patrick Breen (Dr Bradley Meego) Rachel Miner (Laurel Harris)
Anson Mount (Greg) Jamie Forehand (Waiter)

John Henry (Marvin) Woodwyn Koons (Girl) Melinda Relyea (Sherrie)
Marisa Ryan (Nina Grabalski)

Carrie: Carrie tells us a story about a 'lovely couple' called Rob and Elaine, who rented a house in The Hamptons one hot and sticky summer. Elaine invited her two best friends Cindy and Janet, and Rob invited his best friends Ira and Matthew; the plan being that their friends could share both the good times and the exorbitant rent. All was going swimmingly, until one day Elaine came home early to find her husband canoodling with Janet. In the heated atmosphere of the summer house, Cindy got sick of Matthew's terrible jokes, while Ira confessed his true feelings for Elaine . . . This is when Elaine called her friend Charlotte to offer her a great deal for the remains of the summer.

Girl Talk: Over breakfast, Charlotte tries to persuade her friends to go to The Hamptons with her. Despite misgivings, they eventually all agree.

Charlotte: Charlotte meets a twenty-something guy called Greg on the bus to The Hamptons. She pretends to be 27. They talk and laugh and shag, and she meets his friends and they hang out on the beach and get drunk. Everything is going great, right up to the point where he gives her crabs.

Samantha: Sam is under the impression that she acts like she's in her twenties, and it takes the behaviour of an actual twenty-something to bring her to her senses. Meet Nina, Samantha's wisecracking, foul-mouthed assistant. Fresh-faced, ambitious and sarcastic, she point-blank tells Samantha, 'You wouldn't even know what was hot if it wasn't for me.' They row and Nina leaves the firm, taking a copy of Samantha's address book with her. It's scarcely a week later when Samantha receives an invitation to a party hosted by 'Nina G Promotions'. Furious that Nina is using her contacts and what she learned from her to make a career for herself, Samantha attends the party anyway. She wishes to appear magnanimous, at least partially because she's afraid that Nina may be in a position to hire her one day. While Sam is talking to Nina, however, the previously flawless party begins to go badly wrong, and Nina begs for Sam's help. Samantha pitches in and saves Nina's hide with some inspired improvisation, but now that she's convinced she doesn't need to be nice to Nina, she has no qualms about introducing her to Greg . . .

(Outside) The City: The house they're renting has been described as 'shabby chic' but Samantha thinks it's more 'shitty chic'. The holiday in The Hamptons consists of drinking and partying, something that all the women suspect they may be a little too old for. It's not that they feel they shouldn't behave like this, it's just that they don't really want to any more.

Carrie: On the beach Carrie meets Laurel, a 25-year-old girl who says, 'May I just tell you that I worship you.' She loves Carrie's column, wants to be a writer and is keen for Carrie to be her 'mentor'. Rachel Miner's performance is superb, all gawky body language and unsure movements. The actress is actually a lot younger than 25, and this reinforces the age gap between her and Carrie. Laurel's hero worship of Carrie is palpable. Laurel wants to write a memoir about her generation of young women, many of whom are swearing off sex before marriage. After having processed this information Carrie stares at her in blank incomprehension, and then a very good question occurs to her. 'What is it you *like* about my column?'

Fit to Print: In her column Carrie compares the pros and cons of being in your twenties. It boils down to great skin and a consequence-free lifestyle vs horrible apartments and sexually inexperienced men.

Men: Carrie begins a tentative romance with Bradley Meego, a doctor she meets at a book party, but their slowly evolving relationship is just a red herring to distract the audience away from the possibility of Big's return. Which is a shame, because he seems like a good guy.

Also Starring: Bridget Moynahan (Natasha) was born in New York in 1972. Her other acting credits include roles in the movies *Coyote Ugly* (David McNally, 2000) and *Serendipity* (Peter Chelsom, 2001), in which she worked with John Corbett (who plays Aidan Shaw in Seasons Three and Four). She also featured as Marie in the *very Sex and the City*-like (and sadly much abused and consistently badly reviewed) independent comedy *Whipped* (David M Cohen, 1999), a film that I wholeheartedly recommend to anyone who loves this series.

Hey, Big Guy: Suddenly, terribly, Carrie sees Big over the other side of the room. He's with Natasha, a girl he met in Paris. Carrie talks to him, and he tells her that 'the Paris deal' fell through. He planned to call her but hasn't got round to it yet. Their conversation is stilted and awful, and after extracting herself from the situation with as much dignity as she can, Carrie runs away and is sick on the beach. 'Twenty-something girls,' she tells us, 'are just fabulous until you see one with the man who broke your heart.'

And So . . .: 'Twenty-something girls, friend or foe?' This is a big expensive episode, and while it pretends to be about experience vs inexperience, it isn't at all. It's about Carrie realising that the twenty-something girls she and her friends are so hard on are 'simply our youthful doppelgangers who deserved our compassion more than anything else'. Her encounter with Big is a painful, disturbing scene and you can absolutely see why Carrie reacts the way she does.

30
Ex and the City

3 October 1999

Written and Directed by Michael Patrick King

Guest Cast
Chris Noth (Mr Big) David Eigenberg (Steve Brady)
Bridget Moynahan (Natasha) John Enos (Mr Cocky)

La Chanze (Hostess) Peter Davies (Man Diner)
Michael H Ingram (Groomsman) Mark McGann (Carriage Driver)
James Saito (Korean Man)

Carrie: 'Life is all about making choices. Some choices, like who you marry, are *big*, some are even bigger . . .' Like how you deal with an ex-boyfriend. It has been several weeks since the events of **29**, 'Twenty-Something Girls vs. Thirty-Something Women,' and Carrie has just managed to give up referring to Natasha as 'the idiot stick figure with no soul'. She claims to have had an epiphany when she saw Natasha and Big in a restaurant, him stroking her hand. 'They are happy,' she says. 'We are over . . .' Eventually she decides that she should try being friends with Big.

Fit to Print: Carrie tries to work out the insoluble conundrum of 'Can you be friends with an ex?' In mathematics, $A + B = X$. She wonders if there's any answer to her problem.

Samantha: Sam feels that women are for being friends with, whereas men are for fucking. She therefore sees no point at all in Carrie's plan to attempt to be friends with Big, and advises her against it. Later she picks a man up on the street, who she discovers is shockingly well endowed. So big in fact, that she can't . . . er . . . handle it, even after 'two advanced yoga classes and a hit of the biggest Columbian gold she could find'. 'You dated Mr Big,' she tells Carrie. 'I'm dating Mr Too Big.' Carrie calls her 'Goldi-cocks', because she's looking for a penis that isn't too big or too small, but one that's just right.

Charlotte: We are told the story of Taddy, Charlotte's first love. Taddy was a horse who was sold by her father after he threw her in a teen equestrian competition. While jogging in Central Park, Charlotte sees a horse who reminds her of Taddy, and it brings all the memories, both good and bad, rolling back. She decides to go riding, and after a few setbacks, manages to push herself into renewing her acquaintance with the equestrian arts. A not-too-subtle metaphor concerning men and horses is advanced, suggesting that it's all about 'breaking one in' and 'riding' one once you're done. A bit crass, but quite funny anyway.

Miranda: While out shopping for flowers with Carrie, Miranda spots Steve. Panicked by his appearance Miranda grabs Carrie's hand and runs away. A few days later Steve turns up at her apartment and tells her that running away from him was a shitty thing to do. Miranda apologises profusely and then starts to cry, telling him, 'I hadn't seen you in so long, and I missed you and I did that shitty thing. You would never do anything that shitty.' Steve points out that he's just turned up unannounced at her apartment in the middle of the afternoon and called her shitty. This, he says, is a pretty shitty thing to do if you think about it.

Miranda tells Steve that she's never been able to be friends with an ex. She's far more of the 'We loved, thank you . . . I need you to not exist' school of thought. He tells her that they can be friends, even if their lifestyles stop them from being a couple, and asks her to go to dinner with him. Later he goes back to her apartment, ostensibly to get his 'Fire Department of New York' T-shirt back, but they end up having sex – quite a lot of it by the look of them. Afterwards Miranda asks Steve is they're still just friends. Apparently they are, albeit 'friends who have sex'.

Wine and Dine: Big and Carrie have a lunch which runs a whole gamut of emotions and styles, moving from farce to tragedy with huge side orders of pathos and regret. After a few drinks, Big admits that he and Natasha are engaged. Desperately hurt, Carrie leaves immediately, realising that she is not sufficiently over Big to cope with this news. Remembering Charlotte's metaphor, she surmises that she 'broke in Big, and now the idiot stick figure with no soul gets to ride him'. She concludes that the moral of the story is that if you try to be friendly with an ex . . . 'you wind up knee-deep in shit'.

Trivia: Carrie, Miranda and Charlotte obsess over Robert Redford/Barbra Streisand weepie *The Way We Were*

(Sydney Pollack, 1973), and Carrie quotes from it during her final conversation with Big. The films concerns a man, Hubbell (Redford), who marries a safe, uninteresting woman because the prospect of a life with a more complex ex, Katie (Streisand), is too difficult for him. Carrie feels this is a perfect summary of why Big would marry Natasha and not her. Michael Patrick King seems to have a thing for director Sydney Pollack (see **16**, 'They Shoot Single People, Don't They?'), as this is the second time he's invoked aspects of one of his movies.

Hey, Big Guy: Carrie turns up at the very end of Big's engagement party, determined to ask him the question 'that would haunt me for the rest of my life': why wasn't it her?

The answer? 'It just got so hard, and she's . . .' Big stops. He doesn't seem to know what to say. 'Your girl is lovely, Hubbell,' Carrie says, quoting Streisand. When he says he doesn't get it, she replies, 'You never did.' Walking away from Big and out of his life, a thought occurs to Carrie. Maybe she didn't break in Big; maybe he failed to break her in. Maybe some people can't be broken in; maybe they just have to 'run free until they find someone just as wild to run with'.

And So . . .: 'If you love someone, and you break up with them, where does the love go?' There's lots and lots of good stuff in this episode. Miranda and Steve's conversation about 'doing shitty things' is exceptionally funny, even by this series' own standards. All the Big/Carrie angst is beautifully handled too, with Chris Noth making Big strangely vulnerable and nervous, a side to him we've never seen before. Carrie's obvious distress is heartrending and her final scene with Big on the sidewalk is magnificent. Samantha's hysterical, tearful outburst of 'I miss James!' during the girls' discussion of Streisand comes really out of left field, though, especially as (despite the reminder earlier in the episode) the audience will surely have forgotten who he was by now. By this point it's clear that Michael Patrick King's conception of the series relies on Samantha's declared lack of need for a regular boyfriend being mere bravado (see, ooh, any episode in Season Six). This is an effective, impressive season finale.

Season Three (2000)

Created by Darren Star
Based on the book by Candace Bushnell

Executive Producer: Darren Star
Executive Producer: Michael Patrick King
Co-Executive Producer: Jenny Bicks
Co-Executive Producer: John Melfi
Co-Executive Producer: Cindy Chupack
Producer: Sarah Jessica Parker
Co-Producer: Jane Raab
Co-Producer: Antonia Ellis
Associate Producer: Mark McGann
Associate Producer: Amy B Harris

Regular Cast
Sarah Jessica Parker (Carrie Bradshaw) Kim Cattrall (Samantha Jones)
Kristin Davis (Charlotte York/Charlotte York MacDougal)[1]
Cynthia Nixon (Miranda Hobbes)

31
Where There's Smoke . . .

4 June 2000

Written and Directed by Michael Patrick King

Guest Cast
David Eigenberg (Steve Brady) John Slattery (Bill Kelley)
Brad Beyer (Arthur) Michael Lombardi (Ricky) Marceline Hugot (Mary)
Steven Sky Bell (Dr David Gotlieb) Mark Grapey (JJ)
Mike Doyle (Mark) Christopher Haro (Brunch Man)
Lynn Smith (Waitress) Christina Rouner (Nurse)
Brendan Connolly (Fireman)

Carrie: As the season opens, Carrie tells us how New York City is home to a million eligible single men and four very cold single women. Our four heroines are on the ferry

---

[1] Charlotte marries Trey MacDougal in **42**, 'Don't Ask, Don't Tell'. We learn that, after marriage, Charlotte joins Trey's surname with her own in **50**, 'The Real Me'.

heading out to Staten Island, where Carrie is going to be one of the judges at a contest to see which New York firemen get to go on this year's FDNY calendar. It's one of the perks of being a minor New York celebrity.

The City: On the ferry, the four stare at Manhattan Island, which is receding into the distance. 'An island that tiny is big enough to hold all our old boyfriends,' says Miranda. 'Look how small it looks.'

Miranda: When Charlotte points out that Miranda isn't single because she has Steve, Miranda is quick to retort, 'I do not have Steve. There is no having of the Steve ... We're just friends.' It's up to Samantha to point out that Steve and Miranda are having sex, and this is therefore by any definition something other than an ordinary friendship.

Miranda has decided to have laser surgery on her eyes, to enable her to see without glasses or contact lenses for the first time in her life. Despite her doctor's insistence that she needs someone to take her home after the operation, Miranda is convinced that she'll be fine.

Eventually pushed into accepting that this level of self-reliance is pig-headed (speaking as someone who's had the exact same operation, her estimation of how long it will take her to recover is *hopelessly* unrealistic), she asks Carrie to go with her, even though Steve has offered. Miranda wants Carrie there rather than him, as she's her 'friend'. This prompts Steve to ask what *he* is to Miranda; she hasn't decided.

In the end, a deadline means Carrie can't go and so she despatches Steve in her place. He takes care of the drugged-up Miranda, putting her to bed and making sure she takes her pills.

The next morning Miranda wakes up with perfect eyesight and turns to see Steve asleep on the floor next to her bed. 'For the first time in her life,' Carrie says, 'Miranda saw things clearly.' Miranda gently places her hand in Steve's and watches him sleep.

Out and About: The firefighters' party is a riot. Described by Carrie as like 'a quaint European country: the American music was twenty years behind and you could smoke wherever you wanted', it's certainly not lacking in alcohol. Unable to buy Cosmopolitans Miranda picks up four Staten Island Ice Teas, presumably similar to Long Island Ice Teas. She takes one sip and then grins, impressed. 'Hello, I'm drunk,' she says.

There are apparently no eligible men at the firefighters' party. Miranda works this out when she smells Hai Karate aftershave.

Fetishes: Sam's reasons for going to the party are obvious, and she makes no apologies for them. She has a fetish for firefighters and she's determined to indulge it. 'I'm on the fucking ferry, I better see more than just pecs,' she tells her friends. Once there she chats up a fireman named Ricky who is, frankly, really, really, really stupid. She asks what month of the calendar he'll be, and he suggests October because his birthday is in October. Sam simpers and tells him that he should be July, 'or any month that's hot'. Later she uses 'Lower Manhattan' as an (obvious) euphemism, and at one point shouts, 'Dial 911! I'm on fire!' She goes home with Ricky and has sex with him. When Charlotte criticises her for this later, Sam puts her straight and tells her that everyone has fantasies, though Charlotte fantasises 'about a man with a Park Avenue apartment and a big stock portfolio . . . For me it's a fireman with a nice big hose.'

Fashion Victims: Carrie's green and white striped vintage top gets a big thumbs-up, but both Carrie and Miranda wear (seemingly non-fake) fur, which can only get a huge thumbs-down. Carrie pushes her credit card to the limit by buying at least four pairs of Jimmy Choo shoes in one shopping trip.

Charlotte: On the ferry on the way back from the firefighters party, Charlotte is absolutely *wrecked* with booze, singing and dancing and making 'announcements' to the whole of New York by shouting, 'I'm nice and I'm pretty and I'm smart ... I'm gonna meet the perfect guy and ... I'm gonna get married this year!' (see **42**, 'Don't Ask, Don't Tell'). 'If she falls over I will never stop laughing,' says Miranda.

Wine and Dine: The next morning at breakfast, Miranda and Carrie want poached eggs, Charlotte wants to stop her head exploding and Samantha wants to tell them all about her night with Ricky. A discussion of what it is they like about firemen leads Charlotte to exclaim that it's all to do with the inherent heroism of the job – that women really just want to be rescued. 'I'm sorry but it's true – I've been dating since I was fifteen and I'm exhausted. Where is he?'

Fit to Print: Carrie frets at the idea that all women really want in life is to be rescued from it – if Prince Charming had never shown up, 'would Snow White have lain in the glass coffin for ever, or would she have eventually woken up, spat out the apple and gotten a job, a health-care package and a baby from her friendly neighbourhood sperm bank?'

Samantha: Invited to 'hang out' with Ricky and his firefighter buddies, Samantha is appalled to discover that none of the other firemen at his station are as young or fit as he, and that 'hanging out' seems to consist of eating chilli and watching sports on TV. Her evening improves when she and Ricky have sex against the fire engine and she gets to try on various items of firemen's clothing, but as soon as the fire bell rings the atmosphere changes completely, with men screaming at her to hand back their equipment as they've got a job to do. Forced to relinquish her firefighters' clothes at ten seconds' notice, she finds herself nearly naked and embarrassed as hell in front of the entire platoon. Carrie comments that this is a 'rescue fantasy' which has suddenly become something Sam wants to be rescued *from*.

Men: Carrie meets Bill Kelley, a divorced politician, and the 'token straight male judge' at the firefighters event. Carrie tells him that he has terrible taste in men and he explains that this is because he doesn't really dig firefighters. 'I'm more into cops,' he explains. He's appalled to discover that Carrie has never voted, and that she doesn't even know which district of the city she lives in (she only knows it's 'whichever one has [her beloved store] Barneys in', but he works out that, like him, she lives in District 23). After much pursuing, and despite her fear of being hurt again, Carrie goes to a fundraiser with Bill, and rather enjoys herself. She tells him that they'll have to take it slow, and he doesn't seem to mind.

Charlotte meets a man called Arthur, who has *terrible* hair. She thinks he may be her prince and is delighted to discover that they have many mutual friends, and loads of ideas about marriage in common. Unfortunately, beneath his faux-chivalric exterior he's just a well-spoken thug who likes to start fights.

Kisses: Bill Kelley and Carrie frantically make out in a coat cupboard at the firefighters party. He asks her to go home with him but she says 'kissing is enough for tonight'.

And So . . .: 'My hair hurts.' A straightforward slapstick comedy episode with lots of good bits. In some ways it seems designed to act as a manifesto for the way Michael Patrick King sees the series: Carrie has complex personal relationships and is terrified of being hurt, Charlotte is naïve and funny, Miranda can't see the wood for the trees and Samantha is a cartoon character who does ludicrous things, gets hysterical but can always bounce back. All the stuff with Miranda and Steve is wonderfully handled, but the central dilemma of 'Do women really just want to be rescued?' isn't either greatly developed or given any sort of closure. The ending echoes **1**, 'Sex and the City', with Carrie riding away in a mysterious older man's car.

32
Politically Erect

11 June 2000

Written by Darren Star
Directed by Michael Patrick King

Guest Cast
Willie Garson (Stanford Blatch) David Eigenberg (Steve Brady)
John Slattery (Bill Kelley) Anthony Alessandro (Jeff Fenton)
Tommy Crudup (Bob) Elizabeth Maresal Mitchell (Catherine)
Mike Doyle (Mark) Donnie Keshawarz (Greg Miller)
Lisa Sauber (Woman) Sarah Lively (Melinda)
Anthony F Santapaola (Ferry Guy)

Carrie: For the past three weeks Carrie has been dating politician Bill Kelley, and she's spent most of her dates on the campaign trail. She's enjoyed this as it gives her the chance to play at being Jackie Kennedy in retro 60s clothes and wraparound shades. She thinks they make a good team, as she's as adept at fashion as he is at politics. The two disciplines are similar anyway, she explains. They're both about recycling shop-worn ideas and making them seem new and inspiring.

Samantha: In a bar one night, Samantha is chatted up by a handsome, smooth man called Jeff. He charms her and they swap business cards. It's only after he gets down off his bar stool that she realises he's a 'short guy', not exactly a midget or a dwarf but a man who is a great deal shorter than her, none the less. After one date, and a visit to Charlotte's party, Sam is embarrassed into having sex with Jeff, who claims that he'll be the best she's ever had. Unable to resist this possibility, she goes to bed with him and discovers that his claims have certainly got foundation. She later tells Carrie that he 'more than made up for his shortcomings', and that it was 'like having sex with a horny Smurf'. She decides to carry on dating him, especially when she realises just how much he can make her laugh. Great sex *and* funny – this doesn't come along all that often. They date for two weeks which is, as Carrie points out, a long-term relationship compared to Sam's usual one-nighters.

Charlotte: Charlotte is doggedly pursuing her plan to be a wife before the year is out (see **31**, 'Where There's Smoke . . .') and has been inspired by a couple she met at one of Kelley's fundraisers. They met at a party where every single girl was encouraged to take along a man she wasn't interested in, in order to see if any of her girlfriends were. Charmed by this 'one woman's trash is another woman's treasure' vibe, Charlotte throws just such a party. Unfortunately her friends don't seem to catch the spirit of the occasion: Samantha arrives and leaves with the same man (Jeff), Miranda turns up alone and Carrie brings along Stanford, who excitedly observes, 'These guys are in their thirties and these women don't want them, so there may be something here for me!'

Miranda: Steve and Miranda walk through the streets together, and he badgers her about when he'll get to see her next. When she demurs he tells her that he's not dating anyone else, and that furthermore he has no desire to date anyone else. He wants to be with her. Properly. Exclusively. He says that if they have a chance of making it together this time around they should give their relationship the respect of being exclusive. She says she'll think about it. 'So think about it,' he replies, grinning.

Miranda talks to Carrie about this, saying that she's ambivalent and doesn't know if she wants to go forward. She doesn't want to tell him that she suspects she may just be seeing him until something better comes along. Carrie suggests that Miranda make two lists, one of things she likes about Steve and another of things she doesn't like about Steve. She could then see which list is longer. 'That is so judgmental!' Miranda objects. 'You *are* judgmental,' says Carrie. 'You might as well put it to good use.'

Girl Talk: In one of the series' most bizarre scenes, the girls sit around and talk about politics. Sam informs everyone

that she always votes for the most attractive presidential
candidate, as it is better for the country to be governed by
an attractive man; she mentions Richard Nixon (37th
President, 1969–1974), who, she claims, fucked the country
because no one wanted to fuck him. Carrie approves of
(New Yorker) Franklin Delano Roosevelt's (32nd President 1933–1945) taste in hats, although Miranda doesn't
approve of the US's late entry in World War II. Charlotte
twice mentions her college crush on former Vice-President
Dan Quayle. Samantha claims that there was something
homoerotic about Dan Quayle's relationship with 41st
President George Bush. She calls the relationship 'very
Batman and Robin', perhaps not only meaning the long-
running comic hero pairing but also its specific portrayal
in the *very* homoerotic movie flop *Batman & Robin* (Joel
Schumacher, 1997). Charlotte points out that as far as
looks go, no president could hold a candle to John F
Kennedy (35th President, 1961–63). All this appals
Miranda, who with great gravity suggests that it's a good
job her friends weren't involved in the American Revolution, as the founding fathers weren't really much to look
at. Samantha corrects her, mentioning Thomas Jefferson
(author of the Declaration of Independence and 3rd
President, 1801–1809) and his legendary way with women.
'There we were, three girls talking politics,' says Carrie
dryly.

Men: Miranda's list of positive and negative qualities for
Steve isn't going well. An example of the former is his cute
butt, but in the latter column we have his 'dumb jokes'.
She even attends Charlotte's party just in case she spies
anyone better (she doesn't). And then, one night, everything changes for them. Steve tells Miranda that he doesn't
need a quick answer on 'the monogamy thing', but that he
did want to tell her how he feels about her. 'You're the best
woman I ever met, and I wanted you to know it,' he says
quietly. 'I love you, Miranda, I really do.'

Fetishes: Kelley explains at length to Carrie that there's
something he'd like her to do for him that they've not yet

done. He wants to take a shower with her, and have them get each other nicely fresh and clean, and then he wants her to pee on him. Carrie is both stunned and revolted by the whole idea. Sam thinks that this is typical of men in power, whom she believes normally desire humiliation and domination. Things get so bad that Carrie ends up drinking as little as possible every time she sees Bill (including during a visit to an Indian restaurant which serves the hottest curry in New York), ending every date 'parched and nervous'. Eventually she tells him that she simply can't do it; and he responds by telling her that his spin-doctors don't think he should be dating a sex columnist so close to the election because 'it's seedy'. 'I may write about sex, but you like people to pee on you!' points out Carrie, and Bill replies that this may be the case, but it's OK because nobody knows about it.

Fit to Print: In her first piece of politically motivated journalism, Carrie blows the gaff about Kelley's fetish, entitling her column 'To Pee Or Not To Pee: That Is The Question'. Politically, she feels it's the correct thing to do.

And So . . .: 'I don't believe in the Republican Party or the Democratic Party. I just believe in partying.' Bill Kelley's fatal flaw is exposed to first our heroine, and then the public. Good to see Miranda and Steve finding more common ground, and nice to see a strongly comic plot for Samantha that doesn't hinge on embarrassing her. The scenes where Carrie tries not to drink are really funny, largely due to the palpable sense of unease they create.

33
Attack of the 5′10″ Woman

18 June 2000

Written by Cindy Chupack
Directed by Pam Thomas

Guest Cast
Bridget Moynahan (Natasha) Lynn Cohen (Magda)
Barbara Garrick (Celia) Christopher Sieber (Kevin)
Jessica Russo (Waitress) Athena Avella (Beautiful Woman)
Jean de Baer (Spa Manager) Lovette George (Mimi Lebenthal)
Heather Goldenhersh (Jenna) Kate Hampton (Katy)
Linda Powell (Leisle) Christine Jones (Upper East Side Woman)

Wine and Dine: One of the things Carrie likes best about New York is Sunday brunch; you can sleep until noon and still get eggs anywhere in the city. Often Sunday brunches include copious amounts of alcohol and the 'single woman sports pages', otherwise known as *The New York Times'* wedding section. As the four flick through the pages, cooing and criticising in equal measure, Carrie ponders how so many women manage to get so upset about the marital fortunes of complete strangers. That's when Charlotte shows her the picture of Big and Natasha at a wedding – their wedding.

Carrie: Although she at first takes refuge in being as scathing about Big and Natasha's marriage as possible, making comments such as, 'What's next? *Big & Natasha: The Movie*?' and, 'Oh, how original, they fell in love in Paris!', Carrie is entirely unprepared for an accidental meeting with Natasha while out shopping. After discovering that Natasha is helping to organise a 'Women in the Arts' luncheon, Carrie resolves to go – and what's more go looking so fabulous that Natasha will be amazed. When Charlotte questions Carrie's motives (and possibly sanity), Carrie explains that she has met Natasha only twice, once when she was wearing a cowboy hat (see **29**, 'Twenty-Something Girls vs. Thirty-Something Women'), and this time, when she was standing in a changing room in her underwear. Carrie feels there's a deficit to be made up, and she has to demonstrate to Mrs Big that Mr Big's ex has the potential to look something other than a bit crap.

Miranda: Carrie tells us how, after more than a decade of independence, Miranda has finally opened herself up to a relationship; not with Steve, however, but with a

Ukrainian cleaning lady called Magda. Initially pleased with having someone to clear up after her, Miranda is increasingly disturbed by Magda's intrusions into her life. She tries to get her to drink herbal tea instead of coffee, moves her mugs into a different cupboard, hides her hairdryer and buys her a rolling pin so she can 'make pies' (it appears that she feels that making pies is what women should do). She doesn't even approve of Miranda's habit of making her drinks in her 'Law School Class of '90' mug because it's so big.

The big problem arises, however, when Magda opens Miranda's 'goodie drawer' next to her bed. This contains, among other choice items, a vibrator and many, many condoms. Magda is appalled, and while Miranda makes a good stab at defending her perfectly normal life, it's obvious something has changed between them.

One night, when Steve isn't around, Miranda goes to use her vibrator and finds it gone. Worse, it's been replaced with a statue of the Virgin Mary. Carrie concludes that 'Magda was not only cleaning, she was performing an exorcism' and trying to rid Miranda's home of her personal perceptions of sin. Furious, Miranda makes a stand against Magda and argues her down. She points out that if Magda won't stop interfering in her life, then she will find another cleaning lady. 'I don't need another mother,' Miranda points out. 'I have one in Philadelphia and that's near enough for me.' The next time she gets home, the old woman is doing things her way. Victory!

Miranda says that she's 34 years old.

Fashion Victims: For attending the 'Women in the Arts' luncheon Carrie buys herself a really nice pair of tiny, multi-pastel-shaded Manolo Blahnik sandals, and a dress from Bergdorf's, which, she claims, cost her about a month's rent. (Even with her rent-controlled apartment, we're looking at several thousand dollars here.)

Charlotte: Again Charlotte mentions her hatred of her own thighs (see **2**, 'Models and Mortals'), and Carrie points out, 'The problem is not your thighs, sweetie, it's your head.' Charlotte has a problem with semi-public nudity, being entirely unwilling to disrobe in the steam room at the beauty parlour, or indeed anywhere that anyone may see her. Eventually, after multiple attempts by her friends to convince her that this isn't really the sort of thing she should worry about, Charlotte plucks up the courage to drop her towel. Feeling strangely liberated, she luxuriates in the atmosphere, at which point another women looks at her and says, 'I would kill for your breasts.' This makes Charlotte's day.

Samantha: Informed by another customer that Kevin, a masseur at the health club, is known to offer 'something extra' to certain customers, Samantha decides to book an appointment with him. After nearly an hour of massage, and with Kevin having shown no interest in her, Samantha tries to take matters into her own hands, and gets reported to the management for her pains. Banned from the parlour, she points out that this is entrapment. She knows for a fact that Kevin has gone down on several other women customers, and she only went after him because she thought he would be up for it. Kevin is fired, but she's still banned and she's now acquired the enmity of the women for whom Kevin used to provide regular 'services'. Ooops!

Out and About: Dressed to kill, Samantha and Carrie attend the 'Women in the Arts' luncheon only to discover that Natasha isn't there. She's ill and didn't want to run the risk of infecting anyone else by attending the lunch. Robbed of her victory (and she does look, frankly, amazing), Carrie is somewhat deflated. Samantha meets someone who was at college with Natasha and dishes the dirt on her (she once had sex in the communal bathrooms in their dorm, and she put on weight at college), but this doesn't help Carrie feel better.

A few weeks later Carrie receives a note from Natasha, thanking her for attending the lunch. It contains one very minor spelling mistake (substituting 'their' for 'there') which amuses Carrie greatly. Concluding that Natasha is very stupid, she considers her pride restored.

Trivia: The title is a play on *Attack of the 50ft Woman* (Nathan Juran, 1958).

And So ...: 'I'm just not comfortable being naked in public.' Another lovely Cindy Chupack script, (**19**, 'The Chicken Dance', **23**, 'Evolution'), full of amazing moments of pettiness and kindness, humour and humanity, *plus* her trademark flair for writing Charlotte perhaps better than any other writer working on the show. A smashing episode, with a wonderfully irritating little Ukrainian woman who is hilarious in fiction but would be a monumental pain in real life.

34
Boy, Girl, Boy, Girl ...

25 June 2000

Written by Jenny Bicks
Directed by Pam Thomas

Guest Cast
Willie Garson (Stanford Blatch) David Eigenberg (Steve Brady)
Eddie Cahill (Baird Johnson) Donovan Leitch (Sean)
Alanis Morissette (Dawn) Chris Tardio (Matt)
Jenna Rosenberg (Goddess Instructor) Joey Kern (Garth)
Michael Medico (Mark) Eliza Pryor Nagel (Grace)
Torquil Campbell (Joel) Alice Johnson (Woman) Peter Bucossi (Cop)

Out and About: Carrie – 'It's been said that New Yorkers are the most jaded people in the world ... [so] when Charlotte told us that the new show at her gallery would totally blow us away we took it with the proverbial grain of salt.' Despite this, the latest installation by photographer Baird Johnson really does have an affect on Carrie and pals. Its title? 'Drag Kings – The Collision of Illusion and Reality', a series of photographs of women dressed as men. While Miranda simply can't bring herself to believe that some of the pictures are of women at all, the exhibition provokes crises of gender and sexuality in Charlotte, Miranda, Carrie and Sam.

Samantha: Sam once dated a guy who liked to wear her underwear but she never went the other way and wanted to dress up as a guy. She claims to be 'trisexual', meaning that she'll try anything once, but she's aware that her aggressive approach to both relationships and business could be considered traditionally 'masculine'. She has a new aggressive male assistant whose attitude she finds 'annoying, unprofessional and incredibly hot'. They spar and argue and he refuses to be intimidated by her power over him. After a particularly heated row she turns to him and says, 'The bad news is you're fired, the good news is now I can fuck you!' and then proceeds to do exactly that. And across his desk too.

Carrie: Carrie's dating Sean, a twenty-something guy who works on an Internet magazine. She thinks he's a little young for her, but he's fun, sexy and a great kisser, so she copes with her worries about the age gap. She's rather disturbed, though, when he tells her that he's bisexual, or rather that he's previously had relationships with men but currently prefers women. This sets off Carrie's paranoid streak, and while she tries to be cool about it, she's soon accusing him of eyeing up other men, and asking him which he'd choose if offered the choice between a very beautiful woman and a very handsome man. Despite Sean's plea of 'Can you stop making this about their sex? It's all about the person,' Carrie can't leave it alone. In short, she seems to have issues with his level of sexual liberation. Carrie ponders the loss of gender roles: 'If we can take the best of the other sex and make it our own, has the opposite sex become obsolete?'

Miranda: Miranda doesn't seem to have Carrie's difficulties with Sean's sexuality, and agrees with Sam that the next generation is all about sexual expression. She claims that somewhere between Generation X and Generation Y, they blended and went on to create Generation XY.

Despite this, Miranda is having a gender problem of her own. It starts off as a series of domestic disputes with

Steve; sometimes he slides over to her side of the bed in the middle of the night, and he's suggested that he may need a drawer at her place where he can leave his own stuff. She can't handle this level of commitment and becomes aggressive, which leads Steve to comment that sometimes it seems to him that Miranda is 'the guy' in their relationship. He's the one who wants to move in with her, he's the one who pushes for every shred of commitment he can find, he needs her more than she needs him and he said 'I love you' first. She concludes that he's right, up to a point, and has a small crisis about how masculine she believes she has become. 'I will never be a *girlie* girl,' she tells Carrie, who points out that this isn't actually a bad thing. Miranda questions why she's trying to shut Steve out. 'I do love him, I do. So what's my problem?'

She invites Steve round to dinner, saying she'll cook, and plans to tell him that she wants him to move in, but she's late due to problems at work. Despite Steve's attempts to reassure her that it just doesn't matter, she becomes increasingly upset, especially after she drops her shopping on the floor, smashing her not-easily-acquired jar of marinara sauce in the process. 'I do love you,' she tells him, near to tears, but she's afraid because she's never lived with anybody before. 'I'm stubborn, and I like the remote and I can't cook. And I don't do laundry sometimes for, like, two weeks . . . and you're going to see all that and I'm scared and I don't know if I can move forward and I really don't want to lose you.' He tells her not to worry about him – there's no danger of him going away of his own free will.

Charlotte: She isn't impressed by Sean's bisexuality (her innate conservatism coming through again, although this is a bit weird considering **18**, 'The Cheating Curve') and suggests that whether they're gay or straight, people should pick a side and then stay there. However, her epic crush on Baird leads her down a new path when he asks her to pose as a drag king for him, dressing in a man's suit and a false moustache, in order to be photographed for his collection.

Buoyed up by the power that dressing like this gives her, and turned on by the sock shoved down her panties to give her an authentic crotch bulge, for the first time in her life Charlotte *starts* something, grabbing Baird and kissing him hard. They have sex in his office, and she resolves to never see Baird again. The reason? 'She might have been that kind of guy but she'd never be that kind of woman.'

Kisses: Sean takes Carrie to a party being held by his ex-boyfriend, Mark, and Mark's current boyfriend. Here Carrie meets a bewildering array of people who all seem to have slept with/been married to or at least kissed each other at some point. Pushed into playing spin the bottle (which Carrie mocks as a seventh-grade game), Carrie finds herself kissing another woman, Dawn. Although she goes through with it, she leaves shortly afterwards knowing that this world just isn't for her. She does however take some earlier words of Samantha's with her as solace – she may be an old fart, but she's a *hot* old fart.

Also Starring: Alanis Morissette (Dawn) is the multi-platinum-selling artist best known for the 1995 album *Jagged Little Pill* released on Madonna's Maverick record label. Her acting work has been scarce, but she did make an almost silent appearance as God (yes, God), in the controversial but really rather wonderful *Dogma* (Kevin Smith, 1999).

And So . . .: 'Gender's an illusion, sometimes a very beautiful illusion.' A clever, brave episode and a far more compelling and successful glance at the generation behind Carrie's than **29**, 'Twenty-Something Girls vs. Thirty-Something Women'. It's not unlike the (earlier) *Ally McBeal* episode 'In Pursuit of Loneliness', but production schedules mean that the similarities must be entirely coincidental. Carrie's ultimate conclusion is that while she has no problem with Sean and his friends doing what they do (and she certainly wouldn't condemn them for it), it just isn't something she wants to do herself. Which is fair enough, surely?

It's a shame, though, that Miranda worries about being too masculine when the entire appeal of her character is that she manages to avoid the confusion between being strong (which she assuredly is) and being masculine (which she manifestly isn't). The scene of her unburdening herself to Steve is really affecting and strangely wonderful, with both Cynthia Nixon and David Eigenberg acting their hearts out. Kristin Davis, though, doesn't make a remotely convincing man.

35
No Ifs, Ands or Butts

9 July 2000

Written by Michael Patrick King
Directed by Nicole Holofcener

Guest Cast
Willie Garson (Stanford Blatch) David Eigenberg (Steve Brady)
John Corbett (Aidan Shaw) Asio Highsmith (Chivon Williams)
Sundra Oakley (Adele Williams) Ross Gibby (Brad)
Donald Berman (Marty Mendleson) Misi L Lecube (Line Patron)
Prodigal Sunn (South Pole) J D Williams (Sweet Sauce)

Carrie: One Saturday morning Stanford turns up at Carrie's apartment and informs her that there's a beautiful man downtown selling beautiful furniture. All it takes to convince an initially reluctant Carrie to go is a 30-second flash of a photograph of the man in question, furniture designer Aidan Shaw.

On seeing Aidan in the flesh, Carrie describes him as 'warm, masculine and classic American, just like his furniture'. Stanford nods approvingly, saying Aidan's perfect for Carrie. 'I'll come and visit you and the children at your country cabin upstate.'

Carrie has to resort to buying a piece of Aidan's furniture in order to get him to notice her, but it works and he asks her on a date. This, as Miranda points out, makes the chair a justifiable write-off.

On the date, Aidan is unimpressed to discover that Carrie smokes. He tells her that it's nothing personal, but he just doesn't think he can date a smoker. Propositioning him for a second date later in the week, Carrie tells Aidan she can give up smoking. She's been planning to quit anyway, and now she has a reason to try. Beset by nicotine cravings during what she describes as 'the world's longest date', Carrie eventually rushes outside the restaurant, leaving Aidan stranded, to smoke the one emergency cigarette in her purse. She does, too, despite the fact that in her hurry to get it out of her bag she drops it into a pool of stagnant water. Aidan exits the restaurant, stands and watches her, and then tells her that he thinks she has a problem.

Wine and Dine: The girls visit Fusion, a clearly fabulous restaurant (and what's more one run by a friend of Carrie's, former *New York Star* food editor and African-American celebrity chef Adele Williams) that specialises in mixing different cuisines to impressive effect. Items on the menu include a dish of salmon and okra and a pecan and praline pie. Yum!

Samantha: Sam is introduced to Adele's brother Chivon, to whom she immediately takes a shine. They begin to date, rather than 'just fucking', and it quickly becomes apparent that Chivon is more to Samantha than one of her casual lays. A few weeks into the relationship, Adele takes Samantha aside and tells her that she doesn't want her dating her brother. This is not, as you might expect, because she has a problem with Samantha's reputation, or that she is worried that Samantha will break her brother's heart. No, she is simply unwilling to countenance her brother developing a serious relationship with a white woman. At first Samantha ignores her demands, but when the two women are reduced to physically fighting in a club, she is forced to consider surrendering Chivon. In the end, the decision is taken out of her hands, as Chivon seems to be willing to do as his sister says. Unimpressed by this, and reasoning that a man who'll be so bossed around by a relative isn't worth dating anyway, Samantha walks away.

Charlotte: Charlotte has been dating Brad, a man who, when given the opportunity to kiss her, licks her face instead. She complains to her girlfriends, who immediately begin a discussion of bad kissing. Samantha in particular is very forthright on the issue of men who can't kiss. 'If their tongue's just gonna lay there, what do you think their dick's gonna do?' she demands. Despite numerous attempts, Charlotte fails to teach Brad how to kiss even acceptably, so she dumps him.

Men: Stanford meets Marty Mendleson, whom Carrie describes as 'warm, stylish and classic gay, just like his outfit'. She tells Stanford that should he and Marty settle down, she'll 'come and visit you and the swatches at your country cabin upstate'. Stanford is put off, however, by the revelation that Marty collects china dolls, which he keeps on his bed. He has dozens of them, all hugely expensive, all very rare, all dressed and sculpted like various historical figures, mostly royalty. Carrie wonders if even Stanford is enough of a queen to date the queen with the huge selection of china queens. Realising that there are real possibilities between him and Marty, Stanford tries to ignore the doll obsession, but the relationship quickly falters when he accidentally breaks one while thrashing about in the throes of passion.

Miranda: Miranda comes home to find Steve bouncing a basketball around the hallway. He tells her that he's been picked for the most exciting opportunity of his life. At Knicks (New York's premier basketball team) games, they pick out people from the audience to make a shot at the hoop from halfway along the court. If anyone makes the shot, and no one ever has, they receive a million dollars prize money. Steve seems convinced that he can do this, and begins to plan how to spend his million, but Miranda is far more cynical. As she points out to Carrie, there are actual Knicks who can't make a half-court shot. 'I'd have no trouble supporting him if it was a real dream like opening his own bar, but this is just silly.' Carrie points out that Miranda should be there for Steve when he's being silly, but she isn't convinced. After Miranda refuses to go with Steve and watch him shoot hoops, despite having promised that she would, Steve, sick of all her negativity, bursts out, 'I need you to believe in me, even if you think it is fucking stupid!' Realising he's right, Miranda goes and watches him practise shooting hoops. Carrie tells us that Steve never made the million-dollar shot, but having Miranda come out and watch him practising was just as good a prize.

Fashion Victims: Samantha wears what must assuredly be the smallest boob tube in history. Ever.

Kisses: This episode has the series' first onscreen gay kiss, coming a week after the series' first real lesbian one.

Also Starring: Born 9 May 1962 in West Virginia, John Corbett has made appearances in *Duckman* and *The Wonder Years* and played Chris Stevens (the DJ known as 'Chris In The Morning') in *Northern Exposure*. Movie credits include playing Barnes in *Tombstone* (George P Cosmatos, 1993) and a role in *Serendipity* (Peter Chelsom, 2001), in which he worked with Bridget Moynahan, who plays Mr Big's wife Natasha. The multi-talented Mr Corbett is also a qualified hairdresser. You may recognise him from his role in the multimillion dollar-grossing HBO indie flick *My Big Fat Greek Wedding* (Joel Zurick, 2002).

And So . . .: 'I don't usually sleep with men who have nicer accessories than me.' A good strong episode with the plot threads shared out equally between the four (five, if you count Stanford, and as is so often the case this season it seems that we must) lead characters. Adele's racism is no less loathsome for being inverted, and Samantha gives as good as she gets when Adele starts on her. The best bits all feature Steve and Miranda, although Stanford's encounter with the china doll-obsessed man runs a very close second.

36
Are We Sluts?

16 July 2000

Written by Cindy Chupack
Directed by Nicole Holofcener

Guest Cast

David Eigenberg (Steve Brady) John Corbett (Aidan Shaw)
Christopher Orr (Alexander Lindley)
Carl Evans (Samantha's Late-Night Date)
Carol Lawrence (Older Woman) John Cosomano (Policeman)
Kevin Louie (Intern) Caitlin Clarke (Uptight Woman)
Antonio Villacis (Elevator Man) Susan McGinnis (Secretary)
David Lansbury (David) John Freimann (Older Husband)
Julie Follansbee (Freda)

Carrie: Carrie tells us that there are things 'a real New York will wait for'. Carrie would wait for a perfect rent-controlled apartment, the chocolate soufflé at a restaurant she product-places in her column, and a sale of Jimmy Choo shoes. One thing she's not prepared to wait for is sex. After nearly two weeks of romantic dates but no sex, Carrie is wondering why Aidan isn't trying to get her into bed. Even when she less-than-subtly asks him to sleep over, he refuses. When she confronts him about this, he tells her that he just wants to take their relationship slowly. Carrie wonders if thirteen years of dating in Manhattan have conditioned her into diving straight into sex at any opportunity, while making her forget about romance. Eventually, after a date at a blues club, Aidan and Carrie make love. 'For the first time in a long time, I was nervous. Aidan and I were going to sleep together, and it was going to mean something.'

Miranda: Meanwhile, Miranda learns that she has contracted chlamydia from a previous sexual partner, and is told to contact as many of her previous sexual partners as possible and tell them they may be infected. This is, of course, a humiliating experience for her, and she begins to worry about the number of men she's had sex with. The list comes to 42 people, which she feels makes her 'a big, dirty, diseased whore', and she apologises to Steve for this. Steve points out that he doesn't care, and that he's slept with half as many people again as Miranda has. (It's possible, given the way Eigenberg delivers these lines, that he's lying about the numbers to sooth Miranda's worries, which is rather wonderful.) Miranda is surprised by Steve's total and he just grins and says, 'Hey, I'm a bartender and I'm cute,' and kisses her.

Samantha: The residents of Samantha's apartment block are understandably disturbed when an intruder attacks and robs a tenant at gunpoint. Sam initially blames the sub-standard security of the block. However, the security video reveals that the robber snuck in behind someone else's guest: in this case an unnamed man who arrived late at night to have sex with Sam. The other residents blame Samantha for the robbery, and the atmosphere becomes so bad she considers moving out. Samantha explains to Carrie that her neighbours have 'practically chased me with torches, like I was Fuckenstein' and suspects (probably correctly) that 'the dried-up old farts' are jealous of her sexual activities. Carrie reminds Samantha that she has 'a rent-controlled apartment on the Upper East Side' but Sam won't be dissuaded from changing apartments: she requires 'life control' not 'rent control'. So she moves.

Charlotte: Charlotte is dating a man who shouts 'You fucking bitch!' and 'You fucking whore!' as he is orgasming. Is this, Charlotte worries, because she is a whore? Sam retorts, 'If you're a whore, what does that make me?' Charlotte is worried because 'no one wants to marry a whore'. Deciding to confront him, she tells him that she's 'kind of bothered' by what he said to her in bed the other night. He claims not to be able to remember what he said, and poor Charlotte is too embarrassed to repeat it. The next time they have sex, Charlotte immediately draws his attention to what he's *just* said, and he claims that he was lost in the moment and had no idea what he was saying to her.

He tells Charlotte that she's sweet, kind and lovely, and exactly the sort of woman he hopes to marry. He promises to never say 'that' again, and buoyed up by the word marriage, Charlotte forgives him. However, the next – and, as it turns out, last – time they have sex, he finds he can't come. Charlotte lets him shout 'You fucking bitch! You fucking whore!' at her, and immediately he's in ecstasy. 'Oh God! What's wrong with me?' he asks tearfully, rolling away from Charlotte. He stops seeing Charlotte and starts seeing a therapist. Which is, let's face it, no bad thing.

Fit to Print: Sitting in the armchair she bought from Aidan's store, Carrie taps out her latest column. Despite the fact that it's inevitable for single New York women in their thirties to have had a certain number of sexual partners, she now begins to worry, 'Are we sluts?'

The City: Samantha moves into a new apartment in the meat-packing district of the city, right by the Hudson River, where 'whores were whores, men were women, and rents were much higher'. Samantha greets the transvestite hookers standing in front of her new building, and worries that her furniture will be stolen before she gets it all inside.

And So . . .: 'But how many men is too many men?' Confused and occasionally objectionable, 'Are We Sluts?' makes issues of things that shouldn't really be issues. What business of anyone else's is it how many people Miranda has had sex with, or how Sam gets her kicks? Samantha suffers badly for something which isn't actually her fault, while Miranda and Charlotte are pushed into crises concerning their lifestyles, which has a knock-on effect on Carrie. Despite some cool scenes with Sarah Jessica Parker and the consistently impressive John Corbett, this gets dangerously close to judgemental at times. At least Steve has enough of a sense of proportion to not even remotely care how many people Miranda had slept with before they were together. He knows it's irrelevant, he knows it's not his business and he knows that he loves her and she him. End of story.

37
Drama Queens

23 July 2000

Written by Darren Star
Directed by Allison Anders

Guest Cast
Chris Noth (Mr Big) David Eigenberg (Steve Brady)
John Corbett (Aidan Shaw) Kyle MacLachlan (Trey MacDougal)
Amy Redford (Amy Fincher) Ethan Sandler (Dennis Fincher)
Billy Worth (Dr Mark Raskin) Peter Stewart (Single Attractive Man)
Luvada Harrison (Opera Singer) Roy Farfel (Taxi Driver)
Jodi Pynn (Charlotte's Stunt Double)

Carrie: Aidan and Carrie have been seeing each other for
about three weeks, and it all seems to be going well when
one night Carrie wakes up with a start, panicking. It's as
if she's forgotten something. She checks her files for unpaid
bills and missed appointments, but nothing is wrong, and
then it dawns on her, 'What was wrong was for the first
time in my life I was in a relationship where absolutely
nothing was wrong.' She later explains to her friends that
the 'effortless' nature of her relationship with Aidan is
disturbing her. She confides to Miranda that it's possible
she's simply not 'used to being with someone who isn't
doing the ever-seductive withholding dance'. When Aidan
asks Carrie if she wants to meet his parents, who happen
to be in Manhattan this weekend, she panics, unsure if she
can handle something that looks like commitment.
'Aidan's acting exactly the way I wish Big would behave,
and I'm behaving like Big,' she wails.

Samantha: Sam is dating a doctor who regularly prescribes
himself Viagra for recreational use. He doesn't have any
erectile difficulties, he just likes taking it because it 'sends
me on a rocket trip right through your solar system'.
Whatever that's supposed to mean. Sam is impressed by
his stamina while popping Viagra, and a little jealous of the
spaced-out mood it puts him in. She asks him if she can
try it, and while he points out that it is unlikely to have

any physical effect on a woman, he has no objection to her experimenting with it. The effect is dramatic, as Samantha spins giddily, rants, raves and sings herself to orgasm. This is a recreational drug she likes. One she likes a lot. Disturbed by the depth of Samantha's affection for the drug, and a little put off taking it after observing her on it, Dr Raskin writes her a prescription and never sees her again.

Miranda: Miranda is finding a new bliss in domesticity and her quiet, straightforward life with Steve. On a Saturday night, her favourite occupation 'is Steve's laundry, and I have never been happier.' Every night for them is the same, and sex, while good, is now 'functional', Miranda describing it as a race to see who can have an orgasm first. Carrie claims that Miranda and Steve have 'the kind of closeness that only [comes] from true intimacy' and admits to envying them.

However, one night Miranda uncovers something that no one would envy, finding (ahem) skid marks in a pair of Steve's underpants that she's washing for him. Revolted on a visceral level and disturbed by the wider implications, she talks to Carrie. 'When your boyfriend is so comfortable he can't be bothered to wipe his ass, that's the end of romance,' she says, and it's hard to disagree. She wonders if instead of being comfortable she's actually falling into a rut; if Steve's underwear is just a symptom of 'them' becoming boring and careless. Is this relationship good for her? Is she too comfortable? Even through all this paranoia, though, she acknowledges the paradox of her situation. 'We moan when we don't have a boyfriend and we moan when we do.'

But then, just when Miranda is convinced that all the spark has gone out of her life and that she and Steve will be boring and functional for ever, he propositions her in the laundry room and they have sex on the washing machine. Strangely, this bizarrely comic act convinces her that there's excitement, life and humour in their relationship yet.

Hey, Big Guy: While at the opera with Charlotte, Carrie spies Big and Natasha sitting in a box across the theatre from her. Big notices her but Natasha doesn't, and they exchange glances through opera glasses. Carrie freaks out and has to leave, knowing that sitting watching Big and Natasha while at an emotionally fraught opera is not something she can bring herself to do.

Charlotte: Charlotte has bought a new book, the snappily entitled *Marriage Incorporated: How To Apply Successful Business Strategies to Finding a Husband.* The purpose of the book is fairly self-explanatory, and Charlotte plans to use it to ensure that her prophecy (see **31**, 'Where There's Smoke . . .') that she will get married this year is fulfilled. One piece of advice in the book is to spend less time hanging around with dysfunctional single women, i.e. her friends (although how Carrie and Miranda qualify isn't quite explained). Another suggestion is that she try to date the single male friends of the husbands of married women she knows. The book suggests that these people are the singles market's largest untapped resource. Convinced that she should follow this advice to the letter, Charlotte tries to get her never-before-glimpsed married friends, Dennis and Amy, to set her up with their eligible friend Phil, whom she plans to impress by taking him to the opera. Unfortunately, what she gets is *Dennis*, convinced that he's in love with Charlotte and determined to a) procure her for himself and b) keep Phil as far away from her as possible. Pursued into the night by him screaming 'I love you!', Charlotte narrowly avoids being knocked down by a cab. The passenger leaps out to see if she's OK. He's a handsome, dark-haired man in his forties who introduces himself as Trey.

Also Starring: Kyle MacLachlan, who makes an impressive, albeit brief, first appearance as Trey MacDougal, is that rarest of creatures, a genuinely cult actor. Born in Washington on 22 February 1959, he is best known for his starring role as FBI Special Agent Dale Cooper in the massively influential and sadly missed TV series *Twin*

Peaks (1990–1991). The intense, charismatically wooden MacLachlan has had a long working relationship with *Twin Peaks* creator David Lynch, appearing in his movies *Blue Velvet* (1986) and *Dune* (1984), as well as his criminally underestimated *Twin Peaks* movie prequel *Fire Walk With Me* (1992). Other roles include Doors keyboardist Ray Manzarek in rock biopic *The Doors* (Oliver Stone, 1991), Claudius opposite Ethan Hawke's *Hamlet* (Michael Almereyda, 2000) and a role in critically acclaimed split-screen independent picture *Timecode* (Mike Figgis, 2000). Less impressively he was Fred Flintstone's sinister boss in *The Flintstones* (Brian Levant, 1994) and Zack Carey in the truly ghastly *Showgirls* (Paul Verhoeven, 1995).

And So . . .: 'This is nuts. I'm sabotaging the best relationship I ever had.' Carrie's self-destructive and paranoid streaks come to the fore in an episode which seems largely to be marking time. Charlotte's paranoia about Dennis does give the impression that she's going mental, but is eventually proved to be entirely grounded in fact. Which is a relief. The first appearance of Trey, leaping out of a cab to rescue Charlotte from Dennis, is hugely striking and laugh-out-loud funny.

38
The Big Time

30 July 2000

Written by Jenny Bicks
Directed by Allison Anders

Guest Cast
Chris Noth (Mr Big) David Eigenberg (Steve Brady)
John Corbett (Aidan Shaw) Kyle MacLachlan (Trey MacDougal)
Robert LuPone (Len Schneider) Elan Alias (Singer On Yacht)

Carrie: Despite her recent encounter with Big, Carrie and Aidan are still seemingly blissfully happy. Carrie tells us that these days they never leave her bed, and that her mattress has become 'our restaurant, our entertainment centre, our own little New York'. She wonders if they'll be declared missing, and when a search party would be sent out to find them. Aidan grins and answers, 'Spring thaw.'

Men: Charlotte's new beau Trey, with whom she appears to be spending all her time, is a doctor (and therefore well paid); more, he has 'family money,' ensuring he has two of the things that Charlotte considers most important in any potential husband – he's rich and he comes from a 'good family'. Later we see Carrie and Charlotte having their nails done, and Charlotte is telling Carrie about her relationship with Trey. She thinks he may be the one, and as a consequence she's trying not to ruin it by having sex with him too early. She believes that if you don't have sex for a whole year, you become a 'born-again virgin' and 're-grow' your virginity. Later she shows Carrie a Cartier watch that Trey has bought her with the words 'To Charlotte. It's about time I met you' engraved on it.

Wine and Dine: Steve and Miranda are having dinner in a restaurant, and Miranda is distinctly unimpressed with the screaming baby seated at a table near to them. Just as she's complaining about people and their kids, Steve pipes up and tells her that he *likes* babies. And then he spills food down his shirt. As Miranda cleans up his mess, he tells her that her obvious mothering ability indicates that she'd be a great mom and he thinks they should have a baby. Miranda assumes he's joking but it quickly becomes apparent that he isn't. He thinks their child would be 'really cute', and that he could watch *Sesame Street* before going off to work in the bar at night. And then he adds, 'We wouldn't even have to get married.' Miranda dislikes Steve's idea because they've only just moved in together, and because she's currently hugely busy trying to be made a partner at her firm.

Samantha: In her new apartment block, Samantha meets an ageing man with a greying ponytail. He introduces himself as Len, and Sam lets him kiss her hand and leer at her a bit, before turning down his offer of a 'mean white

Season Three (2000)   169

wine spritzer'. Later Sam checks her diary and panics. Her period is five days late, a fact brought into even harsher relief when she realises that the other three are 'all synched up', as Charlotte puts it. Confessing to the others that she is older than they are, Sam tells her friends that she thinks she's menopausal. So depressed is she by this shift in her life that she decides to accept a date with Len, reasoning that if she's menopausal she should only really date people her own age. Bored senseless by Len's prattling about cars and his artificial hip, Sam decides to fuck him to shut him up. As they have sex, something of a miserable experience for Sam, by the look of it, Len looks down at her and says, 'Baby, either you're a virgin or Flo just came to town.' Samantha suddenly comes back to life, surprised and delighted that her period has finally come. Fleeing the old man's apartment, Samantha knows there are 'plenty more hot studs in this hot, pre-menopausal woman's future'.

Miranda: At Miranda and Steve's place, he's watching *Scooby Doo* and eating the biggest bowl of cereal in history, while she's trying to do some important paperwork. She asks him to turn the volume down, and he does, but not by much. She asks again, and he tells her that she'll have to get used to noise when there's a baby around. Miranda tries to dispel any notions of them having a child, but Steve seems more interesting in watching Scooby (and Scrappy), as it's a 'really good' episode (unlikely, if it has Scrappy in it). Miranda goes to bed, telling him to make sure he turns out the lights before he goes to sleep. As Miranda later tells Carrie, she's acting like Steve is a kid, so she ends up nagging him all the time. 'I'm Mean Mommy, and believe me, no one wants to fuck Mean Mommy.' She also tells Carrie that she may be unconsciously sabotaging her relationship with Steve because she secretly knows she could be happy raising a child with Steve. She knows she does want children and her biological clock *is* ticking.

Steve calls Miranda at work and tells her that he knows they're not ready for a baby, but he'd like them to get a puppy instead. They do, but the animal just drives them further apart, Miranda waking Steve up in the middle of the night and shouting, 'Are you happy? We get this puppy and already I'm the only one taking care of it.' She tells him she's sick of him being a big kid all the time. Steve says that they're in a rough patch (which they certainly weren't last week), and Miranda tells him that their relationship is rough all the time, which means that 'it's not good!' Steve asks her if she's giving up on them. The answer is yes. The next morning Miranda is made a partner of her law firm.

Out and About: Carrie is at the launch party for a magazine called *GAB*, held on a yacht floating in New York harbour. Apparently Madonna is there, but we don't get to see her. Charlotte and Trey are there also, and Trey insists on telling Carrie the story of how they met, with Charlotte interrupting and correcting him. The couple have acquired the ability to finish each other's sentences. It's all very sweet.

Standing at the buffet, Carrie literally bumps into Mr Big. Carrie asks him where Natasha is, and he cryptically replies that she 'missed the boat'. After some small talk, Carrie all but runs away from him, but he catches up with her later in the evening and asks her if she's seeing anyone. She tells him she is, and describes Aidan as 'perfect'. Big compliments her on her choice of dress, which makes her uncomfortable. She says it was nice to see him again, and walks away.

Hey, Big Guy: Carrie and Aidan go back to her apartment one night, and while he's making coffee, she checks the messages on her answer phone. One of the messages is from Big, sounding desperately unhappy. Carrie quickly turns the machine off, and Aidan comes into the room and tells her that they're out of filters for the coffee machine. He's going to nip out to a shop on the corner and get some more. Moments after he leaves, Big arrives at Carrie's apartment. He looks like a complete wreck. He asks if Aidan, whom he passed in the hallway, was 'the perfect guy' she told him about on the boat. She asks him what he wants, and he claims to have no idea, but the way he's looking at her belies that sentence. Carrie tells him to go home to his wife and shuts the door in his face. Then she plays the whole message that he left for her; it says everything Carrie always wanted to hear from him, but it's 'a year too late'. Big, she decides, is the 'past come back to haunt me,' and Aidan is her future.

Trivia: Carrie tells Charlotte, who appears not to have heard it before, the story of how she lost her virginity. It involves cannabis and a ping-pong table. Which is amusing.

Also Starring: Robert LuPone (Len) plays Dr Cusamano in the magnificent *The Sopranos*, HBO's *other* hugely successfully, massively sophisticated and multi-award-winning TV show.

And So . . . : 'Hey, Carrie . . . I know you're there. Pick up. I . . . Jesus . . . I miss you. I can't stop fucking thinking about you.' This episode features a second silly and unconvincing break-up for Miranda and Steve (after last season's), and the crisis in their relationship flares up and reaches break-up proportions shockingly quickly, especially since last week's episode was all about how overly comfortable they'd got with each other. It almost seems as if Steve is being written out near the end of the season in case David Eigenberg doesn't wish to return for Season Four, rather than for any plot or character reasons.

Carrie's confusion over Aidan/Big is impressively handled and distressingly affecting, and Kyle MacLachlan demonstrates just how good an actor he really is, stealing every scene he's in, even when he doesn't have any lines.

39
Easy Come, Easy Go

6 August 2000

Written by Michael Patrick King
Directed by Charles McDougall

Guest Cast
Chris Noth (Mr Big) David Eigenberg (Steve Brady)
John Corbett (Aidan Shaw) Bridget Moynahan (Natasha)
Kyle MacLachlan (Trey MacDougal)
Frances Sternhagen (Bunny MacDougal) Bobby Cannavale (Adam Ball)
Kirven Blount (Bean Sprouty Waiter)
Caroline Whitney-Smith (Waitress)

Miranda: It's three weeks since Steve and Miranda split up, but they're still living together while he tries to find somewhere else to live. He sleeps on the sofa, accompanied by the puppy. One morning she accidentally wakes Steve up while going out to work; they small talk in an embarrassed way and Steve apologises for taking so long to find a new place to live. He asks her to look at a new apartment with him. When they get there it's an awful shabby place which Miranda tells Steve he can't possibly live in. (Has she forgotten his old Travis Bickle digs so soon?) A few nights later the puppy is barking outside Miranda's room. She gets out of bed to shout at Steve and discovers that he's not yet come home. This is when Miranda finally realises that she and Steve are over. By the time Steve does come home, Miranda is ready to go out to work. She tells him that she's taken the dog out, made him some coffee, and circled apartments in a copy of the *Village Voice* that she thinks would be good for him. He tells her that he should move out that day and she agrees. But as she goes to work she asks him to keep in touch.

Carrie: It's the first day of the New Designers' Showcase, a fair at which Aidan is exhibiting some of his work. Carrie is helping him, serving as his 'booth bitch' (her term), trying to sell his stuff for him. Aidan goes off to get them coffee, and by startling coincidence Big and Natasha approach her booth. Terrified, Carrie hides behind the desk, but eventually the Bigs notice her, and she tells them that this is her boyfriend's booth, and that she's his booth bitch. Just then Aidan arrives with the coffee, making an awkward situation even more so. Carrie introduces Aidan to Natasha and then 'accidentally' spills coffee on Big so he has to leave. Natasha takes Big away, and Aidan asks

Carrie how she knows the couple. She replies that she knew them in a past life.

Hey, Big Guy: Much later that day Big goes back to Carrie's booth, clearly rather the worse for alcohol. He asks Carrie about Aidan, and she pointedly asks him where his wife is. He tells her Natasha is at an auction for a beige chair. 'Beige,' he says, 'is bullshit,' and goes on to say that everything in his apartment is now beige. Carrie looks at him and says, 'I thought you wanted beige' (see **30**, 'Ex and the City'). Telling Carrie that he's going to reveal a big secret to her, he rolls a programme for the show into a makeshift loudhailer and shouts, 'It's not working. I'm getting out.' Then he leans over and asks her if she knows anyone who might be interested in this information.

Wine and Dine: Dinner at the restaurant for our favourite foursome, and Carrie tells the others that Big is leaving Natasha. Sam regards this as a victory, because Carrie is now happy and Big is now miserable. Charlotte thinks it's sad that Big is leaving his wife after only seven months, and Miranda blames the whole situation on people getting into relationships and especially marriages too quickly. Charlotte takes this personally and tells her that she and Trey are nothing like Big and Natasha. She then confides in her friends that she's off to meet Trey's mother, and she thinks he's likely to ask her to marry him soon. Miranda points out that she's owned underwear longer than Charlotte and Trey have known each other.

Samantha: Samantha is dating a man who is rather keen on her swallowing during oral sex. Sam has a problem with this because she thinks his sperm tastes especially disgusting. She gets him to drink various juices that are supposed to improve the (ahem) flavour, but none of them work. When she later refuses to give him a blow job he's offended, saying he doesn't understand why she can't do something so easy for him. Sam loses her rag at this, saying that men have no idea what women have to cope with. 'Teeth placement and jaw stress and suction and gag reflex, and all the while bobbing up and down, moaning and trying to breathe through our noses. Easy? Honey, they don't call it a job for nothing!' She tells him she has no problem swallowing with the right guy, as long as it doesn't taste too bad. He doesn't believe that he tastes that much worse than anyone else, so Sam gets him to agree to taste his own. If he's fine with it, then she will be too. Ten minutes later he has some on his fingers; he tastes it, and despite the fact that he says it's fine, the expression on his face makes it quite clear that vomiting is an imminent possibility.

Charlotte: Charlotte meets Trey's mother and learns from her that the way to manipulate Trey into doing just about anything is to put your hand on his arm and tell him what you want in a clear, reasonable tone. He always responds with 'All righty!' and goes on to do exactly what he's been told. Later Charlotte and Trey have dinner in a restaurant, and it seems to her that he is about to propose. He's interrupted and she's left hanging on the edge. He eventually tells her she always knows what he wants, and seizing the opportunity, she puts her hand on his arm again and says, 'Maybe we should get married.' What does Trey say? 'All righty!' Charlotte goes over to Carrie's and tells her that she's somehow managed to propose to herself. She's deeply upset that there was no ring and that Trey didn't get down on one knee. She'll now never have a good 'engagement story' to tell people, because the actual events that led to her engagement are so lame. When we next see Trey and Charlotte they're walking down the street, hand in hand. He tells her how delighted his mother was when he told her about their engagement. Charlotte looks sad – she's got everything she wanted but she doesn't like the way she got it. Then they walk past Tiffany's, and Trey stops and tells Charlotte that they should go in and buy the most beautiful ring they have in the store. 'From that moment on, Charlotte would tell *everyone* that right in front of Tiffany's, out of nowhere, Trey popped the question and *she* said, "All righty!" '

Kisses: Carrie goes to stay at the Stanhope Hotel in order to finish some copy she's writing. Big visits her, having found out where she's gone from Aidan. He asks her to have a drink with him, and she politely points out that she has a boyfriend and a deadline, and he has a wife and a drinking problem. They argue and Carries dashes to the elevator. Big follows her and, grabbing her, tells her he made a mistake. He tries to kiss her. She pushes him away and shouts 'Fuck you!' at him. He tells her he loves her, and again tries to kiss her. She pushes him away more gently and this time whispers, 'Fuck you.' He kisses her again, and this time she kisses him back. 'Fuck *me*,' she says. 'And just like that, I lost my head.'

And So . . .: 'I'm engaged, I proposed to myself.' A good mix of stories, the splitting of Steve and Miranda is really sad and contrasts well with Charlotte and Trey's obvious happiness. Carrie completely loses it, cheating on Aidan with a clearly stressed-out Big in one of the series' most passionate and impressive dramatic scenes to date. Trey's habit of constantly saying 'All righty!' is, depending on your point of view, either really funny or incredibly annoying.

40
All or Nothing

13 August 2000

Written by Jenny Bicks
Directed by Charles McDougall

Guest Cast
Chris Noth (Mr Big) John Corbett (Aidan Shaw)
Kyle MacLachlan (Trey MacDougal)
Frances Sternhagen (Bunny MacDougal) Josh Hamilton (George)
Marilyn Alex (Saleslady)

Carrie: Aidan is away in Pennsylvania and Carrie is at a loose end. Haunted by thoughts of her recent night with Big, she tries to occupy herself by filing all her articles, sorting out her shoes (which must take a while) and having the odd crafty cigarette because she knows Aidan can't see her. Eventually she cracks and calls Big. She tells him they have to talk about what they did like adults. They must rise above the physical. 'You can do that?' asks Big quizzically. 'You're married,' she points out. He tells her that he's aware of this, and then says, 'Come on, it was pretty fucking amazing, wasn't it?' She's forced to agree.

They have sex again, despite Big's distaste at being able to smell Aidan on Carrie's sheets, an aroma he describes as 'woodchip'. As they lie around Carrie talks about turning the story of her renewed affair with him into a book, a sort of *Bridges of Madison Avenue*. 'Can I have a beard in the book version?' asks Big. 'I've always wanted a beard.'

Aidan returns to New York and Carrie. He tells Carrie how much he missed her, and then says he has something important to tell her. 'I love you, Carrie, is that too much?' She tells him that she loves him too, and then they make love on the bed from which Carrie has only just removed the Big-scented sheets.

Charlotte: Trey takes Charlotte shopping for china for their wedding at Bergdorf Goodman. The particular set she wants cost $1,300. Trey comments that while it's very nice, he really can't afford it. Charlotte pouts and points out how lovely it looks. Trey confirms that it will indeed 'look lovely under the ramen noodles we'll be forced to eat due to my outstanding china loans' should he buy it for the wedding. She pouts some more, and Trey cracks, buying the china and telling her that he's too crazy about her to deny her anything. And then he asks her to sign a pre-nuptial agreement, which makes her world fall apart. Fretting that they haven't yet walked down the aisle and Trey is already planning for their divorce, Charlotte gets Miranda to look over the papers for her. Miranda thinks it all looks pretty normal and doesn't see any reason why, in principle, Charlotte shouldn't sign it. She claims that she'd never get married without a pre-nuptial agreement:

it's sensible to protect one's assets, especially when 50 per cent of marriages end in divorce. On reading the small print of the contract, Charlotte is appalled to discover that in the event of divorce she'll only get $500,000. It isn't the money that worries her, as she has no plans for divorce. Ever. It's that the contract implies that $500,000 is all she is worth. She resolves to indulge in some hardball negotiations with Trey's aged mother, the impassive Bunny, and so confronts her in a corner during a large party held by Trey's family, at which many prominent New York figures and all of Charlotte's friends are in attendance. Using hard negotiating tactics and implied threats of escalating wedding costs and social embarrassment, Charlotte gets her price upped to a cool $1,000,000. After this conclusion there's a brief, symbolic scene where Trey sweeps in and takes Charlotte away from her friends. They dance and Samantha, Carrie and Miranda leave the party one person short. 'And then there were three,' Miranda comments dryly.

Samantha: Samantha Jones is unwell. She has a terrible, terrible cold and is unable to get out of bed. Permanently coughing and sneezing and unable to sleep, she finds herself frustrated by a broken curtain rail. Ringing around all the men in her address book she can't find a single one who is willing to come over and help her fix it, or even bring her any medicine. One guy offers to come round, with a proviso, but Sam turns him down, saying, 'I can hardly blow my nose, let alone blow you!' Eventually she gets Carrie around to help. Although unable to fix the curtain rail, Carrie is able to mix up Samantha's mother's cure-all recipe from childhood for her. Cough syrup plus Fanta over ice. Strangely, this seems to work, although before it does an incoherent and sobbing Samantha repudiates her entire lifestyle choices: 'It doesn't matter how much you have. If you don't have a guy who cares about you it don't mean shit.' Carrie observes how three days of sleep deprivation have turned Samantha into a whole new woman, that woman being Charlotte.

Sam tells Carrie there are two kinds of guys – the ones
that'll hold your hand and the ones that fuck you. 'The
ones that fuck you aren't worth a damn!' Remembering
her recent indiscretions with Big, Carrie realises that Aidan
is an example of the former and Big is an example of the
latter – and that she's fucked both in the last 48 hours.
Albeit in slightly different senses of the word, perhaps.

Miranda: Since Steve's departure Miranda has wasted no
time in trying to find a new guy, preferably a new,
commitment-free guy who will allow her her own space.
She finds him in George, a guy who works for the same
law firm she does, but in the Chicago office. He's in New
York for business reasons and she's asked to show him the
city. They get on very well and end up making out. Once
George has returned to Chicago, Miranda begins to have
regular phone sex with him. This, she feels, is the kind of
relationship she needs: pressure-free and without the need
to share her living space. She eventually realises, however,
that George is having phone sex with more than one
person. Not quite prepared to be *that* commitment-free,
she hangs up on him.

Hey, Big Guy: Carrie is in bed with Aidan when Big
phones her. He's outside her apartment and threatens to
go up to see her if she doesn't go down and see him. Carrie
lies to Aidan, saying that she's going to walk his dog, Pete,
and then meets Big at the bottom of the stairs, with
Aidan's dog standing next to her like a physical reminder
of her guilt. Carrie angrily reprimands Big for being selfish;
he wants to have two women, the one he can fuck and the
one he can go home to. He corrects her, saying that, quite
simply, he doesn't. He only wants her, and he's going to
tell Natasha about them tonight. The scene then flips on
its head, as the audience and Carrie realise that it's her who
wants two people, one for sex and one for companionship.
She begs Big not to tell his wife. And then Pete runs away.
Carrie panics, shouting at Big to leave her alone, and then
spends several hours searching for the missing dog in the

rain. She eventually returns home only to find that Pete made his way back to her place hours before. Aidan looks after her, supplying her with towels and hugging her. And then he says that he has to ask her a question. 'Are you cheating?' he asks, and before she has a chance to reply, to unburden herself, he continues, 'I can smell the smoke on you.' He hasn't guessed about Big, he just knows she's been smoking again. She apologises, and decides not to tell him about her real cheating. She tells him that she really does want to 'give up', but whether she's talking about Big or tobacco neither she nor we really know any more.

And So . . .: 'The moth to the old flame.' Carrie's betrayal of Aidan makes your skin crawl, as writing and performance combine to make Aidan so utterly decent, likeable, under-standing and *nice* that any kind of mistreatment of him seems like kicking a puppy. In the head. Twice. Big-in-crisis is quite a weird thing to see, and while you can't condone his actions at least he seems to understand that the only way out of the situation is to tell Natasha, apologise for what he's done and leave her for Carrie. Unfortunately he seems to let Carrie talk him out of this. There's not a lot of laughs here, although Charlotte's hard-faced negotiating with Trey's mother is a wonder to behold.

41
Running with Scissors

20 August 2000

Written by Michael Patrick King
Directed by Dennis Erdman

Guest Cast
Chris Noth (Mr Big) John Corbett (Aidan Shaw)
Bridget Moynahan (Natasha) Sam Robards (Tom Reymi)
Mario Cantone (Anthony Marentino) Adrian Reider (Sandwich)
Blanchard Ryan (Saleswoman) Michelle Hurst (Nurse)
Emanuel Loarca (Manager) Keenan Shimitzu (Japanese Businessman)
Janet Papparazzo (Natasha's Stunt Double)

Carrie: In the three weeks since the last episode Carrie and Big have had a series of secret sex rendezvous in a series of hotels, each one seedier than the last. As Carrie observes, 'Our affair, like our hotels, had gone from elegant with crystal to seedy with plastic cups.' Full of guilt, Carrie tells Miranda and her friend is shocked. Carrie begs Miranda to help her, saying that she's too in the middle of the situation to see clearly. 'I need you to yank me out of it', she says, adding, 'I want everyone to get out of this without anyone getting hurt.' 'That's realistic,' replies Miranda, ironically. Her advice? 'Stop. Just stop'.

After a customer at one hotel mistakes Carrie for a hooker ('I've seen you here before. How much?'), she refuses to return there, and they decide to have sex at Big's apartment instead. This will be 'safe' as Natasha is up north in The Hamptons, enjoying herself on the beach.

Miranda: Walking past the same sandwich shop every day, Miranda finds herself offended by the way in which one employee (dressed as a giant sandwich), says 'Eat Me!' She feels it is being sexually threatening, and that this is therefore sexual harassment. After a few days, she complains to the shop. The manager points out that the guy is dressed as a sandwich, and that saying 'Eat Me!' is therefore perfectly in character. Later, and for no readily apparent reason, she comes to like having the giant sandwich man shout at her, and admits to Carrie that she has fantasised about him even though she's never seen his face. Eventually she plucks up the courage to open the guy's mask and look at him. After this, she goes off the idea, even though he is 'kinda cute'.

Samantha: Sam meets Tom Reymi, a well-known permanently single Manhattan socialite, whom Carrie describes as 'the male Samantha'. They swap notes, both having heard of each other, and decide that they have to have sex. It would be the meeting of the best and the best. Going back to Tom's place, Samantha is shown his ceiling-mounted swinging sex chair and immediately wants to try it. 'I've always wanted to run off and join the circus,' she says with a lascivious grin. Then Tom asks her when her last AIDS test was, and Samantha doesn't know how to tell Tom that the only sex test she's ever taken was a quiz in *Cosmopolitan*. He reproachfully says that she should have regular AIDS tests (he does, every few weeks) because given the way they both behave, it's the only responsible thing to do. He won't have sex with her until she's been tested, so seeking advice from her friends, Sam goes ahead with the test, despite being terrified. There the nurse asks her a series of questions about her sexual practices. The answer to all of them is 'Yes' with the exception of 'Do you swallow?', to which the answer is, 'Only when surprised.' Despite Sam's worst fears, the test proves negative. She calls Tom Reymi and has a night of fantastic, completely safe sex in his swing chair. Well, until they break it, anyway.

Charlotte: Charlotte takes a huge number of catalogues displaying wedding dresses to the cafe with her, as she wants her friends to help her find the perfect wedding dress. ('Kill me now,' says Miranda. 'Just take a sharp object and draw it across my throat.') When Samantha hijacks the occasion to discuss whether or not she should have an HIV test, Charlotte is furious. 'We're looking at wedding gowns. Can we please not talk about AIDS right now?' Samantha advises Charlotte to get a stylist to help her finalise her wedding plans. Enter Anthony, the rampantly camp wedding planner who helps Charlotte find the dress she's been dreaming about since she was five years old, and in record time.

Trivia: Carrie quotes the legendary opening lines from Charles Dickens's 1859 novel of revolution and self-sacrifice, *A Tale of Two Cities* ('It was the best of times, it was the worst of times . . .'). She thinks it so precisely sums up her situation that Dickens must have been having sex with his married ex-boyfriend when he wrote it. This is, at best, unlikely.

Hey, Big Guy: After sex at Big's apartment, Carrie informs him that they should stop seeing each other, as the current arrangement isn't fair on either her boyfriend or his wife. Big picks up the phone and again says that it's Carrie and only Carrie that he wants. 'If I make that call, are you going to be there for me?' he asks her, reiterating what he said three weeks before. 'Carrie, in or out?' he presses her. She tells him she needs more time to decide, and he makes it clear that whatever she decides he's going to tell Natasha on Monday.

After he goes to work, Carrie hangs out in his apartment for a while, eating leftover Chinese food and taking a shower. And then Natasha comes home early. Although she tries to sneak out the front door without Natasha seeing, Mrs Big notices her exit and chases Carrie down the fire escape, shouting that she knew they were having an affair but she won't accept them doing it in her house. In her hurry she falls over, smashing her face into the ground. Shocked, Carrie goes back up the stairs to help her. 'I had always assumed the one who would be hurt in all this would be me,' she says, but looking at Natasha's bleeding face, Carrie realises how wrong she has been. She takes Natasha to hospital and waits until Big arrives. Before going in to see his wife, Big asks Carrie about her injuries, and she tells him that Natasha has lost a tooth and needed a stitch in her lip, but thanks to plastic surgery it won't scar. Carrie makes to go, and Big says he'll call her. She says that they are so over they need a new word for over. He doesn't stop her leaving. When she arrives home she finds Aidan there waiting for her, but she doesn't tell him about what's happened.

And So . . .: 'How did we get here? Who are we?' This is a really good if not very *nice* episode as all the plots from the past few instalments begin to pay off. Poor Natasha – what has she done to deserve any of this? It's not as if it was she who broke Big and Carrie up in the first place. Her only 'crimes' are to be younger than Carrie and to have fallen for the same man. Samantha's AIDS fear plotline is an injection of social consciousness into the series, with both Carrie and Miranda admitting to having had more than one AIDS test in their lives and Tom arguing that with the freedom he and Samantha enjoy, there inevitably comes responsibility. This is entirely in keeping with a very dark script, which largely concerns itself with consequences. Charlotte and her stylist's misadventures with dresses are welcome, if temporary, light relief.

42
Don't Ask, Don't Tell

27 August 2000

Written by Cindy Chupack
Directed by Dan Algrant

Guest Cast
Willie Garson (Stanford Blatch) John Corbett (Aidan Shaw)
Kyle MacLachlan (Trey MacDougal)
Frances Sternhagen (Bunny MacDougal) Clark Gregg (Harris Bragen)
Ritchie Coster (Caleb MacDougal) Joe Lapiana (Dwight Owens)

Miranda: With Charlotte's wedding only a week away, Miranda is resorting to new and increasingly desperate ways to avoid being dateless on the big day. She attends singles functions where men and women are organised into pairs, and then rotated through numerous eight-minute 'mini-dates' each. As man after man appears threatened by Miranda's success, she decides to pretend to be an air stewardess. This interests one guy, who informs Miranda he's an ER doctor. After a few dates, and quite a lot of sex, Miranda is worried about her little deception, but her guilt is ameliorated by her discovery that she's not the only one lying. While she has faked being less successful than she is to get a man, he's faked being more successful in order to fulfil his fantasy of scoring with a stewardess. Deciding to let him keep his fantasy, Miranda pretends to be enraged at his lies and dumps him, leaving her to find a last-minute emergency date for the wedding: Stanford.

Samantha: Sam decides to investigate Hibernian regions by sleeping with a Scottish cousin of Trey's she meets at

Charlotte's wedding rehearsal dinner. After seducing him she informs her friends that what has been reported is sadly untrue: Scotsmen *do* wear something under their kilts . . . although it is remarkably easy to get off.

Fashion Victims: The girls go to the fitting for their bridesmaids' dresses at Vera Wang's. Everyone's dress is the same colour, a sort of light champagne, but they're all cut differently according to the individual. The effect is something like the famous *Sex and the City* publicity photograph of the four girls all wearing different little black dresses. Carrie's bridesmaid dress is cut like a boob-tube style top, Miranda's has a bateau neck and Samantha's is very low-cut.

Girl Talk: Carrie decides that she has to tell Aidan about her affair with Big, even though it is now over, because relationships are founded on trust. As Sam says, 'No offence, honey, but I think that ship has sailed.' She thinks Carrie should keep quiet about her indiscretions in the way that she feels men always have. Miranda argues that Aidan will find out eventually, anyway, and Samantha counters, 'He didn't find out when you were fucking Big all over Manhattan. Why would he find out now that it's over?'

Carrie: Carrie tries to convince herself that coming clean with Aidan about Big might be 'the ultimate selfish act; a way to absolve yourself by hurting someone who doesn't deserve to be hurt.' While staying at Aidan's place, Carrie sneaks out to have a cigarette at three in the morning. He follows her out and looks at her, shaking his head and saying that it won't work. Although Carrie initially thinks he means 'them', she realises he's talking about her smoking. She explains that she tried hard to quit, but simply couldn't, and Aidan tells her that it's OK, he can handle her smoking if she really wants to. She reminds him of his refusal to date a smoker, and he smiles and says, 'You're not just a smoker. You're a lot of things.' She's close to confessing her affair with Big to him for a moment, but bottles out.

Fetishes: Charlotte reveals that she and Trey have still not had sex, and Samantha berates her for not taking her future husband for a 'test drive'. Charlotte then confesses that she fantasises about having Trey lick whipped cream from her naked body. Samantha recommends 'low-fat Cool Whip' instead because it's less sticky.

Charlotte: After her bachelorette party, Charlotte goes to Trey's apartment. She's drunk and tells him that, since it's after midnight, and therefore officially their wedding day, they should have sex right now. 'All righty, then,' says Trey, and then picks her up and carries her into the bedroom. Except this doesn't go as planned, and when we cut to Charlotte and Trey in bed, she is devastated. He can't get it up.

Men: As they meet up to go to the wedding, Carrie finally plucks up the courage to tell Aidan that she slept with her ex-boyfriend. 'We slept together and I didn't tell you and I'm sorry.' Aidan asks her if she and Big only had sex once, and she confesses that it was 'many times ... he was married and it was a MESS and I don't know what I was thinking but it is so, so over'. She asks him to forgive her, and he just looks at her with so much pain in his face it's quite hard for the audience to look. She asks him if he'll still go to the wedding with her. He hands her his wedding gift for Charlotte and Trey, a photograph of the love seat he's spent weeks designing and building for them, and then he turns around and leaves without saying a word.

The Big Day: Minutes before walking down the aisle, and moments after Carrie has arrived at the wedding, Charlotte calls Carrie to her side. 'Trey can't get it up!' she says, pulling the veil from her face. Carrie tries to come up with as many reasons and/or excuses for Trey's erectile dysfunction as she can, but Charlotte can't accept any of them. 'He said it happens all the time' she says, her face a picture of misery. Carrie tells her that she doesn't have to get married, she can leave now and everyone else will just have to deal with it, but Charlotte can't bring herself to take that option. 'Charlotte was 34, single, and standing in a $14,000 dress,' says Carrie. 'She was getting married, and not even a low libido could stop her.' And so Charlotte walks down the aisle and into an uncertain future.

Aidan meets Carrie on the street immediately after the wedding and she begs him to take her back, saying that people make mistakes. He explains to her that this is something too big for him to get over quickly, and then he walks away. Carrie rejoins her friends for the wedding photographs, wiping away tears which she hopes people will assume are for the bride and groom.

Trivia: After the first transmission of this episode, the series took a one-week break, with a rerun being shown on 3 September instead of a new episode. This was due to production complications on **43**, 'Escape From New York'. In order to explain this, a specially filmed commercial/apology was run after **42**, 'Don't Ask, Don't Tell'. In it Sarah Jessica Parker sits with her back to us in a director's chair with her name monogrammed on it. She then turns to the camera and introduces herself before saying that she is in place of a preview for next week's episode because 'we don't *have* next week's episode. We're not done yet. We need more time. What you will be seeing next week is a lovely rerun. After that, we'll be back with six new episodes . . . thank you for your indulgence, good night, and godspeed.'

Samantha is convinced that she can pronounce the sentence 'I work in PR' in such a way that whoever she says it to will know she means 'I give great head'. Whatever.

And So . . .: 'I know myself, and this isn't the kind of thing I can get over.' An emotionally bruised and battered Aidan departs with his tail between his legs, despite not having deserved any of his mistreatment at Carrie's hands; and Charlotte faces up to life with a man whom she loves but who may never be able to love her physically. The wedding scenes are impressive but are undercut by such emotional uncertainty that the audience probably doesn't enjoy the day any more than Charlotte or Carrie. Stanford appears (yay!) but isn't given dialogue (boo!). This is almost certainly the least sentimental wedding episode in television history.

43
Escape From New York

10 September 2000

Written by Becky Hartman Edwards & Michael Patrick King
Directed by John David Coles

Guest Cast
Kyle MacLachlan (Trey MacDougal) Matthew McConaughey (Himself)
James MacDonald (Garth) Sarah Michelle Gellar (Debbie)
Edward Kerr (Jason Dique) Will Foster Stewart (Clerk)
Robert Peters (Announcer) Faith Salie (Rina) Vince Morris (Guard)

The City: Carrie describes New York as 'grey, dreary and miserable' although she admits that it may seem this way to her because she's just finished a sordid affair with an ex-boyfriend and been through a painful break-up with her most recent one ... It's just as well, then, that she's heading out of town, with Miranda and Samantha in tow, in order to talk to a Hollywood studio about them taking out an option on her column.

Charlotte: Just before the rest of the gang disappear to LA, Charlotte returns from her ten-day honeymoon in Bermuda with lots of photographs and an improved golf handicap. She confides in Carrie that she and Trey have still not had sex – they tried twice, but she found the process so massively frustrating that she gave up. Carrie tells her that impotence is actually quite common, to which Charlotte replies, 'My husband can't be impotent, he's gorgeous.' She hopes that his problems are just connected to his being nervous about their wedding and the honeymoon, and that once they settle down to normal life the problem will disappear. On Carrie's advice, she devises a strategy to see whether Trey's problem is physical or emotional. She ties a small band of stamps around his penis while he's asleep, because Carrie has suggested that if the band breaks she'll know that he can get an erection, it's just that he has problems doing so while his mind is on it. The paper is broken in the morning, so Trey clearly *can* get an erection, and Charlotte realises that while there's now hope for a physical relationship with Trey, the fact that the problem is either psychological or emotional means that it may be a bigger deal than she initially feared.

(Another) City: 'Later that day three single New Yorkers arrived in the City of Angels.' Due to a huge administrative error, Miranda has to share a room with Carrie. Due to a further administrative error, Carrie discovers that her hotel room, like almost all of California, is a smoking-free zone. Frustrated by Miranda's snoring and driven mad by her inability to smoke without being interrupted by objections, Carrie wonders if things can get any worse. They can, as she discovers upon meeting the people who want to option her work. Enter Debbie, a junior development executive with a big mouth who tells Carrie how much she loves her columns. 'They're just so relatable! It's like I'm you!' Relatable, feels Debbie, equals, 'Big opening weekend, not *X-Men* [Bryan Singer, 2000] big but "chick flick" big.' Translated from Valley-speak this means that she believes the film can make an enormous amount of money in its first three days of release, albeit not as much as a successful blockbuster of the stature of summer 2000's biggest grossing (and arguably best) film. She then says that the guy who came up with the term 'chick flick' to describe a film that primarily appeals to women should have his balls cut off. She tells Carrie that they have a star interested in the project. After a couple of slightly lame guesses – 'That Jennifer Love person . . .' – Carrie gives up. 'Matthew McConaughey!' shrieks Debbie. Carrie is confused by his interest (presumably he wants to play Big), but Debbie assuages her worries by pointing out that McConaughey is a producer as well as a bankable actor, and that he has a reputation for being smart. So she goes off to meet him.

Samantha: Sam meets Garth, who she's amazed to discover is a dildo model, a man whose penis is used as the mould for the USA's second-biggest-selling sex toy. This makes him, as Miranda points out, 'The John Grisham of penises.' Sam is, of course, hugely impressed with this, and resolves to bed him as quickly as possible. She succeeds, but is disturbed when it becomes apparent that he wants more than just sex out of a relationship. He suggests that he move to New York and date Samantha full-time while following his two passions, poetry and porn. Garth, it seems may be the model for a sex toy, but he doesn't want to be treated like one by Samantha. Samantha leaves him, explaining that she's too possessive of her men to 'share' him with the thousands of women who've bought his dildo.

Miranda: Not much for Miranda to do in LA, it seems. She chats to one guy who tells her it's great to talk to a smart and funny woman, which pleases her, but he's almost immediately dragged away by the possibility of chatting to a more available-looking woman with more cleavage on show. This enrages Miranda, who compares herself to New York, with hidden depths and plenty under the surface, whereas the bimbo was more like LA, with everything on show. She's so annoyed she gets drunk in a rodeo bar and rides a Bucking Bronco machine. Sam and Carrie find this very funny indeed.

Men: Matthew McConaughey plays himself as a wide-eyed loser with no idea how to act in civilised company. He describes Carrie's writing as 'sharp, edgy, brutal at times' and 'very New York'. He wants to make a movie concentrating on Carrie and Big, though he can't see why they were unable to make it work. He doesn't seem to get that the Carrie he's talking to is the same person who is in the columns, and goes on to describe Big as 'Such a great guy! I don't know anybody cooler than Mr Big! The only question really is, what the fuck is Carrie's problem?' After this somewhat fruitless meeting, Carrie ponders how it came to pass that she travelled three thousand miles 'to have Matthew McConaughey ask me the same question I've been asking myself for years'. She walks through a mock-up New York street on the Warner Bros lot and while doing so gets homesick for her city. 'No matter how far you travel or how far you run from it,' she wonders, 'can you ever really escape your past?'

Trivia: The title is taken from the Kurt Russell-starring *Escape from New York* (John Carpenter, 1980).

Also Starring: Sarah Michelle Gellar, devastatingly effective as snarling junior executive Debbie, is of course the eponymous heroine of the magnificent *Buffy The Vampire Slayer* (1997–2003), a role she has also played in that series' almost-as-good-but-not-quite spin-off show, *Angel* (1999–2004). A former child star, who appeared in adverts for Burger King at the age of four, she won an Emmy for her role as Kendall Hart in daytime soap opera *All My Children*. Her movie roles include the fabulous Kathryn Merteuil in *Cruel Intentions* (Roger Kumble, 1999), a New York-set take on *Les Liasions Dangereuses*, which if you haven't seen you should, and parts in *Scream 2* (Wes Craven, 1997) and *I Know What You Did Last Summer* (Jim Gillespie, 1997), both of which were, frankly, a bit rubbish. She plays Daphne in *Scooby-Doo* (Raja Gosnel, 2002) and its sequels, alongside her husband Freddy Prinze, Jr as Fred.

Heartthrob actor Matthew McConaughey, so wonderfully, unselfishly self-parodying here, appeared in the historically inept World War II movie *U-571* (Jonathan Mostow, 2000), the history-packed slavery drama *Amistad* (Steven Spielberg, 1997), and the distinctly non-history-making *EDtv* (Ron Howard, 1999). He's also, as the episode states, a successful writer/producer and director as well as actor, with a reputation for being 'smart', which in real life appears well deserved. Pictures he's directed include *Chicano Chariots* (1992) and the really rather good *The Rebel* (1998), in which he also appeared.

And So . . .: 'Every time she licked a love stamp she felt it made a mockery of her marriage.' This is a killingly funny and quietly profound self-reflexive parody episode, which both celebrates and mocks the series of which it is a part. The big-name guest stars (Gellar and McConaughey) are superb, and by the end Carrie appears to have acquired a new sense of purpose. 'I . . . held the key to my escape. I could drive in and have someone tell me the mistakes I made in my past, or I could drive on and figure them out myself,' she says, deciding not to let Hollywood film her life. (She'd be far better off getting some cable station to make a series of it.) Meanwhile, back in New York, Kyle MacLachlan deadpans his way through the funniest material he's yet been given, and Charlotte begins to act, in Carrie's words, 'like a perverted Nancy Drew'. This is an *exceptional* episode, very nearly the best of the entire season.

44
Sex and Another City

17 September 2000

Written by Jenny Bicks
Directed by John David Coles

Guest Cast
Kyle MacLachlan (Trey MacDougal) Carrie Fisher (Herself)
Hugh Hefner (Himself) Vince Vaughn (Keith Travers)
Sam Seder (Lew) Marty Rackham (Ian) Amanda Bentley (Mandy)
Sandra Bentley (Sandy) Lisa Mende (Alicia) Amber Collins (Playmate)
Douglas Weston (Realtor) Will Burke (Bellman)
Jennifer Elise Cox (PR Girl) Chris Huvane (Waiter)
Tara Chocol (Waitress) Eddie Driscoll (Fendi Man)

Charlotte: Back on the East Coast, Charlotte has attended her first black-tie doctors benefit. 'How did I do?' she asks her husband flirtatiously upon their return. He flirts back, saying she did quite well. 'Doctor,' she says to him, 'I have an itch. I was hoping you could help me out.' Trey realises that she's about to try to have sex with him and becomes visibly embarrassed. She tells him they need to consider some 'options', including Viagra. Trey points out that 'Viagra is a killer for men with heart problems' and informs Charlotte that his father died of a heart attack and it runs in the family. He then proceeds to go for a run. This is apparently not the first time he's gone out jogging at bedtime, and Charlotte reasons that if he can run away from their problems then so can she. And she goes and joins her friends in LA.

(Another) City: LA, says Carrie, is a 'land of perpetual sun and perpetual sunbathing'. She's amazed that she is 'actually starting to like LA' as it's a place that New Yorkers are trained to hate, but a few more days in the sun and a couple more shocks may just be enough to dislodge her new-found fondness for the place.

Miranda: Miranda is off to meet New York ex-pat Lew, whom she used to know when he lived on the East Coast. He worked in television back there, and moved coasts when offered a job as a writer on a popular twenty-something sitcom. Meeting him in a restaurant, Miranda is amazed that pale, plump Lew has lost 30 lbs and looks the picture of health. 'Do I look that different?' he asks when she comments on his changed appearance. 'It's a good thing you still wear that hat!' she says, pointing at his New York Knicks baseball cap. She wouldn't have been able to recognise him otherwise.

The change in Lew impresses Miranda, who begins to drop out of her New York state of mind. 'Maybe it's time I stopped being so angry,' she says to Carrie, who pithily asks her what she'd do with all her spare time. Further investigation into the new Lew yields less positive results, however, with Miranda discovering that he chews his food and then spits it out in order to avoid getting fat (no one will hire a 'fat story editor', apparently). He also gets hysterical at the slightest disagreement, leaving Miranda to wonder what happened to the balanced, intelligent man she used to know.

Carrie: Carrie is under the impression that in LA she'll be able to get into movie premieres and after-show parties by flashing her press pass, and is embarrassed to discover that this is not the case. While loitering outside a venue she's been turned away from, she meets a guy called Keith Travers, who says he's there 'representing Matt Damon'. He gets Carrie and Samantha into the party, and while in there asks Carrie for a date. They go for lunch a few days later, and look at a house he says he's thinking of buying. Back at his present house they have sex in the hot-tub before falling asleep in the master bedroom. The next morning Carrie is shocked to be confronted by an enraged Carrie Fisher, who demands to know why Keith, her house sitter, is bringing prostitutes back to her home when he's minding it. Carrie Bradshaw denies being a prostitute, and tells Carrie Fisher (whom she obviously admires) that she's a writer too. 'I'm Carrie, you're Carrie,' she says. 'You write, I write.' Ms Fisher is definitely unimpressed. Equally unimpressed with Keith's lies, Ms Bradshaw makes her own way out. This is, she says 'the perfect end' to her 'week of fantasy'.

Fashion Victims: On an LA street Samantha is sold a fake 2000 season gold-coloured Fendi handbag for $150, about a tenth of the asking price for the real thing. The guy gives her his number, and Sam convinces Carrie to go with her to his house in the Valley (a poor, run-down part of the city) to buy some more. Carrie is unable to bring herself to pay for the bags, as her new sense of purpose won't allow her to indulge in fakery. Even if everyone else was fooled she knows that she would never be. The fake bag becomes a symbol of both Charlotte's marriage (it's she who points this out), because it's perfect on the outside but flawed and obviously fake *inside*, and of LA itself, because it's shiny and beautiful on the outside but ultimately tacky, tarnished and not worth it.

Samantha: Across the crowded party Samantha catches sight of Hugh Hefner. This is, she feels, not a celebrity sighting but *the* celebrity sighting. Samantha has worshipped Hugh Hefner since she was old enough to steal her father's *Playboy* magazines. When Charlotte turns up, all tearful and alone, Samantha suggests that they all go to a party at the Playboy mansion to cheer Charlotte up. 'Why would that cheer her up?' asks an astonished Miranda. 'Does she look like a 22-year-old frat boy?'

Out and About: Nevertheless, they attend, but nothing really goes right once they get there. Samantha has her fake bag stolen and is forcibly ejected after falsely accusing a Bunny of having committed the crime. Charlotte is enraged when a man she's talking to offers to buy her 'some boobs', and Miranda's contempt for the whole occasion is best expressed by her comment upon seeing a pool full of frolicking Bunnies. 'Look, tit soup.' They decide to go. Home. To New York. Right then.

Also Starring: Carrie Fisher, the daughter of Hollywood icon Debbie Reynolds (*Singin' in the Rain*) and actor Eddie Fisher, will forever be remembered as Princess Leia Organa in *Star Wars* (George Lucas, 1977) and its sequels, *The Empire Strikes Back* (Irving Kershner, 1980) and *Return of the Jedi* (Richard Marquand, 1983), although as this episode makes clear, these days she prefers to be thought of as more of a writer than an actress. Highlights of her more-extensive-than-you-think CV of film roles include a startlingly funny cameo as a therapist in *Austin Powers: International Man of Mystery* (Jay Roach, 1997), her debut, as young seductress Lorna, in *Shampoo* (Hal Ashby, 1975) and a part in the Oscar-winning *Hannah & Her Sisters* (Woody Allen, 1986). She's also in *The Burbs* (Joe Dante, 1989), the insipid *Drop Dead Fred* (Ate de Jong, 1991) and the wonderful *When Harry Met Sally* (Rob Reiner, 1987). In recent years she has made a number of guest appearances in TV shows such as *Ellen*, *Ruby* and *Frasier*. As de facto Hollywood royalty from birth, she's had quite a tough time of it, as detailed in her fascinating memoir *Postcards From the Edge*, which she adapted into an excellent film script for director Mike Nicholls in 1990. Other work as a writer includes the celebrated TV movie *These Old Broads* (Matthew Diamond, 2001), featuring her mother, Joan Collins and Elizabeth Taylor, the novels

Surrender the Pink and *Delusions of Grandma*, and an episode of the TV series *The Young Indiana Jones Chronicles* for *Star Wars* creator George Lucas.

Hugh Hefner is the founder of the Playboy Empire, and has somehow managed to become regarded as a lovable national institution in the United States despite being an old pornographer.

The extremely talented Vince Vaughn (Keith) played Norman Bates in Gus Van Sant's superb 1998 remake of Alfred Hitchcock's 1960 classic *Psycho*, and appeared in *The Lost World: Jurassic Park* (Steven Spielberg, 1995). Other films include the tedious, pompous and awful *The Cell* (Tarsem Singh, 2000), and the brilliant *Swingers* (Doug Liman, 1996).

And So ...: 'The sight of all these whitened teeth is blinding.' Not quite as wonderful as the last episode and saddled with the 'message' that New York is better than LA because it's more real, but this is still really rather fine. That said, they do a good job of convincing you of the undesirability of LA's tacky, false, insincere side. As with **43**, 'Escape From New York', there's a real sense of place that comes from the extensive LA filming, and the juxtaposition of one movie star playing herself while another plays a character is pleasingly self-referential. It's just a shame that the semi-frequent pops at *Friends*, itself a great television series, are so smug, petty and unfair.

45
Hot Child in the City

24 September 2000

Written by Allan Heinberg
Directed by Michael Spiller

Guest Cast
Kyle MacLachlan (Trey MacDougal) Kane Peterson (Wade Adams)
Kat Dennings (Jenny Brier) Anita Gillette (Mrs Adams)
Don McLarty (Dr Talley) James Villemaire (Lance Bloom)

Peyton List (Girl #1) Blythe Auffarth (Girl #2)
Zoe Lukov (Sapphire Braces Girl) Ellen Stepansky (Sad Girl)
Gabe Hernandez (Lawyer) April Pressel (Waitress)

Charlotte: Charlotte and Trey go for couples counselling with a doctor whom Trey has had recommended to him through contacts. The doctor tells the couple that he can see that they have trouble verbalising their sexual difficulties, and so advises them to come up with new, innocent names for their genitalia that they won't have trouble saying. Once the names have been decided upon, Charlotte tells her sorry tale about how Trey is unwilling to place his 'Schooner' in her 'Rebecca'. At the end of their first session, Dr Talley tells Charlotte and Trey to go home and lie in bed together, then discuss their fondest sexual fantasises. Charlotte is willing to give it a go, but Trey is unimpressed, looking quizzically at Talley, whom he clearly regards as a crank, and asking him, 'Are you quite sure you went to Yale?'

That night in bed, Charlotte spins a fantasy that is both twee and sordid. She tells Trey about how she is a fairy princess in a forest, riding a unicorn. Suddenly she sees him, a pirate in buckskins, but a prince in disguise. He pulls her off her unicorn and tears off her petticoats . . . . Trey can't summon up the will to reveal his fantasies and simply says, 'I don't deserve you, I'm sorry,' and rolls over.

Later that night, Charlotte hears noises coming from their en-suite bathroom. Thinking that she's made Trey cry, she goes in to talk to him and finds him masturbating furiously to a magazine called *Jugs*. She brings this up at their next therapy session, and Trey claims that it was tension release. 'It helps me sleep!' In Dr Talley's opinion, the fact that the magazine was *Jugs* is a positive thing, as now 'at least we know he isn't gay'. Trey again says he was just using a magazine for tension release, 'It had nothing to do with my wife.' Talley tells Trey that he has to integrate his wife into his sexual routine, as someone who has no problem masturbating to magazines but can't rise to the occasion with a woman he loves has serious issues.

Charlotte herself provides the answer, sticking photographs of her own head over the faces of all the models in Trey's magazines. This he seems to like, and it enables Charlotte to find a use for all the wedding photograph proofs that she doesn't judge as suitable for framing.

Men: Carrie goes to a shoe store to get some Manolos re-soled, only to discover that it doesn't exist any more. In its place is a comic-book store. The guy behind the counter, grungy-looking twenty-something Wade Adams, not only works there but owns the store. Plus he writes and draws his own independent comic. Carrie tells him that she's a writer too, and he asks her if she's ever thought of writing comics. She says she hasn't. Then she notices that teenage boys in the store are looking at her. 'To them . . . you are Wonder Woman,' he says with a smile, indicating that his shop's clientele rarely see girls at all. Does she remember Wonder Woman? Of course she does. Wonder Woman was the one with the super-powered accessories. (Magic bracelets, if you're interested.)

A few days later Carrie receives a beautiful sketch of herself through the post. The envelope also contains Wade's phone number, and she decides to call it. They go on a date, and she goes back to his Central Park-adjacent apartment afterwards. She wonders how he can afford such luxury; the answer presents itself in the shape of a small woman in late middle age. He lives with his parents.

Samantha: Sam is hired to organise the Bar Mitzvah party of thirteen-year-old Jenny Brier. She wants to turn the job down because she doesn't do children's parties but Jenny quickly puts her in her place by explaining about the event's multi-million-dollar budget and A-list guest list. (So A-list that the Clinton family have been invited, although Jenny is sure they'll be too busy to come.) Organising the party brings Sam's friends into contact with Jenny, who is particularly impressed with Carrie. 'You are fucking fabulous. Your column about secret sex? Hello, my life . . .' she says, referring to the events of **6**, 'Secret Sex'. Miranda and Carrie are even more appalled by these 'little women' than

Samantha, 'They sound, and they dress . . . just like us . . .'
is the horrified realisation. The only question is, as far as
Carrie is concerned (and bearing her own recent behaviour
in mind), is it 13-year-olds that are acting like 34-year-olds
or are Carrie and friends behaving like teenagers? The
answer, of course, is a little of both, but her encounter with
Jenny does lead Samantha to appreciate her own childhood, which she loathed at the time, just a little more.

Miranda: In keeping with the 'adolescent trauma' theme of
this episode, Miranda is told by her dentist that she needs
to have braces on her teeth. She gets them fitted but hates
them. Although they will have a positive effect on her
dental health, they have a negative effect both socially and
psychologically, as they make her feel like the awkward
teenager she once was. After one failed date, lots of
food-caught-in-braces trauma and an argument at work,
she decides to do without them. She can't bear to go back
to high school – she only just got out alive the first time.

Carrie: Despite Samantha's advice, Carrie decides to carry
on dating Wade. She enjoys the vaguely childish feeling she
gets from having to work around her boyfriend's parents'
wishes. She also relishes Mrs Adams' hospitality, realising
that living with rich parents is like having servants that you
don't have to pay.
    She and Wade eat Kentucky Fried Chicken, drink and
smoke very expensive Canadian pot at his mom and dad's
place, and have sex at hers. It all seems to be going well,
until one night while they're smoking, his parents come
home early. It seems that the last time they found him
using illegal drugs they told him that if he ever brought
dope into their home again they would evict him. In order
to avoid his fate, Wade tells his parents that they are
Carrie's drugs, and that she brought them to the house.
Mrs Adams asks Carrie if this is true and Carrie says yes.
She did bring them into their house, she's sorry for doing
it, and she'll be sure to take them with her when she goes.
Cue a final scene of Carrie, Samantha and Miranda
playing loud records and getting royally stoned in her

apartment; the very image of thirty-somethings acting more than a little like teenagers, and having a wonderful time.

Trivia: Carrie's answering-machine tape goes, 'Hi, I'm not here, but my shoes are so leave them a message . . .' He he he.

And So . . . : 'We're adults, we have to at least pretend to know better . . .' A smashing script, which remembers that Samanatha is a first-class PR executive for the first time in ages, and mixes a traditional 'Oooh, they grow up so fast these days!' whinge with something a bit more subtle and clever. There's something quite joyous about Carrie's relationship with Wade, and the acknowledgement that adults behaving a bit like kids is more appropriate than kids behaving like adults is refreshingly healthy. Charlotte and Trey's plotline is treated like farce, and played that way it's incredibly funny stuff. The only problem really is that there's no way on earth any of the Bar Mitzvah girls are anything close to as young as thirteen, and this torpedoes the episode's credibility at a couple of crucial points.

46
Frenemies

1 October 2000

Written by Jenny Bicks
Directed by Michael Spiller

Guest Cast
Kyle MacLachlan (Trey MacDougal) Jane Summerhays (Claire Anne)
Dominic Fumasa (Jim) Sherri Parker Lee (Sydney)
Vivienne Benesch (Meg) Rebecca Wisocky (Stephanie)
Bill Dawes (Blond Guy) Kevin Stapleton (Dark Guy)
Jen Nevergole (Girl #1) Catherine Curtin (Girl #2)
Eunice Wong (Girl #3) Jenny Kravat (Woman #1)
Allison Furman (Woman #2) Robin Montague (Woman #3)
Abigail Rose Solomon (Anne) Shelley Dickinson (Liz)
Michael Tenaglia (Guy) Jen Rexford (Jen) Sondra James (Older Woman)

Carrie: Carrie has been asked to teach a class at New York's adult-learning centre, 'A seminar on where to meet men,' she explains to Miranda. 'Apparently I'm an expert.' She decides that it will work because she can offer the (younger) women of the seminar group the benefits of her extra years of experience. 'If you stay single in New York long enough you're supposed to get wiser about dating,' she points out, but as this episode goes on she becomes increasingly convinced that this isn't true, especially after her first class is a disaster and several of her tutees walk out on her. For her second class Carrie decides that she needs to demonstrate to her students that while there's no sure-fire way to meet men, a sure-fire way to not meet them is to sit in a lecture hall full of women. She take the entire class to a bar and they drink and chat. She uses her fee for the lecture to pay for everyone's drinks, and teaches them a few 'on the job' tricks, such as asking a man for a light. She makes five matches that night, and comes away proud of herself.

Charlotte: Charlotte's sex life still hasn't improved. Samantha explains to her that this is because Trey has a Madonna/whore complex. He sees Charlotte as his 'virginal wife', not a 'sexual plaything', and while the models in *Jugs* can arouse him, she can't turn him on because of the way he perceives her. 'Change how he sees you,' Sam advises. It takes Charlotte a while to put Sam's advice into practice, as the two women have a silly argument that leads to them not speaking for several days. Essentially, the now massively frustrated Charlotte contrives to be offended by Sam's lurid tales of her causal bedroom exploits, and very nearly calls Samantha 'a whore'. Sam is understandably upset by this comment, and while Miranda and Carrie hide behind their menus and try to stay neutral, the four don't meet as a group for a while to let things cool off.

Looking for comfort and people to, talk to Charlotte turns to her friends form her college fraternity, who are all WASPy and married. After a few drinks Charlotte becomes irritated by what she regards as her old friends' tweeness and naivety. She inadvertently shocks them by moaning publicly about Trey's impotence, asking drunkenly. 'Don't you ever want to be pounded hard?' Cue a trio of shocked faces. 'I just wanna be fucked . . . really fucked,' she complains, pointing out that she never expected to be so sexually frustrated while married. They all feel that Charlotte's choice of words is really rather inappropriate, and they tell her that they don't want to talk about sex. She realises that this is sometimes how *she* seems to Samantha, and when one of the group nearly calls her 'a whore', it occurs to her that she seems like Samantha to them. Perceptions and behaviour are all relative, she decides, and she leaves to be with her real friends.

Later, she puts Sam's plan into action, buying a beautiful sheer black and red nightgown, which is *very* sexy, and wearing it to bed with Trey. Trey is appalled and asks what she thinks she's wearing: 'You're my wife.' 'I'm not a Madonna and I'm not a whore,' she says, 'but I'm your wife and I'm sexual and I love you.' Amazed, Trey finds himself aroused by this, and they have sex. For a full minute and a half: which Charlotte accepts as a victory of sorts.

Samantha: During her estrangement from her friends Samantha meets Claire Anne, who comes across as a sort of southern Samantha; Ms Jones with a Tennessee accent. They hang together for a while, shouting out things like 'Two hot broads in a hot restaurant!' and egging each other on to drink more, proposition more men and do increasingly outrageous things. However, when Claire Anne goes as far as to sink below a table in a bar and give a man she's just met a blow job, Samantha is appalled. Despite herself, Sam realises that she has lines that can be crossed, and that relatively speaking how she sees Claire Anne is how Charlotte sometimes sees her, and how Claire Anne sees her is how she sometimes sees Charlotte. Like Charlotte before her, she walks away and finds her real friends.

Miranda: Miranda has been stood up. Due to meet a guy she met in Starbucks for dinner, she finds herself hung out to dry. Furious, she telephones his house ready to give him as much verbal abuse as she can muster. When she's put through to his mother she's a little put off, but not sufficiently to stop her berating the woman for how she raised her son. And this is when she's told that he died that afternoon, in the gym, of a heart attack at the age of 35. 'See,' says Carrie later, 'this is why I don't work out.' Miranda agrees to go to the wake, even though she didn't really know the guy, because she feels guilty about chewing out his bereaved mother. Carrie goes with her, and they bump into Jim, a guy Carrie dated eight years before. He asks Miranda out on a date and she agrees to go. Carrie tells Miranda that he's an asshole but Miranda insists that he's cute. She has a great time, so they date again. On the verge of this becoming serious, Miranda invites Carrie out for a drink with them, and it's here that Jim shows his true colours as a ranting, sarcastic, bitter man who wants to get at Carrie because of the way he thinks she treated him. Miranda and Carrie leave Jim shouting in the bar, and as they walk home Carrie does a little dance and says 'I told you so' over and over again. Miranda demands to know how she could have fallen for such an obvious asshole. 'Your date died, you panicked . . .' says Carrie, grinning. 'It's not a big deal.'

Trivia: The title refers to a term invented by Miranda to describe people who are quite like you, and that consequently you should be friends with, but whom you end up competing with instead.

And So . . .: 'Those that can't do teach, and those that can't teach do!' At its heart this is about Charlotte and Samantha learning to appreciate each other. It's also one of the few episodes recently to go out of its way to demonstrate what a good person Samantha is, showing her compassion and kindness and her deep concern for her friends' happiness. 'Frenemies' is a small episode in which very little happens, but what does happen is rather special.

47
What Goes Around Comes Around

8 October 2000

Written by Darren Star
Directed by Allen Coulter

Guest Cast

Bridget Moynahan (Natasha) Kyle MacLachlan (Trey MacDougal)
Frances Sternhagen (Bunny MacDougal)
Timothy Gibbs (Detective Stevens) Jacob Pitts (Sam Jones)
Scott Geyer (Charles) Allison Daugherty (Patty) Steve Harris (Gardner)
Brandon Fox (Mugging Man) Matthew Crane (Man)
Rhonda Cristou (Waitress) Karen Lee (Assistant)
Jason Harris (Male Voice #1) Spike Maclure (Male Voice #2)
Sean Oliver (Male Voice #3) Jodi Pynn (Stunt Carrie)
Bob Coletti (Stunt Man #1) Victor Chan (Stunt Man #2)

Charlotte: 'Two months into her marriage with Trey, Charlotte's life appeared to be a bed of roses. At least, that's how it seemed to an objective outsider ...' Of course, both Carrie and the audience know that Charlotte and Trey have never properly consummated their relationship and that she's an increasingly frustrated and lonely woman, isolated from a man she loves. We see Charlotte and Trey visiting his parents, and watch Trey and his brother play tennis. The MacDougal family estate is impressive, and we hear Trey's mother wax lyrical about the MacDougal family lineage. 'When you marry a MacDougal, you're marrying history,' she tells Charlotte.

Charlotte finds herself attracted to another bit of history, the MacDougals' gardener, the most recent in a long line of gardeners from the same family. She tells her friends about this, and Samantha is as blunt as ever, 'What's the point in being in the suburbs if you're not going to fuck a gardener?' she says, advising her to go for it.

At her next meeting with the gardener she kisses him before she can stop herself. Unfortunately she does so while being observed by her sister-in-law, who tells the family. Strangely the family are nonplussed, seemingly regarding adultery with their gardener's family as a MacDougal tradition. Trey's mother tells Charlotte that she really is a MacDougal now.

Later Trey tells her that it's OK if she cheats on him with the gardener; he says he knows he can't satisfy her, and for the sake of their marriage he's prepared to look the other way. But Charlotte doesn't want a husband who looks the other way, 'I want a husband that takes me in his arms and makes me not want to kiss the gardener.' She tells him that when they get back to New York, they 'should separate for a while'. Trey doesn't look at her, he just sadly says, 'All righty.'

Fashion (Crime) Victims: While out shopping, Carrie somehow manages to get lost somewhere south of Houston St, and there she's mugged at gunpoint. The guy takes her bag, her jewellery and (worst of all) her favourite pair of Manolo Blahniks, which are beautiful pink suede from the 1999 collection. After being through this ordeal Carrie runs around the streets of New York screaming 'He took my strappy sandals!' at the top of her voice.

Fit to Print: Carrie writes a column about 'relationship karma', a theory she has developed based on the idea that how you behave towards people in one relationship affects how other people behave towards you in others. She gets the idea when she falls down some stairs and hurts herself in exactly the way that Natasha did while pursuing her out of Big's apartment (see **42**, 'Don't Ask, Don't Tell').

Miranda: Miranda turns up at the police station to act as Carrie's lawyer after her mugging, and Detective Stevens, who is investigating the case, blatantly hits on her. 'I get mugged and you get him?' asks Carrie, astonished. They date, but Miranda is so nervous that she gets astoundingly drunk. She wakes up the next morning unsure as to whether or not she slept with Stevens, and finds that he's left her a phone number – for her local chapter of Alcoholics Anonymous.

Carrie: Natasha walks into the restaurant where the girls are eating; she sees them, shoots Carrie a look which makes her feel like she's 'Pol Pot or something', and then leaves. Carrie is amazed by the amount of hatred in Natasha's look, and it's up to Samantha to tell her that Natasha and Big's marriage is over. She's left him and is back working for Ralph Lauren. 'I can't believe I'm responsible for breaking up their marriage,' says Carrie, understanding just why Natasha looked at her with such contempt. She resolves to talk to Natasha and apologise to her for what she did.

Samantha: Samantha, due to a complex problem with the telephone exchange, meets a teenage virgin boy who is also called Sam Jones. She thinks he's 'kind of cute', and wonders if she should have sex with him. Give this Sam Jones the great first time she never had. She does, and is disturbed to discover the effect she's had on him. He practically stalks her, ranting and screaming about how he's in love with her, leading her to realise that by 'fucking that Sam Jones she was actually fucking herself'. By having had sex with the other Sam Jones, she's severely damaged her own life. Which is a really bizarre and very funny way of representing Carrie's theory of 'relationship karma'.

Wine and Dine: Now desperate to talk to Natasha, Carrie gets Samantha's assistant to bully Natasha's assistant into telling her where she's having lunch, and there she joins her unannounced. Natasha tells Carrie that if she doesn't leave she'll scream. Carrie says that she's only there to say her piece and then she'll go. And so she does, saying she didn't mean anything like this to happen but she can't take it away. 'So I came here today because I needed to say to you how sorry I am. I am deeply sorry for what I did to you. It was wrong. And I am sorry.' Carrie makes to go, but Natasha stops her and says that she's sorry too. Sorry that *she* met Big, fell in love with him and married him. Sorry that he cheated on her with Carrie, sorry that she ignored it for so long, sorry that she found Carrie in her home and sorry that she chased her down the stairs and broke her tooth. Sorry that even after painful dental surgery one tooth is still a different colour to all the others, and most of all she's sorry that Carrie came to apologise to her, because now, 'Not only have you ruined my marriage, you've ruined my lunch.'

And So . . .: 'The universe may not always play fair, but at least it's got a hell of a sense of humour.' A rumination on 'relationship karma', this script is a welcome return for series creator Darren Star, emotionally complex and filled with his own brand of humour. The bizarrely comic tales of Miranda and Samantha provide a perfectly balanced counterweight to the tragedy of Charlotte and Trey and Carrie's slow realisation as to just how badly she sometimes treats other people. This is the best episode of the season, and Sarah Jessica Parker has never been better than in her brief, awkward soul-bearing scene with Natasha. This is (tragically) Star's last script for the series he created. I don't give out ratings in this book, but if I did this would be an easy 10/10.

48
Cock a Doodle Do!

15 October 2000

Written by Michael Patrick King
Directed by Allen Coulter

Guest Cast
Chris Noth (Mr Big) David Eigenberg (Steve Brady)
John Corbett (Aidan Shaw) Kyle MacLachlan (Trey MacDougal)
Michael Jefferson (Destiny) T Oliver Reid (Chyna) Karen Covergirl (Joe)
Samia Shoaib (Animal Nurse) Emily Cline (Jessica)
Rebecca Boyd (Susan) Vivian Bang (Take-Out Woman)
Angela Ai (Chinese Waitress) Jack Harnett (Hot Guy)
Peter Bucossi (Stunt Co-ordinator) Jodi Pynn (Stunt Carrie)

Wine and Dine: It is less than a month since Charlotte walked out on husband Trey, and the girls are eating egg-white omelettes in the diner. During the course of the meal, Charlotte comes to the dreaded realisation that she'll never be 'single' again; she'll be divorced. She opines that 'the only thing worse than being 34 and single is being 34 and divorced', and it's up to Miranda to point out to her that being trapped in a marriage that doesn't work is worse than either.

Carrie: Carrie is woken up in the middle of the night by what appears to be the sound of roosters crowing. Although initially confused, she eventually remembers that her apartment is distressingly near a vet's. Cursing the fact that 'I let my frenzy for a rent-controlled apartment near Barney's override the fact that it was animal hospital adjacent', she goes over to complain. There the receptionist confirms that what Carrie heard was cockerels crowing – they have just rescued several roosters from an illegal cockfighting ring. The receptionist offers to lock the roosters in the basement rather than let them run free on the roof. Carrie turns her offer down, saying 'They have all that fight trauma – they need fresh air.'

However, after a few more sleepless nights, Carrie cracks and phones the animal hospital to accept their offer.

Samantha: Samantha is also rudely awoken in the middle of the night, but the cause of her discomfort is a crowd of pre-op transsexual prostitutes plying their trade outside her window. She's furious that she is '. . . paying a fortune to live in a neighbourhood that's trendy by day and tranny by night' and begins to wage war on those she sees as responsible.

Sam argues that she knows that TS prostitutes have a place in society but she doesn't think it should be under her window – the 'pseudo-straight married men from New Jersey have to get laid' – She dismisses the prostitutes as 'friendly neighbourhood, pre-op transsexual hookers, half man, half woman, totally annoying', and describes them to Carrie as the 'Up My Ass Players'.

One night later that week she politely asks them to move a little down the street, and they oblige, leading Carrie to comment that 'Samantha always knew how to get her way with men, even if they were half women'.

Later, however, the prostitutes return and the noise they make interrupts Samantha while she's having a night of casual sex in her apartment. She gets out of bed and throws a bucket of water out of the window on to the crowd below. They respond by returning fire with a volley of eggs.

Days later, as a show of reconciliation towards her foes, Sam throws a 'kiss and make up party' on the roof of her building. Several of the prostitutes, plus Charlotte, Carrie and Miranda attend, and they all drink 'Flirtinis', a cocktail described by Carrie as consisting of vodka, champagne and pineapple juice.

Sam claims she pays $7,000 a month in rent.

Miranda: Since splitting up with Steve, Miranda has fallen into a rut that even she describes as 'sitting home with my cat ordering the same thing [from the Chinese take-out] almost every night'. (Chicken and broccoli with brown sauce, brown rice and cold noodles if you're interested.)

She's mortally offended when one night she calls the China Garden to order her now traditional meal and the girl on the other end of the phone both knows in advance what she's about to order and giggles at her.

After some fretting, she decides to go down to the China Garden to confront the girl with the offensive giggle, but upon arrival she sees the girl working the phone and realises that she's simply the sort of person who giggles a lot.

As she goes to leave the China Garden, she sees Steve sitting at what used to be 'their' table. She jokes that she thought she got custody of this restaurant, and he claims he's only there because he loves the place's hot and sour soup. She realises that she keeps going back there because it was filled with happy memories. She and Steve discuss their relationship and her friends' take on it, leaving Steve to respond, 'Only you and I can ever know what happened between you and I. It's nobody else's business.'

She lives at Apartment 4F, 331 West 78th St, and has the phone number of the China Garden on speed dial.

Men: 'That's the thing about New York – you never know what's just around the corner.' While out shopping, Carrie and Miranda see their ex-boyfriends Steve and Aidan sitting at an outside bar. They duck into the open doorway of an apartment building and hide. Miranda says their options are runing the other way or moving into the building they're standing beside. Carrie is horrified. 'We can't run – these shoe straps will break.'

Eventually they pluck up the courage to walk past Aidan and Steve, and rather than blanking them they stop and chat. They're shocked to see that both men have dates.

Distressed, Carrie wonders how Aidan and Steve have managed to move on so quickly when she and Miranda haven't. This is, considering how Carrie treated Aidan, a shockingly shallow and offensive thing to think.

Girl Talk: Our four heroines have a night in at Charlotte's apartment, where they discuss their recent experiences with men. Charlotte claims that after relationships collapse, 'Women sit around moping and men just say "Alright" and then move on.' Sam takes offence at this generalisation. So would most men.

Sam tells Carrie that she looks back so much she should have a rear-view mirror, leading Miranda to comment that 'relationships may appear closer than they are'. The gang's conclusion, despite Carrie's objections, is that men never think anything is their fault. Charlotte swears off all contact with men, saying she's sick of them. Sam thinks she has gone insane.

Later, Carrie and Miranda row about Steve and Big, with Miranda condemning Carrie's *need* of Big's approval and his presence in her life, and Carrie angering Miranda by pointing out how unfairly she treated Steve. Steve showed a few tiny flaws and she decided to get rid of him, cutting him out of her life. 'You are so judgmental!' shouts Carrie.

Fit to Print: Later that night, Carrie sits at her PC and has what may be a moment of epiphany. 'What if everything isn't the man's fault?' She wonders if the problem *isn't* the most recent boyfriend 'or the one before that, or even the one before that . . . Could it be that the problem isn't them, but horror of horrors, it is us?'

Charlotte: Charlotte spends some quality time with the writings of the Dalai Lama, who is now the only man she can tolerate. Her reading is interrupted by Trey, who calls at her apartment to talk to her. 'Since you left I can't stop thinking about you,' he says. She points out that they're separated, but then she realises what's finally happening between them. As Carrie puts it, 'From somewhere deep inside, Trey's cock began to crow.' They have passionate sex against the wall, and afterwards Charlotte asks Trey if their sexual problems actually stemmed from the fact that Trey didn't really want to marry her. He denies that, but then admits that he never really wanted to get married at all, to anyone. He thought 'maybe it was time', and he was amazed that she wanted to marry him, and he knew that if he waited until he wanted to get married he'd never be able to find someone as wonderful as her again. What the future holds for them now neither of them knows.

Hey, Big Guy: Carrie receives a surprise phone call from Big, who asks her to lunch with him. They agree to meet at 2 p.m. at the Boat House Restaurant in Central Park.

Big has painted his bedroom walls red. He describes it as like sleeping in Communist China. Carrie says that a relationship between her and Big is like the red walls: 'A good idea in theory, but somehow it doesn't quite work.'

Big refers to the end of his marriage to Natasha and Carrie claims it was announced on the evening news.

Kisses: Miranda's advice to Carrie when she learns she's agreed to meet Mr Big for lunch is dramatically sensible. 'Don't let him kiss you,' she says. 'That seems to be where you get into trouble.' Unfortunately for both Carrie and Miranda, Big tries to kiss Carrie on the cheek as they meet. She tries to dodge out of the way and ends up falling into Central Park pond – taking him with her.

The City: Carrie reiterates that her apartment is near Barney's, the flagship store of the fashion chain, which is on Madison Avenue. It's famous for treating potential customers as too fat, too poor and, in the men's department, too straight. In **3**, 'Bay of Married Pigs,' Lou and Joe claimed to have registered their civil marriage there.

Fashion Victims: Carry has a 'Cream' baseball cap and wonders if she could get away with a 'Hang in there, baby' halter top. She and Miranda go shopping in her favourite thrift store, where Carrie pays special attention to the 'Two for $5' bin. For her meeting with Big she wears an absolutely gorgeous floral-print chiffon dress (by Richard Tyler) and accessorises it with a beautiful Christian Dior bag. What happens to them when she falls in the (rather polluted and green) pond in Central Park is something that I frankly dread to speculate about.

Trivia: The thumping disco track that plays over the closing credits is 'I Can See Happiness From Here' and appears courtesy of Tommy Boy Music.

And So . . .: 'Oh my God, I'm obsessing again.' This is a fantastically entertaining and emotionally literate season finale; and what's more one that hints at a possible new direction for the series. Charlotte and Trey make steps towards a permanent reconciliation, and having one of the gang happily married is inevitably going to alter the dynamic of the series' four main characters. Samantha gets her best plotline for weeks and Carrie finally seems to be prepared to shoulder some of the blame for her relationship traumas. Of course, if she ends up blaming herself entirely that'll be equally inappropriate. The sunny atmosphere of the roof party ensures that, despite its traumas, the season ends on an upbeat note: all the girls are together and there's plenty of jokes and booze. See you next year, ladies.

Season Four (2001)

Created by Darren Star
Based on the book by Candace Bushnell

Executive Consultant: Darren Star
Executive Producer: Michael Patrick King
Co-Producer/Unit Production Manager: Jane Raab
Co-Producer: Antonia Ellis
Consulting Producer: Jenny Bicks
Supervising Producer: Allen Heinberg
Co-Executive Producer: John Melfi
Co-Executive Producer: Cindy Chupack
Co-Executive Producer: Sarah Jessica Parker
Creative Consultant: Amy Harris
Creative Consultant: Jessica Bendinger
Creative Consultant: Judy Toll
Associate Producer: Mark McGann
Associate Producer: Grace Naughton

Regular Cast
Sarah Jessica Parker (Carrie Bradshaw) Kim Cattrall (Samantha Jones)
Kristin Davis (Charlotte York MacDougal)
Cynthia Nixon (Miranda Hobbes)

49
The Agony and the 'Ex'-tasy

3 June 2001

Written and Directed by Michael Patrick King

Guest Cast
Chris Noth (Mr Big) Willie Garson (Voice Of Stanford Blatch)
Kyle MacLachlan (Trey MacDougal) Costas Mandylor (Friar Fuck)
Yul Vasquez (Phil) Kathleen Bridget Kelly (Sheila)
Aidan Sullivan (Cute Hip Girl) Jonathan Dokuchitz (Danny)
Linda Halaska (Hailey) Annamaria Pace (Hostess) Katie Zeiner (Jill)
David Costelloe (Waiter) Chuck Bunting (Construction Worker)
Douglas McInnis (Construction Worker)

Out and About: The new season begins with upbeat music
and a montage of Carrie and co. heading out to a party –

an engagement party, to be more precise. Danny, a guy they've all known for about ten years and with whom Samantha has apparently had sex, is celebrating his forthcoming marriage in the traditional manner. 'If you are single there is one thing you should always take with you when you go out on a Saturday night – your friends,' says Carrie. Sadly, by the end of the night three out of the foursome are feeling rather bad about themselves.

Charlotte: At the party someone compliments Charlotte on her wedding ring and asks her where her husband is. Charlotte blurts out a string of incomprehensible bits and bobs about her relationship with Trey to this complete stranger. Thoroughly demoralised, she goes to visit Trey in the middle of the night, banging on the door and hollering until he lets her in. 'Thank God – I thought it was the four horsemen of the Apocalypse,' he deadpans. Charlotte explains that she's made some notes about their relationship which she wants to work through with him. 'Whatever it is we're doing, it isn't working,' she explains. Trey tries to get Charlotte to have sex with him, as if this will solve all their problems. He's almost persuaded her when he prematurely ejaculates over her leg.

Miranda: Quizzed at the engagement party about her current dating status, Miranda denies she's seeing anyone special. In fact, she claims that she's 'seeing a whole bunch of unspecial guys', and asks the assembled women if they have 'a completely unremarkable friend or maybe a houseplant' that she could go to dinner with on a Saturday night. Later she tells Carrie that 'society regards people our age as sad'; she makes jokes about being single as a defence mechanism. Her problem is ameliorated for her when she meets an old friend Sheila in the street, and Sheila almost immediately launches into a comedy routine about why she doesn't want kids (it's all to do with fabric stained with chocolate, apparently). Miranda realises that everyone has things in their life that they use as a source of comedy.

Samantha: Sam spends the party chatting up a man called Phil, whom Carrie has dismissed as having no soul. He's a TV agent and says he 'fucking loves it'.

Later, while heading out to do lunch with Carrie, Samantha spots a 'hot priest' standing outside a Franciscan church. She calls him 'Friar Fuck' and seems determined to seduce him. Turned on by his monk's robes, which she describes as '*so* Robin and his merry men', she is subsequently irritated when he rebuffs her advances because of a little thing – called a vow of chastity.

Girl Talk: There's a discussion about the concept of soul mates – and while Charlotte likes the idea that there is someone out there who'll 'complete' everyone, the others recoil from the idea. Samantha points out that believing that there's only one person perfect for everyone makes that ideal 'so unobtainable. You're set up to fail.' It makes the gap between the holy grail of the soul mate and the crushing reality even bigger.

Wine and Dine: Carrie's 35th birthday approaches, and she books a large table at a local restaurant where she hopes to be joined by Miranda et al. Turning up a little early, she is devastated when no one else arrives. At all. After several hours of waiting, she gets fed up and goes home, where she finds messages from all her friends explaining how the traffic in downtown Manhattan prevented them from reaching her until after she'd left the restaurant.

Fit to Print: 'Soul mates, reality or torture device?' Carrie ponders to her laptop.

Girl Talk: Carrie confesses to Charlotte that sitting at her birthday dinner table alone, she felt really sad at not having a man in her life to care about her. 'No special guy to wish me happy birthday,' she sniffs.

Fetishes: Miranda and Carrie both admit to fantasising about Russell Crowe, while Charlotte and Carrie both think George Clooney 'is like a Chanel suit – he'll always be in style'.

Fashion Victims: To attend her failed birthday bash, Carrie really dresses up, with matching (and midriff-revealing) red top and long skirt (Prada) and a beautiful blue woollen coat by French designer Jean-Charles de Castelbajac. Also check out her stars and stripes handbag earlier in the episode.

Trivia: Carrie describes Sam's obsession with the Franciscan monk as 'all very *Thorn Birds*', referring to the Richard Chamberlain-headlining mini-series, the TV event of 1983. Russell Crowe won an Oscar for his performance as Maximus, the slave who defied the Roman Empire in *Gladiator* (Ridley Scott, 2000). George Clooney shot to fame playing Doug Ross in the first four and a bit seasons of *ER*. He's now one of the biggest movie stars in the world with headline roles in contemporary classics such as *Three Kings* (David O Russell, 1999), *Out of Sight* (Steven Soderbergh, 1998) and *O Brother, Where Art Thou* (Joel Coen, 2000).

Willie Garson's cameo on the answerphone is uncredited.

Hey, Big Guy: At exactly midnight on her birthday Carrie phones Big's apartment (his number is 459 1905 and she can tap it in without looking it up still) to leave a message on his answerphone. She knows he's still in England, but she wants to invite him to her birthday dinner in case he's back in New York by that evening. He doesn't make it to the dinner, but as she walks home alone she spots his car outside her apartment. He's brought balloons and champagne, which they drink on the back seat of the limo. She jokingly berates him for being late, and he claims that it's OK because he's still on London time. Carrie points out that London is five hours ahead of New York, meaning that it's now 5 a.m. the day after her birthday in London. Big grins, looks puzzled and says, 'Then I'm really fucking late.' Carrie asks him what he thinks about the idea of soul mates (doesn't she remember **19**, 'The Chicken Dance'?). Big says that he likes the word 'soul' and the word 'mate', but 'other than that . . .'

And So . . .: 'Having three soul mates all nailed down made it a lot easier to spot those great nice guys to have fun with.' Carrie's 35th birthday pushes her into an existential crisis. This episode walks a very thin line between giving up and declaring that *everybody* needs *somebody,* and celebrating the defiantly single attitude that the series proposed at its outset. It's strangely unfocused and seems, rightly or wrongly, a little scared of its ultimate conclusion – which is that if you have good friends and some fun sex, then you don't actually need a permanent partner.

50
The Real Me

3 June 2001

Written and Directed by Michael Patrick King

Guest Cast
Willie Garson (Stanford Blatch) Margaret Cho (Lynne Cameron)
Mario Cantone (Anthony) James McCaffrey (Paul Denai)
Alan Cumming ('O') Daniel Travis (Dave)
Jeff Forney (Photographer) Tony Hale (Tiger)
Luca Calvani (Oscar's Assistant) Jose Llana (Damian)
Jon Antoon (Framer) Marisa Redanty (Doctor)
David A Clark (Man In Black) Adrian Martinez (Delivery Boy)
Fredda Tone (Waitress) Heidi Klum (Herself) Kevyn Aucoin (Himself)
Orlanda Pita (Himself) Ed Koch (Himself)
Peter Bucossi (Stunt Coordinator)

Carrie: Fashion show organiser Lynne Cameron is arranging a show where the clothes will be catwalked by a mix of professional models and 'real people', ordinary New Yorkers who have style. As 'no one is more New York or has more style' than Carrie Bradshaw, she's high on Lynne's list of potential clotheshorses. Having never seen herself as a model, Carrie is reluctant to take the plunge. Later Charlotte points out that Carrie has to do it because, quite simply, she *lives* for fashion. Boxed in by this flawless argument, Carrie agrees.

Samantha: Sam is attempting to only eat organic food, and has taken to drinking hot water with lemon instead of coffee. Unfortunately she's struggling against cravings for a Big Mac all the time. She's also planning to get nude photographs taken of herself. Denying that this is anything to do with exhibitionism, she explains that she wants to have a picture of how she looks now to look at when she gets old, so she'll always remember how 'hot' she was. After the pictures have been taken, however, she shows them to every man she meets, fishing for compliments, but even the guy in the frame shop seems uninterested. Eventually the fat guy delivering her illicit cheeseburger and fries sees the pictures and compliments her on her looks. Cheered up, she gives him an excessively large tip.

Miranda: Miranda gets picked up while working out in her gym. The guy, Dave, asks her out on a date, and tells her that he finds her very sexy. Miranda affects to be confused by this, phoning Carrie and telling her that she considers herself '. . . smart, yes. Sometimes *cute* but never sexy – sexy is the thing I try to get them to see me as *after* I win them over with my personality.' They date once, and his obvious attraction to her buoys up her confidence in herself. They then go out on a second date, where he seems far less keen. Afterwards he doesn't call her. At the gym, he tells Miranda that she struck him as 'full of herself', her newfound confidence in her own sex appeal scaring off the guy that had given it to her.

Charlotte: Unimpressed with her gynaecologist's diagnostic powers, Charlotte switches to Carrie's doctor. She informs her that she has Vulvadinia and prescribes her anti-depressants. Charlotte protests that she isn't depressed – and the doctor tells her that it's her *vagina* that's depressed, not *her*. A bit confused, Charlotte brings it up with her friends. During the course of the conversation she admits that she's never seen herself up close, as she considers female genitalia ugly. Appalled, Sam demands that Charlotte examine herself thoroughly, preferably immediately. All she needs is Sam's pocket mirror and a few minutes in the restroom. Unimpressed by this suggestion, Charlotte eventually examines herself with a mirror in the privacy of her own home; and discovers her genitalia are not as ugly as she previously thought.

Men: Poor Stanford Blatch is desperate for a man, and tells Carrie he's thinking of hiring prostitutes. Carrie is appalled and asks him why he'd do such a thing, 'Carrie, I know what I look like,' he replies. Bemused, she kisses him on the cheek and says, 'Then you can't see what I see.' Carrie and Charlotte try to set Stanford up with Charlotte's wedding planner, Anthony (see **41**, 'Running with Scissors') who we are told is Sicilian (which is definitely not Italian). They hate each other.

Charlotte refers to Stanford looking like actor Ed Harris (as he himself did in **9**, 'The Turtle and the Hare').

Fit to Print: After seeing all the mini perspective crises her friends appear to be going through, Carrie sits at her laptop and ponders, 'Why is it that we can see our friends perfectly, but when it comes to ourselves no matter how hard we look we can never see ourselves clearly?'

The City: Carrie describes the fashionable bar in which she and Stanford are having a quiet drink as located 'on the corner of right now and everyone there, the place to see and be seen', which I can't seem to find in my *New York A to Z*.

Kisses: Miranda snogs Dave on their first date, but not their second. Carrie kisses the photographer Paul Denai, whose work she admires. When Stanford teases her about her 'new boyfriend', she dismisses it, saying it was only a kiss.

Trivia: This episode and the preceding one were shown as a one-hour block on 3 June 2001. The originally aired versions of the episodes only have one set of closing credits (shown at the end of this episode) which covers the cast and crew for both **49**, 'The Agony and The "Ex"-tasy' and

50, 'The Real Me'. These are the first episodes on which series creator Darren Star isn't credited as executive producer. Star had moved on to other projects, leaving the running of the series in the hands of the *other* executive producer, Michael Patrick King, who also wrote and directed these two back-to-back instalments.

Fashion Victims: 'Gucci and Dolce and Dior! Oh my!' chorus Carrie and Stanford as they are shown around the backstage clothes store at the fashion show. When presented with what she's to wear, Carrie initially demurs, 'I have a certain look . . . and I don't think jewelled panties is it', but is eventually persuaded to wear a revealing flesh-baring Dolce & Gabbana bra in black satin and flesh-tone nude rhinestone panties by theatrical costumier William Ivey Long. For the sake of modesty she covers up (a little) with a blue satin belted trench coat, also by Dolce & Gabbana. Her Manolo Blahnik apple-green stiletto sandals are quite breathtaking. Despite her reservations she looks fabulous, although not as fabulous as she did earlier in her spring 2001 black floral satin dress, again from D & G.

Carrie confirms her status as the ultimate fashion victim by telling Paul that when she was very broke she used to sometimes buy *Vogue* rather than food.

Out and About: The time has come for Carrie's catwalk debut, and she's on right before Heidi Klum. There's a nice little 'girls bonding' scene between the two of them and then Carrie struts out – only to fall flat on her face in front of the whole of the New York glitterati. When Ms Klum is forced to step over her, a shocked Stanford shouts out, 'Oh my God! She's fashion roadkill!' Struggling to her feet, Carrie presses on with the show because 'when real people fall down in life they get right back up and keep on walking'.

Also Starring: Alan Cumming is a versatile Scottish actor/writer/director with many stage and screen credits.

He was in the Broadway and London casts of the multi-award-wining musical *Rent*, played a desk clerk with eyes for Tom Cruise in tremendously good non-erotic anti-conspiracy thriller *Eyes Wide Shut* (Stanley Kubrick, 1999) and was villainous computer hacker Boris in perhaps the ultimate James Bond thriller, *GoldenEye* (Martin Campbell, 1996). He also co-wrote (with Forbes Masson) and starred in popular BBC2 sitcom *The High Life* in the mid-90s and plays Kurt Wagner ('The Incredible Nightcrawler!') in the *X-Men* film series.

Ed Koch was the (Democrat) mayor of New York from 1978 to 1990, serving three full elected terms of office. Now a political commentator working in radio and television, he is the author of no fewer than twelve books and countless book, film and restaurant reviews. A trained lawyer, he is also a partner in the law firm Robinson Silverman Pearce Aronsohn & Berman LLP. Credited with restoring financial stability to NYC during his administration, he is widely revered by the people of New York City.

Supermodel Heidi Klum has also played herself in episodes of the New York set sitcom *Spin City*, alongside Michael J Fox.

Kevyn Aucoin is an internationally revered make-up artist whose books *Making Faces* and *The Art of Makeup* are considered set texts by many in his profession.

Orlanda Pita is a real-life celebrity hairstylist for Dolce & Gabbana.

I'm going to go out on a limb and say that Margaret Cho's performance in this episode is *shockingly* awful, but that Alan Cumming is a delight.

And So . . . : 'I don't have time to decipher the levels of queendom in your world right now.' Hmmm. Good bits with Carrie, yet another silly Charlotte-is-a-prude sequence, an underdeveloped Miranda plotline and a dumb Sam story do not a fully rounded episode make! Shame they had to make Carrie fall on her face on the catwalk too. The answer to Oscar's question of 'Do we likee?' has to, be 'Some of it, yeah.'

51
Defining Moments

10 June 2001

Written by Jenny Bicks
Directed by Allen Coulter

Guest Cast
Chris Noth (Mr Big) Kyle MacLachlan (Trey MacDougal)
Craig Bierko (Ray King) Sonia Braga (Maria Diega Reas)
Jim Gaffigan (Doug) Molly Russell (Shay)
Orlagh Cassidy (Park Avenue Woman #1)
Karen Culp (Park Ave Woman #2) Adrian Sevan (Beautiful Woman)
Rob Mounsey (Pianist) Chris Colombo (Stunt Double Driver)

Carrie: Carrie and Big are seeing each other again. They're simply friends, and they're having fun. No sex, no pressure, no pain. 'Now that Big and I weren't playing the dating game we were free to just play, and it had never been better.' All seems to be going well – until Carrie shows an interest in someone else, that is.

Out and About: Carrie and Big go to a tiny jazz club in the East Village. 'Aren't these cats amazing?' he asks. Agog at his fifties slang, she replies, 'Loosen up, baby, we're below 14th St,' he says, grinning, as he orders more drinks. Both Carrie and Big notice the bass player eyeing Carrie up, and eventually he passes her a note asking if Big is her boyfriend. Coyly, she shakes her head.

Later, the bass player introduces himself as Ray King. He's not merely the bass player; he's the owner of the club, and several others to boot. After some chat, he suggests that he, Carrie and Big share a cab back to the part of the city in which they all live. Big reluctantly agrees, and has to be talked out of calling for his limo.

As they ride back to the Upper East Side, Ray chats Carrie up while Big opines that 'cabs are bullshit'. When they arrive back at Carrie's, Big leaps out of the cab with her and waves the driver and Ray on. 'Didn't think I had that groovy jazz club in me, did you?' he says, standing on the sidewalk. Carrie is unimpressed. Ray will think they're together. Big nods. It's all a big joke to him.

Later Ray phones Carrie and asks her to go out with him on Saturday night. She says yes.

Samantha: At an opening at Charlotte's gallery, Samantha meets the beautiful Portuguese artist Maria Diega Reas. Keen to buy some examples of her work, Sam chats to Maria and asks her why there aren't any hot guys at the opening. Maria tells Sam she's gay, so she didn't see the point in inviting hot guys. Sam says that the almost exclusively female crowd may be fine from Maria's point of view, but what is she supposed to do? Maria finds Sam funny and invites her to go to her house for a private viewing of some works in progress. Sam accepts.

Once there, Maria invites Samantha to help her paint, and she agrees. Slowly Sam realises that Maria is trying to seduce her, and backs away. 'I've done the girl thing, once . . . twice, usually involving a guy.' Though it was nice, 'I'm not a relationship person and you're really something.' She asks if she and Maria can be friends.

Charlotte: Dr and Mrs York MacDougal are attending Dr and Mrs Young's cocktail party. Trey is, as he always seems to be these days, feeling rather up for exactly the sort of marital relations he had such problems with last season. 'My estranged wife has a damn fine ass,' he tells her in full view of the other party guests, and then convinces her to have sex with him in the room that Mrs Young has set aside for her guests' coats.

Later Charlotte confides to her friends that she and Trey have had sex in numerous public places including a cinema, a restaurant bathroom and the coatroom at the cocktail party. Fearing her life can be summed up with the phrase 'Fucking against a hand dryer' Charlotte worries about how she should define her and Trey's relationship. 'Is he my boyfriend or my lover or my ex-husband whom I occasionally have sex with in coatrooms?' she asks. No one has an answer.

A few days later Trey tries to convince Charlotte to have sex with him in the back of a moving cab. Charlotte objects

– they are only five blocks from his house. Why can't they go back there and have sex in his bed? Trey is upset, and Charlotte asks if he fears that once they're back in his bed he'll suffer the same performance anxiety as before. He tells her that he doesn't think this is the sort of thing they should talk about in front of a cab driver, and she points out that a few seconds before he was prepared to have sex in front of a cab driver. She storms out of the cab, leaving him on his own.

After a while he calls her and apologises and politely asks her if she would consider making love with him in his bed at home. Smiling, Charlotte agrees. It seems that they may be near to pushing their relationship into something resembling the marriage she's always wanted.

Miranda: Miranda's advice to Carrie vis-à-vis 'having fun' with Big is typically sensible. Hanging with an ex is a 'slippery slope without boundaries. You never know what's gonna happen.'

Miranda herself is dating a newspaper cartoonist called Doug. They've been together about a month, and she's experiencing some barrier problems of her own.

One morning, after staying the night, Doug wanders into the bathroom where Miranda is cleaning her teeth and urinates into the toilet while she's standing there. Shocked by such intimacy, Miranda asks what her friends think about his casualness. Charlotte thinks it's a good thing – it means that he must be her boyfriend as only a boyfriend would be so casual about privacy. Miranda is freaked out. 'I don't want a boyfriend who does that!'

Persuaded by the others to be less uptight, she tries leaving the bathroom door open but is disturbed and revolted by the whole experience. Even worse, a few days later Doug leaves the bathroom door open while he's in there for a . . . longer stint. Faced with this, Miranda decides that, barrier or no barriers, 'An open-door dump [is] definitely worth dumping someone over'.

Fashion Victims: In Ray's jazz club, Carrie wears a Miu Miu black sleeveless pleated dress with Dolce & Gabbana black pumps and a lot of jewellery. Big is suave as hell in his Rene Lezard navy two-button suit.

Samantha wears a matching tortoise-print blouse and skirt from Celine to Charlotte's gallery opening. Personally I think it's horrible, but it clearly does something for Maria.

Also Starring: Craig Bierko is a well-respected New York stage actor whose movie roles include *Fear and Loathing in Las Vegas* (Terry Gilliam, 1998) and *The Long Kiss Goodnight* (Renny Harlin, 1996).

Sonia Braga is a Brazilian actress who largely works in South American cinema and who is consequently, despite her immense talent, is largely unknown in the USA.

Fit to Print: When 'you can date without sex, screw without dating and . . . keep most of your sex partners as friends long after the screwing is over, what really defines a relationship?' asks Carrie's column. The real issue, of course, is 'defining' itself.

Hey, Big Guy: At one point Big says to Carrie, 'I'll watch from down here in case you trip,' which implies he may have been at the fashion show in **50**, 'The Real Me'.

Again they dodge out of giving Big a name as Carrie is interrupted when trying to introduce him to Ray.

Wine and Dine: Ray and Carrie attend the opening of a restaurant, with Samantha and Maria and Big and a model called Shay. Big insists that his appearance is a coincidence, and thanks to a lack of tables, he and Shay end up sharing with Ray, Carrie, Sam and Maria. It's a tense dinner, what with Shay sneaking off to the bathrooms to snort cocaine and Sam warning Big off Carrie, but the food at least is good. Everybody leaves except Maria and Samantha. Maria tells Sam that the way she stood up for Carrie was wonderful. Unfortunately it proved to Maria that she and Sam can't be friends. She's falling for her, and the best thing she can do is stop seeing her before she falls too far. Sam realises that she doesn't want to lose Maria, and suddenly her barriers come down. She opens herself not just to a relationship, not just to sex with a woman, but to a sexual relationship with another women.

And So . . .: 'Carrie likes the jazz man.' This is about boundaries and definitions, the boxes by which people define themselves. It's also warm and funny, and a *great* Samantha episode. The scene where she warns Big about breaking Carrie's heart again is *brilliant*. The way Big both consciously and unconsciously freezes out Carrie's potential boyfriend is subtly played by Noth, who is given a major and largely comedic role in an episode for the first time in what seems like an age. Is he seriously trying to disrupt Carrie's chances with another man, or is he just playing slightly inappropriate practical jokes on her? Noth's performance allows for both interpretations. It's great to have him and the witty, charming, playful side of Big back.

52
What's Sex Got To Do With It?

17 June 2001

Written by Nicole Avril
Directed by Allen Coulter

Guest Cast
Kyle MacLachlan (Trey MacDougal) Craig Bierko (Ray King)
Sonia Braga (Maria Diega Reas) John Grady (Clerk)
Buddy Bowzer (Street Saxophonist)

Carrie: Carrie is still dating Ray. As we join them they've visited three jazz clubs in one night, and then got back to his place to play jazz records. Carrie admits that she doesn't really like jazz, preferring instead something that has a tune she can follow, but Ray argues that she's got to learn to appreciate jazz for what it is, rather than criticising it for not being something that it isn't. 'The beauty of jazz is that it can go anywhere,' he says and then proceeds to seduce her by tickling her and 'playing her' like his double bass.

Samantha: 'Yes, ladies, I'm a lesbian,' announces Sam to her astonished friends, as she admits to her relationship with Maria. Carrie is amazed when Samantha tells her that although they're together they haven't yet had sex because she wants it to be special the first time. Sam also objects to the term lesbian, despite having used it herself. 'That's just a label like Gucci or Versace' she opines. Maria brings out a side of Sam not seen since her relationship with James (see **12**, Oh Come All Ye Faithful): the side that believes that sex can be more than a physical act and that relationships can be fulfilling, exciting things.

Charlotte: Dr and Mrs York MacDougal finally have sex in their marital bed. Charlotte describes the experience as 'almost mind-blowing'. After a second hefty sex session, Charlotte realises that she is ready to move back in with Trey as their relationship is now emotionally, socially and sexually fulfilling. She repeatedly tries to bring it up with Trey over the next few days, but all he seems to be able to talk about is how impressed he is with his own penis. Charlotte sadly tells Carrie that she previously had a relationship but no sex and now it appears that she's doomed to have sex but no relationship. This reminds Carrie of her own current predicament with Ray, and leads to the issue dominating her column.

Some days later, after they've had sex again, Charlotte becomes angry with Trey, demanding to know why he never wants to do anything other than have sex. She storms out of his apartment half-dressed leaving her wedding ring behind.

The next morning Trey knocks on the door of Charlotte's apartment. After a deep breath, he holds up her wedding ring and tells her that she left something behind the previous night. And then he says, 'I want you to move back in and get rid of this old apartment and stay all night every night and wake up next to me every morning and be my wife . . . Charlotte York MacDougal, will you re-marry me?' He places her wedding band back on her finger.

Miranda: Miranda is on strike. She claims to have made the conscious decision not to have sex until 'conditions improve', whatever that means. 'I can't go on any more bad dates,' she says. 'I would rather be home alone than out with some guy who sells socks on the Internet.' Having made this decision she quickly falls into the habit of eating seven chocolate eclairs while watching John Stewart's late-night satirical show on Comedy Central. Eventually going off eclairs, she's tempted to buy a whole chocolate cake, but is put off by the $74.50 price tag. She decides to bake a cheap packet-mix cake (under $5!) which she then eats so quickly she puts what's left of it into the bin to prevent herself from scoffing the lot. Later she goes back and picks the cake out of the rubbish. And eats it.

Girl Talk: The girls are thrown into disarray by Sam's Sapphic confession, with Miranda parodying her: 'Oh, I forget to tell you, I'm a fire hydrant.' Charlotte is unconvinced: 'She just ran out of men,' she claims.

Carrie tells her chums that sex with Ray is the best of her life. She confides that normally to have truly fantastic sex with someone she has to be in love with them, but she feels little for Ray and yet the sex is awesome.

Fetishes: Not a fetish, but Ray walks into Carrie's apartment while she's on the phone and says, 'I want a Bourbon and I want to go down on you. Not necessarily in that order.'

Fashion Victims: Ray's pork-pie hat, which Big rightly parodied last week, turns up again. It still looks silly.

Fit to Print: Faced with the complexities of her friends' lives, Carrie writes a column about how people have sex without relationships and relationships without sex.

Men: Ray gets the boot after two episodes; with Carrie concluding that his babbling, constant inattentiveness, inability to talk about *anything* and obsession with musical instruments are not wild and spontaneous, they're the result of severe Attention Deficit Disorder. She tries to stay with him for the sex, arguing to herself that she should appreciate Ray in the way he wants her to appreciate jazz, by liking him for what he is rather than condemning him for not being something that he isn't – but she eventually cracks.

Trivia: Trey's use of the archaic penis euphemism 'John Thomas' may be inspired by the fact that the director of photography on this (and many other) episodes of *Sex and the City* goes by that name.

And So . . .: 'Trey, I'm on the Mallard!' In the end, Sam and Charlotte get the relationship and the sex, Carrie gets the sex without the relationship but decides to quit, and Miranda gets neither. This episode skilfully mixes Miranda's really funny descent into chocolate-addled madness with pointed character plotlines for the other three. All the performers are really on the ball, but special praise must be reserved for Kyle MacLachlan who manages to deliver the line 'I've never seen my John Thomas so hard' with a straight face.

53
Ghost Town

24 June 2001

Written by Allan Heinberg
Directed by Michael Spiller

Guest Cast
David Eigenberg (Steve Brady) John Corbett (Aidan Shaw)
Kyle MacLachlan (Trey MacDougal)
Frances Sternhagen (Bunny MacDougal) Emily Cline (Jessica)
Sonia Braga (Maria Diega Reas) Joe Petcka (Sean)
Chris Meyer (Bartender) Jennifer Ward (Cashier)

Samantha: Cracks begin to show in Sam and Maria's relationship as Maria starts to realise just how many men Sam has had sex with after meeting three of them in one night. At the same time Samantha is beginning to lose interest, as the amount of sex they have declines and the amount of talking they do increases. She wants to go out, she wants to have fun, she wants *variety* in her life. Maria seems to think that all Samantha is really missing is 'dick', but increasingly Sam and the audience realise that it's not the specific relationship with Maria that's at fault, it's the idea of Sam being in a long-term relationship at all. After an acquaintance of Sam's turns up at her apartment in the early hours of the morning looking for sex, she and Maria have a *massive* row. Sam tells Maria how she feels and Maria voices her disgust at Sam's attitude to casual sex. When Sam says she wants fireworks in her life, Maria responds by throwing a fit and smashing as much of Sam's crockery as she can get her hands on. Even after this Maria remains convinced that all Sam is missing is 'dick', and buys her a strap-on in an attempt to repair the relation-ship. Although using it gives Sam a new appreciation of the effort men have to put into sex, it fails to save their doomed affair. They split up. 'I tried, I really did, but I'm not a relationship person,' Sam concludes to her friends.

Charlotte: Just when we thought Charlotte's marital prob-lems were over, she finds herself embroiled in a series of running battles with his tyrannical mother, Bunny. Not only does Bunny insist on 'helping' them select a new bed for their marital home, she also has a go at 'caring' for Trey while he's ill (a role that Charlotte sees as rightfully hers). Plus she objects to Charlotte's plan to redecorate her and Trey's apartment in something more appropriate to a young, married couple than the hideous, old-fashioned combination of plaid and wooden ducks that Bunny arranged for Trey when he moved in as a bachelor. After a confrontation with Charlotte, Bunny warns the younger woman that she's going to be around for ever. Worried, Charlotte tries to come up with a way to combat the old harpy, but fails. Fortunately, events sort themselves out as Bunny comes tearing into Charlotte and Trey's home to find them having sex. So traumatised is she by the sight of her little boy being ridden by his wife that she never again enters their home without an express invitation.

Miranda: 'New York City can be a terrifying place, but nothing is more frightening than the prospect of bumping into an ex before you've had your morning coffee.' Miranda bumps into Steve early one morning on her way to work. He's delighted to see her, tells her how good she looks, and when she asks him what's new, realises that this means she hasn't got her invitation yet. 'Invitation?' queries Miranda, and Steve explains that after months away from her he's finally taken her advice and opened his own bar.

Wine and Dine: Miranda discovers that Carrie too has been invited to the bar opening. Steve's partner in the venture is Carrie's ex Aidan, the furniture designer she two-timed with the then-married Big. Neither of them wants to go, fearing the consequences of digging up the past.

Girl Talk: There's a lovely scene where Carrie and Miranda sit on Miranda's bed, eat chips and talk about Aidan and Steve. It's not so much what's said, it's the relaxed intimacy of the setting and the warmth of the playing that really make the scene stand out.

Miranda becomes convinced that her apartment is haunted in a neat manifestation of the 'unfinished past' plotlines running elsewhere in the episode. She's told by Samantha and Charlotte (both of whom seem surprisingly confident about such things) that she has to acknowledge the ghost's presence, confront it and order it to leave her property. We don't see whether she does this or not, but Miranda and Carrie decide that this approach is the best one to take with the ghosts of past relationships, and they both decide to attend the bar opening.

Guy Talk: It turns out that Aidan hasn't invited Carrie to the opening at all. It was Steve who did so, partially because he thought (correctly) Miranda would be more likely to come if she could have Carrie's comforting presence by her side and partially because he secretly believes that Aidan and Carrie still have feelings for each other.

Men: A huge welcome back for the superb John Corbett and the equally excellent David Eigenberg, as Carrie and Miranda's exes Aidan and Steve. 'I'm just afraid the way I treated him is gonna haunt me for the rest of my life,' says Carrie of the unfortunate Mr Shaw. You think?

The City: Steve and Aidan's bar, Scout, is on Mulberry St.

Fashion Victims: Stepping out to the opening of Aidan's bar, Carrie combines an Agnes B. pointelle sweater with a black and white floral pattern skirt from Prada (spring 2001 collection). Also check out her awesome 'starfish coat' from Marni. Manolos (what else?) complete the ensemble.

Trivia: Aidan's surname is revealed to be Shaw (on the invitation to the bar opening). Before this episode aired several fan websites seemed to agree that it was Joff. Where this consensus comes from is unclear.

Jessica, Steve's girlfriend from **48**, 'Cock a Doodle Do!', makes another brief appearance.

It's odd that during the conversation about Miranda's apartment being haunted nobody mentions that the previous occupant died in there (see **17**, 'Four Women and a Funeral').

Fit to Print: 'If a relationship dies do we ever really give up the ghost, or are we forever haunted?' wonders Carrie's column this week.

Out and About: After much discussion, soul-searching and arguing, Carrie and Miranda both decide to go to the opening of Steve and Aidan's bar. Sam goes with them. It's a fabulous do, although Carrie's objection that 'It's not a party, it's a parade of our failed relationships!' has a ring of truth about it. Steve and Miranda talk in a civilised manner, while Carrie vainly tries to catch a glimpse of Aidan across the crowded room. He's wearing a suit and has shorn his once long and floppy locks. He looks better than he ever has done, something both Miranda and Samantha notice. Aidan locks eyes with Carrie and then looks down. She feels cheated. Is that it?

Carrie: Carrie sneaks out of the back of the bar to have a cigarette (a bar in which you can't smoke?) and finds Aidan sitting on a dumpster. They share a piece of cake and a few seconds of conversation before Steve comes to the door and tells Aidan it's time for the toast. Carrie suddenly realises something about her and Aidan. She hasn't put the ghost to bed, and meeting him has just made her haunting even stronger. 'What I felt . . . It was real.'

And So . . . : 'I'm still asleep. How could you have had an emotional mini-drama already?' The 'ghost town' of the title is New York itself, haunted by the ghosts of loves lost and abandoned. Ghosts, both metaphorical and (perhaps) literal, haunt our characters as they attempt to reconcile themselves with their pasts. Maria gets possessive about Sam's past life in the way that, say, Steve never did with Miranda, which is unfortunate as it spells the end for the two of them. Charlotte has to deal with Trey's past in the form of his mother, and Carrie and Miranda find themselves haunted by the physical remnants of lost loves. This is an intense episode with a downbeat ending. A goody.

54
Baby, Talk Is Cheap

1 July 2001

Written by Cindy Chupack
Directed by Michael Spiller

Guest Cast
David Eigenberg (Steve Brady) John Corbett (Aidan Shaw)
Kyle MacLachlan (Trey MacDougal) Laura Stepp (Tricia)
Russ Anderson (Cliff) John Bolger (Warren Dreyfous)
Michael Knowles (Marathon Man) Erica N Tazel (Dance Teacher)
Alexandra Palmari (Mary Elizabeth) Cody Arens (Martin)
Jack Rovello (Hank) Erique Cruz DeJesus (Jose)

Dudley Craig Demario (African Drummer)
Tim McCray (African Drummer)

Carrie: Since seeing Aidan at the bar, Carrie has missed him more and more. She's even started phoning him without the slightest idea of what she's going to say and then putting the phone down because she's afraid he'll answer. She describes this process as emotional Russian roulette. 'I think I want him back,' she says to her friends. 'First you have to be willing to accept that after what happened he might not want to hear it,' says Miranda practically. She advises her to find a non-confrontational way of approaching him, such as e-mail. Carrie explains that she's not on the net and has never sent an e-mail in her life, but is convinced by the others that it's worth a try.

She sends him a message, but due to her using the stupid online pseudonym 'Shoegirl' he deletes it without reading it, believing it to be junk mail.

Getting no reply, she gives up and phones him, asking him if he wants to go out with her and Miranda 'as a fun unit'. He's to bring Steve with him.

Samantha: Sam has received a pair of rubber nipples through the post. These are to be worn 'on top' of her own nipples but under her clothes. She believes that this will attract more men as 'nipples are huge at the moment'. She draws her friends' attention to the number of magazine photographs where women's nipples are visible through their clothes. 'It isn't that cold,' she insists. She believes that many people are using rubber nipples and that they're the next big thing.

She's recently been seeing Warren Dreyfous, a guy with whom the sex is fantastic, but there's just one thing wrong with him. He babytalks during sex, referring to Sam's 'tittie-witties' and using all sorts of other slightly sinister banalities. Initially willing to give him a chance ('I finally had to sit on his face to shut him up,' she tells her friends), Sam eventually cracks, asking him to stop his babbling. Mortally offended, he walks out on her during sex.

Charlotte: Charlotte is doing an amazing job of re-decorating her and Trey's apartment, and a discussion on what to do with the room that is currently Trey's study leads to the couple realising that they both want children sooner rather than later.

Miranda: While Carrie frets about Aidan, Miranda is absolutely the most perfect supportive best friend you could possibly imagine. She even goes to dinner with Carrie, Aidan and Steve, despite the trauma that hanging round with her ex gives her, and doesn't even seem to object too strongly to the fact that Steve makes an unwanted pass at her while walking home.

Fetishes: Miranda meets a guy while training for the marathon. They start training together midweek and wind up going back to hers for sex. Miranda is shocked to discover that he likes eating out her anus. She reports this to her friends. Sam's jealous, Carrie's shocked, and Charlotte freaks everybody out by admitting that this is something that she and Trey have tried. 'There's something happening to guys and the ass,' ponders Sam out loud, observing that several men she's been with recently have shown an interest in sexual activity involving the anus. She suspects it's a sea change in sexual fashions. Miranda eventually dumps the guy when she realises that he wants her to return the 'favour' . . .

Fashion Victims: Carrie wears a very preppy vintage rugby shirt which really, really suits her. Also check out her pseudo-schoolwear from Miguel Androver, complete with stripy tie and matching flat cap. Gorgeous.

Out shopping with the girls, Charlotte deliberately juxtaposes a dusty pink Tocca V-neck shell top with a stripy cashmere cardigan by 548. She accessorises with a lovely pink striped satchel from Rada.

Trivia: There's some astoundingly obvious product placement for both Apple and AOL. It's actually even more blatant than the Dolce & Gabbana product placement that runs riot through '50, The Real Me'. Unfortunately, by mentioning it here I've inadvertently continued it.

Carrie points out the basic inequality that grand gestures from men are interpreted as romantic, whereas from women they're generally regarded as bizarre and psychotic.

Fit to Print: 'Thirty-six hours and still no response from Aidan.' Hmmm, autobiographical column?

Out and About: On their double non-date, Carrie becomes convinced that Aidan is up for giving their relationship another try. She gets rid of Miranda and Steve and walks back to Aidan's with him, where she talks about 'them'. When he tells her he isn't interested in pursuing a renewed relationship she's confused, thinking that his body language during the dinner seemed to indicate that he was. She points out that he put his hands on hers. 'I was trying to make you comfortable,' he tells her. He tells her he can try friends but nothing more, and she presses him, saying, 'I love you. I still love you. I just wish that I could be your girlfriend again.' He bursts out an anguished, 'You broke my heart!' and she retreats to the safety of her home.

Later he goes round to her place and they make love without saying a word to one another. He leaves her apartment immediately afterwards, leaving Carrie to wonder if he simply wanted closure. The next day he appears outside her place, with Pete the dog on a lead. Smiling, Carrie offers to join him taking Pete for a walk and he accepts. Carrie, Aidan and Pete step out into the New York streets together.

And So . . .: 'OK, let's give it a try.' With dinner, some charm and a promise that she's changed, Carrie wins back Aidan. This is an unusually Carrie-centric episode in which Sam and Charlotte are reduced to comic relief and a potentially fascinating conversation between Miranda and Steve is pushed off screen by a dumb 'horror-at-a-sex-act' plot of the kind that Charlotte was always lumbered with back in Season One. Still, the real chemistry between Corbett and Parker and the feel-good ending mean this is an episode that leaves you cheery, excited and buzzing.

55
Time and Punishment

8 July 2001

Written by Jessica Bendinger
Directed by Michael Engler

Guest Cast
Chris Noth (Voice of Mr Big) John Corbett (Aidan Shaw)
Ted King (Brad) Gretchen Cleevely (Pia) Susie Misner (Shayna)
Joan Jaffrey Poust (Pedestrian)

Carrie: 'Once Aidan and I were back together it seemed like nothing had ever happened to break us apart . . .' Well, until Big calls Carrie's answerphone to tell her he's back in town and she should call him. After this their relationship gets rather tense – Carrie suspects that Aidan is cheating on her with a girl called Shayna who works at Steve's bar and who is teaching him how to play cards. Her suspicions are further awakened by how cold and distant he seems. He explains that he's just very tired, and that he has to deal with toxic chemicals at the furniture store this week, something he hates doing, but she remains unconvinced. 'It became very clear that I was being punished for my Big mistake,' Carrie says. 'Just how much shit was I willing to put up with?'

Charlotte: Charlotte quits her job, asking, 'What has the gallery ever done for me?' She plans to be a wife and mother, to assist Trey with the social and charitable sides of being a Manhattan society doctor and to continue redecorating their home. Miranda is unimpressed by Charlotte's decision, seeing Charlotte as one of many women who have careers and ambitions until marriage and then 'fold', adopting a far more traditional role in life. Charlotte is angry with Miranda's judgemental response, and argues that if the women's movement is about choice then she has the freedom to choose to be a wife and mother.

Miranda: After coming out of the shower, Miranda puts her neck out while arguing on the phone with Charlotte. Unable to move, she collapses naked on to her bathroom floor and calls Carrie and begs for help. Carrie has a meeting with her editor that day, and knowing how important the meeting is, Aidan offers to go to Miranda's aid in Carrie's place. When he gets there, Miranda is horrified that he isn't Carrie. Although Aidan manages to help her off the floor and then takes her to the chiropractor, Miranda is mortified that he has now seen her both naked and about as undignified as it is possible to be.

Girl Talk: Carrie goes round to see Miranda and takes bagels. She claims that she's there out of concern for Miranda's health, but Miranda correctly deduces that the real reason Carrie is there is for emotional support regarding Aidan. Enraged Miranda shouts, 'You are bullshit. You and your bullshit "cheer me up" bagels! Your boyfriend saw me naked, on the floor, lying on a bath mat.' Carrie apologises for her insensitivity and Miranda provides exactly the kind of support Carrie is searching for: 'Just because you cheated on him does not mean he's cheating on you.' She points out to Carrie that what she sees as Aidan punishing her may actually be her punishing herself.

Samantha: Taking someone else's cab is, for Samantha, right at the top of her list of 'unforgivable acts'. When a man steals her cab in Manhattan, she leaps inside it anyway and scolds him for doing so. Inevitably they wind up having sex and Samantha justifiably takes offence at an off-the-cuff comment he makes concerning the frequency of her waxing. She confronts him about this and asks how he'd feel if she took him to task about how hairy he is. As penance, she makes him shave off all of his body hair, an experience he actually rather enjoys – at least partially because it makes his penis look bigger.

Fit to Print: Carrie decides that relationships and partial lobotomies may be unexpectedly meant for each other, like peanut butter and chocolate. A partial lobotomy would allow someone in a relationship to forget all the attendant pain and hurt, leaving only the memories of fun trips and special holidays. This is a long-winded way of asking a simple question: 'Can you ever really forgive if you can't forget?'

Guy Talk: After Carrie sees Aidan talking to Shayna outside his shop, she yells at him and runs home. He follows her and asks her what's going on. She tells him that she feels he's punishing her and he denies it, although he admits that the idea of having sex with Shayna did cross his mind. She begs him to forgive her, and he puts his arms round her. Carrie knows that while they may never get back to what they had before she cheated on him with Big, they now have something new and different, and that this transitory phase in their relationship is now over.

Trivia: Chris Noth's brief appearance as Big's voice on the phone is uncredited.

And So . . .: 'You have to forgive me.' This is one of the most intense and emotionally powerful episodes of the entire season. The reason for its brilliance is simple – no one is actually right. Charlotte and Miranda argue, and each has very good reasons for saying what they say and believing what they believe. More importantly, although much of what Carrie believes to be Aidan punishing her turns out to be a product of her occasionally prominent paranoid streak, he freely admits that a) he hasn't yet entirely forgiven her for cheating on him, and b) part of him did briefly contemplate sleeping with Shayna in order to make her know how he felt. Because we know how much Carrie hurt Aidan *and* how important making their renewed relationship work is to Carrie, our sympathies are shared around between characters caught in conflict with each other. You'd have to have a heart of purest stone not to feel for them *both*. Elsewhere there are great scenes for Charlotte and Miranda, but an even more silly than usual Samantha subplot is only of the briefest interest.

56
My Motherboard, My Self

15 July 2001

Written by Julie Rottenberg & Elisa Zuritsky
Directed by Michael Engler

Guest Cast
John Corbett (Aidan Shaw) David Eigenberg (Steve Brady)
Becky Ann Baker (Betsy) Mary Pat Gleason (Lucille)
Aasif Mandvi (Dmitri) Peter Onorati (The Wrestling Coach 'Nick')
Elisabeth Canavan (Mourner) Louise Gallanda (Mourner)
Gordon Connell (Minister) Peter Bucosi (Stunt Coordinator)

Wine and Dine: 'The ultimate New York power lunch' is staged with Carrie, Charlotte, Miranda and Samantha convening for an hour in a smart square for sandwiches and chat. Carrie's life consists of Aidan, Aidan, Aidan, Miranda's of work, work and work and Charlotte's has turned into one long round of 'ovulating and decorating'.

Carrie: Carrie and Aidan have exchanged keys to their respective apartments. Charlotte sees this development in the relationship as big, but as Carrie punningly points out, it's the very opposite of 'Big'.

Fetishes: Sam has bought a pamphlet called *1,001 Sexual Positions* from a guy on a corner. She's planning to use them with a guy she's seeing, Nick, who is the wrestling coach at NYU. He's a big lad, and she describes him as 'an extra-strength rubber band'.

Miranda: Miranda's mother has died unexpectedly, and she wasn't with her when it happened. She has to travel to Philadelphia for the funeral, and she asks her friends to go along for emotional support.

Samantha: After hearing of Miranda's mother's death, Samantha is even more emotionally withdrawn than normal. Later she realises that she is now finding it impossible to reach orgasm. After having tried numerous sexual positions and various masturbatory techniques, she gives up, afraid that she has somehow used up her 'quota of orgasms'. Eventually she finds release of a different kind as she breaks down in tears at Miranda's mother's funeral.

Fit to Print: Carrie's computer crashes right in the middle of her writing her column. Traumatised by the loss of something that contained her whole life, she initially refuses to believe that her beloved laptop is gone. Aidan buys her a new computer, but she objects to what she sees as him becoming too involved in her life. Eventually she realises that, much as she had failed to back up her hard drive and support herself technically, she's running away from the emotional support Aidan is offering her.

Trivia: Aidan affectionately calls Carrie 'Ladybird', a probable reference to the nickname of the wife of 36th US President Lyndon B Johnson (1963–1969).

Aidan buys Carrie an Apple iBook and a brand spanking new zip drive, in yet another moment of stunningly unsubtle product placement.

Steve Brady turns up at Miranda's mother's funeral without being asked. Although credited for his role, David Eigenberg doesn't have any dialogue at all.

And So . . . : For a long time this episode looks like it isn't going to work – the paralleling of the three plotlines (Miranda being bereaved, Sam being unable to reach orgasm and Carrie's hard drive crashing) coming across as crass and awful – and yet, somehow, as the funeral scenes draw nearer, the script manages to turn the hard-drive plot into a complex metaphor for trust and Sam's bedroom difficulties stop being comic relief and become a symptom of her emotional recalcitrance. This is a moving, if unsubtle, episode in which Cynthia Nixon turns in an impressive, fraught performance.

57
Sex and the Country

22 July 2001

Written by Allan Heinberg
Directed by Michael Spiller

Guest Cast
Chris Noth (Mr Big) David Eigenberg (Steve Brady)
John Corbett (Aidan Shaw) Kyle MacLachlan (Trey MacDougal)
Frances Sternhagen (Bunny MacDougal)
Noemie Ditzler (Willow Summers – Image On Poster)
William Christian (Stud) Christopher Braden Jones (Farmer Luke)
Theresa Spruill (Nurse)

Carrie: Aidan, it turns out, is one of those types with a fashionably rustic New York country home. He wants Carrie to go there for a weekend away with him. Despite the fact that she describes herself as a 'bona-fide city girl' who would go to a late movie midweek, she reluctantly agrees. Once she gets there Carrie declares the house 'outdated even by civil war standards' and is horrified by the lack of air conditioning, mobile-phone coverage, take-outs and deafening silence. Mention is made of Carrie's inability to cook when she claims, 'The only thing I have ever successfully made in the kitchen is a mess and several small fires.'

Charlotte: Trey and Charlotte are still trying for a baby. Charlotte now has timers and alarms set to go off when she's ovulating so that she and Trey know when it's best to have sex. She turns him down at one point because it isn't the right time. She won't be ovulating for five days so tells him to 'conserve your juices until then so that they'll be at their most powerful'.

Her friends refer to the MacDougal family home in Connecticut as 'The Connecticut Compound'.

Miranda: Miranda's ex Steve Brady has testicular cancer. She's fazed by his casual attitude to his illness, and unimpressed by his doctor. She demands he sees hers. Steve repeatedly claims that his cancer is 'no big deal' until Miranda loses patience with him, shouting, 'It *is* a big fucking deal!' As she tells her friends later, 'First I yelled at him and then I made him cry.' Feeling bad about abusing him in this way, Miranda invites Steve over for beers, Chinese food and watching nonsense kung-fu movies. After a while he objects to the way he feels she's treating him – as an invalid. She says she's trying to apologise for shouting at him, and he tells her that thanks to her outburst he has a better doctor, a clearer diagnosis and an appointment for an operation to remove one of his testicles.

Miranda sits with Steve after he has had his operation. A nurse asks her if she's family, to which she replies that she's Steve's 'call in case of emergency'.

Fit to Print: Trapped in the country with Aidan, Carrie taps into her laptop the following words of wisdom: 'How much of ourselves should we be willing to compromise before we stop being ourselves? When does the art of compromise become compromised?' Eventually she comes to the conclusion that she can handle going out to Aidan's beloved cabin if he adds air conditioning. At the end of the episode she tells us that she learned to love the cabin eventually.

Hey, Big Guy: Carrie has a friendly dinner with Mr Big where he tells her that he's met someone but he can't tell her who. 'Is she your imaginary girlfriend?' Carrie taunts, before Big admits he's seeing Willow Summers, apparently a world-famous actress. (She appears to be modelled, more than anyone else, on Oscar winner and *Tomb Raider* [Simon West, 2001] star Angelina Jolie.)

Samantha: Sam is growing increasingly frustrated that every man she goes out with asks 'What are you doing next weekend?' after they've had sex. Driven to distraction by what she sees as an unwarranted intrusion into her time, she eventually decamps to the country with Carrie and Aidan, where she meets with a seemingly rough farmhand who turns out to be a city worker who moved upstate. They have sex in his barn and Sam is content – until he asks her, 'What are you doing next weekend?' It is, though, a bit weird that Carrie and Aidan dated for so long last year without him mentioning his upstate cabin and the seemingly endless work he's doing to improve it.

Trivia: Carrie quotes from George Orwell's legendary satire *Animal Farm* (1945).

The name of actress Willow Summers may be a play on the names of *Buffy the Vampire Slayer* characters Buffy *Summers* and *Willow* Rosenberg. This seems especially likely given that the film she's starring in has the word 'Angel' featured prominently on the poster. Angel is, of course, the name of another character created for the show.

And So . . .: 'You can't be friends with a squirrel.' Lots of good comedy here, mixing Carrie's overwrought fear of squirrels with her genuine horror at anything other than solidly urban living. Steve's cancer plotline comes out of the blue and is horrifying for both Miranda and the audience, but at least he appears to be well on his way to recovery as the episode ends.

58
The Belles of the Balls

29 July 2001

Written by Michael Patrick King
Directed by Michael Spiller

Guest Cast
Chris Noth (Mr Big) David Eigenberg (Steve Brady)
John Corbett (Aidan Shaw) Kyle MacLachlan (Trey MacDougal)
Noemie Ditzler (Willow Summers – Image On Magazine)
Jack Gwaltney (Allan Janus) James Remar (Richard Wright)
Allan Wasserman (Dr Manuel) Peter Pamela Rose (Willow's Voice)
Roy Farfrel (Stunt Coordinator)

Guy Talk: While playing pool against Steve and Aidan, Sam says a few inappropriate things given that Steve has just had one of his testicles removed, such as: 'I only have one ball left!'; 'It all comes down to one little ball.'

Miranda: Steve tells Miranda that he feels emasculated after his surgery and is considering having a prosthetic fitted. She tries to convince him that it won't be remotely important to any women he might end up dating but he makes it clear that it's important to him. He asks her to attend his appointment at the clinic with him to help him decide. Although fazed by the idea of 'testicle shopping', she does so. The doctor tells Steve that the prosthetics have not yet been fully tested and therefore may not be fully safe. Horrified by this, Miranda talks Steve out of buying one. Later, to convince him he's still 'a man', she has sex with him.

Charlotte: After three months of trying for a baby Charlotte and Trey are depressed that they've had no success. Charlotte tells Trey that her doctor thinks that he should have his sperm tested. He reacts badly to this, which Charlotte interprets as macho behaviour, but Trey explains to her that he's just nervous about discovering he has other problems in the genital area after all his difficulties last year (see **42**, 'Don't Ask, Don't Tell', among others). He goes to a clinic for a sperm count and he turns out to be 'fine . . . No, better than fine.'

Hey, Big Guy: Big has been repeatedly messed around by his movie-star girlfriend (see **57**, 'Sex and the Country') and he phones Carrie in search of emotional support. 'She can reach me, but I can't ever get her,' he explains, meaning in terms of being able to contact her both physically and emotionally. Later, after Carrie and Aidan have gone upstate to his cabin, Big calls and tells her he's been dumped by Willow. He needs someone to talk to. Carrie reluctantly invites him to the cabin. He turns up in the middle of the night and proceeds to get very drunk, moaning about how badly Willow has treated him. Despite everything, Aidan insists that Big sleep on the sofa rather than drive back to New York in his state.

Fashion Victims: Big in casualwear just doesn't seem right, somehow.

Playing pool, Sam looks awesome in a turquoise knit dress by Thierry Mugler.

Samantha: Sam goes for a PR job with Richard Wright, the hotelier. He's rather patronising, so when he tells her that he doesn't want to hire her she puts two and two together and comes up with basic sexism. 'What does he think I'm going to do?' she rages to her friends. 'Get my period and ruin his empire?' It later turns out that the real reason he doesn't want to hire her is that she's had sex with his architect and he doesn't want to have to deal with the potential emotional fallout. Rather than accept this, Samantha gets angry, telling Wright that if she was a man he'd have congratulated her on the fuck and given her the key to her office right away. She then storms out on the brink of tears. Later he calls her to tell her that he's impressed by her 'balls', and that she's hired despite his reservations.

Trivia: It's a bit plot-convenient that the first time we ever see Big too drunk to drive is the first time we ever see him without his chauffeur.

Aidan comes up with a complex metaphor about him being The Green Hornet and Mr Big being Batman and how, when they met, although everyone expected Batman to be proved the greater hero, it was The Green Hornet who came out on top. This is a reference to the three episodes of the 1960s *Batman* TV series that guest starred Van Williams (as The Green Hornet) and Bruce Lee (as Kato), the stars of US TV's *other* popular superhero/crime series (you guessed it) *The Green Hornet*. The episodes were 'Tut's Case is Shut' (29 September 1966) and the two-part story 'A Piece of the Action'/'Batman's Satisfaction' (1 and 2 March 1967). So now you know.

Men: The morning after he spends the night on Aidan's couch, Carrie convinces Big that he should try to get to know Aidan. Bluntly, if they can't get along then there'll be no room for Big in Carrie's life. Initially the guys get on OK, shooting hoops, but this quickly becomes a fight as the two knock hell out of each other in the mud. Pete the dog bites Big, trying to protect his master, and this brings the fight to an end. Then they all have breakfast together and the now sober Big explains his relationship with Willow to Aidan, who begins to feel some sympathy for his hated one-time rival.

Fit to Print: 'Maybe men and women aren't from different planets as pop culture would have us believe.'

And So . . .: 'I might feel like less of a man or something.' This is a clever and well-worked attempt to argue that much-vaunted differences between men and women are actually far less significant and nowhere near as absolute as some people choose to believe – with the two sexes' attitudes and outlooks constantly growing closer. The final scene, when Aidan and Big begin to bond over breakfast, is, for me, the funniest moment in the entire season.

59
Coulda, Woulda, Shoulda

5 August 2001

Written by Jenny Bicks
Directed by David Frankel

Guest Cast
David Eigenberg (Steve Brady) John Corbett (Aidan Shaw)
Kyle MacLachlan (Trey MacDougal) Peggy Gormley (Dr Peck)
Lucy Liu (Herself) Josh Burrows (Chad) Craig Chester (Hermes Clerk)
Stuart Rudin (Man) Maggie Lacey (Hostess) Sally Mayes (Nurse)
Peter Bucosi (Stunt Driver)

Miranda: Miranda is pregnant – the result of her one-night stand with Steve. She can't believe it – with Steve only having one testicle and her having one lazy ovary it seems improbable that it could happen at all. 'It's like the special Olympics of conception,' she claims. She's determined to have an abortion as a) she doesn't want to get back together with Steve *and* b) she simply doesn't have enough time in her life for a baby right now. She calls the clinic and asks for an appointment: 'I'm pregnant and I need not to be.' She decides that she can't even tell Steve as he'll want her to keep the baby.

She feels particularly bad about telling Charlotte as she knows how hard Charlotte has been trying for a baby.

Charlotte: It's been three months since the last episode, and five months since Trey and Charlotte started trying for a baby. Having discovered that Trey's sperm count is perfectly acceptable she has begun to blame herself for their failure to conceive. She and Trey visit another doctor for her to have some fertility tests, and she discovers that her body produces an unusually high amount of anti-sperm antibodies. Her chances of conceiving naturally are fifteen per cent of normal. Charlotte points out that she spent her entire twenties terrified of getting pregnant, and now it turns out that she could have been 'screwing around' to her heart's content.

Samantha: Samantha is booked to represent actress Lucy Liu. This is partially because Lucy approves of Sam's no-nonsense attitude and partially because she notices Sam tipping a waitress 25 per cent of the total bill. Lucy claims that she was once a waitress and is therefore always impressed by such generosity.

Girl Talk: Samantha reveals that she has had two abortions but doesn't elaborate with the details. Carrie had one way back in 1988 – the father was a waiter at The Saloon, they had sex once and she never told him that she was pregnant. Eventually Miranda backs out of having an abortion, deciding that at 35 and with only one ovary this may be her last chance to have a child.

Carrie: Aidan asks Carrie if she has ever had an abortion and she lies. Later she admits that she lied and he asks her why. She tells him that she was afraid he would judge her for something she did when she was in her early twenties.

Fashion Victims: Samantha desires a $4,000 Birken handbag, for which there is a five-year waiting list on top of the extreme price tag. Consumed by her desire for the bag, she claims that it's for Lucy Liu – and gets to skip the queue. Unfortunately for Sam the store deliver the finished bag to Lucy's hotel rather than to her, and while Lucy quite likes the bag she is unimpressed by Samantha's abuse of her name and fires her.

Check out Lucy in her 'J'adore Dior' shirt and combat pants. Cool, different and very sexy.

Also Starring: Lucy Liu, here appearing as herself, played Ling Woo in *Ally McBeal* (1998–2001). Her film work includes *Charlie's Angels* (Joseph McGinty Nichol, 2000) and its sequel, *Shanghai Noon* (Tom Dey, 2000), the Oscar-winning *Chicago* (Rob Marshall, 2002) and the glorious *Kill Bill – Volume One* (Quentin Tarantino, 2003). She is, as Samantha says, 'a big, big fucking star' and she's only going to get bigger.

Trivia: Carrie is still using her old laptop, so presumably she took the one Aidan gave her back (see **56**, 'My Motherboard, My Self'). It's also worth mentioning that at one point she refers to *the* great sitcom of the late 70s/early 80s, *Taxi*, and one of its cast, mulleted heart-throb Tony Danza.

And So . . .: 'No judgement!' The script to this episode very carefully walks a difficult line, absolutely refusing to make any moral judgements about the topic of abortion and instead simply illustrating the multiple responses of different people placed in similar situations. Carrie telling Aidan that Miranda is pregnant with Steve's baby puts him in an absolutely untenable position which he somehow manages to rise above. Samantha messes up really badly by abusing Lucy Liu's name and profile in an ultimately failed attempt to acquire a pricey accessory – rather stupid of her, really.

60
Just Say Yes

12 August 2001

Written by Cindy Chupack
Directed by David Frankel

Guest Cast
Chris Noth (Mr Big) David Eigenberg (Steve Brady)
John Corbett (Aidan Shaw) Kyle MacLachlan (Trey MacDougal)
Frances Sternhagen (Bunny MacDougal) James Remar (Richard Wright)
Greg Ainsworth (Co-Pilot) Gustavo Santamarina (Gelati Guy)
Scott Geyer (Charles MacDougal)

Carrie: Carrie's apartment building (which is city owned
and rent controlled, lest we forget) is going co-op, meaning
that residents have to either buy their apartments or move
out. Carrie is furious – she doesn't have the money to buy
her place. Aidan points out that *he* does. He says that he
could buy her apartment and one next to it and they could
knock the adjoining wall through and live together. She
asks him if this would make him her roommate or her
landlord, and he counters that it'd make him a bit of both.
He asks her to consider his idea.

A few days later, when attempting to clear up after
Aidan, Carrie finds a boxed engagement ring in with his
possessions. Suddenly she knows what's coming next.

Girl Talk: 'I saw the ring and I threw up,' Carrie tells the
girls at the diner. She goes on to explain that the trauma
of the idea of marriage was so huge that her stomach just
turned. She also tells them that she hated the ring. Can she
marry someone who doesn't know her well enough to pick
out a ring that accurately reflects her tastes? 'Wrong ring,
wrong guy,' is Sam's advice, until Miranda confesses that
she picked out the ring with Aidan. Carrie is unsure
whether or not she should accept his proposal should it
come. Is she ready for marriage?

Samantha: Talking to Richard Wright (see **58**, 'The Belles
of the Balls') about the possibility of Carrie accepting

Aidan's proposal, Sam demands to know why everybody has to get married and have children. 'It's so clichéd!' Wright agrees with her, asking, 'Who needs a wife when you have a life?' Hours later they're having sex on his private jet while heading to Rio.

Charlotte: Charlotte and Trey's attempts to have a baby are now reaching epic proportions. He's giving her hormone shots every night to boost her chances of conceiving and she's getting increasingly emotional as her desperation increases and her hormones run wild. After a particularly epic display in public, Trey asks Charlotte is she'll stop taking the hormones – and then if they can stop trying so hard for a baby. He tells her that he thinks he could be happy with just the two of them. They should try to conceive naturally through the traditional method of just having sex. Charlotte turns away from Trey, deeply upset.

Miranda: 'I don't know why they call it morning sickness when it lasts all day fucking long,' says Miranda, understandably fazed by the amount of vomiting she's doing now that she's two months gone. She finally gets round to telling Steve that she is pregnant and that the baby is his. She says he doesn't have to help support the child in any way, but that he can see the baby as it grows up it if he wants to. 'It's my decision and it's just something I want to do for me,' she explains.

Late one night Miranda opens the door of her apartment to find Steve on his knees, holding out a ring to her. 'Are you fucking crazy?' she shouts. 'That's your answer?' he replies, agog. She tells him that she doesn't want to marry him, and he responds by saying he doesn't want to marry her. She then quite sensibly demands to know what the fuck he thinks he's doing. He explains that he wants to be more to their child than someone who sees him in the playground occasionally. She tells him that he can play a major part in the raising of their child, but he questions her logic. '. . . Raise a kid together and not be together?' he asks. 'How can that work?' 'We'll figure it out,' she replies. '*We'll* figure it out?' he returns. She smiles at him.

Trivia: Aidan sings 'It's Not Unusual', the Tom Jones hit, in the shower.

Trey says that he's 43 years old.

Fit to Print: Anticipation of Aidan's impending marriage proposal leads Carrie to consider how you really know. 'Are there signs? Fireworks? Is it right when it feels comfortable or is comfortable a sign that there aren't any fireworks? How do you know when it's right?'

Hey, Big Guy: Carrie is failing to grab a cab on a busy street when Big's limousine rolls up and he leans out of the window and shouts, 'Hey, lady! Need a ride?' Carrie hops into the back of the limo. 'Admit it. You drive around looking for me, don't you?' she teases him. She tells him about Aidan and finding the ring, and he tells her that Aidan isn't the guy for her. She counters that Aidan may be the guy for her, but that she isn't ready for marriage yet. Big thinks she won't ever be ready, 'You're not the marrying kind.'

Out and About: The New York Scottish Society's Annual Highland Fling, which Trey's family attend, continuing to labour under the misapprehension that they're Scottish because some people that they're related to left there centuries before.

And So . . . : 'I love you, Carrie. There's no one I could love more. I want to live my life with you. What do you think?' says Aidan, kneeling in a New York Street. Carrie looks at the ring. It isn't the one she saw before – it's squarer in shape and with a bigger stone. It's also stunningly beautiful. She gasps. Aidan tells her he had another one, but he changed it for something more 'her'. Carrie looks at Aidan and says yes. This is a brilliant episode. Full marks.

61
The Good Fight

6 January 2002

Written by Michael Patrick King
Directed by Charles McDougall

Guest Cast
John Corbett (Aidan Shaw) Kyle MacLachlan (Trey MacDougal)
James Remar (Richard Wright) Robert John Burke (Walker Lewis)
Francis Beers (Mrs Cohen)

Carrie: Aidan has moved in, and Carrie is already feeling a little cramped. He's blocked one of the doors to her bathroom and, worse, has brought house plants. When the old lady who lives next door, and whose apartment Aidan has bought (see **60**, 'Just Say Yes'), informs the already squabbling couple that she won't be moving out for another month, all hell breaks loose. Aidan says he needs more space for his stuff (which he does) and Carrie gets cross when he tries to throw out some of her old stuff to make room (and who can blame her?). The row really gets out of control when Pete the dog starts chewing on an irreplaceable 1996 London Blahnik.

Later, they both apologise to each other, and Carrie explains to Aidan that she needs an hour to 'decompress' after finishing work each day. Eh? She's a freelance writer – she doesn't go to work, she sits at home and works irregular hours on her laptop, or carries it to coffee houses. She's talking rubbish here.

Samantha: Sam is still working for, and still having sex with, Richard Wright. She offers to give him a blow job in his glass-portioned office at one point, and later tells the girls about how fabulous she considers his dick to be. 'It's dick-tastic,' she explains. Richard gives her a long-stemmed pink rose, which she throws in the bin for lack of interest. It's pretty obvious that Sam is falling for Richard in a more permanent way, and he for her, but she doesn't want to admit it. She goes over to his apartment, to find he has set out a pool-side table for a romantic dinner for two. She berates him for this, telling him that she wants no part in such things, and they have sex in the pool instead. Later they dance, and Samantha finds herself crying. Is she really that afraid of intimacy?

Charlotte: Charlotte wants to have her friends over for a girls' night in. Trey thinks this is a good idea, until he's informed that he's not invited. The atmosphere between Charlotte and Trey has not been good since they stopped trying for a baby; with Charlotte finding the fact that they have a baby room but no baby to put in it quite traumatic. At one point Trey gives Charlotte a cardboard cutout of a baby because he seems to think that this will stop her feeling a void where a baby should be. He genuinely means it as a joke, and doesn't intend it to hurt her, but it's a very stupid and massively insensitive move.

Miranda: After a blind date with a guy so nice she wishes she'd made more effort, Miranda begins to wonder whether it's OK to have sex while pregnant, and specifically if it's OK to have sex with someone who isn't the baby's father. Eventually she decides it is, and goes to bed with him.

Wine and Dine: Charlotte's girls' dinner goes very badly: Trey forgets that he isn't supposed to be there, and both Miranda and Samantha have to rush off. Trey and Charlotte argue about the cardboard baby, and Trey ends up being exiled to the guest room.

Trivia: This episode, and the following five, were shot for inclusion in Season Four, and then held back until early 2002 (see **67**, 'Anchors Away'). Although referred to by HBO as the 'bonus season', they follow directly on, in story terms, from the previous episodes – and make far more sense if treated as part of Season Four.

Note: From this episode onwards the title sequence has been re-edited to remove the shot of the twin towers of the World Trade Center. It is, of course, the first episode shown after the 11 September 2001 attacks on New York and the Pentagon. As the episode was shot long before 11 September, there is no mention of the events of that day or the effects they had on New York and New Yorkers.

There was some press speculation on both sides of the Atlantic as to how the series would deal with such a trauma affecting the city where it was set. In the end the series, like NBC's *Friends*, simply ignores that day and its repercussions and while, for example, Carrie's apartment (given its often-stated location on 73rd Street) is not much of a walk from what is now 'Ground Zero', the repercussions of this are simply avoided. These 'bonus season' episodes and the subsequent fifth season move, without comment, from a pre-9/11 world to a post-9/11 one, but without acknowledging those events. This is because, simply, they're too terrible to be incorporated into sitcom or light drama. Episode **66**, 'I Heart NY', is a sort of love letter to New York, and it's the closest the series comes, indeed could feasibly come, to 'dealing' with 9/11.

And So . . .: 'When two halves move in together, it makes a whole lot of stuff.' Domestic bliss doesn't begin well for Carrie and Aidan, and Charlotte and Trey seem to be moving further apart. Samantha can't face up to her feelings for Richard, either. Well, at least Miranda's having fun. Pure sitcom with a dose of trauma. Ordinary.

62
All That Glitters . . .

13 January 2002

Written by Cindy Chupack
Directed by Charles McDougall

Guest Cast
Willie Garson (Stanford Blatch) John Corbett (Aidan Shaw)
Kyle MacLachlan (Trey MacDougal) James Remar (Richard Wright)
Mario Cantone (Anthony Marentino) Murray Bartlett (Oliver)
Daniel Sarafin Sauli (Max) Chris Payne Gilbert (Gordon)
Tracy Tobin (Celeste) Joe Duer (Gorgeous Gay Guy)

Out and About: Annoyed that an exhausted Aidan doesn't want to go out on a Saturday night, preferring instead to veg out in front of the TV with a big bucket of Kentucky Fried Chicken, Carrie organises a girls' night out with the three usual suspects. Miranda's only proviso is that they go somewhere where she won't feel fat because she's pregnant; somehow this translates into them heading out to a gay bar.

Samantha: Sam starts popping Ecstasy at the bar; and then heads over to Richard's place because she's heard that sex on E is meant to be amazing. (Sam's got to her age and with her lifestyle and has never yet taken E? Come on . . .) Staying true to the tradition that E dismantles your inhibitions, Sam finds herself telling Richard that she loves and that she is *in love* with him, but instantly regrets it. The next morning she swears off taking E ever again, and hopes that Richard won't mention it. Later she realises that she wishes her statement had meant something to him, and that this means he means something to her.

Carrie: Carrie returns from her night out with the girls to find Aidan asleep in bed with his big bucket of KFC next to him. She tries to get him to have sex but he claims to be too tired and to have eaten too much chicken. He asks her to rub his tummy and she does so – but under protest.

Charlotte: Through an old friend, Charlotte meets a designer on *House & Garden*, who suggests that they might like to photograph Charlotte and Trey's home for an upcoming issue. Charlotte is delighted, as this has been her fantasy since she used to wear her mother's pearls and read *H&G* as a child. The shoot goes ahead and it looks as if, due to the state of their relationship, Trey won't be in the photographs. Charlotte orders him to take all his stuff out of the spare room anyway, to give the illusion that they are the perfect suburbanite Manhattan couple for the purposes of the photographs. They have a sombre, resigned 'argument' and agree to split up; Trey will move back to the Connecticut compound, and Charlotte can keep the apartment given that she's now sold hers.

On the day of the shoot, Trey offers to be in the photographs, saying that he can at least do this for her. And so, a month later, the readership of *H&G* sees Dr and Mrs MacDougal presented as the happy couple that they simply aren't – false smiles and all.

Miranda: At the gay bar Miranda meets Max, a junior executive from her firm she was unaware is gay. Almost as an exchange for this piece of information she tells him that she is pregnant. Later he lets it slip at work that she is pregnant, although to be fair to him he is defending her against charges of being asleep at her desk (and therefore, someone suspects, an alcoholic) at the time. She freaks out at him and demands to know what he'd think if she told everyone that he is gay. Of course she then realises that there's someone else in the room. Max enquires if Miranda would like to phone his grandparents next.

Men: Oliver, an Australian gay man new to New York who uses Carrie's columns in the *New York Star* as a survival guide. They hang out together for a while, Carrie using him as a substitute boyfriend because of her boredom with Aidan, but she tires of it after a while and returns home to Aidan. To be fair to Aidan, on every occasion he doesn't want to go out he's genuinely wiped out by overwork, and on every occasion he does want to go out Carrie doesn't want him to.

Stanford: Stanford semi-jokes that, by hanging out with Oliver so much, Carrie is neglecting him, cheating on him with another gay-man-boyfriend-substitute. 'He doesn't love you like I do,' he points out, and reminds her how long they've known each other.

Fit to Print: Carrie muses about whether it becomes more necessary to shake things up in your life the more you settle down. 'At what point do separate interests become separate bedrooms?'

And So . . .: 'Gay boyfriends are the loopholes of monogamy.' Isn't it a bit disturbing the way Charlotte and Trey can work together to create a beautiful lie but can't manage to work out their relationship? It's a shame to see Kyle MacLachlan leave the series, even if there is, in all honesty, nowhere left for his character to go (well, apart from the idea that they might just make him and Charlotte a happy couple, something the writers seem to be studiously avoiding). Nice to see Stanford for the first time in an age, but it's a shame his dress sense has gone into even further decline.

63
Change of a Dress

20 January 2002

Written by Julie Rottenberg and Elisa Zuritsky
Directed by Alan Taylor

Guest Cast
John Corbett (Aidan Shaw) James Remar (Richard Wright)
Lynn Cohen (Magda) Molly Price (Susan Sharon) Marc Grapney (JJ)
Andre de Shields (Pat) Lisa Tharps (Tammy) Alice Spivak (Rita)
Nancy Shayne (Viola) Carprice Benedetti (Judith McBain)

Samantha: Sam discovers that Richard has been sleeping with someone else as well as her, even though she herself has been 'exclusive' to him for quite a while. She's actually surprised by how hurt she feels by this, especially as the two of them haven't even discussed becoming exclusive. She tries to get a quick revenge on Richard by having sex with gossip columnist JJ in the restrooms of a club, but he fails to rise to the challenge.

Charlotte: In order to try and get over her impending divorce, Charlotte takes up tap-dancing lessons – and the dancing turns into an elaborate metaphor for her life. She refuses to dance alone, and becomes very emotional when asked to do so.

Miranda: Miranda admits to Carrie that she still isn't feeling 'maternal' despite being several months' pregnant, and wants to know if this makes her a bad person – or potentially a bad mother. She 'fakes' her reaction to her sonogram, feeling absolutely no emotion at all when she first sees her baby on the screen or when she's told she's having a boy. She spends the next few days fake-grinning at people and pretending to be happy about her situation when she's still having absolutely no reaction at all. Later, after she feels her baby kick for the first time she experiences, with some relief, her first maternal feeling.

Fit to Print: Carrie wonders whether people really want to get married or whether they're just programmed by society into thinking they do.

Carrie: Carrie is feeling under pressure to plan her wedding, and begins to wonder if she is ready, or if she'll ever be ready. She goes wedding-dress shopping with Miranda, but this just freaks her out, especially when one of the dresses she tries on causes her to break out in hives. She tells her friends that she believes this is her body physically resisting the concept of marriage. After much soul-searching she decides to tell Aidan that she doesn't want to marry him. In doing this she demands to know why he is so keen to marry her, and it transpires that, despite everything they've been through, he wants to marry her so quickly because he still doesn't trust her. They fight, and the next day Aidan moves out of their conjoined apartment and out of Carrie's life.

And So . . .: 'I can't believe I'm back here again.' For what seems like the tenth time in the lifetime of the series, one of our heroines and her significant other break up as the season's end approaches. It all seems so arbitrary, and driven by the logic of television production rather than the characters. Carrie's fear of marriage has been presented as coming out of her longstanding antipathy towards the institution. This episode, in the space of a scene, tries to turn this concept on its head, making the very idea of them getting married at all originate in Aidan's lack of trust in Carrie. This makes it his problem and encourages the audience to sympathise more with her than with him.

While this would be a viable plot/character strand if better
executed, it doesn't convincingly come across in either this
or the immediately preceding episodes. In fact, who was it
that reinstigated their relationship? It wasn't Aidan, was it?
It just seems like a convenient way to write John Corbett
out. Again. The fact that the whole storyline is a rerun of
the Miranda/Steve living together plot from Season Two
doesn't help either.

64
Ring a Ding Ding

27 January 2002

Written by Amy B Harris
Directed by Alan Taylor

Guest Cast
Chris Noth (Mr Big) David Eigenberg (Steve Brady)
John Corbett (Aidan Shaw) James Remar (Richard Wright)
Dina Pearlman (Ruby Rosen) Robert Gomes (Roger)
Joan Rosenfels (Delia the Broker) Stephanie Cannon (Linda)
Charles Parnell (Salesman) Lynda Gravatt (Bus Waiter)
Paul Albe (Repairman)

Carrie: Aidan clears the last of his stuff out of Carrie's
apartment, leaving behind a letter that gives her thirty days
to buy her apartment back from him. Understandably
thrown into a panic by this, she begins to worry about how
she's going to afford real estate, especially when the bank
tells her she's an undesirable candidate for a loan.

Fashion Victims: As the spectre of homelessness begins to
haunt Carrie, she speculates that she will be a Fendi bag
lady, or possibly the old woman who lives in her shoes. She
does have a lot of shoes, after all. Carrie realises that she's
spent over $40,000 on shoes in her adult life, and Miranda
helpfully points out that this would be enough to cover the
down payment on her apartment.

Samantha: Sam discovers that all the gifts she has received
from Richard are actually picked out by his assistant, who

is also responsible for writing the notes that accompany them. These notes have been a great source of frustration to her recently, as they're always signed 'Best' or some other non-committal phrase. She asks the assistant to sign one of the cards 'Love' and he agrees to do so. Later, when Sam opens a present from Richard in his presence the card is there. She reads the card out loud, emphasising the word 'love'. Richard tells Samantha he loves her; she smiles and says, 'And I love . . .', points at her gift, 'this'.

Charlotte: Now that Trey is gone, Charlotte begins looking for work. She doesn't need a job due to both the nature of the prenuptial agreement she and Trey signed and his decision to let her have his apartment, but she decides that she needs something to fill her time now she's not the socialite wife of a Manhattan society doctor. No one, it turns out, will hire her so she becomes a volunteer at the Museum of Modern Art instead.

Hey, Big Guy: Carrie visits Big at his office to tell him the sad story of her recent troubles. He gives her a cheque for $30,000 and tells her she can pay him back whenever. Miranda later points out that this generosity means that Big has power over Carrie and, thinking better of accepting it, Carrie tears the cheque up.

Wine and Dine: Out for a Chinese meal with the girls, Carrie is moved when both Sam and Miranda suggest that they can lend Carrie $15,000 each to help her cover the down payment on her apartment – but refuses their generosity knowing that neither of them can really afford to lend her that much cash at once.

Girl Talk: Hanging around her apartment, fixating upon how much she'll miss it, Carrie is suddenly seized by a terrible rage, and charges round to Charlotte's place to confront her. Why didn't Charlotte offer to lend Carrie money when the others did? Especially given that she can easily afford it? Charlotte points out that Carrie is 35 years old and that she needs to stand on her own feet at some point in her life. It's good advice, but Carrie points out that Charlotte is living off a divorce settlement so she can't really take the moral high ground on this one. Later they have lunch, and they both apologise. Charlotte tells Carrie that she wants her to have the engagement ring Trey gave her in order to pay for the apartment. 'Will you take this ring?' Charlotte asks. 'I will,' replies Carrie.

Miranda: At Miranda's place, Steve and Miranda are drawing up schedules to allow them to spend separate time with their baby once it's born. Miranda treats it like any other legal transaction, working things out in the most minute details, but Steve rightly points out that they're both going to have to be flexible about this as children aren't exactly like trains. She says she's absolutely desperate for sex, and she's certain nobody would want to have sex with her in her current condition. He says he does, but he isn't sure if it's allowed by their contract. 'Fuck the contract,' says Miranda, 'and please fuck me.'

And So . . .: 'Life gets complicated.' This is trying to be a ringing (bad pun intended) endorsement of the series' creed that friendships are better than relationships, but keeps falling over the amazingly selfish portrayal of its lead character. There are some great scenes with Steve and Miranda, and Sam's subplot is sharp and funny, but the whole thing somehow fails to gel. That Charlotte giving Carrie her ring is partially to free herself from her own past isn't given as much emphasis as it should be, either, and it just comes across as though Charlotte has simply caved in to Carrie's demand that her friend support her.

65
A 'Vogue' Idea

3 February 2002

Written by Alan Heinberg
Directed by Martha Coolidge

Guest Cast
James Remar (Richard Wright) Candice Bergen (Enid Frick)
Ron Rifkin (Julian Fisher) Rachel Nichols (Alexa)
Magaly Coliman (Gretchen) Grace Naughton (Wendy)

Carrie: Carrie has written her first article for *Vogue*, but immediately finds herself clashing with her unsympathetic editor, Enid, who wants Carrie's pieces to be less obviously by Carrie Bradshaw. Carrie seeks solace from Julian, a middle-aged *Vogue* big shot, who assures her that her work is easily good enough, and pours her several Martinis into the bargain. Carrie rewrites her article, and is pleased when it's accepted for publication in *Vogue*. She is less pleased when Julian comes on to her, and she realises that was the only reason he was nice to her in the first place.

Samantha: Still, amazingly, with Richard, Sam is informed by her beau that what he wants for his birthday is a threesome with her and Alexa, a ravishing young restaurant hostess of his acquaintance. Sam reluctantly acquiesces. Richard is disturbed when, during the sex, Alexa starts calling him 'Daddy', and he immediately demands that she leave. He then tells Sam that he is seriously thinking about trying 'the monogamy thing' with her.

Miranda: Charlotte throws a baby shower for Miranda, but it soon becomes clear that she is doing this as a way of exploring her own frustrations at not having a baby or a husband than as a celebration of Miranda's pregnancy. Charlotte's high-powered attitude to the baby shower – all must-have gifts and toy storks – freaks Miranda out a bit too. And who can blame her? When Charlotte sees that one of Miranda's gifts is a Tiffany silver baby rattle just like the one Trey gave her, she begins to cry.

Also Starring: Candice Bergen is best known as the eponymous heroine of *Murphy Brown*, one of the big TV hits of the late 1980s. Her movies include such diverse projects as the epic *Gandhi* (Richard Attenborough, 1982), the ludicrous *Miss Congeniality* (Donald Petrie, 2000) and the fantastic Art Garfunkel/Jack Nicholson-starring *Carnal Knowledge* (Mike Nichols, 1971). She also provided the voice of the 'female' computer in *2010: The Year We Make Contact* (Peter Hyams, 1984) albeit under the wonderful pseudonym, Olga Mallsner.

Ron Rifkin has appeared in numerous television shows, and is best known for his role as Arvin Sloane in *Alias* (2001–), and in films, such as *LA Confidential* (Phil Alden Robinson, 2002), *The Negotiator* (Curtis Hanson, 1997) and *The Sum of All Fears* (F. Gary Gray, 1998).

Trivia: Carrie's dad left when she was five years old and her mother raised her alone.

And So . . .: 'How much does a father-figure figure?' Bits and bobs of cod-Freudian ideas flit sluggishly around an unfunny and rather bland episode. It's all a bit uninspired, really, but Candice Bergen's cameo is good, Ron Rifkin is as terrific as you might expect and Kristin Davis's breakdown is rather affecting.

66
I Heart NY

10 February 2002

Written by Michael Patrick King
Directed by Martha Coolidge

Guest Cast
Chris Noth (Mr Big) David Eigenberg (Steve Brady)
Kyle MacLachlan (Trey MacDougal)
Frances Sternhagen (Bunny MacDougal) James Remar (Richard Wright)
Terry Maratos (Eric) Pete Corby (Bobbo)
Tom Cappadona (NYC Cab Driver) Geneva Carr (Nurse)
Miriam Green (Doctor)

Carrie: Bored and lonely, depressed because it's autumn, Carrie goes to see Big, takeaway pizza in hand. She discovers that his apartment is empty of furniture, and, though he's still there, he won't be for long. He's bought a huge chunk of Napa, California, and is moving there. She asks him out on one final date, telling him he owes it to 'us' – to himself, to her, and to New York City.

Girl Talk: Carrie decides to ask her friends their opinion on her having sex with Big one last time. Miranda thinks it's a terrible idea, but Carrie decides to go ahead with it anyway, should the opportunity arise.

Men: While volunteering at MOMA, Charlotte spots Trey and his mother walking through the museum; this brief glimpse is enough to push her into accepting a date with Eric, a guy who turns out to be tedious, bitter and strangely aggressive. Better luck next time, eh?

Samantha: Samantha is becoming very possessive of Richard, and is convinced he's cheating on her with someone else. The fact that she got into the 'relationship' with him precisely because she doesn't want commitment or monogamy is now beside the point: she's fallen in love with Richard and there's nothing she can do about it. She begins to follow him around the city, wearing a ludicrous disguise, in an attempt to catch him at one of his infidelities. She eventually does and, crying and screaming, she smashes a triptych picture of three hearts she bought for him, snarling, 'Now your heart's broken too.'

Miranda: Steve and Miranda are together when she goes into labour and is rushed to hospital. Miranda rings Carrie – interrupting her final date with Big – and Carrie rushes to the hospital to see her friend. Miranda has a baby boy, delivered in the series' most moving scene to date. Miranda tells Steve that the boy's first name will be Brady, like Steve's last name, making his name Brady Hobbes – the perfect mix of the two of them.

Hey, Big Guy: Big likes 60s American rock outfit, Blood, Sweat & Tears and owns Andy Williams's version of *Moon River*. Carrie is clearly at her most wrong ever when she describes this inarguably great record as 'corny'. .

Returning to Big's flat alone after Miranda has had her baby, Carrie finds him finally gone and two items left on the floor for her – a copy of this record labelled 'for if you get lonely' and a plane ticket to California in Carrie's name labelled 'for if I ever get lonely'.

The City: This episode is dedicated to 'our city of New York ... Then, now, and forever'. Given when it was originally shot this episode must have had some editorial surgery performed on it during autumn/winter 2001. Although it doesn't mention the events of 11 September, and indeed clearly takes place before them, it's a love letter to the city of New York and a look back to a time before the traumatic events of that day. The final scene as Carrie wanders around the Park reflecting on how life, people and even Cities change – but the things that you love remain the things that you love for ever – is brilliant.

And So ...: 'Don't disappoint us.' All the scenes with Carrie and Big are wonderfully bittersweet, Steve and Miranda's time on screen is perfection itself and the episode's own little eulogy to the much-battered people of New York is also superbly handled. This episode is so good that the fact that Samantha's plotline is out-of-character, repetitive rubbish honestly doesn't matter a bit. Well, not much.

Season Five (2002)

Created by Darren Star
Based on the book by Candace Bushnell
Executive Consultant: Darren Star
Executive Producer: Michael Patrick King
Executive Producer: Sarah Jessica Parker
Executive Producer: Cindy Chupack
Executive Producer: John Melfi
Producer: Jane Raab
Associate Producer: Mark McGann
Associate Producer: Grace Naughton

Regular Cast
Sarah Jessica Parker (Carrie Bradshaw) Kim Cattrall (Samantha Jones)
Kristin Davis (Charlotte York)[1] Cynthia Nixon (Miranda Hobbes)

67

Anchors Away

21 July 2002

Written by Michael Patrick King
Directed by Charles McDougall

Guest Cast
David Eigenberg (Steve Brady) James Remar (Richard Wright)
Mario Cantone (Anthony Marentino) Lynn Cohen (Magda)
Sylvia Miles (Joan) Jamie Gustis (Paul Watkins)
Daniel Sunjata (Louis LeRoy, USN) Diego Lopez (Bill Hope)
Seth Consentino (Sweet Young Sailor) Mark Deklin (Ship Officer)
Michael Hollick (Dickie Sailor) Chandra Wilson (Police Officer)
Vincenetta Gunn (Lina) Philip Levy (Deli Manager)
Chris Tschupp (Cute Rain Guy) Tom Myler (Joseph)

Samantha: It's 'Fleet Week' – the week that a host of US
Navy ships converge on New York harbour and then a
horde of sailors converge on New York's clubs and bars.
Normally Samantha would be cock-a-hoop about the

---

[1] Charlotte abandons the 'MacDougal' suffix before her divorce is
finalised (**72**, 'Critical Condition'), reverting to 'York' in **67**, 'Anchors
Away'.

possibilities, but she's too busy pining over Richard/being angry with him (depending on her mood). He keeps leaving messages – many, many messages – on her phone asking to take him back and forgive his infidelities, but she's too angry even to think about acquiescing. She's not too angry, however, to listen to his messages again and again (see **Men**).

Carrie: 'When you are single and live in New York there are no end of ways to end your day,' says Carrie, and goes on to prove it by spending all her leisure time in museums and going to the famous Paris cinema in order to see French films on her own. Judging by the beatific smile on her face as she guzzles chocolates from the box and watches *Joie Pour Deux* on her own she's perfectly happy. Well, until Charlotte makes an insensitive comment about 'Great Loves', anyway. One that sends the heroine off at the deep end again (see **Fit to Print**).

Miranda: It's about three weeks since Miranda gave birth to Brady and she is, in Carrie's words, 'moving slowly away from her old life'. During the conversation about 'Great Loves', Miranda flat-out denies that she does, or has ever, seen Steve that way and claims that neither of her relationships with him shook her to the core. Samantha doesn't seem to like the fact that Miranda carries Brady around with her a lot of the time and isn't mollified by Miranda's insistence that she should just think of baby and carrier as 'an extra big purse'. Miranda is not at all happy at being bundled into a taxi by Samantha for getting in the way during a projected shopping trip and even less happy to find Steve in her house. He's been let in – and made a sandwich! – by her housekeeper.

Days later Miranda is completely freaked out when the end of the umbilical cord attached to Brady's navel falls off (as it is, of course, meant to do). She's even more freaked out when the cat steals it and starts playing with it, flicking it around the floor and carrying it in its mouth. She calls Steve, unable to bring herself even to try to grab the blackened fleshy lump from the moggy. Steve turns up and rescues the baby detritus, leaving Carrie's voiceover to comment that, while Miranda may not have agreed that Steve was a core-shaker, she could rely on him to be there for her when she was shaken to the core.

Charlotte: Determined either to rediscover her old self, or create a new self, after the collapse of her marriage to Trey, Charlotte changes her name back to Charlotte York and replaces the name plate on her front door to prove it. It's been six months since she had sex, and she plans to be as 'not Charlotte' as possible at the Naval dance. Assuming any of her friends agree to go with her. Eventually they do (see **Out and About**).

Girl Talk: It's a nightmare when one of your friends has a baby. Miranda can't talk to, or listen to, Carrie because she's preoccupied with the difficulty of getting Brady to breastfeed and Carrie can't talk to, listen to, or even *look* at Miranda when she's breastfeeding.

Men: Samantha gives in to Richard's begging for a second chance. Or seems to. She goes to meet him in a restaurant, allows him to get comfortable and then throws a Martini in his face. Then she goes out with some sailors.

Fetishes: Like I said – sailors, lots of sailors.

The City: Carrie feels that New York is the perfect place in which to be single because 'the city is your date ...' Intending to prove this she sets off for the Guggenheim one Thursday afternoon, not realising that the Guggenheim doesn't open on Thursdays. Then she gets caught in a rainstorm (Carrie's frequent squeaky little shriek/scream noises as she does so are really, really funny) and winds up trapped under an awning with a cute guy. Instead of seducing him, she successfully freaks the hell out of him by jabbering at him in an 'endearing' way, making jokes about marriage and telling him far too much about her break-up with Aidan. He runs away. Literally.

Wine and Dine: Sitting in a strange diner, Carrie meets a woman in late middle age who tells her that single girls such as they both are should stick together. While Carrie is still boggling from this, the woman informs our Ms Bradshaw that she split up with a man in 1982 and never really recovered because she spent too long telling herself that someone or something else would come along. She's now reduced to grinding up lithium and putting it in her ice cream in order to lift her mood. Not an enviable fate.

Charlotte insists that Samantha use the euphemism 'sushi' for 'cunnilingus' when Brady is about, even though Miranda doesn't mind, since Brady is not able to speak or understand yet.

Fashion Victims: This episode features one of Carrie's best ever outfits – the entirely vintage ensemble of striped miniskirt and red jacket which goes really well with her newly curly hair. Fantastic.

Trivia: The first episode of the series' almost startlingly short Season Five which was arranged and planned as a mere seven-episode block in order to work around cast members' other acting commitments and Sarah Jessica Parker's pregnancy. Presumably the decision to delay the final six episodes of the previous season to January/ February 2002 was in part taken when it was unclear how many, if any, new episodes could be produced with the intention to air them in 2002. To spend a whole calendar year off the air was obviously unacceptable as it would have meant that it, by then a certified heavy hitter in TV awards, would fail to qualify for a whole rash of awards ceremonies. A year is a long time in TV, long enough for a series to be forgotten. This very sensible decision, combined with the veritable briefness of the Season Five, had a couple of knock-on effects.

Season Six was also cut into two separate chunks and shown in two blocks, one in midsummer and the other in midwinter, just like the Season Four had been. Except that this time there was no pressing business reason. That initial splitting of Season Four also means that the divisions between 'seasons' from this point on are largely arbitrary. The gap between the two 'halves' of Season Four is just as big as the gap between Season Four and Season Five. The gap between the two halves of Season Six is as big again and the extra-size Season Six (twenty episodes!) means that each 'half' of Season Six is larger than the 'full' Season Five. This guide uses the divisions between seasons as (currently) used by the production company and the episode order/divisions exhibited by the (excellent) DVD box-sets of the series.

Fit to Print: 'Does that flame of adventure still flicker inside of all of us or, when it comes to being carefree single girls, have we missed the boat?' Carrie and her column grapple with the idea that being 'carefree' is harder now, somehow, and that Miranda's new responsibilities have changed things in their peer group.

Hey, Big Guy: Big is mentioned in the context of people only having room for two great romantic loves in their adult life. Big would be one of Carrie's (Aidan would be the other).

Out and About: After much consideration, consultation and temporary rejection Carrie, Charlotte and Sam visit the US Navy bash where all three are big hits. However, all three go home alone out of choice. Charlotte, in a most un-Charlotte-like moment, is persuaded to flash her right breast at a relative stranger and decides that that's enough 'danger' for the night. Carrie turns down an officer because, while he's nice, he doesn't like New York, and Samantha crawls out drunkenly to listen to her messages from Richard again. Clearly her recent actions against him haven't ameliorated her feelings.

And So . . .: 'Maybe the past is like an anchor holding us back.' A zingily good opening episode which manages, for perhaps the first time, to make it clear that our leads are growing older and that their priorities are changing, and it does so without implicitly criticising their previous existences. Lots of good Sam comedy is complemented by suggestions of a sea change in Charlotte's behaviour and more subtle shifts in Carrie's and Miranda's. A good 'un.

68
Unoriginal Sin

28 July 2002

Written by Cindy Chupack
Directed by Charles McDougall

Guest Cast
David Eigenberg (Steve Brady) James Remar (Richard Wright)
Amy Sedaris (Courtney Masterson) Molly Shannon (Lily Martin)
Lynn Cohen (Magda) Cheryl Bricker (Dr Grayson)
Danton Stone (Patrick) Matt Servitto (Gabe) Anne Meara (Mary Brady)
Joseph O'Brien (Father Andrew)
Sorrel Dove Tomlinson (Affirmation Girl)
Lisa Leguillou (Woman in Love) Erin Stutland (Waitress)

Wine and Dine: At the diner, the girls wait to order while Carrie discusses how her life has led her to compose columns on socks and French fries. When the waiter arrives Carrie orders fries (it might need to be a two-part column), Miranda goes for the Denver Omelette (onion, green peppers, ham, bacon, peppers and Tabasco sauce) and hash browns, Charlotte has veggie scrambled eggs and wheat toast and Sam says, 'I'll have the fruit plate and I'm back with Richard . . .' Silence. For a moment. And then Charlotte asks, 'Richard, whose death we've been plotting?' It's a fair question, but Sam has given in and taken him back.

Carrie: Carrie is on the run from her editor, Gabe, because she's terrified of being told that her column is to be discontinued. She believes that her currently non-existent sex life is having an adverse affect on her writing and that there is only one possible result to this: 'I am not getting laid, therefore I am getting laid off.' In fact, she couldn't be more wrong. Clearwater Press want to collect her columns into a book. All she has to do is write an introduction and a dedication. Sam, for one, is delighted for her as she says that anyone who is anyone has to have a book.

Samantha: Yes, it's true. Sam is back with Richard, having forgiven him and accepted his excuse that he cheated on her because he was 'scared' of their relationship. She seems quite affected by this explanation, which is odd as it sounds like cynical sixth-form pat to everyone else. Richard buys Sam a vast diamond ring as a 'sorry' present and Carrie refers to it as the 'Canary-Diamond-I'll-Try-Not-To-Cheat-And-Eat-When-Scared Ring'.

When told that Steve and Miranda are spending all their non-working time baby-proofing their apartment, Sam, continuing her mini-war against Miranda's new parental status, points out acidly: 'I'll tell you how to baby-proof, use a condom.'

Miranda: Steve, who is apparently Catholic, wants Brady baptised into the Church of Rome. Miranda, an atheist, attempts principled opposition to this idea but falls in line to please Steve's 'ma'. As Steve points out, there'll be cake and a party, a chance to take lots of photos and, in the end, what does it matter 'if you don't believe it's just water on the kid's head'? Steve's ma is comically Catholic, foul-mouthed, implicitly racist, drunken, ranting, doesn't approve of them not being married (does she know they're not even together?) and really quite funny; but Steve's sudden status as an Irish Catholic after always apparently being played as New York Jewish is a bit of a surprise.

When Miranda discusses the baptism service with the priest, she makes a few stipulations: there's to be no mention of Catholicism, no original sin, no renouncing of Satan, indeed no mention of Satan, the devil or hell at all. The priest raises an eyebrow, leaving Steve to comment that Miranda doesn't support Satan, just that she won't talk about him.

Men: It's announced as Carrie's opinion that men who are too good-looking aren't very good in bed, because they have never had to be. She might not actually mean this: it comes up in a string of non sequiturs designed to distract Charlotte.

Patrick, Steve's drunken second cousin, cracks onto Carrie at the baptism. She's obviously slightly afraid of him.

Fashion Victims: Carrie's woollen pseudo-Jamaican hat-thing, Charlotte's amazing pink sheepskin Christian Lacroix jacket (jaw-dropping, let me tell you). Carrie's flower-on-head-like Chanel Couterre hat and Narciso Rodriguez little black dress combo at Brady's baptism are pretty special too.

Fit to Print: 'The worst thing about not being in a relationship is when your job is writing about relationships' apparently.

Trivia: 'The little church that would' is a reference to 'The Little Engine That Could', Walter Pappy's inspirational 1978 children's story of determination – often seen as a great feminist parable.

Reference is made by Carrie to the less-than-rosy state of the United States economy in 2002. A rare intrusion of real-world logic into the series.

Charlotte: Charlotte has started going to a creepy love-cult. It's a sort of sinister blend of fire and brimstone televangelist Christianity, Pyramid Selling and the Moonies. She drags Carrie along once Carrie is, in her own words, 'one bad date from cynicism', but Carrie sees that the cult is really having a negative affect on her friend's state of mind: the cult leader keeps insisting that the reason Charlotte can't find love is because she isn't really 'out there'. Carrie gives the lecturer a lecture about the extent to which Charlotte really is out there after all.

And So . . .: 'What's the harm in believing?' Heaven, hell, purgatory limbo and everything between are the thematic buzzwords in this episode, which mines the punning homophonic sound of Sin and Cynicism. So, Charlotte joins a freaky cult, Samantha believes in Richard, Miranda doesn't believe in God and Carrie doesn't believe in herself. Carrie's brought out of this funk by Miranda who tells her friend that she wants her to be Brady's godmother because 'I don't know if I believe in any of this, but I believe in *you*.' It's also a deeply self-referential instalment. It contrives to demonstrate how the book *Sex and the City* (upon which the TV series is partly based) came to be published and goes on to suggest that a TV series may be based on Carrie's book.

69
Luck Be an Old Lady

4 August 2002

Written by Julie Rotenberg & Elisa Zuritsky
Directed by John David Coles

Guest Cast
David Eigenberg (Steve Brady) James Remar (Richard Wright)
Lynn Cohen (Magda) Matt Skollar (Cute Guy)
Victoria Labalme (Denise) Lou Bonacki (Photographer)
Alex Corrado (Bernie) Iris Almario (Terry) Brendan Connor (Jerk #1)
Richard Byrne (Jerk #2) Rick Jaeckel (Dealer) Victor Verhaeghe (Rob)
Paul Urcioli (David) William Jay Marshall (Herman) Hope Clarke (Lee)
Michael Buscemi (Male Croupier) Paul Lazar (Ken)

Carrie: As this week begins Carrie is out on her first blind date in a decade. She gets stood up. Moaning, with considerable justification, to her friends later, she argues she's reached rock bottom since her feelings have been hurt by someone who is a complete stranger. She wonders why she should bother with dating anyway, risking a lousy time when she could guarantee a good time by hanging with her girlfriends. What can she get out of a date that she couldn't get out of a night with the girls? Pausing, Samantha smiles and points out, 'Honey, you're cute but I'm never gonna fuck you . . .'

Charlotte: Charlotte's 36th birthday is coming up, and she's decided to 'stick' at 35. This will be her 35th birthday part two, or her 'thirty faux' birthday as Carrie points out. Samantha's opinion is that it would be the smartest thing Charlotte has done in a number of years if she lies about her age. Charlotte is determined to not celebrate her birthday at all and is helped in this ambition by all her friends being indisposed on the big day. Carrie objects to this and Richard suggests that Carrie, Miranda and Charlotte accompany him and Sam to Atlantic City (free flights and accommodation) in order to celebrate Charlotte's birthday. Carrie forces the others to agree.

Men: Steve's spectacular fear at looking after Brady for a whole weekend is really funny. He's frightened he might 'break him' and virtually throws a fit when he thinks he might have scratched the baby's skin with his fingernail. What's less funny is that his worrying causes Miranda and Carrie to miss their flight, so they have to get a long-haul bus to Atlantic City instead.

(Another) City: Atlantic City to be precise, where Richard knows the names of all of the staff at the Taj Mahal Hotel which sends Sam off into a paranoid funk (see **Samantha**). Carrie loves the fact that you can smoke in the casinos, unlike virtually any public building in New York City, about as much as she loves the peppermint saltwater candy.

Miranda: Miranda gets really into the gambling and dice rolling once in the Casino of Atlantic City, loving it right until the moment she pauses, when suddenly she has to go and have a lie-down and some chocolate. This is apparently what she's like post-natal.

Guy Talk: There's an absolutely brilliant scene in which a large man demands that Miranda 'move her fat ass'. The girls are understandably shocked at this blatant, unnecessary and frankly unfounded vileness and Miranda points out that her ass is the size it is because she's just had a baby. 'What's your excuse?' demands Carrie, 'Having triplets?' The whole house applauds her.

Girl Talk: Carrie strongly implies that she and Miranda are the same age and that Charlotte is around a year younger than both of them. Samantha claims to be 37 – as ridiculous as it's meant to be. This is another episode where all four of our heroines fret about their ages, with Miranda getting Charlotte an 'old maid' card game as a joke present and Charlotte taking the joke very badly. Carrie initially talks about her same-sex friendships as her insurance against an unhappy old age (she takes this point of view after seeing all the cheerful old ladies on the bus she and Miranda take to Atlantic City) but after seeing an elderly couple joking and flirting with one another, clearly very much in love and lust after many, many years, she changes her mind.

Fetishes: Richard gives Samantha a really very tacky-looking and staggeringly uncomfortable-sounding string-of-pearls thong and offers to give her a 'pearl necklace' to go with it. Charlotte assumes he means an actual necklace made of pearls and is 'enlightened' by Samantha.

Fashion Victims: In the casino Carrie wears an amazingly revealing (cleavage and belly) patchwork top from Balenciaga made by combining quilted liberty print pastel pieces with pieces of Eurotron – a sort of metal mesh material. It's really very odd.

Charlotte buys a dress which Carrie labels 'Atlantic Slutty'. It's a flattering, if obvious, look for Ms York.

Fit to Print: 'If we know the house always wins, why gamble?' ponders Carrie, thinking about both the gaming tables and the 'lottery of love'.

Trivia: Carrie makes a reference to the concept of 'Groundhog Day' when the Burkseville, Ohio, groundhog pokes its head out of a hole and, depending on a series of arcane rules, its movements determine how many more weeks of winter there are in the USA. No, not many others believe it either.

There's a shot of a spinning roulette wheel from above that the director seems to have taken directly from *Little Caesar* (Mervyn Le Roy, 1931), the classic gangster picture.

'Knitting is the new yoga,' according to Charlotte.

Samantha: Absolutely convinced that Richard is either cheating on her, or has cheated on her, or will cheat on her,

Samantha descends into total paranoia about their relationship. Unable to cope with the worry, she dumps him
and returns his ring (see **68**, 'Unoriginal Sin'). The problem
with dumping him while still in Atlantic City, though, is
that all four girls have to return to New York on the bus.

And So . . .: 'Hoping to hit the jackpot.' Beneath the glitz
and the higher-than-usual-quotient of stupid jokes, there's
also a really worthwhile point here about the difference
between appreciating the time you spend with your friends
and using your significant friendships as a place to hide
from realisations about what you want from life. (It's a
point that goes at least equally for men too.) The
different-from-usual locations help make the episode stand
out from the pack. The end, with the four girls laughing
together on the bus, is one of the season's, indeed the
series', warmest moments.

70
Cover Girl

11 August 2002

Written by Judy Toll & Michael Patrick
Directed by John David Coles

Guest Cast
Willie Garson (Stanford Blatch) Amy Sedaris (Courtney Masterson)
Craig Gass (Tom) Judy Gold (Barnes & Noble Clerk)
Nick Scotti (Worldwide Express Guy) Molly Shannon (Lily Martin)
Sean Palmer (Marcus) Nikki E Walker (Weight Watchers Woman)
Gillien Goll (Sad Woman) Miranda Black (Samantha's Assistant)
Anne Rutter (Almost Divorced Woman) Michael Zeppetello (Himself)

Carrie: Carrie's publisher has some horrible ideas for her
book cover, including a really bad cover mock-up which
features her head Photoshopped onto a naked model's
body running through New York.

Samantha: After the disastrous ideas for the cover of
Carrie's book, Samantha offers to do Carrie's PR work on
the project for the token payment of two Martinis and a

lunch. As a result of this we see the exterior of Sam's PR firm offices (and her 'Samantha Jones' logo) for the first time ever when Carrie visits Sam's office. There is an incident which itself leads to the two of them having a hefty row.

It's not clear how long it is since Samantha chucked Richard, but she's already trying to seduce the delivery boy (successfully, I might add) by offering to suck him off without the slightest encouragement. Carrie walks in while Samantha is on her knees and dashes out – leaving both women angry.

Charlotte: Self Help or Self Hell? Looking for an on-the-page pick-me-up in the continuing wake of her split with Trey, Charlotte buys the kind of self-help books that propose to offer a solution to lonely singletons. The horrors of being in the aisle of a bookstore full of these things, trapped with monstrous-looking people and crying women, isn't quite enough to put her off buying more. The list of books she might like based upon her recent purchases (including *I'm Alright – Now* and other choice items) is, however.

Miranda: Miranda meets Tom while at Weight Watchers. She's there in order to get rid of her 'baby fat' and he's there because he eats too much when he's upset. They bond over a shared love of Krispy Kreme glazed doughnuts and wind up having sex. Tom is, it turns out, a bit of a hero when it comes to cunnilingus, but Miranda can't cope with his habit of kissing her immediately afterwards. Her criticism of him for this triggers his get-criticised-need-to-eat-reflex and he dumps her in order to go look for food. Summing up, Carrie notes, 'Miranda met an overeater and he overate her!' Tom is the series' first one-episode comedy partner for one of the four main characters in an age and his plotline seems like a throwback to Season Two. Nice performance from Craig Gass though.

Men: Stanford! Yay! He's met someone whose name is Marcus – a Broadway-level dancer who shares Stanford's love of exotic coffee. When Carrie asks him if she's too judgemental, he demurs, saying that the two of them 'Judge! That's our hobby. Some people do arts and crafts, we judge,' which, while comforting to Ms Bradshaw, feeds nicely into Carrie's column.

Fit to Print: 'Are we being too quick to judge judgement?' Carrie's column wonders if, in our desire to avoid being critical of others, we occasionally abandon the sense of our own opinions.

Fashion Victims: While book-shopping, Carrie wears cargo pants from Balenciaga. You have to go on a list to get those, you know. Her new Megan Park bag is pretty special too, as is her Juicy Couture hooded top which she somehow manages to wear in a manner which means she doesn't look like a non-league football manager. Also while shopping, Charlotte goes casual with jeans and a black long-sleeved T-shirt with a pink polo player and pony on it. No, it's much better than it sounds, honestly. Carrie's vintage Sex Pistols T-shirt (Vivienne Westwood) is completely brilliant, but some of the stuff Samantha comes up with for Carrie to wear at the cover shoot for her *Sex and the City* book . . . isn't. Carrie protests at some of Sam's selections, claiming that, at their age, they can't get away with the same things any more and they should be covering up. That plural personal pronoun further upsets Samantha who sees Carrie as dragging her into her own decisions on growing older. Referring to both Carrie's accidental, implicit criticism of her dress sense and what she sees as Carrie's judgement of her blowing the delivery boy, Sam proclaims, 'I will wear whatever, and blow whomever, I want, as long as I can breathe and kneel.' As long as this attitude is going to encourage her to wear items like the Gucci satin motorcycle jacket she sports here.

And So . . .: 'Isn't she fabulous?' A very ordinary, fun episode with little to say and a row between Samantha and Carrie which is over almost as soon as it starts. There's an awful lot of discussion of oral sex, though.

71
Plus One Is the Loneliest Number

18 August 2002

Written by Cindy Chupack
Directed by Michael Patrick King

Guest Cast
Willie Garson (Stanford Blatch) Candice Bergen (Enid Frick)
Issac Mizrahi (Issac Mizrahi) Amy Sedaris (Courtney Masterson)
Ron Livingston (Jack Berger) Harold Keenan (Harold Keenan)
Frances Sternhagen (Bunny MacDougal)
Mario Cantone (Anthony Marentino)

Carrie: Carrie bumps into a nice guy called Jack Berger
while visiting her publisher to discuss the launch party for
her book. He's recently written a very funny first novel
which 'speaks to men in the same way that your column
speaks to women' – albeit not strongly enough to prevent
the book from littering discount stores across New York.
The two of them walk through the city together discussing
publishing and having what Carrie calls 'one of those great
first dates that you can only have if they aren't an actual
date'. As he heads off home she asks him on what she
thinks *is* an actual date, to be her 'plus one' guest at her
book's launch party. He says he'd love to but his girlfriend's parents are visiting them and he won't have the
time. Jack pops into the party to say 'good luck' anyway,
but it's clear that he's not interested in Carrie, nor even
really aware that she's interested in him.

Samantha: Visiting her plastic surgeon for her regular
Botox injection, Sam is persuaded to go for a chemical peel
instead. This results in her face looking like boiled lobster
flesh so that she dreads even the possibility of going out.

Charlotte: Charlotte is finally ready for a new relationship,
taking a nice young man home to spend the night. The next
morning, however, her not-quite-yet-ex-husband's mother,
Bunny MacDougal, turns up at her apartment to catch her
out; it turns out that the other residents of the block are

spying on her at Bunny's request. Bunny insists she has the right to do this because, although Trey gave Charlotte the apartment, it wasn't technically his to give, and it is still registered in the MacDougal family name.

Miranda: Miranda is back at work now, trying to juggle her career with Brady and making some attempt to get back into dating. Walker, a business contact with whom she had one night of great sex long ago, asks her out again. She doesn't tell him she now has a baby and invites him to come to Carrie's launch party because she's already got the babysitting arrangements sorted out for that night. He comes along, they hit it off again and end up kissing passionately against the wall. He invites himself back to her place and she has to tell him about the baby. Although not keen on children, he goes to her place anyway, but their sex is interrupted by Brady's crying from the next room.

Girl Talk: Carrie bumps into *Vogue* editor Enid in a restaurant and asks her how she juggles her work and love life. Enid claims to have a time-share on a man: she sees him on one side of the park; his other woman sees him on the other. Enid's wisdom gets her an invite to Carrie's party. There, however, Enid panics when she sees her beau and his other woman. Are they on the wrong side of the park, Carrie asks? Enid runs off yelling that they're beneath the part of New York which is split by the park. Who has jurisdiction in this part of the city? 'East Side, West Side, who the hell knows down here?' squeals Enid, causing Carrie to wonder if she should find a new role model.

Wine and Dine: At Carrie's party there are little cakes with pink-icing stiletto shoes on them. They look delicious and Ms Bradshaw scoffs a fair few. Charlotte's friend Anthony decides to pull the shrimp waiter and succeeds. After the party Carrie and her chauffeur go for hotdogs.

Fashion Victims: Carrie wears an Anna Molinari feather dress to her book party and its contrasting layers of black and white look really good on her. Samantha, thanks to her chemical peel, feels the need to turn up with something covering her face. Cue a custom-made feather hat and veil, handmade by Philip Treacy who makes hats for the British Royal Family.

Also Starring: The *New Yorker*'s Harold Keenan and critic Issac Mizrahi both cameo as themselves attending Carrie's party, presumably to add some real-life New York flavour to the occasion.

Fit to Print: 'Why does one minus a plus one feel like it adds up to zero?' Carrie wonders why it is that in New York people need three things: a career, a relationship and an apartment, and whenever they have two out of the three it just shows up the lack of the third one.

Men: Jack Berger, whom Carrie can't date because he's happily attached, collects playing cards. Years before he'd noticed that there are often odd playing cards lying around on the street (this is actually true of most large cities). Jack's ambition is to collect a whole set of spare cards. After her party, on her way into her car, Carrie notices another playing card, a Jack in fact, lying in the gutter. Carrie takes this as a sign that the universe is telling her that nice men do exist.

And So . . .: Cindy Chupack turns in another lovingly constructed, thematically immaculate little playlet of an episode where absolutely everything works. It's worth noting that I don't get free hotdogs every time I put a book out – but then I don't look like Carrie Bradshaw.

72
Critical Condition

25 August 2002

Written by Alexa Junge
Directed by Michael Patrick King

Guest Cast
Willie Garson (Stanford Blatch) David Eigenberg (Steve Brady)
Heather Graham (Heather Graham)
Mary Testa (Cabaret Singer Debbie Cass)
Peter Ratray (Sharper Image Salesman)
Victor Browne (Attorney Matthew Bloom)
Robert John Burke (Walker Lewis)

Carrie: Carrie is afraid of her book reviews. Very afraid. Especially the review by Mitchiko Cathatani of the *New York Times* who, according to Carrie, might be brilliant but can be very tough and, according to Stanford, is 'impossible to pronounce'. In fact, the first time Carrie mentions her by name, Stanford thinks she's talking about an appetiser.

Miranda: 'I'm a bad neighbour and a bad mother,' wails Miranda at one point. She now considers herself to be pretending even to be a lawyer. Brady is crying non-stop all night every night. Miranda isn't sleeping, nor are her neighbours, and the baby surely isn't sleeping. It's all a bit of a nightmare and Miranda can't bring herself to see Steve right now because she's worried she'll ask him to marry her merely to get some more help with Brady. One of her neighbours complains about the noise and Miranda points out that she has a baby. No dice. Her neighbour points out that if Miranda took any notice of other people in their block she'd know that. A few days later the neighbour returns in a better temper. She lends Miranda a vibrating/rocking baby chair which, as if by magic, makes Brady stop crying. Miranda regards this as a miracle and almost starts crying herself with sheer relief.

Samantha: Sam unwinds by getting drunk and stoned after an (obviously strenuous) day of leg and bikini waxes and plans to use her favourite vibrator. But it shorts out. Taking it back to the store where she bought it she is informed that it's a back massager, not a vibrator, chiefly because the store doesn't admit to selling vibrators. Regardless, they give her a replacement item and Sam spends some happy time advising the other women in the shop on their choice of sex aids. She's an expert, you see.

Sam is also being bullied by Carrie into acknowledging that Miranda has had a baby and that this has had an effect on her life. Miranda is their friend and she needs support and help. Shamed at last, Sam turns up at Miranda's place unannounced and offers Miranda the hair and beauty appointment that she had previously booked for herself: 'Here I am, Mary Fucking Poppins,' she announces. Yes, she's offering to babysit. Once Miranda has gone out, however, Brady's new rocking baby chair breaks. Sam's solution to the immediately crying-again baby problem is to place her newly acquired (and thankfully not yet used) 'back massager' into Brady's chair.

Girl Talk: Carrie meets a girl in the toilets at a club who recognises her both from her column and because, er, she dated Aidan right after Carrie did. Then she pulls a face which basically says, 'Oh My God He Was Like, So Fucked Up By What You Did To Him!' and moves on. Carrie is traumatised by this encounter and her trauma is increased by her discovery, via Sam, that this girl, Nina Katz, is the Talent Booker for *Saturday Night Live*.

Charlotte: During Charlotte's divorce negotiations there's no mention of the terms of the prenuptial agreement she and Trey signed in Season Three (**40**, 'All or Nothing'), wherein Charlotte was entitled to a simple $1 million pay-off from the MacDougal family in the event of divorce. While she is right that Trey said she could keep the apartment (**63**, 'Change of a Dress') and that Bunny is being an evil old harridan, it's hard to see how Charlotte's pursuit of the deed and title to the place (which is obviously worth far more than $1 million) isn't a refutation of the spirit and the letter of an agreement *she* wanted. Unfortunately, Trey is out of the country during the negotiations, denying the viewers one more appearance by the brilliant Kyle McLachlan (McLachlan was actually out of the country, appearing on the London stage in the superb *On an Average Day* during filming, so this is a kind of in-joke), but the telegram he sends ordering his lawyer to give Charlotte what she wants is a great deus ex machina ending. That the telegram says 'Charlotte was a wonderful wife, she did nothing wrong,' also goes to show that everybody gets good reviews sometimes.

The City: There are, says Carrie, three inevitable things that every New Yorker has to put up with sooner or later: having your purse stolen; witnessing some random public urination; seeing a gay friend's boyfriend in a musical revue. Hell, if life's that bad she should move to London.

Men: Charlotte meets Matthew Bloom, of Bloom and Goldenblatt, who is handling her divorce from Trey. She *really* fancies him and is therefore faced with the dilemma of needing to fight ugly (Bunny, Trey's mother, is fighting the other side of the divorce for the MacDougal clan) in front of a man to whom she wants to appear beautiful. The solution is easy – cue Harry Goldenblatt, Matthew's fellow attorney and partner. He is balding and comically unself-conscious, casually spitting bagels out of his mouth as he enters the room, and Charlotte doesn't have an issue with fighting ugly in front of him. So she switches lawyers.

Fashion Victims: A tired, baby-stressed and unwashed Miranda asks if she can wear a baseball cap in to work. 'With what shoes?' is Carrie's instant reply. Outfits of note this week include Carrie's green terry dress, which is a Retro 70s sort of thing, courtesy of Juicy Couture. While good, this is nowhere near as good as the 'girl meets boy' dress by Robert Funk that Carrie wears for her chat with Steve (who, in baseball casuals, looks dreadful). Samantha's white Escada trouser suit is nice, but the bright red Versace top she wears with it isn't. Stanford's pink and white candy-striped jacket is typically Stanford – i.e. horrible.

Also Starring: Heather Graham, who cameos as herself here (looking *stunning* in casuals), is one of the biggest female movie stars of recent years. Her pictures include *Austin Powers – The Spy Who Shagged Me* (Jay Roach, 1999), one of the funniest films ever made, *Killing Me Softly* (Kaige Chen, 2002), one of the stupidest and *Boogie Nights* (Paul Thomas Anderson, 1997), one of the most needlessly long. Viewers with longish memories will re-member her as Annie Blackburn, the girlfriend of Dale Cooper (Kyle MacLachlan's character, strangely) in the second season of *Twin Peaks*.

Trivia: A magazine with Sarah Jessica Parker on the cover is clearly visible on one of the newspaper stands early in the episode (just before Carrie notices the man randomly urinating against the wall). I suppose one could stretch the point and argue that Carrie herself is now so famous that she appears on magazine covers, but it's an odd, acciden-tal, intrusion of reality.

Marcus appears in a song from horribly overrated musical *Chicago* which was turned into a horribly over-rated and entirely soulless film in 2002.

Carrie mentions Gwyneth Paltrow who won an Oscar for *Shakespeare in Love* (John Madden, 1999), and also name-checks Sir Ian McKellen who, bewilderingly, *didn't* win an Oscar for *God and Monsters* (Bill Condon, 1998). Mitchiko Cathatani is a real-life, Pulitzer prize-winning journalist, chiefly on New York-based publications.

Fit to Print: 'When it comes to life and love, why do we believe our worst reviews?' Carrie's tizz over her book reviews, and her encounter with Nina Katz, lead her to worry that exes might be badmouthing her all over the city. Worse, Nina could be badmouthing her to A-list celebrities – say, a Gwyneth Paltrow or an Ian McKellen. (Though why Gwyneth or Sir Ian might be interested in the details of Carrie's messy break-ups with Aidan is anybody's guess.) Worried that she's being paranoid but determined to tackle Nina about this the next time they bump into one another, Carrie next sees Ms Katz in the street where she's accompanied by (woo!) Heather Graham. This delights Stanford ('Ms Graham, you are fabulous, may I buy you a pretzel?') but when she's told Carrie's name, Heather pulls the same face Nina pulled earlier. Ouch!

And So ...: 'That's a terrible thing to think about me!' Angst about the public reception of your written work doesn't strike me as a universal theme, somehow, and the attempt to tie this into the 'reviews' one receives from ex-partners is only semi-successful. That said, this fifth season, like the fourth before it, does seem to be moving away from episodes that the majority of people can relate to and moving towards being more of a soap/sitcom relating to a specific group of people – which is a common development with long-running TV shows. So, while this is a bit of a shapeless episode and not really *about* anything, it's also above-average in terms of sheer entertainment value. Stanford is always good value for money; the scene where Steve and Carrie discuss Aidan is both funny and horrifying and Heather Graham's face-pulling cameo is an effective punchline (Stanford, though, goes one better with his non-sequitur: 'Have you ever been to Bavaria?')

73
The Big Journey

1 September 2002

Written by Michael Patrick King
Directed by Michael Engler

Guest Cast
Chris Noth (Mr Big) Mario Cantone (Anthony Marentino)
Evan Handler (Harry Goldenblatt) Molly Shannon (Lily Masterson)
Roscoe Ormon (Train Waiter) Charles Techman (Porter)
Frank Ensenberger (Mr Winkle Groupie) Mr Winkle (Mr Winkle)
Robert Peters (Bachelor #1) Jason Kolotouros (Bachelor #2)
Jack McCarthy (Bachelor #3)

Out and About: Carrie is doing a series of readings and book signings in San Francisco. She is, she insists to the others, 'very big' there. What she means, as Miranda points out, is 'Big is in San Francisco'. Carrie plans to go on the train, rather than fly, and is going to book a room on the long-haul rail journey.

Samantha: Sam is suffering from a 'been-there done-that existential crisis' and thinks that New York should change its name to Same York. She's bored and lets everyone know it. Carrie suggests that Sam come with her to San Francisco, suggesting that two girls on a train will be just like the film *Some Like It Hot*. It isn't, of course. It's rather dull with tacky dining cars full of Amish people and heavily drinking married men, and Sam and Carrie's accommodation on the train is so small that the toilet is also the shower. Viewing it, Sam claims that she's 'beginning to understand why there was a murder on the Orient Express'. Sam later admits to suffering a 'mid-life thing', but gets over it in a minimum of screen time.

Fashion Victims: Charlotte's suede top is, er, top. Carrie's Vivienne Westwood blue plaid dress is a tad traditional, but really works, while Sam's vile Thierry Mugler green jacket really doesn't – not even by combining it with her white houndstooth Escada skirt can she save it. Mr Winkle's stripy blue top is awesome.

Miranda: Miranda and Samantha come up with the idea of a chain of male brothels open for women. Sam suggests calling the chain 'Starfucks'.

Fit to Print: Part of Carrie's reason for going to San Francisco is to see Mr Big with whom she's convinced she will inevitably have consequence-free sex. Buoyed by this thought and by Miranda and Sam's plan for brothels, as well as Charlotte's new-found preparedness to have sex rather than hunt husbands, Carrie pens the following: 'Certain women of a certain age are all after a certain thing – and that certain thing does not involve a certain ring. Are we the new bachelors?'

Charlotte: Harry Goldenblatt comes over to Charlotte's apartment so that she can sign her final divorce papers and she informs him that she's thinking of selling the home his divorce negotiations have won for her. He tells her that he knows of a smaller bachelor pad which is for sale and he can show it to her, although it may be a bit too 'male' for her tastes. While showing her around, Harry hits on her, utilising all the tacky paraphernalia of the apartment (pre-programmed stereo system, dimmers). Charlotte leaps on him and they have sex. Which is ironic, given that she hired him as her lawyer because she was too attracted to his partner.

Later, while discussing this encounter with her gay pal, Anthony, Charlotte wonders how to keep her 'relationship' with Harry down to just the sex. Anthony suggests she keep the conversation to a minimum, for example, just the phrases 'fuck me' and 'get out'. Charlotte and Harry have sex on another occasion and, despite his pleas for a dinner date, Charlotte insists, with Sam-like efficiency, that they are not in a relationship and he is just 'a great fuck'.

Hey, Big Guy: 'This Mr Big character, does he have a real name?' asks a man with a raised hand at one of Carrie's book readings. It's Big. After the reading he goes back to her hotel room where she virtually jumps him. Big, however, insists that she come to dinner and there they discuss her book which Big says he saw in a shop 'right there in the window, next to the real books. Cute cover.' He says he had no idea he hurt Carrie as much as the book makes clear he did. He used to read her column, of course, but seeing them all stacked up together in one place was difficult reading for him. They go back to her hotel room, where Carrie tries to seduce him again, but he doesn't seem to notice, saying he doesn't want her to get hurt again. Big asks her to talk to him some more about the book, in particular this part on page 39 ... The next morning Carrie wakes up fully clothed. She and Big *haven't* had sex. Carrie gets up to go to another book reading but then Big calls her back. Only now do they have sex. Carrie and Sam head back to NYC first class.

Also Starring: Evan Handler, as Harry Goldenblatt, has (like Kristin Davis), a CV of guest parts in the best TV has to offer: he played democratic fundraiser Doug Weyland for three weeks on *The West Wing* (10–24 October 2001) and has also guested on the ninth season of *Friends* (in 'The One Where Rachel Goes Back to Work' on 9 January

2003). Film work includes playing David in *Natural Born Killers* (Oliver Stone, 1994) and, surprising no one who has seen him, as Larry in a biopic of *The Three Stooges* (James Frawley, 2002).

And So . . .: 'It's not the journey, it's the destination.' It's great to see Big again, good that even in this short season the producers could get him involved, even if only for one week, and terrific that Chris Noth is given a chance to add another layer to his underrated and quietly complex performance in the role. There's also a really funny strand about Carrie having to share her book tour platform with 'Mr Winkie', a cute, miniature dog who is apparently massive on TV and with kids and who has apparently also written a book. The subplot about Carrie having a spot on her face is strangely pointless.

74
I Love a Charade

8 September 2002

Written by Cindy Chupack and Michael Patrick King
Directed by Michael Engler

Guest Cast
Willie Garson (Stanford Blatch) David Eigenberg (Steve Brady)
Ron Livingston (Jack Berger) Evan Handler (Harry Goldenblatt)
Sean Palmer (Marcus) Elizabeth Regen (Amy)
Julie Halston (Bitsy Von Muffling) Nathan Lane (Bobby Fine)
Melissa Short (Cassandra) Andrea Langi (Shayne) Daniel Ziskie (Judge)
James Remar (Richard Wright)

Out and About: Carrie and co. are seeing Carrie's friend Bobby Fine in his piano cabaret bar act thing. It's a sort of blend of jokes and piano tunes and it ends with Bobby announcing that he's going to marry the amusingly named Bitsy Von Muffling in the Hamptons later that summer. Carrie laughs – she's always assumed that Bobby was gay and is convinced that he's joking, but he's absolutely serious. He invites them all to the wedding.

Miranda: Miranda is unimpressed with Bobby's announcement, claiming that he is obviously gay (he has, to be fair,
just said 'Mr Broadway has to go tinkle' when referring to
himself) and that this is a marriage of, at best, convenience
and companionship. As Bobby and Bitsy tell everyone
about their love, Miranda tells her friends that it is the
'love façade' that she finds 'the most offensive part'. Later,
Miranda finds Steve asleep on her bed after he's been
looking after Brady. Prompted by nothing but the smell of
lilacs and an upsurge in feelings for Steve, she quietly,
quickly seduces him and they have sex. She takes responsibility for this action, but worries it will upset their 'exes
who are friends and who have a baby' dynamic, and she
dashes off to the Hamptons with the girls, declaring, 'I'm
a fucking fugitive. Literally.'

Samantha: Sam plans to go to the wedding and decides to
use Richard's house for a party the day before so that the
girls can have a longer stay out there.

Charlotte: Charlotte is still having regular sex with Harry
Goldenblatt. He's been invited to the wedding too, and so
they decide to go together. Charlotte confesses to the
others that Harry isn't her type because 'He's bald and
short and he eats with his mouth open.' She also notes that
he's hairy everywhere except on his head and that she finds
this slightly disgusting. Although he embarrasses her at
Samantha's party, and at the wedding, she's impressed by
his white suit, charm, self-deprecating wit ('I'm sure you'll
hate my moves on the dance floor, but this is the chance
that every man must take . . .') and obvious affection for
her. She tells him that she thinks she might be falling in
love with him and he responds by saying that he's been
falling in love with her on a minute-by-minute basis since
the moment he first saw her. He says their romance can't
ever go anywhere, not only because she 'could have any
blue-blooded guy in the room' and will tire of him, but also
because there's no way his Judaism will let him marry a
Gentile in all conscience.

Fit to Print: In the light of Bobby's odd marriage plan and her own determinedly single status, Carrie pens a column where she wonders what it is that is needed to make a relationship work 'til death us do part'.

Also Starring: Nathan Lane may be most recognisable to audiences for his role in *Mouse Hunt* (Gore Verbinski, 1997), but most of his work has been on Broadway. He won Tony awards for his roles in *The Producers* and *A Funny Thing Happened on the Way to the Forum*.

Men: Carrie bumps into Jack Berger (see **71**, 'Plus One Is the Loneliest Number') by accident and, discovering that he is now single, she asks him to Samantha's party. However, once he's there she frightens him off by pouring forth at embarrassing length on the topic of her and Aidan. He flees: 'He literally couldn't get away from me fast enough,' she pouts, saying that it wasn't *really* her that frightened Jack, 'It was the Zsa Zsa Zoo, it makes me crazy . . .' Jack turns up at Bobby and Bitsy's wedding (technically he's not crashing as the groom invited the entire clientele of a restaurant Jack happened to be in the night before) to let Carrie know that she didn't, on reflection, freak him out that much.

Trivia: James Remar's cameo as Richard on the answerphone is uncredited. This is par for the course on this series (see **55**, 'Time and Punishment').

Fashion Victims: Carrie's David Dalrymple's House of Field's pink dress; with her hair backcombed and a bejewelled Judith Lieber clutch bag in her hands – she looks simply wonderful.

Miranda dresses Brady in Ralph Lauren so that he'll be swish enough to be accepted at Samantha's party (to which he's specifically not been invited because he's 'Mr Shitty Pants', poor kid). Sam's orange pool-side mini-dress could damage your eyes if seen on a 100Hz TV.

And So . . .: 'What do we do now?' 'Dance.' It's about halfway through this episode that you realise that Harry

Goldenblatt is the series' most memorable creation since Stanford Blatch. Although there's much good verbiage (Charlotte – 'I love "Cats!"' Bobby – 'Medic!') this is primarily a heartfelt episode dealing with the feelings of the four main characters. Carrie's absurd mixed metaphor about drowning her sorrows in a third piece of cake is a real rewind-the-tape-and-listen-again moment.

Season Six (2003)

Created by Darren Star
Based on the book by Candace Bushnell
Executive Consultant: Darren Star
Executive Producer: Michael Patrick King
Executive Producer: Sarah Jessica Parker
Executive Producer: Cindy Chupack
Executive Producer: John Melfi
Co-Executive Producer: Jenny Bicks
Producer: Antonia Ellis
Producer: Jane Raab
Associate Producer: Mark McGann
Associate Producer: Grace Naughton

Regular Cast
Sarah Jessica Parker (Carrie Bradshaw) Kim Cattrall (Samantha Jones)
Kristin Davis (Charlotte York/Charlotte York Goldenblatt)[1]
Cynthia Nixon (Miranda Hobbes)[2]

75

To Market, to Market

22 June 2003

Written and Directed by Michael Patrick King

Guest Cast
David Eigenberg (Steve Brady) John Corbett (Aidan Shaw)
Victor Webster (Chip Kilkenney) Ron Livingston (Jack Berger)
Evan Handler (Harry Goldenblatt) Wallace Lanham (Willy)
James Biberi (Detective) Bernardo Irzarri (Juan)
Amish Patel (Cab Driver) Tony Ray Rossie (Truck Driver)
Travis Wright (Irate Driver)

Out and About: The sixth series picks up with Carrie having overslept in the city that never sleeps. She's due to ring the 9.30 bell to announce the start of trading at the

---

[1] Charlotte adds Harry's surname to hers after their marriage in **82**, 'The Catch'.
[2] Miranda's surname doesn't change after her marrriage to Steve in **88**, 'The Ick Factor'.

New York Stock Exchange because today is the day that
her paper, the *New York Star*, goes public – i.e. people will
be able to buy shares in it, which Charlotte later does.

The City: Sam is incensed that the meatpacking district
into which she moved (see **48**, 'Cock a Doodle Doo!') is
growing increasingly fashionable, increasingly gentrified
and increasingly expensive. When Miranda orders a burger
that costs $20 Sam comments that the only thing that you
could spend $20 on in the area when she moved in was 'a
hand job from a tranny'. It becomes clear that all the
prostitutes, transvestites, transsexuals and other assorted
streetwalkers of Sam's district now know her by sight and
she's grown to love the local colour of an area she once
hated and is resisting its changing. She's particularly
enraged to discover that a Pottery Barn (a chain store
offering mid-price, bland furnishings catering to middle-
aged tastes) will be opening near her.

Miranda: While changing Brady and larking around with
Steve, Miranda gets poo all over her face. This is actually
very funny. During the subsequent horseplay, Miranda
suddenly realises that she's completely in love with Steve,
always has been and that they belong together. She's been
lying to herself for years. Freaked out by this sudden
self-realisation, she picks an argument with Steve and
chases him out of the apartment. She then confides in
Carrie, telling her 'I'm in love with Steve . . .' 'I can believe
it,' deadpans Carrie, 'I just can't believe you admitted it.'

Samantha: A new guy moves into Sam's building. He's an
attractive stockbroker with a six-pack and stock tips. They
start having semi-regular sex at Sam's instigation and he
gives her stock-market tips (turning 'mutual fun into
mutual funds'). He's eventually arrested for insider trading, and it turns out that he's a prolific philanderer who
gives away information to everyone he sleeps with.

Charlotte: Increasingly in love with the 'so not her type'
Harry Goldenblatt, who promised his late mother on her
death bed that he would only marry another person of

Jewish faith, Charlotte tries to find out if it's possible that he could change his mind, asking if the 'whole Jewish thing' is really that important. But it is. She even asks him to change his mind during sex, when he's seconds away from orgasm, and he agrees that perhaps Judaism isn't really that important. The next morning, however, he rightly points out that 'asking me to renounce Judaism during sex is a clear manipulation . . .'

He says that he didn't explain to her about how important Judaism was to him initially because he couldn't believe that 'a shikzah Goddess' like her could really fall for 'a Putz' like him and therefore he never thought it would come up. Harry tells Charlotte that the main reason he needs to marry within his religion is that he would like his children to be brought up within their heritage. And so she feels she has to tell him that she possibly can't have children. He says that they could adopt or work something else out. She's very important to him and other considerations can be worked through later. Impressed with his 'humour, compassion and acceptance', Charlotte begins to consider the real possibility that Harry Goldenblatt is the *one*.

Fit to Print: Is dating really that different to the Stock Market? i.e. Carrie wonders: 'When it comes to finance and dating, why do we keep investing?'

Men: Carrie is due to go on her official first date with Jack Berger (it's obviously not all that long since the events of the previous episode); they're planning to go for dinner and to a movie. Jack calls her saying: 'It's Jack. Berger, not Kerouac. Just wanted to clear that up.'

Carrie bumps into Aidan in the street: he's hale and hearty and carrying a baby around with him – his son, Tate. He married another furniture designer. Carrie's pleased to see him so obviously happy.

Trivia: Berger mentions Jack Kerouac, beat poet and author of the classic adolescent text *On The Road* (1957). He also claims he's 'The Candy Man', a nickname for Rat

Pack hero Sammy Davis Jnr (1925–1990). Carrie realises
what he's doing and queries this, so he brazenly suggests,
'Sammy Davis ripped me off!' 'You don't feel the need to
use the Junior?' queries Ms Bradshaw.

Fashion Victims: Carrie gets all tangled up in a Calvin
Klein silk tank dress topped by a vintage floral print opera
coat (direct from Sarah Jessica Parker's closet). She tries to
find her balance in platform Miu Miu shoes. Charlotte's
brown tweed Ralph Lauren jacket and a pair of Levis are
simple, smart and sexy. Sam's horrid banana-covered top
defies further description. Carrie's ridiculous headscarf
looks decidedly odd.

Also Starring: A return visit for Ron Livingston's Jack
Berger; now single and interested in Carrie. Ron was in
Band of Brothers, HBO's World War Two mini-series in
which he played Captain Nixon, and *The Practice* where
he used to be a regular as Assistant District Attorney Alan
Lowe. Born in 1968, he went to Yale with fellow actor
Edward Norton.

And So . . .: 'I so cannot be in love with Steve . . . how can
I have been wrong all these years?' This is a very focused
season opener which seems to know exactly where it, and
the season, is going. Mixing trauma, farce, character
comedy and serious character stuff it's a really impressive
scripting juggling act. Miranda going loopy over Steve and
completely losing it when he announces he's seeing someone else is really funny and Carrie's scalp-crawlingly awful
date with the graphic designer guy is *excruciating*.

76
Great Sexpectations

29 June 2003

Written by Cindy Chupack
Directed by Michael Patrick King

Guest Cast
David Eigenberg (Steve Brady) Ron Livingston (Jack Berger)
Evan Handler (Harry Goldenblatt) Lynn Cohen (Magda)
Jason Lewis (Jerry Jerrod) Pierre Epstein (Rabbi Minsch)
Julia Murney (Rival Raw Woman) George Manns (Janitor)
Elaine Kussack (Rabbi's Wife) Kimberly Campoli (Cocktail Waitress)
Anthony Stewart-Jones (Jules) Victoria Velero (Mimi)
Angelina Hong (Sales Girl) Rochelle Aytes (Hostess)

Wine and Dine: Carrie makes a pun of 'Berger' and 'Burger', talking about how he's as delicious as the first few bites of a really good Burger.

Samantha takes her friends to a restaurant where they don't cook the food; it's all vegan non-dairy and less than 118 degrees. The soup is chilled and the special of the day is leek papaya patties served with zucchini enchiladas. Miranda and Carrie go for a pizza afterwards in order actually to consume some food. Sam decides to go for the waiter.

Miranda: Still mourning the idea of her and Steve getting back together, Miranda describes her Tivo (solid state TV programme recorder) as her boyfriend and she's devastated when Magda accidentally breaks it. After hours on the phone to the support people she still can't get it to work and then the man who is meant to come around and repair it doesn't turn up. Steve fixes it almost without the slightest difficulty and then dashes off for what he says is a hot date, leaving Miranda cheerful about her technology but increasingly miserable about Steve's role in her life.

Samantha: Sam hunts down and seduces the waiter from the restaurant, fighting off (or paying off!) several competing women in the process. She and the waiter then have sex in an unusually large (for television, anyway) number of positions and she doesn't get any sleep.

Charlotte: After careful consideration about the possibility of marrying Harry, Charlotte decides that she must convert to Judaism. When Charlotte announces this to her friends, using the words, 'I'm becoming a Jew,' the incidental music stops and they all look at her in silence for a moment. Even funnier is the reluctance of Harry's local Rabbi even to talk to her about the possibility of her conversion. 'We're not interested,' he tells her when she turns up, and then closes the door in her face.

Men: Berger's excuse for not phoning Carrie is a stroke of genius: 'A sixty-foot raccoon was attacking the village and I had to trap it and kill it and stuff it . . . I might have rabies.'

Carrie: Carrie is now dating Jack Berger, but they've not yet had sex. She and Jack click so well in all other aspects of life (even his kissing is awe-inspiring apparently) that she's sure the sex will be fantastic. It isn't. It's terrible. On both occasions they do it. Carrie frets and panics, asks the girls for advice and decides against telling him. She decides to get some sexy underwear, some sexy bedroom shoes and then get really, really drunk before the next time she and Jack have sex. She thinks this will remove her inhibitions. In the end all that happens is that she passes out before they have the chance to have sex. The next morning they talk about their failure to have good sex (indeed, on the previous night, any sex at all) and after some discussion they go for it again, and this time it works.

Trivia: The title is a pun on that of Charles Dickens's 1860 novel *Great Expectations*, but you almost certainly knew that.

Fashion Victims: At their all-girls-together dinner, Carrie wears an Alberta Ferretti beaded dress with a vintage satin cape from the La Reina shop. Nice rhinestone necklace, too. Charlotte's cleavage-enhancing ruffled corset from Ralph Lauren may be her best ever outfit. Miranda's black Moschino, coupled with a black bandeau by Alberta Ferretti, is certainly *her* best outfit in a long while – a sign that her period of dull-dressing post-baby blues is over. Sam's disastrous purple fake fur muffler is the mistake of the show.

(Another) City: The episode's writer makes up a TV show which Miranda is watching on BBC America. It's apparently about a black man from Brixton and a white woman from Hampstead Heath and their strange romance when he moves into the flat above her hat shop. Leaving aside the spectacular non-issue of what American TV (still-clearly-crippled-by-the-after-effects-of-segregation) would call 'interracial relationships' in London and the fact that you can't be *from* Hampstead Heath (unless you're a rabbit or a squirrel; you can be from Hampstead, yes, but from Hampstead Heath?), the clips we see manifestly aren't British television. They're in an aspect ratio of 16:9 and are shot in single camera video. British TV just isn't made like that. The culture crash romance of Jules and Mimi is obviously meant to echo thematically the Charlotte/Harry culture clash romance, but the very *concept* just doesn't function in a British context.

And So . . .: 'We should be smoking, not chokin'.' This is easily the most drunk we've ever seen Carrie get. A smart little look at the things that can unexpectedly go wrong based upon expectation, there's an enormous amount of good comedy herein. The episode is also superbly directed, including a huge swinging pan in Carrie's apartment (just after Berger says, 'We gotta make the bed more like a restaurant!') and the brilliantly constructed scene with the overlapping shower curtains.

77
The Perfect Present

6 July 2003

Written by Jenny Bicks
Directed by David Frankel

Guest Cast
Chris Noth (Mr Big) David Eigenberg (Steve Brady)
Ron Livingston (Jack Berger) Evan Handler (Harry Goldenblatt)
Lynn Cohen (Magda) Jason Lewis (Jerry Jerrod)
Pierre Epstein (Rabbi Minsch) Jennifer Coolidge (Victoria)
Ericka Kreutz (Purse Party Woman)

Miranda: Miranda finds condoms in Brady's nappy changing bag where they've obviously been accidentally left by Steve. She gets angry at him, ostensibly because he's exposing their baby to contraceptives, but actually because she's realised she's still in love with him and the knowledge that he's in a relationship with someone else is upsetting to her. As Carrie says, 'some of Miranda's baggage had shifted during the fight . . .' As if to prove the invalidity of Miranda's general point about Steve not taking parenthood seriously compared to her, Brady falls off the chair and starts to cry while she is lecturing Steve on how he should be more focused on the baby.

Out and About: Victoria, a never-before-seen old friend of the entire gang, has had a bad break-up and has invited them over. They go en masse to offer emotional support. When they get there they discover that Victoria has decided that her destiny lies in designing, making and selling her own bags. Sam is unimpressed, snarling that she'd prefer to carry a colostomy bag when she is presented with one particular example. At this 'purse party', Samantha meets Jerry, the waiter whom she successfully pursued in **76**, 'Great Sexpectations', and she chases after him again. They end up having sex against the wall outside Victoria's apartment, but they're discovered by Victoria. This sudden intrusion of carnal activity sends Victoria into a spin and she has a hysterical, screaming, ranting fit in the middle of her own party.

Charlotte: Charlotte is accelerating her studies in Judaism: she unconsciously utters her first 'Oi!' at one point and is delighted, as this means she's well on the way to being thoroughly assimilated into her new life. Ever the straight-A student, she has thrown herself into her conversion classes and is determined to do this right and not be a 'meat-eating vegetarian'. The hardest thing, she finds, is being prepared to give up Christmas – she labels Rabbi Minsch, who instructs her that she'll have to leave her Christian traditions behind, as 'The Minsch who stole Christmas'.

Carrie: Carrie is having a fine old time with Berger (even the sex is now good) until she sees him hear a message on his answerphone from his ex-girlfriend. He swears at the answerphone twice while flipping it the double finger. Convinced he's actually a lunatic with serious rage issues, Carrie later confronts him about this and he explains that 'she cheated on me, that's how it ended, she broke my heart and killed me and then I was dead'. Which is quite sweet.

Also Starring: Boston-born Jennifer Coolidge appeared on Broadway with Cynthia Nixon in the successful revival of Clare Boothe Luce's *The Women*, presumably the cause of her appearance here. She is most recognisable as 'Stifler's Mom' in the *American Pie* film series (Jesse Dylan, 1999, 2001, 2003).

Hey, Big Guy: Big phones Carrie one night and they have phone sex. She tells the girls and admits that this is something that she and he have done on occasion since he moved away. She decides this has to stop now that she's serious about Jack and phones Big again to tell him so. During the conversation, a new Big style tip emerges: while a Jacuzzi is apparently still a cliché, a Hot Tub is retro.

Fit to Print: 'He has a past, I have a past – do our pasts really have to have a present?' Carrie wonders. And do you as a couple have a future if your pasts are in the present?

Fashion Victims: Carrie's Rebecca Taylor rainbow silk dress over cargo pants from Zara at the 'purse party' is terrific. Miranda's clothes sense continues its upward trend this season with her pink pinstripe (Zenobia). Charlotte is charming in Chanel separates and a leather Louis Vuitton bag. Sam mixes up an Armani halter and a lovely Gucci satin jacket, much better than her other one (see **70**, 'Cover Girl'). Best of all is Carrie's very ordinary striped T-shirt (get one on any market) with a very out-of-the-ordinary goddess pattern dress by cult Brazilian bikini designer Rosa Cha for an awe-inspiring effect. As a prelude to phone sex, Big and Carrie talk about the red Gucci dress she wore when they were going out.

And So . . .: 'It's not baggage, it's Big-ige.' The theme of whether or not the past should be allowed to dominate the present is a little obviously expressed, but there's some exceptional character material in here and Chris Noth's appearance is a rare treat. It's a shame, though, that it's announced in the opening credits and not left as a surprise 'Easter egg' for the audience – as John Corbett's was in **76**, 'Great Sexpectations'.

78
Pick-a-Little, Talk-a-Little

13 July 2003

Written by Julie Rottenberg and Elisa Zuritsky
Directed by David Frankel

Guest Cast
Evan Handler (Harry Goldenblatt) Ron Livingston (Jack Berger)
Jason Lewis (Jerry Jerrod) Patti Karr (Mrs Collier) Yaani Kinf (Marcy)
Liza Lapira (Pam) Birgit Darby (Jane) Nick Gregory (Paul)

Charlotte: 'Good morning, Mrs Collier, I'm a Jew now, how are you?' says our Charlotte when faced with one of her neighbours for the first time since her conversion. She seems to be really getting into her newly found Judaism (see **77**, 'The Perfect Present'. She's preparing Harry traditional Shabbat meals and singing traditional Jewish songs and enjoying herself immensely. She's even practising her new signature, 'Charlotte York Goldenblatt', despite Harry not yet having proposed. She insists they have an understanding about their future.

However, when Charlotte insists that Harry can't watch baseball on Shabbats a row ensues. 'I gave up Christ for you, you can't give up the Mets?' she demands, and he points out that if they continue like this life will be long and dreary if every time she wants him to do something like take out the rubbish or tidy up, she uses the 'I gave up Christ for you' line. Charlotte responds by telling Harry that when people see them together, they wonder what she's doing with *him*; making it clear that, as much as she's denied it before, she thinks she is frankly too good for him and that normally she'd be out of his league. Harry quietly says that he knew some people would think that, but that he had no idea that she was one of them. Then he walks out and later sends someone else around to pick up his TV from Charlotte's. Has New York now got one more single Jewish girl?

Carrie: Carrie feels that there is no greater sound than your friends laughing at your new boyfriend's jokes. She's taken Berger to meet the others and they all love him, taking his advice and finding him charming and amusing.

Fetishes: Sam is still enjoying regular sex with Jerry and is delighted to be with somebody who likes to 'fuck outside the box'. Fantasies they've played out include Jerry as a burglar who ties Sam up and forces her to have sex with him; Jerry as an accountant who takes his fees in kind from the penniless Sam and Jerry as a government agent who coerces Sam into sex in return for immunity from prosecution. Later he tells her he's come up with something hotter to play and Sam is amazed that there is anything hotter than 'secret service sluts'.

Samantha: Once she and Jerry have abandoned their role playing, she finally discovers his surname (Jerrod, making him Jerry Jerrod – his parents have much to answer for) and that he's a recovering alcoholic who regularly attends Alcoholics Anonymous (AA) meetings. These are very important to him. Sam describes herself as 'demanding, stubborn, self-sufficient and always right' both in the office and in the bedroom.

Fit to Print: Carrie loves Jack's new book, *Hurricane Pandora*, but makes the mistake of telling him about the one thing that she doesn't like first – the fact that one of his female characters, a hip New York gal, wears a 'scrunchie' in her hair. Stung by this criticism, and the joky way it is put to him, Jack becomes very withdrawn. Carrie complains about this later to Miranda, commenting that while she accepts that she was needlessly light-hearted and 'sassy' ('sass will bite you on the ass' points out Miranda), he was demonstrating a shocking lack of perspective – especially as the two of them had only recently said 'I love you' for the first time.

Carrie's own column this week builds off her experiences with Jack, opening with the lines, 'When does criticism that is constructive become destructive? Are there times when the ladies should just shut the fuck up?'

Also Starring: Jason Lewis, by now a semi-regular fixture as Jerry Jerrod (a.k.a. 'Agent Smith'), is a model turned actor born in California in 1971. His other actor jobs include appearances in *CSI: Miami* (playing Jimmy Hutton in 'Grand Prix', first transmitted on 10 November 2003), and several episodes of Darren Star's *Beverly Hills 90210* (as Rob Andrews, in March and April 1997).

Miranda: Jack explains something to Miranda that she finds very liberating: when a guy declines to come in for coffee or says that he can't stay because he has an early meeting, it's simply cover for the fact that he's not that keen. Carrie, Charlotte and Miranda come up with dozens of reasons for not calling or leaving early that they've heard from men over the years, but Jack is firm. They're all just code for 'I'm just not that into you'. Miranda considers that she's emerging into a brave new world in which she's not constantly trying to read more or less into 'signals' from men than she should.

When Carrie raises the subject of needlessly nitpicking at friends and partners, Miranda answers, 'All women pick, it's in our DNA, it's our way of showing that we care,' leading Carrie to compare nitpicking to its literal forebear, the female ape or monkey picking nits and lice off her male companion.

When invited over to Charlotte's to cook Jewish food, Miranda is astonished by the turn of events: 'We're wearing aprons, [Carrie,] do *you* own aprons?'

Wine and Dine: Unfortunately for Miranda, her new world of liberation doesn't last very long. Out on a blind date with a friend of Harry's, she is cheerfully laid back when he excuses himself from the evening. She tells him that it's OK, that she knows he's not that into her. He denies this and, still cheerful, she tells him that he should be brave enough just to tell the truth. So he does. He has diarrhoea and *this* is why he's rushing off home.

Fashion Victims: Carrie's winning streak in the clothes stakes continues; her combo of a vintage yellow Mickey Mouse T-Shirt under a simple man's white tuxedo jacket. It might just be me, but Charlotte looks really hot in her little white Jewish veil. Sam's gold lamé-in-pieces thing she wears for one of her fantasy dates with Jerry is very revealing and vaguely reminiscent of Jane Fonda's costume in *Barbarella* (Roger Vadim, 1968).

Trivia: Isn't there so obviously something about the way that Sam says 'Agent Smith' that seems designed to make you recall *The Matrix* (The Wachowski Brothers, 1999) and its less popular sequels.

And So . . .: 'Saying I love you is easy, what comes next is a little scrunchier.' Funny and truthful, this is the best episode of the season so far. Jack's extreme prissiness about bad reviews is the first real dent in the character's armour, but Carrie's talking him out of it is wittily written and beautifully played by a more-than-usually great Sarah Jessica Parker.

79
Lights, Camera, Relationship

20 July 2003

Written by Michael Patrick King
Directed by Michael Engler

Guest Cast
Willie Garson (Stanford Blatch) David Eigenberg (Steve Brady)
Ron Livingston (Jack Berger) Jason Lewis (Smith Jerrod)

Mario Cantone (Anthony Marentino) Amy Sedaris (Courtney)
William Abadie (Tony) Gloria Votsis (Prada Salesgirl)
Brian Delante (Actor) Constance Barron (Actress)
Lincoln Hudson (Photographer #1) Anthony Grasso (Photographer #2)

Charlotte: Now that Harry has left her, Charlotte is ostensibly looking for other dates. Carrie tries to coax her into trying out a friend of hers who is a 'perfect' being, 'straight single and works for Prada', but Charlotte refuses because he's not Jewish and she's not going to change just like that, even though Sam tries to explain to her that 'this Prada item may be off the rack' very soon. Charlotte quietly admits that she's not really looking as she's not over Harry just yet.

Samantha: Sam initially refuses to attend a play in which Jerry is appearing, but later relents. She doesn't like the play (she doesn't like theatre generally) but approves of his public nudity in it. In order to help 'her man', Sam offers to do the PR for his play (for which he's being paid $30 a week!) for free as they have no one else, and turns the opening night into a star-studded gala, making Carrie go and getting all the literati and glitterati to turn up. She also suggests that Jerry get a new stage name as 'Jerry Jerrod' is awful. Drawing on their recent sex games, she chooses 'Smith Jerrod' for him.

Fashion Victims: Carrie buys Jack a shirt which she describes as the 'I never say "Fabulous!" Fabulous Shirt'. Her vintage green gridiron top (Miami Dolphins?) with a white 55 on is great.

Miranda: Miranda is, according to Carrie, currently performing her one-woman show entitled, 'I'm not in love with Steve.' One day, when Steve brings Brady round, he also brings Miranda a treat – 'I scammed you a cupcake, it's chocolate, I had to fight for it!' he says, referring to a toddler's birthday party that Brady has been to at the park. Miranda is clearly crazy about Steve, a fact even she acknowledges, and they wind up making cupcakes together at his apartment. Miranda is horrified to discover that they are actually for his new girlfriend, Debbie, but carries on helping anyway, blinking back tears.

Fit to Print: The crisis with Jack causes Carrie to wonder: 'As women's roles evolve and change we assume that men's do as well ... are the men of today less threatened by a woman's power or are they just acting?'

Carrie: Carrie's publisher sends her a big fat advance cheque for the French edition of her book and she's obviously delighted. Jack seems a little put out and later, talking to her publisher who is also Jack's publisher, Carrie discovers that Jack's contract with the publishing house has been cancelled. She theorises that he's threatened by her success, especially after he starts racing around on a motorbike in a classic male-compensation-issues manner. She tells him that being on the back of the bike frightened her, and he admits that he is threatened by her success. They attend the Sam-organised bash at Jerry's play together, but he runs out on Carrie after being embarrassed by the press interest in her.

Trivia: From this episode onwards Jerry is credited as 'Smith Jerrod', using the name Samantha comes up with for him. Sam starts occasionally to call him 'Smith' as well. For the sake of clarity we'll stick with 'Jerry'.

Sam memorably announces 'shit motherfucker fuck shit' when she discovers she has to go to Jerry's play and then explains to the girls that she has to go to the theatre! ('They finally made that mandatory?' deadpans Carrie).

And So ...: 'Oh, now you went and told the truth!' Charlotte's refusal to abandon her recently acquired Judaism is both funny and charming while Jack's fear of Carrie's success is as bizarre as it is reprehensible, but at least he has the decency to know that he's behaving strangely and is out of line. Everyone cheers for Stanford's sudden reappearance at the end.

80
Hop, Skip, and a Week

27 July 2003

Written by Amy B Harris
Directed by Michael Engler

Guest Cast
Chris Noth (Mr Big) Ron Livingston (Jack Berger)
Evan Holder (Harry Goldenblatt) Jason Lewis (Smith Jerrod)
Lynn Cohen (Magda) Doris Beclack (Lemore)
Lee Shepard (Maurice White) David Pittu (Jonathan)
Alice Gold (Barbara) Catherine Wold (Elaine)
Peter Hermann (David) Angela Scott (Jury Duty Woman)
Rosemarie Dewitt (Fern) Randy Schein (Average Date)
Nate Lombardi (Waiter) Ryan Ross (Gay Guy)
Ann Coatney (Jewish Single #1) Lisa Jolley (Jewish Single # 2)
Sara Barnett (Catholic Schoolgirl #1)
Casey Killoran (Catholic Schoolgirl #2)
Holland Hamilton (Catholic Schoolgirl #3)

Wine and Dine: Charlotte is out on a disastrous date, one
organised by one of the cavalcade of comedy Jewish
mothers whom she has befriended at temple and all of
whom are trying to marry her off to their sons. Spotting
Carrie and Jack, Charlotte gets Carrie to ring her and ask
for help. Charlotte leaves and, once her date has gone,
dashes back into the restaurant and eats with Carrie and
Jack. Sadly their dinner is going almost as badly as hers
did. Carrie is claiming to have a parsley allergy in order to
avoid their being any parsley garnish on her food, which
Jack regards as needlessly histrionic. Charlotte flees as Jack
and Carrie begin to row. Later he says that he needs time
to think; he's going to his house in the Hamptons for a
week and he'll let her know whether he thinks that they can
make it work when he gets back. Carrie is upset but
doesn't see what else she can do. Jack accepts that his
behaviour caused by his jealousy at Carrie's career success
is unreasonable, but he doesn't know if he can overcome it.

Out and About: Carrie is doing jury duty for the City of
New York. She tries to excuse herself on the grounds that

she works for herself and is irreplaceable and it is impossible for anyone to cover for her, but the clerk refuses her request, possibly because she recognises her.

Miranda: Miranda is feeling increasingly guilty about leaving Brady and is afraid he will come to regard Magda as his mother. One day at work she's called in and is told that she isn't successfully managing her cases; one of her colleagues, Fern, seems to have grassed her up, presumably with the intention of picking off Miranda's caseload for herself. Miranda apologises but is both angry and offended. Her righteous fury is something to behold. She points out that nobody works harder than she does and that the weekend her mother died she was back in the office by Monday morning. She volunteers to limit her hours to 55 (yes, 55!) a week.

Fashion Victims: Carrie's brilliant black high-waisted Jean Paul Gaultier baggy trousers combine with her black braces make her look like she's wearing a huge pair of dungarees. She finishes off the look with a vintage red-patterned white shirt and matching Miu Miu red shoes. Sam's pink plastic earrings and terrible top with a thin neon green neck and blue, white and green pattern work much less well. Charlotte's red and white top from Miu Miu is perfect first-date wear (shame about the date). Carrie goes shopping at the Century 21 discount store and gets an Anna Molinaro dress and a Dolce Kimono so cheap she's practically leaping around the place in excitement.

Fit to Print: While Jack is away indulging in his thinking time, Carrie turns the experience of waiting for him to come back into a column. She wonders how people who are actually in the mess are every able to sort it out: 'Do we need distance to get close?'

Samantha: Sam arranges for Jerry to appear in an advert for Absolut vodka. He's naked except for a bottle of the Swedish beverage covering his penis. He's unhappy about this 'exposure' and tells Sam that his AA buddies are ashamed of him advertising alcohol, while his Mother is busy buying up every copy of every magazine that runs the advert that is on sale in his home town in ease his grandmother accidentally sees it. Sam dismisses these people as 'drunks, nobodies and prudes'.

Jerry is also upset by the amount of gay interest he gets after the advert appears in Times Square. Sam explains that this is all according to plan – the gays are first in line, but they will be followed by the girls and then the industry, she explains as if talking to a small child. Later they row about this and Sam is upset. The row even causes her Botox-controlled face to frown; or, as Carrie says, causes something which is 'as close to a frown as Samantha and her dermatologist Dr Peterson would allow'. Sam's mantra is, however, borne out when Jerry is set on by screaming schoolgirls in the street and then, a few days later, offered an acting job as a model/hustler/junkie in a movie directed by Gus Van Sant.

Hey, Big Guy: Big calls Carrie's mobile and his tone: 'I'm with two men in plaid pants and I'm carrying a nine iron, greetings from California . . .' suggests he's actually begging for death. When Carrie queries his taking part in a golf game he responds that he's only doing it so that he can have the Scotch after the game, which sounds much more like the Big we know and miss.

Charlotte: At a Jewish single mixer, and having already turned down both a date and casual sex (with the same guy), Charlotte overhears the other Jewish single girls worrying that all the cute guys have gone, leaving home only 'the fatties and the baldies'. Charlotte looks around, hoping that one of the baldies will be 'her baldie'. She sees Harry across the crowded room and rushes over to him; she tells him that she's missed him, she loves him and she doesn't care if he never marries her, she just wants to be near him. She says she'd be lucky to have him on any terms and she apologises for saying that he wasn't good enough for her. 'Of all the synagogues in all the cities, you had to walk into mine,' he says and then gets down on one knee: 'Charlotte York, will you marry me?'

Carrie: Jack comes back to Carrie's apartment bearing flowers and apologies; he says he loves her and thinks they should try and make their relationship work. They hug and kiss and cry. He stays over that night but the next morning Carrie is alone. Jack has left a Post-it note saying, 'I'm Sorry, I can't – Please Don't Hate Me' on her laptop. He's gone.

And So . . .: 'A pineapple?' 'A coconut!' 'So *close* . . .' There's an awesome dramatic sucker punch in this episode; the way it gets Charlotte and Harry back together and then, immediately after, seems to get Carrie and Jack Berger back together – only to have him abandon her and end the episode with her alone, near to tears and cold. Nice? No, but it's great television – one of the most upsetting moments in the whole series. Poor girl.

81
The Post-it Always Sticks Twice

3 August 2003

Written by Liz Tuccilo
Directed by Alan Taylor

Guest Cast

Jason Lewis (Smith Jerrod) Michael Showalter (Billy)
Brent Crawford (Peter) David Wilson Barnes (Andrew)
Gabe Doran (Frankie) Alani Vazquiez aka LA LA (MTV Interviewer)
Kate Albrecht (Girl on TRL) Cherelle Cargill (Bride)
Deadre Aziza (Bachelorette #1) Janine Green (Bachelorette #2)
Jeanine Serrales (Bachelorette #3) Kim Director (Gracie)
Michele Santopietro (Nicole) Suzanne Didonna (Corinne) Orfeh (Anna)
Zofia Boerucka (Hostess) Katherine Brecka (Woman)
James Hanlon (Cop) David Wheir (Ethan) Amo Gulinello (Dave)
Ciaran Tyrrell (Paul) John Deblasio (Businessman)

Carrie: Carrie tells her friends about her recent break-up with Jack Berger and bemoans the fact that she feels the relationship was a waste of her time. She considers leaving an aggressive message on his answerphone of the 'Hey, it's me, you're a dick!' kind, but realises that that would just be descending to his level. Sam says that the way to never be someone's ex-girlfriend is to never be anybody's girlfriend (see **Samantha**) and tells Carrie that she's suffering from something close to post-traumatic stress syndrome in the aftermath of the Berger break-up. Carrie decides that they all have to go out and do something spectacular that night because she doesn't want to remember that day as the day she was dumped by Post-it note.

Charlotte: Charlotte now earnestly believes in the interconnectedness of all things – explaining to her friends that if she'd never married Trey then she'd never have got divorced, never have needed a divorce lawyer, never met Harry, never fallen in love with him and never gotten engaged to Harry. Carrie's Post-it note break-up must therefore be of use, in some way, at some point in the future, Charlotte insists. Later she revises this theory while drunk – wishing that her marriage to Harry was to be her first so that she could make it the big and special day she wants it to be. She thinks that big second marriages are somehow unseemly. While out on Carrie's big night, though, she meets a group of girls who are having a bachelorette party. Coincidentally, they ask her to take a photograph of them and, when Carrie tells them that Charlotte got engaged today, they insist that she's in the photograph too. She begins to swap wedding planning stories with them so that, in Carrie's words, 'Charlotte's inner judge was silenced by some very loud bachelorettes.'

Miranda: Getting ready for their big night out for Carrie to forget Berger, Miranda tries on – and fits into – her too-small jeans that she's kept around in the vain hope that they will one day fit again. And this is that day. 'In my skinny jeans! For the first time since 1985!' she shrieks at her friends. Sam compliments her on her 'cute little ass' which she says she'd never noticed before and Miranda, renewed with confidence, spends the whole night getting hit on and chatting up younger men. It's not, as Carrie voice-overs 'a state of behind' but 'a state of mind'.

Fashion Victims: Jerry is due to go on MTV and, as his publicist, Samantha has informed all the most fashionable fashion houses. TRL, Gucci and D & G have all sent suits for him to wear, but Jerry isn't interested – he's going to wear his jeans and a sleeveless shirt. Appalled, Sam worries that the kids won't look up to him unless he's wearing clothes that they are completely unable to afford. She convinces him to wear some excessively expensive sunglasses. Sam's tiny 'New York Dolls' dress is bonkers apparel for someone of her age, but somehow she makes it work splendidly.

Samantha: Jerry refers to Samantha – while talking to only her, mind – as his 'girlfriend', which upsets her. It's not a label she's happy with and she tells him not to mention 'girlfriends' to anyone, ostensibly because it's a bad idea for anyone who is a sex symbol to be considered attached. When he tells the MTV audience that he's dating but there's 'no one special', exactly as she instructed him, she's suddenly struck by the fact that she's not happy with the label 'nobody special' either. This provokes her to grab, quite literally, the nearest man to her – with unexpected consequences (see **Out and About**).

Fit to Print: Pondering on Charlotte's chat about everything happening for a reason, Carrie pens the following: 'Why are we in such a rush to move from confused to Confucious? Do we look for lessons to lessen the pain?'

Trivia: The title is from *The Postman Always Rings Twice* (Bob Rafelson, 1981), a movie title which has been riffed on before by TV series such as *Moonlighting*.

Out and About: Sam guestlists all her friends at a new bar called Bed which is apparently fabulous and, not surprisingly, full of beds on which the guests sit or lie (although it can't be that fabulous, given that it's playing a remix of the Tom Jones version of 'Sex Bomb'). There Carrie bumps into some friends of Jack's who don't know they've broken up and drunkenly lectures them on the horrors of being dumped by Post-it note. Her friends drag her away.

Outside, while walking past some younger guys, they smell cannabis and, inspired, they go to a rough bar to try and buy some because Sam's usual dealer isn't available. ('Damn those dealers and their summer houses!' deadpans Carrie.). Carrie has decided to get high (for the first time in a long time. They get thrown out of the bar after Sam has cracked onto another woman's boyfriend, but not before she's purchased a pre-rolled spliff. Carrie starts smoking it in the street but is picked up by a policeman for doing so. When Carrie explains that she's smoking because she was dumped by Post-it note, he doesn't believe her; so she shows him it. Appalled that anyone would do this to her he lets her off with the more minor misdemeanour of 'Smoking [tobacco only] in a Bar'.

Wine and Dine: A stoned Carrie and company eat ice cream in the diner just before the end credits roll. 'I said Doobie!' cackles Carrie as she monopolises Samantha's ice-cream split.

And So . . .: 'They're not strangers, they're our new friends with pot!' It's brilliant to see Miranda regain confidence in her own general brilliance and attractiveness after all her doubts over recent episodes and this is generally a life-affirming, giggly episode; somewhat surprising after the end of last week's instalment but no less welcome for that. A really good episode to show to friends who doubt that the series is both funny and clever. Isn't the policeman's disbelief and sudden compassion just great? And if Miranda and Carrie think that only women have 'skinny jeans' hidden away then there are obviously some secrets still left in the world. Oh, and *all* the men I've asked think that the Post-it note break-up is completely unacceptable. A terrific episode all round.

82
The Catch

10 August 2003

Written by Cindy Chupack
Directed by Alan Taylor

Guest Cast
Willie Garson (Stanford) David Eigenberg (Steve Brady)
Evan Handler (Harry Goldenblatt) Mario Cantone (Anthony Marentino)
Jason Lewis (Smith Jerrod) Sean Palmer (Marcus) Lynn Cohen (Magda)
Pierre Epstein (Rabbi Minsch) Brian Callen (Howie Halberstein)
Paul Cannon (Drew) Eleni Fuiaxis (Debbie)
Michael Raab (Photographer)

Carrie: Carrie's been asked to do an article for a magazine about the Bungee Jumping style trend for swinging on a large trapeze in public. She takes Stanford with her for moral support when she tries it, ignoring his taunts about whether she wants to skip it and go to Jeffries for the sale they're having on stripes. She grits her teeth and bears it. 'Two hours later, I was hooked,' she says.

Men: Harry tries to match up Carrie with Howie, a friend of his who is doing best man duties at the wedding and is only going to be around for a week. Carrie can't see why she should have a fling with a guy who is only going to be around for a few days: 'It's expiration dating . . . what's the point?' she asks her friends. Sam insists that that is exactly the point. Carrie considers herself to be too old for a fling, but decides to go along with it anyway. She goes out with Howie, who is cute and funny, and they have sex. Terrible, boring sex where he vibrates the bed in a comedy 'boing boing' manner with his frenzied thrusting, and Carrie lies there visibly (to the audience if not Howie) bored. She also gets a crick in her neck as a result of this process. It was, she says, 'teenage sex' in the sense that he'd got no idea what he was doing and she'd rather have been somewhere else. When he invites her back to his hotel the next day (which is also Charlotte's wedding day) she refuses and makes clear that this was a 'fling'. He gets upset, drunk and delivers a bizarre rant of a 'Best Man' speech which contains the word 'Bitch!' and the phrase 'You used me for sex!' shouted in her direction.

This episode has the largest role ever for Charlotte's gay friend Anthony. He describes Howie's crazy Best Speech as 'a mazzeltov cocktail' and throws water at Miranda when she accidentally sets fire to her notes at the wedding ('Sorry, hun, good speech though' he deadpans). Earlier, while arranging the wedding's details, he screams into the phone at some poor functionary about all the candles they want and, on seeing Charlotte in her wedding dress for the first time, calls her 'Audrey Hepburn-owitz'. When Harry asks if Charlotte is the most wedding-obsessed woman he's ever known, Anthony claims that this is far from the case. He apparently knew a girl who gave herself a stroke before the wedding, but 'pulled it together for the big day'. Can Anthony have his own spin-off series, please?

Miranda: Steve's girlfriend Debbie, whom Miranda has not met on the grounds that once she's met her, she becomes real, has been buying Brady presents for a while and has now started buying Miranda presents and giving them to her via Steve. Ms Hobbes is particularly angry about an aromatherapy candle, as she tells her friends at lunch. Miranda refuses to meet Debbie, but Steve brings her around with him anyway the next time he has to pick up Brady. Miranda hides under the bed until they go.

Fashion Victims: For a change, Stanford looks *brilliant* in his purple suit with matching tie and shirt. Charlotte's beautiful wedding dress is by Badgley Mischka, the designing duo. It's all ruffles and lace and off-the-shoulder wondrousness. When Carrie goes trapezing she's wearing ordinary Nike baby-blue sweatpants, but with a really nice Ella Moss pink and raspberry-red striped top. Miranda's wearing an orange dress from Versus which looks great with her hair colouring. You can only see this last item in long shot in the last scene of the episode, though.

Fit to Print: Troubled by her inability to let go of the trapeze and take a chance, which isn't really a chance, Carrie wonders if this is a result of getting older: your adolescence and twenties are so often about just having fun – why does this seem to stop in your thirties? 'In life there's no safety net; when did it stop being fun and start being scary?'

Charlotte: Charlotte is desperate for the York/Goldenblatt marriage to be announced in the *New York Times* and the couple have a special photo session in Central Park in anticipation. She gets her wish, but there's a smudge on the photograph on every copy of the paper which makes it look as though she has a moustache: 'I'm having a Jewish wedding and I look like Hitler.'

She develops the theory that her wedding is cursed because Harry accidentally saw her in her wedding dress a few days before; on the day itself there are so many mini-mishaps that she hides in the bathroom and cries between the ceremony and the reception. Carrie finds her and points out that Charlotte has already had the perfect wedding – followed by the not so perfect marriage. Maybe the slightly shambolic wedding is a good omen. Carrie smiles sadly at Charlotte and tells her, 'You have a wonderful man who loves you, who will be there to catch you when you fall . . .' She asks her to open her eyes and look at all the great things about her life.

And So . . .: 'Nothing's casual any more, even when it says so on the invitation.' Lucky Cindy Chupack gets to write *another* Charlotte wedding day episode, one full of subversions and reversals and comedy disasters. From Howie's psychotic, ranting, best-man speech to Miranda setting fire to her notes, Charlotte spilling red wine on her wedding dress and Harry being unable to break the traditional Jewish glass-wrapped-in-a-cloth, this is a comedy of errors with a secret heart. Lovely.

83
A Woman's Right to Shoes

17 August 2003

Written by Jenny Bicks
Directed by Tim Van Patten

Guest Cast
Willie Garson (Stanford) Evan Handler (Harry Goldenblatt)
Blair Underwood (Dr Robert Leeds) Tatum O'Neal (Kyra)
Lynn Cohen (Magda) Marion McCorry (Board President)
Brian Sullivan (Chuck) Samantha Buck (Margot)
Dolores Duffy (Cataract Lady) Greta Cavazzoni (Salesgirl)
Ashley Stewart-Jones (Jules) Victoria Varlero (Mimi)
Patrick O'Sullivan (Milo) Kelly O'Sullivan (Allegra)
Greg Harr (Younger Man) Genevieve Elma (Mother)
Chris Mongiardo (Waiter) Liam Broggy (Noisy Two-Year-Old)
Seamus Davey Fitzpatrick (Singing Toddler)

Carrie: The single New Yorker's weekend is for purchasing, says Carrie, and who are we to argue? She's out buying presents for her friend Kyra's baby and later when she and Stanford go to Kyra's house for the baby party they are invited to leave their shoes at the door. Carrie reluctantly does so and is appalled when, as she goes to leave, she discovers that her shoes have disappeared; presumably taken by another guest on their way out. Her $485 Manolo Blahniks are gone. After a few days of subtle pressure, Kyra offers to pay for the shoes, but when she discovers that they were $485 she tells Carrie that she will only give her $200. Apparently, she feels she shouldn't have to pay for Carrie's extravagances. What she's clearly missing is that she's actually paying for her own decision to make people take off their shoes before they enter her house and her refusal to find out which of her friends took Carrie's Manolos. It's a clear-cut case of accepting responsibility for your actions, but this doesn't stop Kyra lecturing Carrie on her needlessly expensive shoes and saying that, as a person with 'a real life' i.e. children, she appreciates what's important and what isn't. Carrie's shoes aren't that important. Eventually, Kyra buckles further and buys Carrie new shoes.

Samantha: Samantha is enraged by Carrie's and Kyra's encounter and rants about how people with children expect special treatment and that while she doesn't personally dislike children (although of course she does) there are places where children shouldn't be taken, and parents shouldn't demand that others make allowances for their decision to reproduce. Faced with a noisy child in a restaurant, she grits her teeth and bears it, but when she's told by the management that she can't use her cellphone because of the noise, she points out that she's making far less noise than the screaming, ranting, plate-smashing, food-spilling child on the other side of the restaurant. The waiter tells her they have no policy on that.

Miranda: Miranda's apartment block housing association is interviewing new tenants. One prospective tenant is a young black doctor called Robert Leeds whom Miranda is deeply in lust with the moment she sees him. After Leeds's interview is over and he's gone, Miranda implies to the other members of her residents' association that the reason they don't want to let Robert Leeds move in to their apartment block is because they're racists. In fact there are genuine, if pernickety, questions about his suitability and Miranda is overkeen on him because she fancies him so much. He does move in and he and Miranda become friends after he treats Brady for chicken pox.

Fashion Victims: Shockingly there's another big score for Stanford here: his dark blue suit with green lined patterning, green shirt and green and blue diagonal stripes is great. Carrie commits absolute Fashion Crime for the first time with her retro T-shirt featuring the logo of blundering progressive Rock dinosaurs, *Yes* (one can only assume she's never heard one of their songs).

Carrie (eventually) gets a pair of beautiful, silver rhinestone-studded Manolo Blahniks out of Kyra. She tries them out with a pair of Joe Jeans and a lovely Club Monaco floral blouse. She looks, quite simply, *hot* in this particular get-up.

At lunch Miranda looks great in a one-shoulder-on, one-shoulder-off green dress from Ilya, which again achieves the difficult-to-manage thing that is matching her hair colour, while Charlotte looks fresh and pretty in her pink floral dress from Plenty.

Also Starring: Blair Underwood (born 1964) starred as Jonathan Rollins in *LA Law* from 1987–1994 although the years since haven't seen him find a publicly visible vehicle for his talents.

Tatum O'Neal is the daughter of Ryan O'Neal and the ex-wife of tennis superstar John McEnroe. Born in 1963, she became the youngest person ever to win an Oscar in 1973, winning Best Supporting Actress for her role in *Paper Moon* (Peter Bogdanovich, 1973). Her other films include the lead in *International Velvet* (Bryan Forbes, 1978).

Trivia: A lot of online resources and fan sites list this episode as being called 'No Shoes, No Services'. Why they do this when there's a very clearly marked title onscreen (and it's 'A Woman's Right to Shoes') is anybody's guess.

Miranda's insanely implausible made-up BBC America TV show *Jules and Mimi* (see **76**, 'Great Sexpectations') makes another appearance. Given the obviously semi-graphic sex scenes I believe in it even less than previously.

And So . . .: 'Sometimes I can be a little rigid.' Kyra's behaviour relating to Carrie's shoes is grotesquely patronising, unacceptable and borderline evil. Her eventual acquiescence to her responsibility to replace Carrie's shoes comes around far too late in the episode for her to be redeemed in the eyes of the audience. Sam's confrontation with the mother who is simply incapable of disciplining her child is an example of pure Jones righteousness.

This is a clever episode that manages to take a look at the way that married people, and people with children, are selfish and self-centred (which of course is very different to the way that single, childless people are selfish and self-centred, which the series concerns itself with every week). Most TV series wouldn't dare to criticise the behaviour of any child (regardless of how extreme) or their parents.

Of additional interest, there's a really clever shot where the teabag abandoned by Harry looks vast due to being inches from the camera – part of a nice subplot about Harry trying not to be a slob around Charlotte.

84
Boy, Interrupted

24 August 2003

Written by Cindy Chupack
Directed by Tim Van-Patten

Guest Cast
Willie Garson (Stanford Blatch) Blair Underwood (Dr Robert Leeds)
Mario Cantone (Anthony Marentino) Sean Palmer (Marcus)
David Duchovny (Jeremy Wade) Geri Halliwell (Phoebe)
Benedick Bates (SoHo House Manager)
Jon Ingle aka Lady Bunny (Prom MC) Dolores Duffy (Mrs McCaffrey)
Marcella Guarino (Blonde Knicks Dancer)
Lucas Kerr (Male Pool Attendant) Denia Brache (Cleaning Lady)
Grainne de Buitlear (Female Employee)

Carrie: Carrie didn't go to her high school reunion, so when her high school sweetheart calls her about a one-to-one reunion, she can't resist going to meet him for drinks. She sets up an emergency escape plan to make sure she can get out of the happy reunion if it proves to be not so happy, but in fact Jeremy is even better than she remembers. He's single, good-looking and obviously keen on her. She cancels her escape plans and they have dinner. Later he walks her home and they discuss whether or not she should kiss him goodnight – they have kissed before after all: 'We were in a lip lock for most of nineteen eighty-two,' Carrie points out. They kiss and she takes him up to her apartment. They don't have sex, but they do start dating. Carrie is immediately very happy but wonders what she has been doing for twenty years if the right guy was the one she already had in high school.

Samantha: It's a New York summer and Samantha is slowly boiling to death in the heat of the meat-packing district; she can't use the pool around the corner as the club it's in has a waiting list and she's been waiting for admission and membership for six months. After she inadvertently gets hold of a card belonging to another member, she starts abusing it: she doesn't actually charge anything to it, but merely uses it to get her and the girls (including Stanford) in. Eventually she is rumbled by staff and, while the others make their escape, she holds off security.

Miranda: Miranda's new neighbour, Doctor Robert, offers her free tickets to a Knicks game. He can get courtside seats at any time because he's actually the team's doctor and he specialises in sports medicine. Miranda thinks she's being asked out on a date but in fact he's just giving away a ticket. Wondering whether he sees her as a charity case, Miranda takes the tickets and goes along with Charlotte. Eventually Dr Robert overcomes Miranda's fears by telling her outright that he likes her, and they kiss.

Men: When Carrie asks Jeremy to stay the night he demurs, and then he admits that he's currently staying in a psychiatric facility nearby. Later they discuss his need for therapy and further work, she visits him at the institute and they have a nice picnic (well, as nice as one interrupted by a less well patient running across the lawn screaming 'faeces!' can be). He also gives her a bag of marbles, deadpanning that if he loses any more of his he'll know where there are some stashed. He explains that he didn't immediately tell her he was having treatment because he didn't think 'Hi, I might be crazy, would you like to share an appetizer?' was an appropriate way to begin their first conversation in twenty years. Carrie is willing to give the relationship a try, until he reveals that he'll be in the treatment facility for about ten months to a year. They promise to talk when he's not obligated to return to the centre to check in and Carrie leaves, thinking about how her break-up with the guy who thought he was crazy was the sanest break up she'd ever had.

Charlotte's gay chum Anthony gets another fantastic line when talking about Chelsea: '[You] can't swing a dick without bumping into someone you know.' Oh, and another 'Hello! Wake up and smell the KY!'

Wine and Dine: Cafeteria is a fashionable restaurant in Chelsea.

Guy Talk: Anthony shows Charlotte an advert in an old magazine he's got which proves that Stanford's boyfriend Marcus was once a gay escort – not much of a step away from being a prostitute. Stanford finds out from Samantha about this and splits up with Marcus, claiming that it isn't the escort thing that bothers him but the fact that Marcus couldn't tell him. He's especially upset as they were due to go to the Lesbian, Gay and Transgender Prom of New York and Stanford missed out on his own high school prom back in the day; Carrie agrees to go with him.

Fashion Victims: Carrie's glorious empire-waisted chocolate-striped sundress by Ella Moss. No wonder Jeremy falls in love with her all over again. Charlotte's pin-ruffled Tulseh top is good, but what is it with Charlotte and ruffles this season?

Also Starring: Geri Halliwell was one fifth of the Spice Girls and as such scored eight UK number one hits between 1996 and 1999. She left the Spice Girls acrimoniously and her initial success as a solo artist included the number one hit singles 'Look at Me' and 'Lift Me Up', but long-term solo success has proved more elusive. Her cameo performance here shows that she's no actress – eyes fixed on Kim Cattrall's forehead like some boggle-eyed loon, delivering every line (all four of 'em) with a breathtaking lack of conviction or interest. Dismal is the word.

David Duchovny (born 1960) was the star of FOX TV's phenomenally successful *The X-Files* (1993–2001), which made him one of the most highly paid actors in the history of television and gave him the chance to write and direct several (extremely good) episodes into the bargain. He left the show at the end of its penultimate season but returned for the final episode a year later. Since then he's starred in the Sci-Fi comedy *Evolution* (Ivan Reitman, 2001) and appeared in extreme modelling comedy *Zoolander* (Ben Stiller, 2001). He's a New Yorker, incidentally.

Trivia: Charlotte was a cheerleader in high school; the audience discovers this when Charlotte wonders outloud if she ever told Miranda that she was. 'No, because you knew I would mock you endlessly', replies Miranda. He he he.

Out and About: After Marcus and Stanford have split up, Carrie agrees to attend the Lesbian, Gay and Transgender Prom with Stanford, in order to spare him the indignity of going alone (he has to attend as he's on the committee). They're proclaimed 'The Queen and Queen'. They're dancing and Marcus arrives and tries to cut in. He explains to Stanford that he didn't tell him about his time as an escort because he was embarrassed and regarded it as part of his past, whereas Stanford is part of his future. The two dance as Carrie looks on, her faith in love restored.

And So . . . : 'I can't, I have to visit my boyfriend at the asylum.' David Duchovny's guest turn is typically brilliant, a laid-back and very detailed performance from a charismatically wooden actor who does just enough for you to realise that this is precisely monitored acting. This is yet another superb Cindy Chupack screenplay; one of the very best of the show's whole run with even more wit on display than normal, and the odd hint of meta-fiction ('I don't think my story could end like that,' says Carrie). The central dilemma is, for once, universal. Who hasn't wondered what would have happened had their first love really lasted for ever or what it would be like to see your high school love again? The real love story is, of course, Stanford and Marcus, and if you aren't deeply happy for them as they dance close at the end then you're a terrible human being. This is a simply brilliant episode, one of the show's half dozen best – it even has a slapstick Samantha subplot which resolves without humiliating her. Perfect.

85
The Domino Effect

7 September 2003

Written by Julie Rottenberg and Elisa Zuritsky
Directed by David Frankel

Guest Cast
Chris Noth (Mr Big) David Eigenberg (Steve Brady)
Blair Underwood (Dr Robert Leeds) Jason Lewis (Smith Jerrod)
Irene Glezos (Fran) Julie Halston (Bitsy Von Muffling)
Hoon Lee (Dr Mao) Melidda D Madison (Carol)
Elizabeth Canavan (Barb) Irene Glezos (Fran) Tonye Patano (Ruby)

Carrie: Some New York nights are huge, even gigantic, says Carrie. She also acknowledges that some of them are just 'Big'. Carrie meets Big for dinner and asks him why he's in New York. He tells her he's in the city for routine heart surgery – an angioplasty. Unable to cope with the idea of his dying or being seriously ill, she bursts into tears.

Samantha: Smith is back from his movie shoot with Gus Van Sant and is still obviously very keen on Samantha. Despite their having tried out virtually every sexual experience in her repertoire, there's one kind of intimacy she's still not happy with. She won't hold hands with him. So desperate is she to avoid this that she snatches her arm away and then falls down a hole in the street, breaking her toe in the process. Telling Carrie about Smith's 'twisted' behaviour, Samantha asks for sympathy but fails to get it: Carrie mocks Sam's horror at this simple public display of affection. Eventually Sam cracks and she and Smith start holding hands in public.

Charlotte: Charlotte attends the alternative medical surgery of Dr Mao in order to get acupuncture treatment which she hopes will help her and Harry to conceive a child.

Miranda: Miranda's new doctor-neighbour-boyfriend is not only sexy and professional, but he can also cook! He and Steve meet in the most unfortunate of circumstances: Steve lets himself into Miranda's apartment one afternoon to pick up something of Brady's, not knowing that Miranda has secretly taken the day off work in order to spend it in bed with Robert. Turning away too quickly from the sight of his ex and her doctor naked and writhing, Steve smashes his nose against the doorframe and starts gushing blood all over the place. Robert, being a doctor, quickly tries to treat Steve and uses an old hospital trick to staunch the bleeding. He puts half a tampon up each of Steve's nostrils, leaving Steve both indebted to him and more or less thoroughly emasculated.

Telling the girls about it later, Miranda admits that there's a part of her which is amused by the way Steve found out about her great new relationship: 'the sex and the bloody nose and the doctor boyfriend'. She queries whether it's terrible that she is amused. Er, yes, Miranda, it is, since you're looking for opinions.

Later Miranda sees Steve's new girlfriend Debbie in the park and she's simply stunning. There are uncomfortable moments and fumbled exchanges and later still Steve seems to be about to say something of great importance to Miranda, but he gets interrupted.

Hey, Big Guy: Carrie tells the girls about Big's heart and Miranda asks if he's on the waiting list to get one. She's suitably ashamed when Carrie tells them what's actually the matter with him. After his op, which he comes through tired but unscathed, Big checks himself out of hospital early and goes back to his hotel. Carrie meets him there and reveals that she has brought a variety of board games and 'amusements' – including dominos – to keep him occupied during the period where he's not allowed to be excited by anything. He, in return, calls her Sniffles – referring to her habit of breaking into tears whenever his illness is mentioned – and is obviously, if not ostentatiously, grateful.

A couple of times he raises the spectre of the idea of them being together again and in a permanent way, for example, asking only half-jokingly if playing board games together is what they'd be like in their 70s. 'You and me? The Early Bird Special?' he asks at another point, referring to the

American restaurant tradition of letting retired couples who want to eat early in the evening do so at a discount rate. Carrie ignores these comments, but looks after Big, sleeping next to him as he slips in an out of consciousness in some pain. The next day he seems fine and says that he feels like himself again. His emotional outreaching appears to have stopped, leaving Carrie to ponder again on the lost 'them' and acknowledge that she couldn't wait another five years for another sentimental moment from Big.

And So ...: 'Life's short, you might want to consider holding his hand.' While the Steve/Miranda encounter is riveting stuff, the central issue is, of course, the way that Big's heart stopping working properly (literally) causes it to start working properly (metaphorically), i.e. he opens up to Carrie. To see both of the series' long-running on-and-off relationships shift slightly in one episode is a treat for long-time fans. It's a very sweet and nicely played episode which is difficult to do justice to on paper. Chris Noth successfully makes Big vulnerable, which isn't easy to imagine and is even harder to watch.

86
One

15 September 2003

Written by Michael Patrick King
Directed by David Frankel

Guest Cast
David Eigenberg (Steve Brady) Evan Handler (Harry Goldenblatt)
Blair Underwood (Dr Robert Leeds)
Mikhail Baryshnikov (Aleksandr Petrovsky)
Beth Lapides (Performance Artist) Lynn Cohen (Magda)
Anne Meara (Mary Brady) Eleni Fuiaxis (Debbie)
Andrew Stewart-Jones (Jules) Victoria Valero (Mimi)
Albert Makhtsier (Russian Cab Driver)
Marina Kotovnikov (Russian Waitress)

Carrie: Carrie accompanies Charlotte to a New York gallery to see a new performance art installation in which a woman is sitting silently and without eating in a replication of a New York apartment. She's planning to do this for three weeks. Charlotte is touched by the installation, but Carrie is unimpressed, saying that all over Manhattan depressed women are already doing that. She argues that, without the audience, this would just be a normal Friday night when a girl is waiting for a man to call. She giggles at the woman and is noticed by a tall man in early middle-age whom Charlotte recognises – the artist, Aleksandr Petrovsky.

Miranda: It's Brady's first birthday and Miranda is arranging a party attended by her and Robert, Steve and Debbie, Miranda's friends and some members of Steve's family (Carrie agrees to come on the guarantee there will not be a clown – she doesn't believe there is anything scarier). A few days before the party, Miranda finds herself in a position where Robert tells her that he loves her and she is unable to reply. She phones Carrie, telling her that she must be fucked up because she can't tell people she loves them. She was always certain that that wouldn't be the case when the right guy came along and keeps repeating how 'fucked up' she is. At the party she and Steve are alone for a moment as they prepare Brady's cake: maybe it's because it's their child's first birthday, maybe it's seeing how much Steve's Ma loves Debbie, maybe it's her recent crisis with Robert, or perhaps it's a combination of all these things, but Miranda just blurts out to Steve that she loves him and then starts crying and apologising. She says she knows that it's inappropriate and that she's causing trouble by saying this when he's happy with Debbie, but she couldn't stop herself. Steve is shocked, but he isn't unhappy. Far from it. He smiles at her and says, 'I mean, c'mon . . . Miranda, you're The One.' Three weeks later they're back together.

Charlotte: Charlotte discovers that she is pregnant and announces this to her friends. After three weeks, however, she miscarries. Emotionally devastated, she withdraws to the point were she can only sit on the sofa watching TV. She tells Miranda that she can't bear to go to Brady's birthday party and Miranda understands. When the day of the party arrives, however, Charlotte, having been taught about grit and determination by a biography of Elizabeth Taylor, glams up and goes along to help her friend celebrate her child's birthday.

Samantha: Samantha has started wearing reading glasses in public and, when questioned, announces, 'I need glasses and I am not ashamed, I have a sexy young man who loves to fuck me and I'm not ashamed . . .' She even admits that she is 45 (making her a couple of years younger than the actress playing her). Her newly discovered ability to cope with her age will only go so far. Sam is, at Jerry's request, growing her pubic hair back but is horrified to discover that some of it is grey and fears that no man will want to sleep with her if she has 'Grandma's pussy'; she repeats a proverb she's heard which is that if you pluck one grey hair out 'six more will come to its funeral'. She tries home-dying her pubic hair but leaves the dye on too long and it goes a spectacular orange. Not Miranda's-head-hair orange but really bright orange. Even Carrie runs out of patience with Samantha when she traps her in Miranda's bathroom during Brady's birthday party and flashes her to prove that the colour really is as bad as she's saying (Carrie, visibly afraid, discovers that there really is something in the world that she finds scarier than a clown). Carrie tries to persuade Sam simply to tell Jerry what has happened as she's sure he won't have an issue with it. Sam can't and instead shaves her brightly coloured hair off, telling Jerry that she's a busy girl and she doesn't have the time available for him to be 'searching around down there'.

Girl Talk: Steve's comedy Ma appears again – she brings her own beer to the party. She has also, much to Carrie's horror, hired a clown.

Men: Aleksandr was one of the defining artists of the 1970s and a regular at Studio 54. He seems amused by Carrie's negative and slightly contemptuous reaction to the art installation – amused in the sense that he finds it charming.

When Carrie says that she doesn't believe the woman is really there 24/7 and that if they turned up at 3 a.m. she'd have gone out to McDonalds, he seems even more entertained. Later on he phones Carrie and asks her to visit the gallery with him saying that they should go and check at 3 a.m. to find out. Carrie is sure he isn't serious and says so. He replies, 'I am serious, she is serious, you are the only one who is not serious.' Carrie agrees to meet him for a late (1 a.m.) dinner beforehand. They go to a Russian restaurant where they eat black bread and fruit and drink water. Carrie asks him about his time as the 'number-one hot guy at Studio 54' and he replies that he remembers 'Martha Graham's face, Andy Warhol's wig – that's about it'. He's more interested in the future. He's obviously very interested in her.

Trivia: There's some more of Miranda's unfeasibly unconvincing TV nonsense, *Jules and Mimi* (see **76**, 'Great Sexpectations').

Kisses: Aleksandr pays off the taxi driver (who is also Russian) and tells him to come back in a moment so that he and Carrie can say a 'proper goodnight'. They wind up kissing enthusiastically against the wall as Carrie's voice-over reflects that Aleksandr tastes like black cherries.

Also Starring: Mikhail Baryshnikov who joins the series as Aleksandr in this episode has had one of the most fêted careers in modern dance. Born on 28 January 1948 in a Latvia which was part of the Soviet Union, he yearned to be, and then trained to become, a ballet dancer and was accepted by the Kirov Ballet in 1966. While touring Canada with the company in 1974 he claimed political asylum and set out to become an American citizen. His was one of a number of high-profile defections by sporting and artistic figures during the early 1970s. He joined the American Ballet Theater (of which he was latterly Artistic Director) and the New York City Ballet and fought stereotypical notions surrounding male dancers. His ability, looks and charm led to him having a series of high profile relationships with American actresses and public figures, including one with Jessica Lange which resulted in his only child, daughter Katherine. He was nominated for an Oscar for his first film role in *The Turning Point* (Herbert Ross, 1977) and has acted occasionally since. Mostly, though, he has preferred to work as a director of Ballet since retiring as a dancer.

And So . . .: 'Of all my odd dates, this was number one.' Michael Patrick King's best episodes are all about Steve and Miranda – he did, after all create them way back in **20**, 'The Man, the Myth, the Viagra' – and the scene between Steve and Miranda in the cupboard is terrific stuff and something a lot of viewers have been waiting a long time for.

The initial appearance of Aleksandr, laconically played by Mikhail Baryshnikov, gives the episode a unique atmosphere caused by his laid-back performance and 'Russian' perspective.

The Charlotte subplot, which sounds awful and crass on paper, is sensitively handled and comes across as life-affirming onscreen.

87
Let There Be Light

4 January 2004

Written and Directed by Michael Patrick King

Guest Cast
David Eigenberg (Steve Brady) Jason Lewis (Smith Jerrod)
Mikhail Baryshnikov (Aleksandr Petrovsky)
Blair Underwood (Dr Robert Leeds) James Remar (Richard Wright)
Francine Roussel (Violette) Polina Nikforova (Irene)
Bayne Gibby (Co-ordinator) Chris Hale (Party Host) Brian Nishi (Lee)
Anan George (Padma) Maggie Rizer (Party Girl #1)
Jull Latiano (Party Girl #2) Giselle Jones (Fragrance Girl)
Mark Agnes (Barney's Employee)

Kisses: It's three weeks since the last episode and Carrie hasn't seen Aleksandr since; she receives a mysterious letter from him asking if she wants to go for a walk and when she meets him he tells her he has been in Holland for three weeks. They make out on a park bench and Carrie nearly gets carried away. In fact, she tells her friends later that it was only common decency which prevented her from consummating her relationship with Aleksandr out in the open, in public and indeed in front of some schoolchildren. She tells her friends, 'Ladies, I am thinking of taking a lover,' and seems to regard the whole thing as an enormous jape. Later Aleksandr takes Carrie back to his spectacular apartment block and they have sex. The next morning he introduces her to his staff and makes her pancakes for breakfast. Suddenly self-conscious, Carrie wonders how many times in his fifty plus years Aleksandr has done this, beginning to doubt if they have a future and worrying that Aleksandr is, in fact, simply using her as a lover.

Charlotte: Charlotte is looking to buy some new scents, including one called 'Cucumber and Basil'. 'Why would you want to smell like a salad?' Samantha very sensibly asks. Carrie describes Charlotte's ideal smell as 'classic, clean with just a hint of neuroses'. Informed by her doctor not to try and get pregnant for two months, Charlotte decides to volunteer helping the blind. Her volunteer leader tells her that the best way to understand what she's dealing with is to go to a public place with a blindfold on and get a friend to lead her around. Carrie comes out with her but abandons her in Barney's in order to answer a phone call from Aleksandr. Tut tut.

Miranda: 'Hey, how lucky are we?' Steve asks Miranda as they ride up in the elevator towards what is now their apartment. Not as lucky as they think, as Robert gets into the lift with them resulting in a supremely uncomfortable experience for all. When she's told, Carrie opines that time in a lift with an ex is the only thing she knows of that is more uncomfortable than even a bikini wax. Miranda tries not to use the lift in future, only to discover that Robert has had the same idea. They have a truly awful conversation on the stairs one time and Miranda begins to fear that Robert is going to try and make her and Steve's lives a misery. When some of Steve's stuff is wrecked while they leave it unattended during his move into their apartment, Miranda is convinced that Robert has damaged it in revenge. Steve dashes off to Robert's apartment to tell him what he thinks of him, but discovers Robert nearly naked with two honeys. Steve concludes that not only has Robert got better things to do than damage his luggage, but that he's honestly over Miranda. Steve apologises to Robert and leaves. While he doesn't actually lie to Miranda, he just tells her that Robert won't be troubling them any more – leaving Miranda with the illusion that Robert is still crazy about her and that Steve confronted him and won.

Fit to Print: After spending her first night with Aleksandr, Carrie is suddenly insecure and worried about where her relationship is going – despite previously only being interested in 'taking a lover'. She finds herself asking herself lots of questions, such as 'Does he like me?' 'Will he call again?' 'Where is this all going?' She adds to her column, 'When it comes to men even when we try and keep it light how do we wind up in the dark?'

Samantha: Jerry has been invited to a party for the thirty hottest people under thirty in New York. Samantha is about to dismiss the whole enterprise but then she discovers that it's being hosted by her ex, Richard Wright (see **66**, 'I Heart NY' among many others). In the light of this, she suggests that Jerry should go to the party and that she should go with him. There she meets Richard and begins to ignore Jerry. She and Richard go upstairs to have sex during the party and Sam casually dismisses Jerry from her life as she does so. But she doesn't enjoy having sex with Richard. At all. And she realises that she hates herself for what she's doing to the loyal and caring Jerry.

She leaves and finds Jerry waiting for her for no other reason than he wanted to make sure that she got home OK. Samantha is unsure of what she's feeling, but she seems to be appreciating Jerry more.

Girl Talk: There's a really nice scene with Carrie and Sam wandering through an autumnal New York street talking about their lives; and an even nicer one as Charlotte and Anthony wander through the park against a dazzling background of brown leaves. This contains some more classic Anthony dialogue, including his opinion that Charlotte's plan to volunteer to help with the blind is 'very Jackie O' (i.e. Jackie Onassis), and his claim that Charlotte talks about her need for a baby so much that not only they but also 'the homeless guy on the corner of 57th and 7th' knows how important it is to her.

Men: Without his staff of three, Aleksandr insists he would be on the street with a sign saying 'will do art for food'. He can speak French as well as Russian. When Carrie tells him that she can't see him any more because she can't be one of many girls, he tells her that there are no other girls. He also admits that, though he does keep some emergency phone numbers, Carrie is the only person he is seeing at the moment. Mollified, she begins to look at the sculpture he's making and asks what it all is. He grins and replies with a phrase full of multiple meanings, 'I don't know. It's too soon to tell.'

Fashion Victims: Jerry wears a 'Fuck Yoga' T-shirt. Anthony cannot think of anything worse than 'stonewashed jeans with a matching jacket'.

Trivia: Carrie's address is reiterated as 245 East 73rd Street. This episode was the first one in the second block of Season Six episodes shown. The division appears to be fairly arbitrary as the action follows on more or less directly from the end of the previous episode (the three-week gap is mentioned in voice-overs in both) and they share the same writer. This is the first episode in which Jason Lewis is credited as part of the opening 'Guest Star' cast rather than on the end credits alongside the minor characters and surprise appearances.

And So . . .: 'The only place this is going is loverville . . .' It's a shame that *Sex and the City*'s only ever major black character becomes all psycho and rage driven in a pseudo-

Othello manner after being dumped by Miranda, but at least he's not quite as mad as Miranda is convinced he is.

Aleksandr serves up surprises along with his pancakes and, while Carrie may not know where their relationship is going, the reassuring thing is that, from the audience's point of view, it appears to be somewhere interesting. It is hard, though, to shake the idea that many of Carrie's problems with men come from the fact that she 'presents' a 'version' of Carrie to prospective partners rather than simply being herself as she is with her friends. This is especially odd given that all of her friends do seem able to 'be themselves' with potential partners.

88
The Ick Factor

11 January 2004

Written by Julie Rottenberg and Elisa Zuritsky
Directed by Wendy Stanzler

Guest Cast
David Eigenberg (Steve Brady) Evan Handler (Harry Goldenblatt)
Jason Lewis (Smith Jerrod) Mikhail Baryshnikov (Aleksandr Petrovsky)
Blair Underwood (Dr Robert Leeds) Lynn Cohen (Magda)
Anne Meara (Mary Brady) Heather MacRae (Judge)
Michael Hobbs (Dr Bevel) Sylvia Kauders (Fighting Wife)
Berni Padden (Fighting Husband) Raushanah Simmons (Bartender)
Io Tillet Wright (McDonalds Worker) Jean Brassard (French Waiter)
Jonah Spear (Jefferson Waiter)

Carrie: Aleksandr has written a short piece of piano music called 'The Girl With The Sparkling Eyes' about Carrie and has developed the habit of reading poetry to her out loud. While Charlotte thinks these gestures are romantic, Samantha and Miranda are convinced that they can't possibly be sincere. 'Ick!' exclaims Miranda.

Charlotte: Harry sets out to prove that he can be as romantic as Charlotte is convinced Aleksandr is being, and takes her for a seven-course meal in a French restaurant. They have a fabulous time, but they also both get food poisoning. Harry has some sympathy for ideals about romance, insisting that there's a difference between the real and the unreal and both exist, just like real ice cream and the whipped air variety.

Miranda: Steve and Miranda are, in a touchingly silly scene, getting cheerfully drunk outside a bar, both of them wrapped up against the autumn cold, when they spot an old couple grumbling at one another. This leads to a discussion about what they do and don't want in their lives and this finishes with Steve saying that whatever else happens he doesn't want to lose Miranda again. So she asks him to marry her.

Miranda announces her forthcoming marriage to her friends, but denies that she's 'engaged'. She wants her wedding to mean something, to be able to recite her vows to Steve in front of her friends and intends to hold the ceremony as soon as she can – well, as soon as she can find a venue that doesn't make her feel sick. She's also resolutely opposed to having anything at her wedding which resembles the 'millions of cookie cutter weddings' she's attended and heard about. Freaked out by Miranda's attitude – which also extends to gifts – Charlotte panics and suggests that their friend will only be happy if they buy her 'a stapler, wrap it in brown paper and smear some dog poo on it!' The ceremony eventually takes place outdoors with a small selection of family and friends and is rather lovely. Magda makes everybody clap 'Is happy time! Clap! Is happy time!' Those wacky Ukrainians, eh?

Fit to Print: Carrie tells Aleksandr that her column is predicated on the assumption that romance is either dead or phoney. Later, she worries that it's actually neither but, that in a world of irony, distance and lack of sincerity, people are incapable of taking genuine romantic gestures as being genuine and have lost the ability to appreciate romance. 'Have we become romance intolerant?'

Out and About: Aleksandr takes Carrie to the opera as a surprise and he's bought her a brand new Oscar De La Renta dress so that she will have something appropriate to wear. Outside the Opera House and within hearing distance of a small outdoor orchestra, Aleksandr asks Carrie to dance. She describes this as the most romantic moment of her life and promptly faints. When she wakes up she tells Aleksandr that they have to take this more slowly – she's an American and she can't cope with such unencumbered romanticisms. So they go to McDonalds instead.

Samantha: Samantha has discovered that Jerry has been listed the number one hot guy to watch by a magazine and seen herself, as his girlfriend, featured in most of the pictures of him taken by the paparazzi. Looking at all these pictures she becomes obsessed with the idea that her breasts are too small and books an appointment to talk to a surgeon about having them enhanced. Her friends aren't terribly impressed, insisting she's both intelligent and competent and that it would be perverse for her to feel validated by having larger breasts. She insist that she isn't going to have 'the watermelon freakshow kind' and any work done will be subtle. At her appointment, however, the plastic surgeon is worried by a small lump he finds in her breast and insists that she have a biopsy. Initially convinced that this is nothing serious, Samantha discovers that this isn't the case. On the way to Miranda's wedding she tells Carrie that she's been informed that she has breast cancer.

And So . . .: 'Just the way Miranda wanted it.' A very odd mixture of comedy, tragedy and really very touching scenes of friendship. This is a slow, thoughtful episode. The wedding scenes are charmingly unpretentious and Kim Cattrall excels with the more serious material she's given to play here.

89
Catch-38

18 January 2004

Written by Cindy Chupack
Directed by Michael Engler

Guest Cast
David Eigenberg (Steve Brady) Evan Handler (Harry Goldenblatt)
Jason Lewis (Smith Jerrod) Mikhail Baryshnikov (Aleksandr Petrovsky)
David Deblinger (Dr Pinkner) Julia Sweeney (Sister Anne Marie)
Amy Von Freymann (Receptionist) Jonathan Espolin (Paparazzo)

Samantha: While Samantha's 'lumpectomy' has gone
smoothly, her doctor advises her that she should have a
course of chemotherapy as a precaution in case there is a
microscopic cancerous element left. Samantha asks what
the likely reasons are for her contracting cancer and is told
that 'lifestyle choices' play a part and that, statistically,
women who've not had children are more likely to get
cancer. Sam takes this news badly, saying that the doctor
has just effectively said 'I'm a whore who needs chemo'.

She decides to change doctors, but the one that she
wants isn't available, indeed is booked up for appointments months ahead. She resolves to wait around in his
office on the off-chance that she can get a drop-in
appointment. While there she begins talking to another
woman who is there for exactly the same reason. Sam asks
her what she does and it turns out that she's a nun. While
a little mollified that those society sees as morally good are
as cancerous as those that society sees as morally bad, Sam
soon gets over this slightly obnoxious bit of self-justifica-
tion and forms a bond with the woman. Samantha
name-drops everyone she can think of from the New York
glitterati in an attempt to swing an appointment but it
fails. Just when she's on the verge of giving up hope, the
doctor's acerbic receptionist sees a photograph of Samantha and Jerry in the celebrity magazine she's poring
over and realises that Sam is his girlfriend. Sam barters
with the smitten receptionist, swapping a visit to the centre

from Jerry for appointments with the city's best cancer doctor for herself – and for her cloistered nun friend.

Miranda: Miranda and Steve are going away together for four days over a long weekend; staying in a cabin resort somewhere upstate. Her friends ask if the trip is actually her honeymoon and she emphatically denies this, being someone entirely opposed to 'the bullshit' surrounding weddings. Sam tells her to accept that it's her honeymoon because a honeymoon is 'basically sex with room service', and who doesn't want that? When Miranda points out that it can't be their honeymoon because they are taking Brady, Carrie and Charlotte volunteer to split the baby-minding duties for the weekend. And just like that, Miranda is on her honeymoon.

The first thing she notices when they get there is that there's no TV – and then that she's forgotten her cellphone charger. Steve tells her not to worry as she's not going to need it as it's just the two of them – which makes Miranda worry more. With the limited charge left on her phone, she calls Carrie in a panic complaining that she's bored, that 'sex is the only thing on the itinerary' and that she misses news and current affairs and mental stimulation. She and Steve spent two hours sitting on the couch by the fire in silence – 'He was looking into my eyes, I was looking into the remote.' She even deplores the fact that she's not allowed to be sarcastic while on her honeymoon. Later she realises how important a few days of quiet away from the city are to Steve and she apologises to him for being so tense and for being an asshole. Steve agrees that she is, 'but you're my asshole'. Reacting exactly like every member of the audience, Miranda comments, 'That's sweet and also gross at the same time.'

Charlotte: Brady sees Charlotte and Harry having sex. Charlotte panics and calls Miranda, entirely hysterical, convinced they've psychologically scarred Brady for life. Miranda isn't bothered, telling Charlotte, 'He doesn't know what he's looking at, he doesn't know where his nose is . . .'

Carrie: Looking after Brady – and in particular a moment when someone mistakes her for his mother – leads Carrie to wonder about having children of her own. She realises that, at 38 years old, if she wants children she might have to make the decision of when and with whom in the near future. The age of her fifty-something boyfriend is also a factor. He tells her that he already has a child, Chloe, who is now 22 and lives in France with her mother, his ex-wife. He also tells her that he's had a vasectomy. Conversations with her friends convince Carrie that she should talk to Aleksandr about *them* being parents. She tells him that she thinks she could 'be' with him 'properly' and asks if his vasectomy is reversible. He acknowledges that vasectomys are reversible, but says that his is never going to be. He tells Carrie that it is extraordinary to be a parent and that he would never want her to miss out on it on his account. However, he's already had a family and he's too old to do it again.

Fit to Print: Carrie wonders about the shoulds, woulds and wants of existence; do women want perfect weddings, perfect honeymoons and babies or are they just made to feel that they should? Does this pressure come from society or from inside the individual? 'Why are we shoulding all over ourselves?'

And So . . .: 'It's a death trap – we're just going to strap a pillow to the baby and hope for the best.' The scene at the café at the beginning of the episode is brilliant. It's not strikingly brilliant in scripting terms but just watch the detail in the performances, how comfortable everyone is in the parts they've been playing for six years, how precise and yet casually improvisational all the actors are.

90
Out of the Frying Pan

25 January 2004

Written by Jenny Bicks
Directed by Michael Engler

Guest Cast
David Eigenberg (Steve Brady) Evan Handler (Harry Goldenblatt)
Jason Lewis (Smith Jerrod) Mikhail Baryshnikov (Aleksandr Petrovsky)
Dana Ivey (Trudy Stork) Jonathan Hadary (Vincent)
Billy Longo (Cab Driver) Cindy Cheung (Nurse)
Anthony Veneziale (Bartender)

Out and About: Aleksandr has been showing Carrie all the
parts of New York she doesn't know, the odd, interna-
tionalist, non-American parts. They've been to international cinemas and small restaurants and now Aleksandr
wants to visit somewhere he's never been before – Carrie's
apartment. As he looks around, he says that the apartment
is very like her. 'Small and artless?' she asks and he shakes
his head – 'warm'.

Carrie: Later, Carrie and Aleksandr have their first row
when, while they're talking about Samantha's problems, he
mentions a friend of his who died of cancer. Carrie sees
this as insensitive. Aleksandr tries to explain that he's
simply trying to be realistic but Carrie is too upset and
storms out.

Samantha: Samantha's new doctor agrees with her old one,
and she's now on a course of preventative chemotherapy.
Carrie, Charlotte and Miranda meet her at her chemo
clinic and are introduced to her nurse, who wonders if they
are all as much fun as Samantha is. 'We try,' says Miranda.
What's far from fun is that Samantha's hair is beginning
to fall out as a result of her chemotherapy. She tells Carrie,
'Every time the wind blows I have to check that I'm not
bald.' The premiere of Jerry's film for Gus Van Sant
(which is called *Needles, CA*) is coming up and Samantha
wants to look her best for it. Despite announcing that 'I'm
going to kick cancer and that red carpet's ass!' she tries on
a variety of wigs but is unimpressed by any of them – they
all have names like 'Candy' and are horribly obvious. The
man in the shop tries to tell Sam that he has provided wigs
and advice to many women with cancer but she cuts him
off, saying that she has a premiere not cancer. She tells
Jerry that she can't come along but he insists; she tells him

he can't cope with her cancer and he is equally insistent that he can. Jerry finds Samantha shaving her head and shaves his in solidarity with her, going almost bald at the premiere while she wears a deliberately outrageous pink wig.

Charlotte: None of Charlotte's eggs, as donated for IVF, have proved suitable. Charlotte is despondent at this news and spends most of the following few days running through Central Park ostensibly 'keeping fit' but more probably running away. She meets an elderly lady who is walking her show dogs, including one called Princess Dandyridge Brandywine (which sounds like a character in a book by Tolkien) whom Charlotte adores. The old woman, Mrs Stork, doesn't care for Princess because she failed as a show dog (one of her legs is too short) and after she hears about Charlotte and Harry's problems conceiving, she gives Princess to Charlotte as a gift. She and Harry rename the dog Elizabeth Taylor Goldenblatt after her favourite actress.

Miranda: Steve and Miranda are looking for somewhere else to live as her place is too small for the two of them, an ever expanding Brady, Steve's dog and Miranda's cat. They look through the property section with Miranda tutting at the descriptions being used for places they've already seen; why not call one particular example what it is – a 'crack house on an air shaft'? Steve finds a house in Brooklyn but Miranda as a Manhattan girl makes it clear that she's not moving to Brooklyn under any circumstance; by definition she doesn't like anything not Manhattan. Steve points out that he's from Queens and she seems to like him, but she remains unconvinced. She eventually goes to see the house and realises that it's perfect. They buy it. Not only is Miranda no longer in the dating game, she's left Manhattan behind as well.

Girl Talk: There's a really well-played and affecting scene where Samantha insists on talking to Carrie about the possibility of her cancer killing her. It's a shocking intrusion into both the rhythm of the series and Carrie's life.

Fetishes: The metropolitan obsession with coffee practically counts as a fetish these days. Aleksandr is shocked to discover that Carrie doesn't have an espresso machine – 'You call yourself a writer?' he asks, understandably horrified. Later he makes Carrie an espresso at his place. She doesn't like its bitterness, saying she's going to have milk in it 'Then it's not espresso,' Aleksandr points out.

Fashion Victims: Carrie's astonishing red top and layer lace ruffles skirt combination – it's *stunning*.

Also Starring: Dana Ivey who cameos as Trudy Stork is the American equivalent of a great dame of the British theatre. Fearsomely talented, she's from Atlanta, Georgia, and has won more theatrical awards than you could shake a stick at.

Fit to Print: 'Denial: Friend or Foe?' Carrie types. When denial can save you from 'pain, fear or Brooklyn' what's wrong with not facing facts? After writing this, and talking to Samantha, Carrie begins to understand what Aleksandr was trying to say. They talk again about cancer and he tells her poignantly that when his friend with cancer, Sofie, died he was devastated by the sheer scale of the pain he experienced. He hadn't been prepared for it, because he denied the very possibility of her dying: 'I didn't want you to be surprised like I was,' he tells her.

And So . . .: 'I have to face up to it.' Aleksandr is being brutally pragmatic, yes (and very Russian), but he isn't being cruel and that's what Carrie, with help from Samantha herself, comes to realise. Even his apparent insensitivity is actually a reflection of his great sensitivity and maturity. Mikhail Baryshnikov is quite brilliant in this episode, whether killing a mouse with one blow with a frying pan or talking quietly and slowly about the death of a friend. This is a sharply written episode which is probably the series' most serious instalment. Kim Cattrall once again shines when given more serious material to work with.

91
The Cold War

1 February 2004

Written by Aury Wallington
Directed by Julian Farino

Guest Cast
Chris Noth (Mr Big) Willie Garson (Stanford Blatch)
David Eigenberg (Steve Brady) Jason Lewis (Smith Jerrod)
Evan Handler (Harry Goldenblatt)
Mikhail Baryshnikov (Aleksandr Petrovsky)
Mario Cantone (Anthony Marentino) Sean Palmer (Marcus Adant)
Laila Robins (Audra Clark) Mark Margolis (John Paul Sandal)
David Frei (Dogshow Judge) Delaine Yates (1st PR Girl)
Smar Ross (2nd PR Girl) Brian Nishi (Lee) T R Pescod (Tom)
Adam Nee (Fan) Shaun Zaken (Waiter) Josh Annex (Gay Guy on Street)
Jolly Abraham (Woman on Street)

Carrie: When Carrie discovers that Aleksandr is preparing for a big solo showing of his work – his first major exhibition in six years – she realises that they never discuss their work, or indeed any of the other important aspects of their lives, with each other. She worries that they have nothing in common and that, therefore, their relationship will not last as it will never be 'complete'. She explains her vision of a couple sharing everything together or 'at least their passions'. Miranda tells her that every relationship is different and that she should evaluate her relationship with Aleksandr on its own terms. She also considers Carrie's being greedy: 'You want passions on top of passion?'

Samantha: Samantha is now quite into the experimental wig thing and sports a number of outlandish styles during the course of this episode, claiming that she's decided to turn 'a little hair loss into a lot of hair gain'.

A fan of Jerry's takes a photograph of Jerry out for a drink with Samantha, Marcus and Stanford. The photograph ends up in *Tattle Tale* magazine (which Miranda reads and loves) where, thanks to Sam being cut out of the picture, it's used to heavily imply that Jerry is gay. 'I'm a beard in a wig,' Sam notes with some amusement. Her friends are amazed, they thought she'd be angry but she tells them that after cancer it's very difficult to worry about the small stuff and, besides, 'Once the gay rumours start you're really a star.'

She soon changes her tune, however, when she realises the extent to which the Manhattan 'in' set now assumes that Jerry really is gay and that she's merely *pretending* to be his girlfriend. Miranda reminds her about not worrying about little things, but Sam puts her straight about how these rumours affect her reputation for having a spectacular sex life. She's particularly incensed when a gay friend of hers asks her for Jerry's phone number and then laughs in her face when she insists that he's not gay and that she is the only person who is having sex with him.

Sam works out the best way to prove that she's having sex with Jerry. They make a porn tape and leak it to the paparazzi. The 'Smith Jerrod is Gay' rumours are scotched and everyone is happy. Well, everyone except for Miranda who accidentally sees some of the tape while surfing for celebrity gossip online. As Carrie says, 'Samantha's hot tape cured Miranda's love of gossip for good.'

Miranda: Miranda is tired after walking all the way from the subway station to her and Steve's new house in heels. Steve suggests that she carry her shoes and walk home in sneakers but Miranda refuses: 'You can take me out of Manhattan, but you can't take me out of my shoes.'

Charlotte: Charlotte is convinced that her new dog, Elizabeth Taylor Goldenblatt, is missing being a show dog, so she enters her for a few competitions. Eventually she wins one in front of an audience of her friends, despite the dog being on heat during the show. Later Harry persuades Charlotte to let the dog roam free in the park for a while rather than being on her lead all the time. Charlotte is horrified to find that – before she can stop it happening –

the on-heat Elizabeth Taylor is coupling with a variety of other dogs. 'Elizabeth Taylor got gang-banged in the park!' shrieks Charlotte to her friends. 'That's *so* 80s!' mutters Samantha who is understandably only half-listening. Charlotte refers to the dog as her 'little girl', which again leads to sarcasm from Sam, who thinks that, after her experiences, she's probably now a woman.

Men: Charlotte's friend Anthony helps her with walking the dog and taking it to the show. Once when they are out on the street he seems put out by the amount of attention the dog's getting: 'That dog is getting more cruised than me and we're on the corner of gay and gay!' he claims. Later, when drying the dog's hair with a hairdryer, he shouts 'This was not the kind of blow job I was hoping for today!'

Trivia: Chris Noth only appears as a voice on the answerphone and isn't credited onscreen for his 'appearance'.

Hey, Big Guy: Coming back from four straight days at Aleksandr's, Carrie finds four messages on her answerphone, all of them from Big. The first couple are cheery, the second two are less so, Big worrying that he's done something to upset her. He says he called her mobile phone but he must have copied the number down wrong, unless she's secretly 'a ticked-off guy named Paco'.

Fit to Print: Aleksandr reads out loud a bit of Carrie's column that he thinks is particularly witty: 'It's my belief that the last time anyone enjoyed the sixty-nine position was in 1969.' Carrie's lack of anything in common with Aleksandr leads her to wonder if, even if the romance is hot and passionate, there can be anything permanent if you don't have anything in common. 'Without sharing your worlds can even the hottest relationship keep out the cold?'

Guy Talk: Carrie asks if Aleksandr would like to meet some of her friends; he enthusiastically agrees but on the night that they've arranged he doesn't turn up and instead sends champagne and his apologies. He says he's working too hard on pieces for his show to spare the time. After the girls have been drinking for a while, Carrie takes them all back to the apartment to meet Aleksandr anyway, but he asks them to leave because he's so busy. The girls depart, apart from Carrie, who goes alone to Aleksandr's bed, but later goes into his workshop to tell him that what he did was rude. She finds him nearly distraught, worrying about what the world will think of his new show. He tells Carrie that it's been said that 'the world is waiting with breath that is bated' for his new pieces and when he looked at them today they seemed 'stupid, flat, needless, childish' and he had a crisis of confidence. She tells him that he is brilliant at what he does and says that, while she doesn't understand his life and work, she can listen to his problems for him. The episode ends with them deep in discussion about each other's lives.

And So . . .: 'It worked for Paris Hilton.' The best Sam comedy plotline in ages is combined with some really nice work form Sarah Jessica Parker and Mikhail Baryshnikov. The nature of Aleksandr's crisis stretches the show's normal depiction of relationships in interesting ways. The dog show plotline, though, is really very dull indeed.

92
Splat!

8 February 2004

Written by Jenny Bicks and Cindy Chupack
Directed by Julian Farino

Guest Cast

Willie Garson (Stanford Blatch) David Eigenberg (Steve Brady)
Evan Handler (Harry Goldenblatt) Jason Lewis (Smith Jerrod)
Mikhail Baryshnikov (Aleksandr Petrovsky)
Sean Palmer (Marcus Adant) Wallace Shawn (Martin Grable)
Candice Bergen (Enid Frick) Kirsten Johnston (Lexi Featherston)
Ronald Guttman (Andre DiBachi) Sakina Jaffrey (Rama Patel)
Demetrious Kalkabnis (Dorado Waiter) Tom Deckham (Pet Store Guy)

Charlotte: Charlotte discovers that Elizabeth Taylor Goldenblatt is pregnant after her antics in the park with the eight or nine mutts.

Girl Talk: Carrie's *Vogue* editor Enid is organising a party and she asks Carrie to come along, bring Aleksandr and also a single friend of his; not a date for her exactly, but someone for her to pair with in a party which is going to be mostly couples. At the party Enid dislikes the friend that Aleksandr brings along (He's a Hobbit!) but is smitten with Aleksandr himself. In a free moment Carrie asks Enid what she thinks she's up to very obviously putting moves on her boyfriend. Enid defends herself by saying that Aleksandr is in her age bracket, not Carrie's, and that Carrie is the one at fault for 'swimming in my pool'. Enid says she's in No Man's Land and that, as a single fifty-something woman, she has a tiny pool of men in which to fish – so small it's 'a wading pool'.

Also at the party is Lexi, an 80s party girl once known to Carrie, Charlotte, Miranda and Sam who is now, in her own words, 'forty fucking years old'. She's lost any dignity she might once have had and is a comedy character, snorting coke in the lavatories, ranting and being needlessly rude to everyone. She's a caricature of Carrie, and the sort of person you might think Samantha was if you only watched the series' trailers and not the show itself. While trying to open a window so that she can smoke without having to go outside in the snow, Lexi slips off her Manolo Blahniks and out of the window – and eighteen storeys down to her death. The New York papers' headlines read: 'The End of an Era' and 'The Party's Officially Over'.

Wine and Dine: Carrie and Aleksandr throw a dinner party for themselves, Charlotte and Harry, Jerry and Samantha, Marcus and Stanford and Miranda and Steve. A few hours beforehand, he asks Carrie to come to Paris with him – not merely for the opening of his show, but for an indefinite period of time. She won't need to get rid of her New York apartment because he'll cover the payments for her. In

Paris they can live in a hotel while he refurbishes his apartment on the Left Bank of the Seine.

Samantha: Sam is entirely supportive of Carrie's plan to move and also casually uses the word 'boyfriend' to describe Jerry for the first time. When Carrie worries about 'her' being able to function in Paris, Sam scolds her lack of confidence. 'Believe me, your fabulousness will translate.'

Trivia: Aleksandr has described his new show as one consisting of 'large-scale light installations, integrated with video images'.

(Another) City: Aleksandr describes Paris as the greatest city on Earth, leading Steve to grin and remind him that he is talking to New Yorkers. Aleksandr shakes his head: 'New York is wonderful, but nowhere on Earth is like Paris.'

Also Starring: Kristen Johnston was Sally in aliens-on-earth sitcom *Third Rock From the Sun* (1992–2000) for NBC and appeared in *Austin Powers – The Spy Who Shagged Me* (Jay Roach, 1999).

Carrie: After considering Aleksandr's suggestions for a long time, Carrie agrees to go to Paris with him. She doesn't want to leave New York but she doesn't want to lose him either and she knows she has to make a choice. Aleksandr's jet-set lifestyle, multiple homes and constant flitting form one side of the world to the other mean that she won't have to give up her old life, just live it only part of the time. She can still work as some kind of writer and the whole idea opens up new worlds for her. Her recent encounters with Lexi and Enid have also clearly shaken her world-view and complacency. She's so sure she wants to go that she realises that it doesn't even really matter what her friends think.

Fit to Print: After Aleksandr's offer, Carrie writes a column which acknowledges that while 'the unexamined life is not worth living' the real danger is if the process of examining *becomes* your life. Is that being alive or is it just procrastination? Have all those lunches and late-night phone calls made her all girl talk and no girl action, she worries. After accepting Aleksandr's offer, Carrie resigns from the *New York Star* and ends her column. They weren't keen on her proposed 'American Girl in Paris' new direction (for which she doesn't blame them, saying a 'New York Paper' needs a 'New York Girl') so she just decided to stop. She suspects they will hire a new 29-year-old with a whole new set of problems to carry on her work.

Miranda: Miranda is grumpy all through Carrie and Aleksandr's dinner party and doesn't even ask Aleksandr any questions about himself. It seems out of character but is really just a sure indication that she doesn't approve of him. She later complains to Steve that Aleksandr is pretentious and Steve tells her that she just doesn't think that anyone could be good enough for her or her friends. It took five years for her to come round to the idea that he might be, after all.

After Lexi's funeral, when Carrie tells Miranda that she's going to Paris Miranda is upset and appalled that Carrie has given up her job. She tells her that her column is who she is. 'It's not who I am, it's what I do,' Carrie points out and says that this is all really about Miranda – while Carrie continues to stay in New York and to write her column, Miranda doesn't have to feel that life has changed. As far as Carrie sees it she has a choice between staying in New York to 'write my life' or going to Paris to 'live my life'. Miranda shakes her head and Carrie demands that Miranda just admit that she doesn't like Aleksandr. Miranda does just that. Don't *you* go to Paris with him then,' retorts Carrie. She walks away from Miranda, leaving her alone in the street.

Out and About: As the episode ends, Carrie and Aleksandr slide through a snowbound New York on a horse-drawn sleigh.

And So . . .: 'We are done with the question portion of the programme.' An episode that is mercifully free of obvious 'jokes' about Paris and the French, 'Splat' uses the move to Paris as a means of examining the decision-making process and not as an opportunity for 'witticisms' about blue cheese. Enid and Lexi are both, in their own ways, parodies of Carrie – one is a potential future for her if she never takes a chance and the other is a convenient package of what some might see as her worst excesses. Her death, in one of the least dignified ways imaginable, decrying New York in the process, is almost entirely comic and symbolic. An episode with a title like this isn't really taking the death-by-falling of a character terribly seriously, is it?

93
An American Girl in Paris (Part Une)

15 February 2004

Written by Michael Patrick King
Directed by Tim Van Patten

Guest Cast
Chris Noth (Mr Big) Evan Handler (Harry Goldenblatt)
Jason Lewis (Smith Jerrod) Mikhail Baryshnikov (Aleksandr Petrovsky)
Anne De Salvo (Sheila) Cecile Casel (Chloe) Jennifer Gelfer (Mona)
Thomas Chabrol (Andre) Karine Plandtadit-Begeout (Fabienne)
Yett Gottesman (Waitress) Adam Ludwig (Bellhop)
Samuel Delfiner (Bellman) Philppe Beglia (Clerk)
Michael Cohen (Doorman #1) Eric Nagger (Doorman #2)
Guillaume Veyre (Fussy Salesman) Isabelle Tanakil (Dior Shopper)
Agathe Bodin (Female Parisian Friend #1)
Sacha Rukavina (Female Parisian Friend #2)
Sarah Pratt (Female Parisian Friend #3)
Laetizia Venezia Tarnowski (Female Parisian Friend #4)

Hey, Big Guy: Among the many phone messages Carrie picks up on her last evening in New York is one from Big. He's in New York and he'd like to see her. Deleting the voicemail, Carrie heads out to her final dinner with the girls which she sees as their own Last Supper. Big is waiting outside in his car; they sit and talk, he cracks jokes about the Mountain coming to Mohammed and claims that Carrie's recent policy of ignoring his phone calls meant he was 'starting to feel like a needy chick'. He mentions his recent heart surgery and tries to tell Carrie that he's been thinking about them and their relationship. Carrie is appalled by this announcement, coming as it does at a point when she's about to embark on a new life. She asks him if he has a radar about when she might be happy; only then does he turn up to 'shit all over it'. Big tries to carry on talking about them but she stops him. 'Forget you know my number, forget you know my *name*!' she tells him, and walks away.

Wine and Dine: Carrie, Charlotte, Miranda and Sam's final dinner together needs to be held in the early evening due to the time of Carrie's flight. Miranda says this makes them like senior citizens who eat cheaply in the late afternoon. Carrie tells them all about Big's visitation and compares him to The Boy Who Cried Wolf and says that it is six years since she met Big. 'I want to thank you all' she tells her friends 'for being there' and wonders what her life would have been like if she'd never met them. As they eat their meal, conversation becomes maudlin. Charlotte cries – in fact, everybody cries. 'I'm going to miss you, you cunt,' says Sam, in an attempt to clear away the atmosphere of sincerity. By the next morning, Carrie has gone.

(A European) City: Carrie is making a decent fist of learning French. Arriving in Paris, she manages to speak enough comprehensible French to get by. She gives a little squeal of delight when she realises that she can see the Eiffel Tower from her hotel window.

Fashion Victims: Carrie hits Dior in Paris after a week there and instantly slips over, sliding across the floor scattering her possessions. In the process she loses her necklace that spells out 'Carrie' which upsets her greatly. As she tells Aleksandr, it's worthless but also priceless, a cheap piece which has great sentimental value (as she bought it on a day out with her friends).

Carrie: Increasingly upset and increasingly alone, Carrie doesn't get to see Aleksandr as much as she'd like to, as he's far busier with his show than he anticipated. Her lack of ability to speak enough French – despite her best efforts – sees her excluded from conversations, trapped, alone and quiet.

Samantha: Sam is involved in organising a benefit dinner to raise money for breast cancer research and she's not seeing eye to eye with some of her co-organisers. They are committed to some kind of promotion involving cookies, but Sam thinks that women who are suffering from breast cancer need more inspiration than a biscuit. So a suggestion is made. Why doesn't she give them exactly that? Why doesn't she do an inspirational speech? Later, Sam rehearses her speech in front of Jerry who finds it stilted and hollow. He tells her that, at his Alcoholics Anonymous meetings, the speakers who stay real are the most inspirational for the listeners. Sam insists that she knows PR and goes ahead with the speech as written. It's embarrassing and stilted and not helped by the hot flushes that she's getting as a result of the chemotherapy. 'Fuck this,' she says and abandons the speech. She speaks from the heart, talking about what she's been through, what they've all been through. She takes her wig off, revealing her shaven scalp. One by one most of the women in the hall, inspired by Samantha's defiance, honesty and courage, stand up and remove their wigs.

Charlotte: Charlotte is picking up Carrie's mail for her and forwarding it to Paris. One day she's sorting Carrie's post when the telephone rings. Carrie's answerphone cuts in but Charlotte can still hear the message being recorded. It's Big, asking for forgiveness and if Carrie is happy. Charlotte picks up the phone and invites Big to join her and the others for lunch.

Guy Talk: Big joins Charlotte, Sam and Miranda at their usual café. He literally takes Carrie's place at the table and begins to talk to the girls about his relationship with

Carrie. He says he knows he's never been particularly popular among them and that he has caused Carrie pain. He knows he's made a number of mistakes when it comes to Carrie and ruined it more than once; he also acknowledges that they know her far better than he does, actually better that anyone else does. He tells them that he does love Carrie and wants to know if she'd ever take him back. He asks if she's happy and if Paris is working – 'I wouldn't want to wreck that for her,' he says. If they honestly tell him that she's better off without him, he promises to leave: 'I'll be history'.

Miranda: Despite their recent rows, it's Miranda that Carrie phones when things get tough and Miranda that the other girls defer to when Big asks for advice. 'Go get our girl,' she tells him.

And So . . .: 'I do love her.' The first half of the episode is bright, charming and cheerfully bilingual and from it you can easily imagine a seventh season set, and filmed, entirely in Paris. The second, though, is progressively uncomfortable as Carrie seems more and more like a fish out of water. There's the odd flash of obviousness here (Carrie is jealous when she sees Aleksandr embracing a beautiful girl, but it's his twenty-something daughter) but the script is generally very carefully constructed with lots of reversals of expectation and a low key 'cliff-hanger' which enables the audience to feel the pressure that Carrie is feeling without blaming Aleksandr.

94
An American Girl in Paris (Part Deux)

22 February 2004

Written by Michael Patrick King
Directed by Tim Van Patten

Guest Cast
Chris Noth (Mr Big) David Eigenberg (Steve Brady)
Evan Handler (Harry Goldenblatt) Jason Lewis (Smith Jerrod)

Mikhail Baryshnikov (Aleksandr Petrovsky) Lecy Goranson (Amber)
Lynn Cohen (Magda) Mario Cantone (Anthony Marentino)

Wine and Dine: Carrie meets Aleksandr's ex-wife for lunch and later discovers that the chic and remote Juliette approves of her thoroughly. This, combined with the discovery of her French fanbase in a bookshop, gives Carrie reasons to believe that she may be able to like life in Paris after all.

Samantha: Sam and Jerry both dye their cropped hair bleach blond, he again doing it in sympathy with her post-chemotherapy baldness. More distressing for Sam is that the chemotherapy has robbed her of her sex drive. She tries to encourage him to have sex with other people saying she, above all others, knows how important sex is to people. He refuses and insists that she'll get her sex drive back, saying that, in winter the trees are bare, but that doesn't mean they're no longer alive. He insists that he can wait 'until spring' and, while he's away, he sends her some flowers that haven't yet bloomed as a symbol of how their relationship will grow. Sam misses Jerry terribly and phones him and says she's changed her mind – she'd prefer it if he didn't have sex with other people; 'I haven't, and I won't' he says. Days later Samantha is asleep and she's woken by Jerry coming into her apartment and telling her he loves her. 'You flew back to tell me that?' she asks. 'Can you think of a better reason?' he replies.

Fashion Victims: Carrie's red and black polka dot dress is awesome; Juliette is impressed with Carrie's vintage bag (and so am I). It is inside this bag, in a tiny divet behind a small rip in the lining, that she finds her 'Carrie' necklace which she lost in **93**, 'An American Girl in Paris (Part Une)'.

Miranda: Increasingly erratic behaviour from Steve's always erratic mother Mary (she calls Brady 'Stevie' and doesn't know who Miranda is) causes Steve to take her to the hospital. It turns out she's had a small stroke, resulting in significant aphasia and memory loss. Steve goes over to her apartment (which he hasn't been inside for a while; he normally picks her up in the hallway) and discovers that it's a roach-infested mess. Worried for her health and safety he starts talking about getting a cleaner and a nurse but, despite the fact that she and Steve's Ma have never got on, Miranda says that this isn't necessary and insists that Mary should come and live with them. One day the increasingly disorientated Mary disappears and Miranda has to comb the streets to look for her. She finds her pulling food out of bins and takes her home. Not wishing to scare Steve she bathes Mary before Steve gets in from the bar in a scene which seems designed to acknowledge Miranda's acceptance of Mary as part of her family through her connection with Steve.

Men: Jerry is making a movie about Atilla The Hun in Canada (it's cheaper to film there, as anyone who knows anything about movie and TV production over the last ten years knows), which ties in nicely with the current holiday vogue for faux-historical epics like *Troy* (Wolfgang Petersen, 2004) and *Alexander* (Oliver Stone, 2004).

(A European) City: The Paris that Tim Van Patten's camera finds is not that of postcard clichés nor a backdrop for Carrie's angst – it's a beautiful, stylish place with flaws and shining moments all of its own. Van Patten borrows shots and camera movements from Godard when displaying Paris and this is appropriate not only for the location, but for the series – which began with an episode that borrowed a dozen visual tricks from the French New Wave. Despite largely filming in a city thousands of miles from the series base there's a real sense of the series house style coming full circle, coming home.

Carrie: Aleksandr has a panic attack before the unveiling of his show to the museum curator. He is scared that the curator of the gallery will think that he's a stupid old man, past it and effectively useless. Carrie agrees to go with him despite the fact that she has arranged to meet a group of Parisian Carrie Bradshaw fans for a party.

When Aleksandr gets to the museum, his hand clasped in Carrie's he's so scared, they hail him as a genius and he effectively abandons her to be praised by the Paris art hierarchy. After seemingly hours of waiting for Aleksandr to prise himself away from them and even speak to her Carrie leaves to go to the Carrie Bradshaw fans party. But it's over.

Going back to her hotel she confronts Aleksandr about his selfishness and points out that in Paris she's useless, an appendage to his life. In New York she had a life and a job; in Paris she doesn't, and she didn't give up her job and her life just to walk the streets of Paris on her own. She realises that she, indeed no other person, will be as important as his work to him. 'I am someone who is looking for love, real love,' and she realises that this is not what they have. After he accidentally slaps her, she walks out of his hotel room and out of his life and heads to the hotel reception to book herself a separate room.

Charlotte: Charlotte and Harry are still trying to adopt and they meet a couple from North Carolina who are expecting a baby. They realise halfway through that the couple have decided to keep the child and demand to know why they even bothered coming to see them. The impoverished pair admit that they'd never seen New York. Harry is upset and feels used but Charlotte tries to comfort him, shrugging and joking that they're Jews, 'we've been through worse than this'. Which is *brilliant*. Later, Harry receives a letter that confirms that they have been selected to adopt a Chinese orphan. The couple look adoringly at the photograph, 'That's our baby,' whispers Charlotte.

Hey, Big Guy: Big (whose name is, remarkably boringly, John) makes his first appearance in the episode in what is also the entire series first literal heart-missing-a-beat moment. His car pulls up behind Carrie in the street and neither he nor she notice one another even while the audience sees both of them.

Later, as Carrie, having split up with Aleksandr, frets on the floor of the hotel looking for the stones that have come off the necklace Aleksandr gave her, Big walks in simply

looking for a room. There's a magical moment of sudden
recognition, which moves into near total farce as Big
decides to beat Aleksandr up and Carrie has to chase him
around the hotel begging him not to. In the only way she
can think of to stop him, Carrie trips him up, which is
possibly the single funniest thing in the whole 94-episode
run of the show – so funny that even the characters laugh
out loud at it. Big tells Carrie that she's 'The One' and
apologises for his reticence before.

Together they return to America, to New York, to her
friends, to her apartment. 'Are you coming up?' Carrie
asks, and, in a nod to the last line of the very first episode,
Big grins and replies, 'Abso-fucking-lutely.'

And So . . .: 'Can you believe this is finally happening?'
This is a slower-, and slightly longer-, than-usual episode,
but one paced enormously skilfully; 'An American Girl in
Paris (Part Deux)' is an emotional experience which builds
and builds to an ending of punch-the-air delight and real
emotional catharsis. Carrie's return to the diner is simply
glorious. The way the plot strands, and different scenes, are
intercut with one another in the last ten minutes or so is
blissful. Any charges that this programme is shallow are
undercut utterly by the marvellous scene where Magda,
who started off as a comedy cleaning lady, maternally
kisses Miranda on the forehead and whispers to her about
the nature of family love. There isn't a single performance
in here that is anything less than note perfect.

This is a lovely piece of television and a textbook
example of how to make the last episode of a long running
TV series work. If you've gotta go out, then this is how you
should go out.

Appendix One: Sex and the Matrix

Written by Mike Bender
Edited by Steve Welch
Directed by Joel Gallen

Cast: Sarah Jessica Parker (Carrie Bradshaw) Kim Cattrall (Samantha Jones) Kristin Davis (Charlotte York Mac-Dougal) Cynthia Nixon (Miranda Hobbes) Jimmy Fallon (Neo) Laurence Fishburne (Morpheus) Vince Vaughn (White Rabbit)

Notes: A spoof which combines the apparently irreconcilable worlds of *Sex and the City* and *The Matrix* (The Wachowski Brothers, 1999) as made for, and shown as part of, the 2000 MTV Music Awards. *Saturday Night Live* star Jimmy Fallon takes over Keanu Reeves's roll of Neo while *Sex and the City* guest star Vince Vaughn makes a spectacular fool of himself as the White Rabbit. Laurence Fishburne is spared maximum indignity by only appearing in footage from *The Matrix* itself. Probably best not to think about it too hard.

Appendix Two: Awards and the City

The sheer number of awards that Sex and the City won (never mind was nominated for) over the course of its six-season, 68-month, 94-episode run on HBO is immense. This list covers the most prestigious and the most interesting, and is not meant to be complete. (It's worth noting that most of the series' award nominations have come from Guilds or Unions, demonstrating how much those who work on the show are respected by their peers.)

The series' two principal film editors, Michael Berenbaum and Wendy Stanzler, have both separately won an 'Eddie' award for their work on the series. The 'Eddie', which is handed out by the American Cinema Editors, USA is widely prized in the industry because it is a prize for film editing voted for only by film editors. Michael Berenbaum won for **50**, 'The Real Me' in 2002 and Wendey Stanzler won for **69**, 'Luck Be an Old Lady' in 2003. Stanzler was also nominated on two other occasions, in 2001 for **41**, 'Running with Scissors' and in 2004 (co-nominated with Berenbaum) for **82**, 'The Catch'.

The series' writing has come to the notice of the Writers' Guild of America who nominated individual episodes of the series a startling ten times for 'Best Writing, Episodic Comedy'. This is another set of awards voted for by those working within the profession it rewards. Cindy Chupack (my favourite Sex and the City writer) has been nominated four times, for **23**, 'Evolution', **33**, 'Attack of the 5'10" Woman', **60**, 'Just Say Yes' and **71**, 'Plus One Is the Loneliest Number'. Jenny Bicks has picked up two nominations for **17**, 'Four Women and a Funeral' and **83**, 'A Woman's Right to Shoes'. Michael Patrick King can also boast two nominations (for **30**, 'Ex and the City' and **66**,

'I Heart NY') as can the writing team of Julie Rottenberg and Elisa Zuritsky (for **56**, 'My Motherboard, My Self' and **63**, 'Change of a Dress').

The Directors Guild of America has also nominated the series every year since 2000. In 2000 itself Victoria Hochberg was nominated for **20**, 'The Man, the Myth, the Viagra'. In 2001 Allen Coulter was up for a gong for **48**, 'Cock a Doodle Do!' In 2002 no less than three of the series' directors were up for DGA awards: Michael Patrick King for **50**, 'The Real Me', Michael Engler for **56**, 'My Motherboard, My Self' and Allen Coulter for **51**, 'Defining Moments'. The next year only Michael Patrick King would be nominated, this time for **71**, 'Plus One Is the Loneliest Number'. 2004 was King's third year in a row for a nomination for this award (for **76**, 'Great Sexpectations') but again he didn't win. Neither did Michael Engler for **80**, 'Hop, Skip and a Week', but Timothy Van Patten, nominated for directing **84**, 'Boy, Interrupted' did.

The New York-based clothes designer, Patricia Field, who was responsible for much of the series' look, was nominated for a Costume Designers Guild Award every year between 2000 and 2004. She won for the first two years. Presumably after that the awards voters thought that somebody else ought to be given a chance. Personally, I think the clothes got better year-in year-out.

In 2002 the Screen Actors Guild finally gave the series' four leading ladies the 'Outsanding Ensemble Cast' award they'd blatantly deserved from the beginning. The year before, Sarah Jessica Parker had, equally deservingly, won Outstanding Performance by a Female Actor and the SAG obviously decided that it was time to give the other three their due credit.

The American Comedy Awards have twice nominated Sarah Jessica Parker as 'Funniest Female Performer in a TV Series Leading Role' – once in 2000 and again in 2001. In 2000 they also nominated the series as 'Funniest Television Series'.

Sarah Jessica Parker won a Golden Globe for her performance as Carrie three years in a row between 2000 and 2002. Kim Cattrall won one for playing Samantha in 2003; that year not only Parker but also Cynthia Nixon missed out despite being nominated. The series won Best Television Series – Musical or Comedy in 2001 and 2002 and was nominated again in 2003. In 2004 Cattrall, Kristin Davis and Cynthia Nixon were all nominated as Supporting Actress but none of them won, presumably the result of the vote being split within the series' fans. Parker though, regained her crown and took home a fourth Golden Globe in five years.

The most influential and respected TV awards are, of course, the Emmys. Virtually since its inception, *Sex and the City* has been gaining nominations for what are often called 'The TV Oscars'. In 1999 the show was nominated for 'Outstanding Comedy Series' and Sarah Jessica Parker for 'Outstanding Lead Actress in a Comedy Series'. Neither won. In 2000 the series was up for nine Emmys; these were 'Outstanding Comedy Series', 'Outstanding Lead Actress in a Comedy Series' (Sarah Jessica Parker), 'Outstanding Supporting Actress in a Comedy Series' (Kim Cattrall) and nominations for sound-mixing, costumes, casting and art direction. Both Michael Patrick King and Cindy Chupack were nominated for 'Outstanding Writing for a Comedy Series' for **30**, 'Ex and the City' and **23**, 'Evolution' respectively. None of the nominees won. In 2001 the show was nominated ten times; for Art Direction, Casting, Costumes, Directing (Charles McDougall for **39**, 'Easy Come, Easy Go'), Hairstyling, Sarah Jessica Parker, Kim Cattrall and make-up. None of those won either, but the tenth nomination, 'Outstanding Comedy Series', did. It was a triumph for HBO and a neat little statue was duly given to everyone who is named as a producer on that year of the show (look it up!). The next year the show won three Emmys: one for Casting, one for Costuming and one for Michael Patrick King for directing **50**, 'The Real Me'. The series also garnered unconverted nominations for King as a writer, for Cindy Chupack (for writing **60,** 'Just Say Yes'), for Cynthia Nixon, Kim Cattrall and Sarah Jessica Parker, for Frances Sternhagen (she played Charlotte's mother-in-law Bunny MacDougal), for 'Outstanding Comedy Series' and for hairstyling. In 2003, Jennifer McNamara finally won an Emmy for casting the series. Her fellow nominees (the art direction team, the costumiers, director Michael Engler for **74**, 'I Love a Charade', the hairstylists, Sarah Jessica Parker, the make-up team, editors Wendy Stanzler and Michael Berenbaum, and Kim Cattrall) were less fortunate. The series also failed to win a second 'Outstanding Comedy Series' award.

Appendix Three: The Book

Sex and the City, written by Candace Bushnell

Carrie: One of the book's major characters is Carrie Bradshaw, a 'friend' of the narrator and an obvious author substitute. She dates 'Mr Big' and is a lot more like the TV version of Sam. In fact, everyone is a lot more like the TV version of Sam. Samantha's suggestion that women go out and have sex 'like men' originates with Carrie in the book, not Sam.

Miranda: There is a character called Miranda Hobbes, but she's a forty-year old cable executive with long dark hair who doesn't appear very much.

Charlotte: A character called Charlotte makes a couple of appearances, but she's an English journalist (in fact, the same one Carrie is telling the story about at the beginning of **1**, 'Sex and the City').

Samantha: Samantha Jones is a movie producer. The character most like Samantha (in attitude, and in that she works in PR) is called Sarah. Samantha's obsession with the movie *The Last Seduction* (John Dahl, 1994) is clearly sourced in a mention in the book of Carrie having seen it as part of research for something.

Girl Talk: The character Amalita Amalfi (see **5**, 'The Power of Female Sex') appears and is almost exactly the same as the television version, although she is involved in substantially different events.

Hey, Big Guy: Mr Big, surprisingly, leaps off the page fully formed. You can even hear Chris Noth delivering his lines. The final line of the book is 'Carrie and Mr Big are still together'.

Men: Skipper Johnston appears, but he isn't the character from the TV show either. He's far, far more cynical and has a different job.

Stanford Blatch's theory that only in the gay community can one find romance (see **1**, 'Sex and the City') is the pet idea of the book's unnamed narrator. The TV series' Skipper's belief that love conquers all, given space, and that what Manhattan lacks is space, is a verbatim transcript of something said by the character Donovan Leitch in the book.

There is a character called Capote Duncan who isn't really the same character with that name from **1**, 'Sex and the City' at all.

There is a section which is clearly about film director Oliver Stone, but he's fictionalised as Gregory Rocque, a filmmaker who made *G.R.F.* (standing for Gerald Rudolph Ford) and *The Monkees,* clearly referring to Stone's pictures *JFK* (1993) and *The Doors* (1991). This is very silly and nowhere near as clever as it thinks it is.

Trivia: One line in the epilogue becomes the basis for **31**, 'Where There's Smoke . . .'

Episode **2**, 'Models and Mortals' is related to the section of the book called 'Meet the guys, who date models!'

A character called Jolie Bernard is a rough basis for Laney Berlin, seen in **10**, 'The Baby Shower'.

And So . . .: 'It's going to end badly.' This is not a novel, it's a collection of newspaper columns linked together with the faintest breath of ongoing narrative – and it shows. Some characters are introduced several times and some not at all. There are too many nearly identical characters for one to keep track of, and 'Carrie' is sometimes a friend of the narrator and sometimes the narrator herself. The narrator is never explicitly named and often disappears for several pages at a time. Candace Bushnell's book is not really very like the series which claims to be based on it. Reading it after seeing the TV show is an odd experience; it's an embryonic version of what's onscreen. It's as if someone's put the pilot episode in a meat grinder, resulting in a random collection of often unrelated bits and bobs. Darren Star's 'created by' credit on the TV show, which conceptually seems vainglorious for something based on a previous work, is therefore entirely justified. Without Darren Star, the programme we all enjoyed for nearly six years and have been looking at over the last 369 pages would not exist in anything like the form that it does. Even the episodes made after his departure from the series have more in common with his version of *Sex and the City* than Candace Bushnell's. His contribution in taking the title, some names and a dozen sentences from this book and melding them into the HBO TV series *Sex and the City* quite simply cannot be overstated.

Appendix Four: Sex and the Silver Screen?

Rumours about a *Sex and the City* theatrical motion picture began circulating before the series had even finished. News stories suggested a screenplay – and possibly theatrical directorial debut – by Executive Producer Michael Patrick King, and the reunion of the series' four main stars. King was quoted as saying that he hoped to have a first draft script completed for May 2004.

It is unusual for an American television series to move to the big screen so soon after its televisual conclusion, and even more unusual for it to take its television cast with it as it does so. While 'revivals' of long-dead TV shows are common, they usually involve wholesale recasting of roles with the original stars present only in cameos. *Star Trek*, perhaps the most successful TV-to-film transition, remains a notable exception (though not a series one would normally compare with *Sex and the City*). *The X-Files – Fight The Future* (Rob Morrow, 1998) not only used the entire TV cast but was actually made *between* seasons of the TV show.

Less than a month after the screening of the final episode of *Sex and the City*, the plans for the film seemed to be falling apart; at least if one believed the press reports. There was much newspaper and Internet talk of feuds between the series' stars, both during the production of the series and over terms for the motion picture. One site found itself claiming that Kim Cattrall and Sarah Jessica Parker both expected to receive in excess of $10 million for re-creating their roles on the big screen and that the $5.4 million they had each allegedly been offered was, more than any personal animosity, the reason for the delay. Nothing has been confirmed by any of the interested parties.

By 9 March 2004, studio briefings were strongly implying that not only had no deal been reached to make the
picture, but that no deal could or would be reached. Even
if this is now the case it would be unwise to work on the
assumption that there will never be a *Sex and the City*
movie, TV movie or revival, perhaps with or perhaps
without, the show's original stars. In a world where
Starsky and Hutch can be presented as a multi-million
dollar movie 27 years after it began on television and
Warner Bros hires one of the producers of *Buffy The
Vampire Slayer* to revive *Lost in Space* for them, it
becomes increasingly difficult to believe that the series'
characters, format or title, won't find revival in some form
in the near or distant future.

We live in an age where it seems impossible to kill a
brand – let alone a good idea – and *Sex and the City* is,
and remains, simply that. A good idea for a TV show
which became, with a lot of hard work, a very, very good
TV show. As an epitaph for a television series, you can't
really look for anything better.